STATISTICS
FOR THE
BEHAVIORAL
AND
SOCIAL SCIENCES

SECOND EDITION

STATISTICS
FOR THE
BEHAVIORAL
AND
SOCIAL SCIENCES

A BRIEF COURSE

Arthur Aron
Elaine N. Aron

State University of New York at Stony Brook

Prentice
Hall

Upper Saddle River, New Jersey 07458

Library of Congress Cataloging-in-Publication Data

ARON, ARTHUR.
    Statistics for the behavioral and social sciences : a brief course / Arthur Aron, Elaine N. Aron.—2nd ed.
        p. cm.
    Includes bibliographical references and index.
    ISBN 0–13–026186–6
        1. Social sciences—Statistical methods. 2. Social sciences—Data processing. I. Aron, Elaine. II. Title.

HA29.A745 2002
300′.1′5195—dc21

                                                    2001021906

VP, Editorial Director: *Laura Pearson*
Acquisitions Editor: *Jayme Heffler*
Editorial Assistant: *April Dawn Klemm*
Senior Managing Editor: *Mary Rottino*
Production Liaison: *Fran Russello*
Editorial/Production Supervision: *Marianne Hutchinson (Pine Tree Composition, Inc.)*
Prepress and Manufacturing Buyer: *Tricia Kenny*
Art Director: *Jayne Conte*
Cover Designer: *Bruce Kenselaar*
Director, Image Resource Center: *Melinda Lee Reo*
Manager, Rights & Permissions: *Kay Dellosa*
Image Specialist: *Beth Boyd*
Photo Researcher: *Karen Pugliano*
Senior Marketing Manager: *Sharon Cosgrove*

Credits appear on page xviii, which constitutes a continuation of the copyright page.

This book was set in 11/2 Times Roman by Pine Tree Composition, Inc., and was printed and bound by Von Hoffmann Press, Inc. The cover was printed by Phoenix Color Corp.

© 2002, 1997 by Pearson Education, Inc.
Upper Saddle River, New Jersey 07458

Printed in the United States of America
10   9   8   7   6   5   4   3   2   1

ISBN 0-13-026186-6

Prentice-Hall International (UK) Limited, *London*
Prentice-Hall of Australia Pty. Limited, *Sydney*
Prentice-Hall Canada Inc., *Toronto*
Prentice-Hall Hispanoamericana, S.A., *Mexico*
Prentice-Hall of India Private Limited, *New Delhi*
Prentice-Hall of Japan, Inc., *Tokyo*
Pearson Education Asia Pte. Ltd., *Singapore*
Editora Prentice-Hall Do Brasil, Ltda., *Rio de Janeiro*

Brief Contents

Contents

8 Introduction to the *t* Test   152

9 The *t* Test for Independent Means   178

10 Introduction to the Analysis of Variance   199

11 Chi-Square Tests and Strategies When Population Distributions Are Not Normal   231

12 Making Sense of Advanced Statistical Procedures in Research Articles   265

Appendix

Tables   289

Preface to the Instructor

The heart of this book was written over a summer in a small apartment near the Place Saint Ferdinand, having been outlined in nearby cafes and on walks in the Bois de Boulogne. It is based on our 35 years of experience teaching, researching, and writing. We believe that this book is as different from the conventional lot of statistics books as Paris is from Calcutta, yet still comfortable and stimulating to the long-suffering community of statistics instructors.

The approach embodied in this text has been developed over three decades of successful teaching—successful not only in the sense that students have consistently rated the course (a statistics course, remember) as a highlight of their undergraduate years but also in the sense that students come back to us years later saying, "I was light-years ahead of my fellow graduate students because of your course," or "Even though I don't do research, your course has really helped me understand statistics that I read about in my field."

In this second edition of this *Brief Course* we have tried to maintain those things about the book that were especially appreciated, while reworking the text to take into account the feedback we have received, our own experiences, and advances and changes in the field. However, before turning to the second edition, we want to reiterate some comments we made in the first edition about what we have done differently than other statistics texts.

What We Have Done Differently

We continue to do what the best of the newer books are already doing well: emphasizing the intuitive, de-emphasizing the mathematical, and explaining everything in clear, simple language. What we have done, however, differs from these other books in nine key respects.

1. ***The definitional formulas are brought to center stage*** because they provide a concise symbolic summary of the logic of each particular procedure. All our explanations, examples, practice problems, and test bank items are based on these definitional formulas. (The amount of data to be processed in our practice problems and test items are reduced appropriately to keep computations manageable.)

Why this approach? To date, statistics texts have failed to adjust to technologic reality. What is important is not that the students learn to calculate a correlation coefficient with a large data set—computers can do that for them. What is important is that students remain constantly aware of the underlying logic of the procedure. Consider the population variance—the average of the squared deviations from the mean. This concept is immediately clear from the definitional formula (once the student is used to the symbols): $\text{Variance} = \Sigma(X - M)^2/N$. Repeatedly working problems using this formula engrains the meaning in the student's mind. In contrast, the usual computational version of this formula only obscures this meaning: $\text{Variance} = [\Sigma X^2 - (\Sigma X)^2/N]/N$. Repeatedly working problems using this formula does nothing but teach the student the difference between ΣX^2 and $(\Sigma X)^2$!

Teaching computational formulas today is an anachronism. Researchers do their statistics on computers now. At the same time, the use of statistical software makes the understanding of the basic principles, as they are symbolically expressed in the definitional formula, more important than ever.

It is a mystery to us why statistics textbooks have not changed their methods with the advent of statistical software, but we are convinced that the change is overdue. Of course, because computational formulas are both historically interesting and occasionally needed—and because some instructors may feel naked without them—we still provide them in a brief footnote wherever a computational formula would normally be introduced.

2. ***Each procedure is taught both verbally and numerically—and usually visually as well—with the same examples described in each of these ways.*** Practice exercises and test bank items, in turn, require the student to calculate results and make graphs or illustrations and also to write a short explanation in layperson's language of what the statistics mean. The chapter material completely prepares the student for these kinds of exercises and test questions.

It is our repeated experience that these different ways of expressing an idea are very important for permanently establishing a concept in a student's mind. Many students in the social and behavioral sciences are more at ease with words than with numbers. In fact, some have a positive fear of all mathematics. Writing the lay language explanation gives them an opportunity to do what they do best and, if they are having trouble, forces them to put the procedures in front of them in the verbal form they process best.

3. A main goal of any introductory statistics course in the social and behavioral sciences is to ***prepare students to read research articles.*** In fact, the way a procedure such as a *t* test or chi-square is described in a research article is often quite different from what the student expects from the standard textbook discussions. Therefore, as this book teaches a statistical method, it also gives examples of how that method is reported in the journals. The practice problems and test bank items also include excerpts from articles for the student to explain.

4. The book is ***unusually up-to-date.*** For some reason, most of the introductory statistics textbooks we have seen read as if they were written in the 1950s. The basics are still the basics, but the subtleties of the way statisticians and researchers think about those basics today has changed radically. Today, the basics are undergirded by a different appreciation of issues like effect size, power, accumulation of results

through meta-analysis; the central role of models; and a whole host of new orientations arising from the prominent role of the computer in our analyses. We are much engaged in the latest developments in theory and application of statistics. We believe this book reflects that engagement. For example, we devote an entire chapter to effect size and power, discussing how to handle situations in which assumptions are violated, we cover data transformations (this widely used approach is easily accessible to introductory students but is rarely mentioned in current introductory texts).

5. The book is written to *capitalize on the students' motivations*. We try to do this in two ways. First, our examples, while attempting to represent the diversity of social and behavioral science research, emphasize topics or populations that students seem to find most interesting. The first example is from a real study in which 151 students in their first week of an introductory statistics class rate how much stress they feel they are under. Also, in our examples, we continually emphasize the usefulness of statistical methods and ideas as tools in the research process, never allowing students to feel that what they are learning is theory for the sake of theory.

Second, we have tried to make the book extremely straightforward and systematic in its explanation of basic concepts so that students can have frequent "aha!" experiences. Such experiences bolster self-confidence and motivate further learning. So often textbooks constantly beat their readers over the head with just how oversimplified everything they are learning is. Instead, we try to inspire readers with the depth of what can be learned, even in an introductory course. It is really quite inspiring to *us* to see even fairly modest students glow from having mastered some concept like negative correlation, the distinction between failing to reject the null hypothesis and supporting the null hypothesis, or the idea of independence in a chi-square analysis.

6. *The final chapter looks at advanced procedures* without actually teaching them in detail. It explains in simple terms how to make sense out of these statistics when they are encountered in research articles. Most research articles today use methods such as hierarchical and stepwise multiple regression, factor analysis, structural equation modeling, analysis of covariance, and multivariate analysis of variance. Students completing the ordinary introductory statistics course are ill-equipped to comprehend most of the articles they must read to prepare a paper or study for a course. This chapter makes use of the basics that students have just learned to give a rudimentary understanding of these advanced procedures. It also serves as a reference guide that they can keep and use in the future when reading such articles.

7. The accompanying *Student's Study Guide and Computer Workbook* focuses on mastering concepts and also includes instructions and examples for working problems using a computer. Most study guides focus on plugging numbers into formulas and memorizing rules (which is consistent with the emphasis of the textbooks they accompany). For each chapter, our *Student's Study Guide and Computer Workbook* provides learning objectives, a detailed chapter outline, the chapter's formulas (with all symbols defined), and summaries of steps of conducting each procedure covered in the chapter, plus a set of self-tests, including multiple-choice, fill-in, and problem/essay questions. In addition, for each procedure covered in the chapter, the study guide furnishes a thorough outline for writing an essay explaining the procedure to a person who has never had a course in statistics.

Especially important, our *Student's Study Guide and Computer Workbook* provides the needed support for teaching students to conduct statistical analyses on the computer. First, there is a special appendix introducing the language and procedures of SPSS/for Windows. Then, in each chapter corresponding to the text chapters, there is a section showing in detail how to carry out the chapter's procedures on the computer. (These sections include step-by-step instructions, examples, and illustrations of how each step of input and output appears on the computer screen). There are also special activities for using the computer to deepen understanding. As far as we know, no other statistics textbook package provides this much depth of explanation.

8. We have written an ***Instructor's Manual that really helps teach the course***. The *Manual* begins with a chapter summarizing what we have gleaned from our own teaching experience and the research literature on effectiveness in college teaching. The next chapter discusses alternative organizations of the course, including tables of possible schedules and a sample syllabus. Then each chapter, corresponding to the text chapters, provides full lecture outlines and **additional worked-out examples not found in the text** (in a form suitable for copying onto transparencies or for student handouts). These worked-out examples are particularly useful, as creating examples is one of the most difficult parts of preparing statistics lectures.

9. Our ***Test Bank*** **section of the** ***Instructor's Manual*** **makes preparing good exams easy.** We supply approximately 40 multiple-choice, 25 fill-in, and 10 to 12 problem/essay questions for each chapter. Considering that the emphasis of the course is so conceptual, the multiple-choice questions will be particularly useful for those of you who do not have the resources to grade essays. This supplement also includes computational answers to each textbook chapter's practice problems that are not given in the text. (The textbook provides answers to selected practice problems, including at least one example answer to an essay-type question for each chapter.)

About this *Brief Course*

We were thrilled by the enthusiastic response of instructors and students to the first and second editions of our *Statistics for Psychology* (Aron & Aron, 1994, 1999), as well as the positive comments of reviewers, including the most encouraging evaluation in *Contemporary Psychology* (Bourgeois, 1997).

The *Brief Course* was our answer to the many requests we received from instructors and students for a textbook using our approach that is (a) more general in its focus than psychology alone and (b) shorter, to accommodate less comprehensive courses. Of course, we tried to retain all the qualities that endeared the original to our readers. At the same time, the *Brief Course* was not a cosmetic revision. The broadening of focus meant using examples from the entire range of the social and behavioral sciences, from anthropology to political science. Most important, the broadening informed the relative emphasis (and inclusion) of different topics and the tenor of the discussion of these topics. The shortening was also dramatic: This *Brief Course* is about half the length of the original, making it quite feasible to do the whole book, even in a quarter-length course.

Influences on the Second Edition

We did the revision for the second edition in San Francisco. We hope that this has not resulted in a loss of whatever romance the first edition gained from being written in Paris. On the other hand, this edition has been leavened by some beautiful views of the Bay.

More important, this revision is enriched by our experience teaching with the first edition and by the experience and encouragement of scores of instructors who have written to us about their experiences using the book. This revision is also informed by our own use of statistical methods. The last five years have been a very productive time for the two of us in our own research programs in personality and social psychology. (For overviews of our main research programs, see A. Aron, E. Aron, & Norman (2001) and E. Aron & A. Aron (1997). Perhaps particularly useful has been that one of us (AA) has served as associate editor for the *Journal of Personality and Social Psychology* during the last several years. This has kept us in touch with how the best researchers are using statistics (as well as how reviewers rate their colleagues' use of statistics).

Specific Changes in the Second Edition

1. *Writing.* We have thoroughly reviewed every sentence, simplifying constructions and terminology wherever possible. It is hard enough to learn statistics without having to read complicated sentences.

2. *Updating examples.* We have replaced over 50 examples from the first edition with newer ones. This is particularly important for the sections on how to understand and evaluate research articles. The whole point of these sections is for students to see how statistics actually look when reported in current research. In reviewing the old examples and finding new ones, we were struck by quite a few subtle changes in the way statistical results are being reported. For example, five years ago interaction effects in analysis of variance were generally reported with line graphs—today they usually use bar graphs (see Chapter 10).

3. *Adjustments to enhance pedagogy and better meet the needs of instructors using the book.* These have been mostly small changes, but there are a great many of them. Perhaps what will seem most obvious to those who have used the first edition is that we have added a section on levels of measurement and significantly revised our chapter on correlation and regression. We have also made even more of an effort than in the first edition to use multicultural examples whenever possible.

4. *Some changes we have not made.* The 9 points noted earlier in this introduction remain as the central, unique features of this book. Also, except where we felt we could make a major improvement in pedagogy, we have not changed the major teaching examples in each chapter, for two reasons. First, instructors using the first edition told us that they have built their lectures around their experience using these examples and don't want to have to start from scratch with new ones. Second, these examples include tables showing all the details of computation. By keeping these examples the same, we minimize the chance of errors creeping in.

Keep in Touch

Our goal is to do whatever we can to help you make your course a success. If you have any questions or suggestions, please write or contact us by email (**aron@ psych1.psy.sunysb.edu** will do for both of us). Also, if you should find an error somewhere, for everyone's benefit, please let us know right away. When errors have come up in the past, we have had good success in getting them fixed in the very next printing.

Acknowledgments

First and foremost, we are grateful to our students through the years, who have guided our approach to teaching by encouraging us with their appreciation for what we have done well, as well as their various means of discouraging us from persisting in what we have done not so well.

We remain grateful to all of those who helped us with the first edition of the *Brief Course* as well as to those who helped with the first and second editions of the larger book. For their very helpful input on the development of this second edition of the *Brief Course,* we want to thank Carol Pandey, L. A. Pierce College; Stephen L. Chew, Samford University; Malina Monaco, Georgia State University; Michael Biderman, University of Tennessee at Chattanooga; Dennis Jowaisas, Oklahoma City University; Rod Gillis, University of Miami; Marie A. Roman, DePaul University; Sally Radmacher, Missouri Western State College; Robert Shamansky, Simpson College; and Maria Czyzewska, Southwest Texas State University.

In addition, we want to express our appreciation to the following individuals who told us about errors in the first edition: Harley Baker, Kathy Bechstein, Doug Cornford, Hamze Dodeen, O. H. Gordon, Jeff Joireman, Dennis Jowaisas, Beth Morling, Richard Wielkiewicz, Thom Yantek, and Shuqiang Zhang. We also particularly want to acknowledge Sheryl Skaggs for her assistance in locating many of the new examples for this edition.

Arthur Aron
Elaine Aron

Credits

Data in tables 3–9, 3–10, 8–7, 8–8, 9–4, 9–5, 10–7, 10–8, 11–7, 11–8, and 11–9 are based on tables in Cohen, J. (1988). *Statistical power analysis for the behavioral sciences* (2nd ed.). Copyright © 1988 by Lawrence Erlbaum Associates, Inc. Reprinted by permission.

Introduction to the Student

The goal of this book is to help you *understand* statistics. We emphasize meaning and concepts, not just symbols and numbers.

This emphasis plays to your strength. Most social and behavioral science students are not lovers of mathematics but are keenly attuned to ideas. And we want to underscore the following, based on our 35 years' experience in teaching: ***We have never had a student who could do well in other college courses who could not also do well in this course.*** (However, we will admit that doing well in this course may require more work than doing well in others.)

In this introduction, we discuss why you are taking this course and how you can gain the most from it.

Why Learn Statistics? (Besides Fulfilling a Requirement)

1. ***Understanding statistics is crucial to being able to read research results.*** In most of the social and behavioral sciences, nearly every course you take will emphasize the results of research studies, and these usually include statistics. If you do not understand the basic logic of statistics—if you cannot make sense of the jargon, the tables, and the graphs that are at the heart of any research report—your reading of research will be very superficial.

2. ***Understanding statistics is crucial to doing research yourself.*** Many students eventually go on to graduate school. Graduate study in the social and behav-

ioral sciences almost always involves *doing* research. Often learning to do research on your own is the entire focus of graduate school, and doing research almost always involves statistics. This course gives you a solid foundation in the statistics you need for doing research. Further, by mastering the basic logic and ways of thinking about statistics, you will be unusually well prepared for the advanced courses, which focus on the nitty-gritty of analyzing research results.

Many universities also offer opportunities for undergraduates to do research. The main focus of this book is understanding statistics, not using statistics. Still, you will learn the skills you need to do some of the most common statistics used in the kinds of research you are likely to do.

3. *Understanding statistics develops your analytic and critical thinking.* Social and behavioral science students are often most interested in people and in improving things in the practical world. This does not mean that you avoid abstractions. In fact, the students we know are exhilarated most by the almost philosophical levels of abstraction where the secrets of human experience so often seem to hide. Yet even this kind of abstraction often is grasped only superficially at first, as slogans instead of useful knowledge. Of all the courses you are likely to take in the social and behavioral sciences, this course will probably do the most to help you learn to think precisely, to evaluate information, and to apply logical analysis at a very high level.

How to Gain the Most from This Course

There are five things we can advise:

1. *Keep your attention on the concepts.* Treat this course less like a math course and more like a course in logic. When you read a section of a chapter, your attention should be on grasping the principles. When working the exercises, think about why you are doing each step. If you simply try to memorize how to come up with the right numbers, you will have learned very little of use in your future studies—nor will you do very well on the tests in this course.

2. *Be sure you know each concept before you go on to the next.* Statistics is cumulative. Each new concept is built on the last one. Even within a chapter, if you have read a section and you do not understand it—*stop*. Reread it, rethink it, ask for help. Do whatever you need to do to grasp it. (If you think that you understand a section but are not sure, try working a practice problem on it at the end of the chapter.)

Having to read the material in this book over and over does not mean that you are stupid. Most students have to read each chapter several times. Each reading in statistics is usually much slower than that in other textbooks. Statistics reading has to be pored over with clear, calm attention for it to sink in. Allow plenty of time for this kind of reading and rereading.

3. *Keep up.* Again, statistics is cumulative. If you fall behind in your reading or miss lectures, the lectures you then attend will be almost meaningless. It will get harder and harder to catch up.

4. *Study especially intensely in the first half of the course.* It is especially important to master the material thoroughly at the start of the course. This is because everything else in statistics is built on what you learn at the start. Yet the beginning of the semester is often when students study least seriously.

If you have mastered the first half of the course—not just learned the general idea, but really know it—the second half will be easier. If you have not mastered the first half, the second half will be close to impossible.

5. ***Help each other.*** There is no better way to solidify and deepen your understanding of statistics than to try to explain it to someone having a harder time. (Of course, this explaining has to be done with patience and respect.) For those of you who are having a harder time, there is no better way to work through the difficult parts than by learning from another student who has just mastered the material.

Thus, we strongly urge you to form study teams with one to three other students. It is best if your team includes some who expect this material to come easily and some who don't. Those who learn statistics easily will really get the very most from helping others who have to struggle with it—the latter will tax the former's supposed understanding enormously. For those who fear trouble ahead, you need to work with those who do not—the blind leading the blind is no way to learn. Pick teammates who live near you so that it is easy for you to get together. Also, meet often—between each class, if possible.

A Final Note

Believe it or not, we love teaching statistics. Time and again, we have had the wonderful experience of having beaming students come to us to say, "Professor Aron, I got a 90% on this exam. I can't believe it! Me, a 90 on a statistics exam!" Or the student who tells us, "This is actually fun. Don't tell anyone, but I'm actually enjoying . . . statistics, of all things!" We hope you will have these kinds of experiences in this course.

Arthur Aron
Elaine N. Aron

Displaying the Order in a Group of Numbers

1

CHAPTER OUTLINE

WELCOME to *Statistics for the Behavioral and Social Sciences: A Brief Course*. We imagine you to be as unique as the other students we have known who have taken this course. Some of you are highly scientific sorts; others are more intuitive. Some of you are fond of math; others are less so, or even afraid of it. Whatever your style, we welcome you. We want to assure you that if you give this book some special attention (perhaps a little more than most other textbooks require), you *will* learn statistics. The approach used in this book has successfully taught all sorts of students before you, including people who had taken statistics previously and done poorly. With this book, and your instructor's help, you will learn statistics and learn it well.

Given that you *can* learn statistics, you still have to decide if you want to make the effort it will require. Why would you want to do that, except to meet a requirement of your major? (Not a very energizing motive.) First, you will be far better equipped to read research articles in your major. Second, you'll be on your way to being able to do your own research if you so choose. Third, just as your muscles would become stronger as the result of weight training, your brain will be sharper as a result of this course.

Think of statistics as a tool that extends a basic thinking process that every human employs: You observe a thing; you wonder what it means or what caused it; you have an insight or make an intuitive guess; you observe again, but now in detail, or you try making some little changes in the process to test your intuition. Then, you face the eternal problem: Was your hunch really confirmed or not? What are the chances that what you have observed this second time will happen again and again, so that you can announce your insight to the world as something probably true? Statistics is a method of pursuing truth. At least statistics can tell you the likelihood that your hunch is true in this time and place, with these sorts of people. (The truths of statistics also depend on how carefully you have collected your information, but good research design is another topic altogether.) This pursuit of truth, or at least of future likelihood, is the essence of science. It is also the essence of human evolution and survival. Think of the first research questions: What will the mammoths do next spring? What will happen if I eat this root? It is easy to see how the accurate have survived. You are among them. Because your ancestors exercised brains as well as brawn, you are here. Do those who come after you the same favor of thinking carefully about outcomes. Statistics is one good way to do that.

The Two Branches of Statistical Methods

There are two main branches of statistical methods:

descriptive statistics

1. Descriptive statistics. Social and behavioral scientists use descriptive statistics to summarize and make understandable, to describe, a group of numbers from a research study.

inferential statistics

2. Inferential statistics. Social and behavioral scientists use inferential statistics to draw conclusions and inferences, which are based on the numbers from a research study, but go beyond these numbers.

The first three chapters of this book focus on descriptive statistics. This topic is important in its own right, but it also prepares you to understand inferential statistics. Inferential statistics are the focus of Chapters 4 through 12.

Frequency Tables

In this chapter, you learn to use tables and graphs to describe a group of numbers. The purpose of descriptive statistics is to make a group of numbers easy to understand. Tables and graphs help a great deal.

An Example

Aron, Paris, and Aron (1995), as part of a larger study, gave a questionnaire to 151 students in an introductory statistics class during the first week of the course. One question asked, "How stressed have you been in the last 2½ weeks, on a scale of 0 to 10, with 0 being not at all stressed and 10 being as stressed as possible?" The 151 students' ratings were as follows:

4, 7, 7, 7, 8, 8, 7, 8, 9, 4, 7, 3, 6, 9, 10, 5, 7, 10, 6, 8, 7, 8, 7, 8, 7, 4, 5, 10, 10, 0, 9, 8, 3, 7, 9, 7, 9, 5, 8, 5, 0, 4, 6, 6, 7, 5, 3, 2, 8, 5, 10, 9, 10, 6, 4, 8, 8, 8, 4, 8, 7, 3, 8, 8, 8, 8, 7, 9, 7, 5, 6, 3, 4, 8, 7, 5, 7, 3, 3, 6, 5, 7, 5, 7, 8, 8, 7, 10, 5, 4, 3, 7, 6, 3, 9, 7, 8, 5, 7, 9, 9, 3, 1, 8, 6, 6, 4, 8, 5, 10, 4, 8, 10, 5, 5, 4, 9, 4, 7, 7, 7, 6, 6, 4, 4, 4, 9, 7, 10, 4, 7, 5, 10, 7, 9, 2, 7, 5, 9, 10, 3, 7, 2, 5, 9, 8, 10, 10, 6, 8, 3

It takes a while just to look at all these ratings. Looking through them gives some sense of the overall tendencies, but this is hardly an accurate method. One solution is to make a table showing how many students used each of the 11 values the ratings can have (0, 1, 2, and so on, through 10). We have done this in Table 1–1. We also figured the percentages each value's frequency is of the total number of scores.

Table 1–1 is called a **frequency table** because it shows how frequently (how many times) each rating number was used. A frequency table makes the pattern of numbers very easy to see. In this example, you can see that most of the students rated their stress around 7 or 8, with few rating it very low.

Frequency tables sometimes give only the raw-number frequencies and not the percentages, or only the percentages and not the raw-number frequencies.[1]

An Aside: Variables, Values, and Scores

Another way of saying what a frequency table does is to say that it shows the frequency of each **value** of a particular **variable.** A value is simply a number, such as 4, –81, or 367.12. A value can also be a category, such as male or female or a person's religion.

TABLE 1–1
Number of Students Rating Each Value of the Stress Scale

Stress Rating	Frequency	Percent
10	14	9.3
9	15	9.9
8	26	17.2
7	31	20.5
6	13	8.6
5	18	11.9
4	16	10.6
3	12	7.9
2	3	2.0
1	1	.7
0	2	1.3

Note: Data from Aron, Paris, & Aron (1995).

frequency table

value

variable

---

[1]In addition, some frequency tables include for each value the total number of scores with that value and all values preceding it. These are called *cumulative frequencies* because they tell how many scores are accumulated up to this point on the table. If percentages are used, cumulative percentages also may be included. Cumulative percentages would give, for each value, the percentage of scores up to and including that value. The cumulative percentage for any given value also is called a *percentile*.

A variable is a characteristic that can have different values. In short, it can vary. In our stress example, the variable is level of stress. It can have values of 0 through 10. Height is a variable, social class is a variable, score on a creativity test is a variable, number of people absent from work is a variable, dosage of a medication is a variable, political party preference is a variable, and class size is a variable.

score

On any variable, each person has a particular number or **score** that is that person's value on the variable. For example, Chris's score on the stress variable might have a value of 6; Pat's score might have a value of 8. We often use the word score for a particular person's value on a variable. This is because much social science research involves scores on some type of test.

Social science research is about variables, values, and scores. We will be using these terms throughout the book. The formal definitions are a bit abstract. In practice, you will find that what we mean when we use these words usually is obvious.

How to Make a Frequency Table

Here are the four steps for making a frequency table.

1. **Make a list down the page of each possible value, starting from the highest and ending with the lowest.** In the stress rating results, the list goes from 10, the highest possible rating, down through 0, the lowest possible rating. (Even if one of the ratings between 10 and 0 had not been used, you would still include that value in the listing, showing it as having a frequency of 0. For example, if no one in the class had given a stress rating of 2, you would still include 2 as one of the values on the frequency table.)

2. **Go one by one through the scores, making a mark for each next to its value on your list.** This is shown in Figure 1–1. It is a good idea to cross off each score as you mark it on the list.

3. **Make a table showing how many times each value on your list was used.** To do this, add up the number of marks beside each value. It also is wise to cross-check your work by adding up these totals. You want to be sure that their sum equals the total number of scores.

4. **Figure the percentage of scores for each value.** Do this by taking the frequency for that value and dividing it by the total number of scores. (You usually will need to round off the percentage. There is no fixed rule

FIGURE 1–1
Creating a frequency table of stress ratings. (Data from Aron et al., 1995)

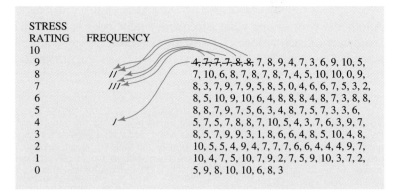

STRESS RATING	FREQUENCY	
10		
9		4, 7, 7, 7, 8, 8, 7, 8, 9, 4, 7, 3, 6, 9, 10, 5,
8	//	7, 10, 6, 8, 7, 8, 7, 8, 7, 4, 5, 10, 10, 0, 9,
7	///	8, 3, 7, 9, 7, 9, 5, 8, 5, 0, 4, 6, 6, 7, 5, 3, 2,
6		8, 5, 10, 9, 10, 6, 4, 8, 8, 8, 4, 8, 7, 3, 8, 8,
5		8, 8, 7, 9, 7, 5, 6, 3, 4, 8, 7, 5, 7, 3, 3, 6,
4	/	5, 7, 5, 7, 8, 8, 7, 10, 5, 4, 3, 7, 6, 3, 9, 7,
3		8, 5, 7, 9, 9, 3, 1, 8, 6, 6, 4, 8, 5, 10, 4, 8,
2		10, 5, 5, 4, 9, 4, 7, 7, 7, 6, 6, 4, 4, 4, 9, 7,
1		10, 4, 7, 5, 10, 7, 9, 2, 7, 5, 9, 10, 3, 7, 2,
0		5, 9, 8, 10, 10, 6, 8, 3

about how many decimals to use when rounding off the percentages. A rough guideline would be with fewer than 10 values, round to the nearest whole percentage; with 10 to 20 values, round to one decimal place; with more than 20 values, round to two decimal places. Note that because of the rounding, the total of your percentages usually will not be exactly 100%.)

A Second Example

Tracy McLaughlin-Volpe and her colleagues (2001) had 94 first- and second-year university students keep a diary of their social interactions for a week during the regular semester. Each time a student had a social interaction lasting 10 minutes or longer, the student would fill out a card. The card included questions about who were the other people in the interaction, and about various aspects of the conversation. Excluding family and work situations, the number of social interactions of 10 minutes or longer over a week for these 94 students were as follows:

48, 15, 33, 3, 21, 19, 17, 16, 44, 25, 30, 3, 5, 9, 35, 32, 26, 13, 14, 14, 47, 47, 29, 18, 11, 5, 19, 24, 17, 6, 25, 8, 18, 29, 1, 18, 22, 3, 22, 29, 2, 6, 10, 29, 10, 21, 38, 41, 16, 17, 8, 40, 8, 10, 18, 7, 4, 4, 8, 11, 3, 23, 10, 19, 21, 13, 12, 10, 4, 17, 11, 21, 9, 8, 7, 5, 3, 22, 14, 25, 4, 11, 10, 18, 1, 28, 27, 19, 24, 35, 9, 30, 8, 26

Now, let's follow our four steps for making a frequency table.

1. Make a list of each possible value down the left edge of a page, starting from the highest and ending with the lowest. In this study, the highest number of interactions could be any number. However, the highest actual number in this group was 48, so we can use 48 as the highest value. The lowest possible number of interactions is 0. Thus, the first step is to list these values down a page. (It might be good to use several columns so that you can have all the scores on a single page.)

2. Go one by one through the scores, making a mark for each next to its value on your list. Figure 1–2 shows this.

3. Make a table showing how many times each value on your list was used. Table 1–2 is the result.

4. Figure the percentages of scores for each value. We have *not* done so in this example because with so many categories, it would not help much for seeing the pattern of scores. However, if you want to check your understanding of this step, the first three percentages would be 1.06%, 2.13%, and 0%. (These are the percentages for frequencies of 1, 2, and 0. We have rounded to two decimal places.)

Grouped Frequency Tables

Sometimes there are so many possible values that a frequency table is too awkward to give a simple picture of the scores. The last example was a bit like that, wasn't it? The solution is to make groupings of values that include all values within a certain range. For example, consider our stress example. Instead of having a separate frequency figure for the students who rated their stress as 8 and another for those who rated it as 9, you could have a combined category of 8 and 9. This combined category is a range of values that includes these two values. A combined category like this is called an **interval**.

48 - /	31 -	15 - /
47 - //	30 - //	14 - ///
46 -	29 - ////	13 - //
45 -	28 - /	12 - /
44 - /	27 - /	11 - ////
43 -	26 - //	10 - 7HL /
42 -	25 - ///	9 - ///
41 - /	24 - //	8 - 7HL /
40 - /	23 - /	7 - //
39 -	22 - ///	6 - //
38 - /	21 - ////	5 - ///
37 -	20 -	4 - ////
36 -	19 - ////	3 - 7HL
35 - //	18 - 7HL	2 - /
34 -	17 - ////	1 - //
33 - /	16 - //	0 -
32 - /		

FIGURE 1–2
Creating a frequency table of students' social interactions over a week. (Data from McLaughlin-Volpe et al., 2001)

interval

TABLE 1–2
Frequency Table for Number of Social Interactions During a Week for 94 College Students

Score	Frequency	Score	Frequency	Score	Frequency
48	1	31	0	15	1
47	2	30	2	14	3
46	0	29	4	13	2
45	0	28	1	12	1
44	1	27	1	11	4
43	0	26	2	10	6
42	0	25	3	9	3
41	1	24	2	8	6
40	1	23	1	7	2
39	0	22	3	6	2
38	1	21	4	5	3
37	0	20	0	4	4
36	0	19	4	3	5
35	2	18	5	2	1
34	0	17	4	1	2
33	1	16	2	0	0
32	1				

Note: Data from McLaughlin-Volpe et al. (2001).

grouped frequency table

This particular interval of 8 and 9 has a frequency of 41 (the sum of the 26 scores with a value of 8 and the 15 scores with a value of 9).

A frequency table that uses intervals is called a **grouped frequency table.** Table 1–3 is a grouped frequency table for the stress ratings example. (However, in this example, the full frequency table has only 11 different values. Thus, a grouped frequency table was not really necessary.) Table 1–4 is a grouped frequency table for the 94 students' numbers of social interactions over a week.

Making a grouped frequency table involves combining the individual values into the intervals (groups of adjacent values). There are some rules about how this is done. Most important, there should be about 5 to 15 intervals. Also, all intervals should be of the same size (except that sometimes researchers use a different size for the highest or lowest interval). If you study the examples closely, you will see that we have followed some additional principles. The low end of each interval is always a multiple of the interval size. (For example, if the interval size is 3, then the low end of the intervals contains multiples of 3, such as 0, 3, 6, 9, and so on.) It also is standard to make the intervals a round number, such as 2, 3, 5, 10, or a multiple of 10. (Table 1–3 uses intervals of 2 each. Table 1–4 uses intervals of 5 each.)

The big question in actually designing a grouped frequency table is determining the interval size and the number of intervals. There are various guidelines to help researchers with this, but in practice it is done automatically by the researcher's computer. Thus, we will not focus on it in this book. However, should you have to make a grouped frequency table on your own, the key thing is to experiment with the interval size until you come up with an interval size that is a round number and that creates about 5 to 15 intervals. Then when actually setting up the table, be sure you set the low end of each interval to a multiple of the interval size and the top end of each interval to the number that is just below the low end of the next interval.

TABLE 1–3
Grouped Frequency Table for Stress Ratings

Stress Rating Interval	Frequency	Percent
10–11	14	9
8–9	41	27
6–7	44	29
4–5	34	23
2–3	15	10
0–1	3	2

Note: Data from Aron, Paris, & Aron (1995).

Kinds of Variables

Most of the variables social scientists use are like those in the stress ratings example. The scores are numbers that tell you how much there is of the thing being measured. In the stress ratings example, the higher the number the more stress. We call this kind of variable a **numeric variable.** Numeric variables also are also called *quantitative variables.*

Social scientists use two main kinds of numeric variables. The kind of variable used most often is a variable in which the numbers stand for aproximately equal amounts of what is being measured. This is called an **equal–interval variable.** Take grade point average (GPA). This is a roughly equal-interval variable—for example, the difference between a GPA of 2.5 and 2.8 means about as much of a difference as the difference between that of 3.0 and 3.3.

The other kind of numeric variable social scientists often use is where the numbers only stand for relative rankings. This is called a **rank-order variable.** An example is rank in one's graduating class. Notice that with a rank-order variable, the difference between one number and the next does not always mean the same amount of the underlying thing being measured. For example, the difference between being second and third in your graduating class could be a very dissimilar amount of difference in underlying GPA than the difference between being eighth and ninth. There is somewhat less information in the rank-order variable. It is less precise. (Rank-order variables are also commonly referred to as *ordinal variables.*)

There is also a kind of variable that is not about numbers at all, but which refers just to categories. This is called a **nominal variable** (it is also sometimes called a *categorical variable*). With a nominal variable, such as gender or religion, the values are names or categories. (The term *nominal* comes from the idea that its values are names.) For example, the values for gender are female and male. A person's score on the variable gender is one of these two values. Similarly, hair color has values, such as brown, black, and so forth. Sometimes frequency tables are used for nominal variables so that the table gives the frequency for each value or category of the nominal variable.

In this book, we focus mostly on numeric variables. However, rank-order and nominal variables also are fairly common in the social and behavioral sciences. We discuss some statistical procedures specifically designed for using rank-order and nominal variables in Chapter 11.

numeric variable

equal–interval variable

rank-order variable

nominal variable

TABLE 1–4
Grouped Frequency Table for Numbers of Social Interactions during a Week for 94 College Students

Interval	Frequency	Percent
45–49	3	3.2
40–44	3	3.2
35–39	3	3.2
30–34	4	4.3
25–29	11	11.7
20–24	10	10.6
15–19	16	17.0
10–14	16	17.0
5–9	16	17.0
0–4	12	12.8

Note: Data from McLaughlin-Volpe et al. (2001).

Histograms

A graph is another good way to make a large group of scores easy to understand. "A picture is worth a thousand words"—and sometimes a thousand numbers. One way to graph the information in a frequency table is to make a special kind of bar chart called a **histogram.** In a histogram, the height of each bar is the frequency of each value in the frequency table, and all the bars are put next to each other with no space in between.

histogram

A histogram looks a bit like a city skyline. Figure 1–3 shows two histograms based on the stress ratings example, one based on the ordinary frequency table and one based on the grouped frequency table. (When making a

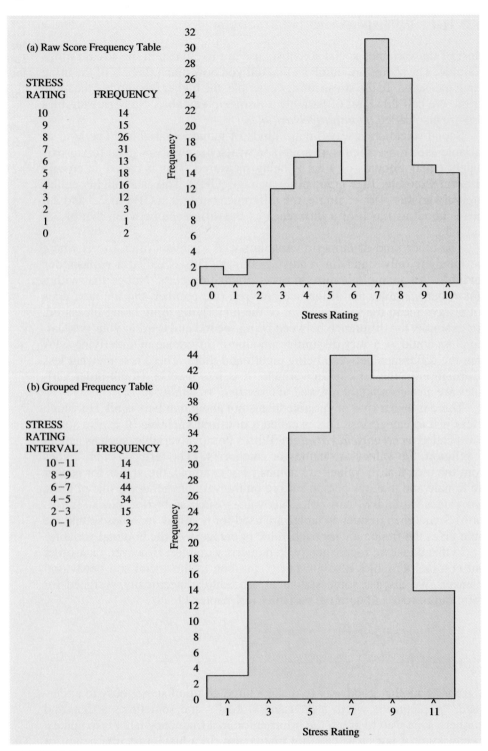

FIGURE 1–3
Histograms based on (a) a frequency table and (b) a grouped frequency table for the Aron et al. (1995) data.

histogram for the frequencies of the different values of a nominal variable, the bars are usually separated, making the familiar bar graph.)

How to Make a Histogram

Here are the four steps for making a histogram:

1. **Make a frequency table.**
2. **Put the scale of values along the bottom of a page. The numbers should go from left to right, from lowest to highest.** For a grouped frequency table, the histogram is of the intervals. Mark only the midpoint of each interval, under the center of each bar. The midpoint is the middle of where the interval starts and the next interval begins. (To get the midpoint, take the bottom of the next interval minus the bottom of this interval; divide this by 2; then add this to the bottom of this interval.)
3. **Make a scale of frequencies along the left edge of the page.** The scale should go from 0 at the bottom to the highest frequency for any value.
4. **Make a bar for each value.** The height of each bar is the frequency of the value it is placed over. Making a histogram is easiest if you use graph paper.

Additional Histogram Example

Figure 1–4 shows a histogram based on the grouped frequency table for the example of the numbers of students' social interactions in a week.

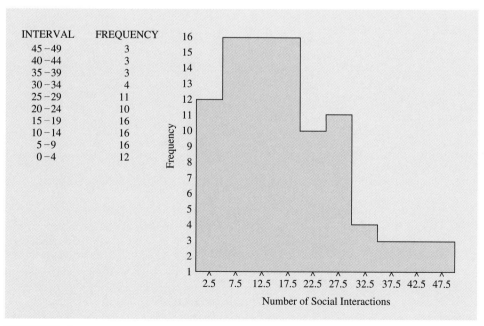

FIGURE 1–4
Histogram for number of social interactions during a week for 94 college students, based on grouped frequencies. (Data from McLaughlin-Volpe et al., 2001)

Frequency Polygons

frequency polygon

Another way to graph the information in a frequency table is to make a special kind of line graph called a **frequency polygon.** In a frequency polygon, the line moves from point to point. The height of each point shows the number of scores that have that value. This creates a kind of mountain-peak skyline. Figure 1–5 shows the frequency polygon for the frequency table in the stress ratings example.

How to Make a Frequency Polygon

Here are five steps for making a frequency polygon.

1. **Make a frequency table.**
2. **Place the values along the bottom.** Be sure to include one extra value above and one extra value below the values that actually have scores in them. You need the extra value so that the line starts and ends along the baseline of the graph, at zero frequency. This creates a closed or "polygon" figure.
3. **Along the left of the page, make a scale of frequencies that goes from 0 at the bottom to the highest frequency in any value.**
4. **Mark a point above each value for the frequency of that value.**
5. **Connect the points with lines.**

Additional Frequency Polygon Example

Figure 1–6 shows the five steps in making a frequency polygon based on the grouped frequency table for the students' social interactions example.

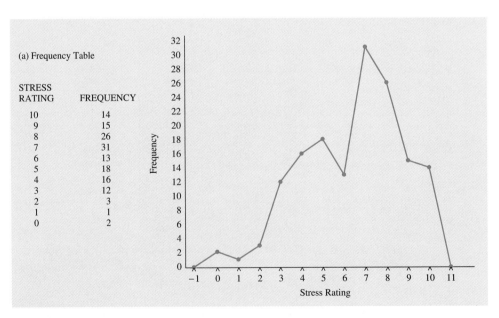

FIGURE 1–5
Frequency polygon based on a frequency table for the Aron et al. (1995) data.

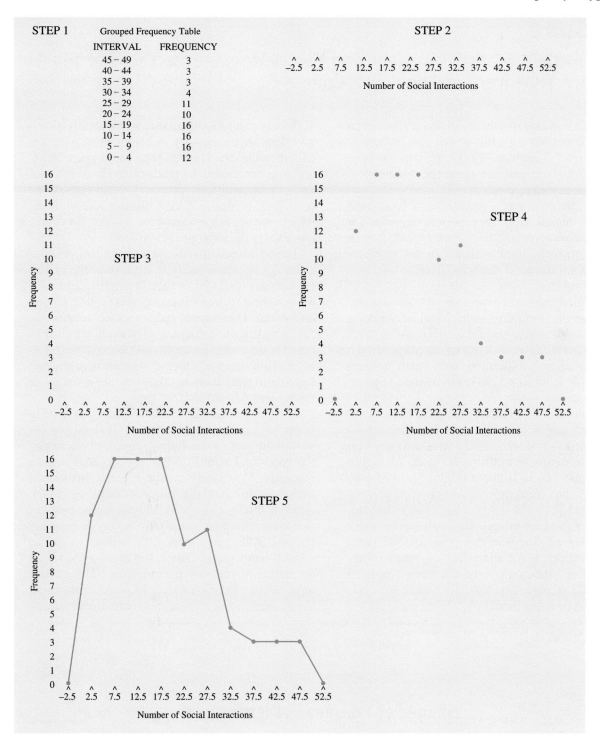

FIGURE 1–6
Five steps in making a frequency polygon based on the grouped frequency table for number of social interactions during a week for 94 students (data from McLaughlin-Volpe et al., 2001) Step 1: Make a frequency table. Step 2: Place the values along the bottom. Step 3: Along the left side of the page, make a scale of frequencies that goes from 0 at the bottom to the highest frequency in any value. Step 4: Mark a point above each value for the frequency of that value. Step 5: Connect the points with lines.

BOX 1-1

Math Anxiety, Statistics Anxiety, and You: A Message for Those of You Who Are Truly Worried About This Course

Let's face it: Many of you dread this course, even to the point of having a full-blown case of "statistics anxiety" (Zeidner, 1991). If you become tense the minute you see numbers, we need to talk about that right now.

First, this course is a chance for a fresh start with the digits. Your past performance in (or avoidance of) geometry, trigonometry, calculus, or similar horrors need not influence in any way how well you comprehend statistics. This is largely a different subject.

Second, if your worry persists, you need to decide where it is coming from. Math or statistics anxiety, test anxiety, general anxiety, and general low self-confidence each seems to play its own role in students' difficulties with math courses (Cooper & Robinson, 1989; Dwinell & Higbee, 1991).

Is your problem mainly math/statistics anxiety? There are wonderful books and websites to help you. Do a search, or try **mathanxiety.net, mathpower.com,** or **mathmatters.net.** We highly recommend Sheila Tobias's (1995) *Succeed with Math: Every Student's Guide to Conquering Math Anxiety* (but there are also other books described at these websites). Tobias, a former math avoider herself, suggests that your goal be "math mental health," which she defines as "the willingness to learn the math you need when you need it" (p. 12). (Could it be that this course in statistics is one of those times?)

Tobias explains that math mental health is usually lost in elementary school, when you are called to the blackboard, your mind goes blank, and you are unable to produce the one right answer to an arithmetic problem. What confidence remained probably faded during timed tests, which you did not realize were difficult for everyone except the most proficient few.

Tobias claims that students who are good at math are not necessarily smarter than the rest of us, but they really know their strengths and weaknesses, their styles of thinking and feeling around a problem. They do not judge themselves harshly for mistakes. In particular, they do not expect to understand things instantly. Allowing yourself to be a "slow learner" does not mean that you are less intelligent. It shows that you are growing in math mental health.

Is your problem test anxiety? Then you need to learn to handle anxiety better. Test taking requires the use of the thinking part of our brain, the prefrontal cortex. When we are anxious, we naturally "downshift" to more basic, instinctual brain systems. And that ruins our thinking ability. Anxiety produces arousal, and one of the best understood relationships in psychology is between arousal and performance. Whereas moderate arousal helps performance, too much or too little dramatically reduces performance. Things you have learned become harder to recall. Your mind starts to race, and this creates more anxiety, more

Shapes of Frequency Distributions

frequency distribution

A frequency table, histogram, or frequency polygon describes a **frequency distribution.** That is, these show the pattern or shape of how the frequencies are spread out, or "distributed." Social scientists also find it useful to describe this shape in words. (Describing the shape of a distribution is important both for the descriptive statistics we focus on in this chapter and also for the inferential statistics you will learn in later chapters.)

arousal, and so on. Because during a test you may be fearing that you are "no good and never will be," it is important to rethink beforehand any poor grades you may have received in the past—most likely these reflected your problems with tests more than your abilities.

There are many ways to reduce anxiety and arousal in general, such as learning to breathe properly and to take a quick break to relax deeply. Your counseling center should be able to help you or direct you to some good books on the subject. Again, there are also many websites about reducing anxiety.

Test anxiety specifically is reduced by, first, overpreparing for a few tests, so that you go in with the certainty that you cannot possibly fail, no matter how aroused you become. The best time to begin applying this tactic is the first test of this course: There will be no old material to review, success will not depend on having understood previous material, and it will help you do better throughout the course. (You also might enlist the sympathy of your instructor or teaching assistant. Bring in a list of what you have studied, state why you are being so exacting, and ask if you have missed anything.) Your preparation must be ridiculously thorough, but only for a few exams. After these successes, your test anxiety should decline.

Also, create a practice test situation as similar to a real test as possible, making a special effort to duplicate the aspects that bother you most. If feeling rushed is the troubling part, once you think you are well prepared, set yourself a time limit for solving some homework problems. Make yourself write out answers fully and legibly. This may be part of what makes you feel slow during a test. If the presence of others bothers you, the sound of their scurrying pencils while yours is frozen in midair, do your practice test with others in your course. Even make it an explicit contest to see who can finish first.

Is your problem a general lack of confidence? Is there something else in your life causing you to worry or feel bad about yourself? Then we suggest that it is time you tried your friendly college counseling center.

Lastly, could you be highly sensitive? A final word about anxiety and arousal. About 15 to 20 percent of humans (and all higher animals) seem to be born with a temperament trait that has been seen traditionally as shyness, hesitancy, or introversion (Eysenck, 1981; Kagan, 1994). But this shyness or hesitancy seems actually due to a preference to observe and an ability to notice subtle stimulation and process information deeply (Aron, 1996; Aron & Aron, 1997). This often causes highly sensitive people (HSPs) to be very intuitive or even gifted. But it also means they are more easily overaroused by high levels of stimulation, like tests.

You might want to find out if you are an HSP (at **www.hsperson.com**). If you are, appreciate the trait's assets and make some allowances for its one disadvantage, this tendency to become easily overaroused. It has to affect your performance on tests. What matters is what you actually know, which is probably quite a bit. This simple act of self-acceptance—that you are *not* less smart but *are* more sensitive—may in itself help ease your arousal when trying to express your statistical knowledge.

So good luck to all of you. We wish you the best while taking this course and in your lives.

Unimodal and Bimodal Frequency Distributions

One important aspect of a distribution's shape is whether it has only one main high point (one high "tower" in the histogram or one main "peak" in the frequency polygon). For example, in the stress ratings study, the most frequent score is a 7, giving a graph with only one very high area. This is called a **unimodal** distribution. If a distribution has two fairly equal high points, it is called a **bimodal** distribution. Any distribution with two or more high points is also called **multimodal.** Finally, if all the values have about the

unimodal
bimodal
multimodal

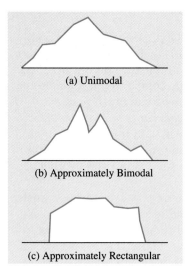

FIGURE 1–7
Examples of (a) unimodal, (b) approximately bimodal, and (c) approximately rectangular frequency polygons.

rectangular

symmetrical

skewed

FIGURE 1–8
Fictional examples of distributions that are not unimodal: (a) A bimodal distribution showing the possible frequencies for different levels of quality of work of employees who come to the attention of higher-level managers. (b) A rectangular distribution showing the possible frequencies of students at different grade levels in an elementary school.

same frequency, it is called a **rectangular** distribution. These frequency distributions are illustrated in Figure 1–7.

The information we collect in social science research is usually approximately unimodal. Bimodal and other multimodal distributions occasionally turn up. A bimodal example would be the distribution of number of employees whose names have come to the attention of higher-level managers. If you made a frequency distribution for the quality of work of such employees, the high points in a graph of these would be at the values indicating that the quality of work was either very poor or very high. An example of a rectangular distribution is the number of children at each grade level attending an elementary school. There would be about the same number in first grade, second grade, and so on. These examples are illustrated in Figure 1–8.

Symmetrical and Skewed Distributions

Another aspect of the stress ratings example is that the distribution was lopsided, with more scores near the high end. This is somewhat unusual. Most things we measure in the social sciences have about equal numbers on both sides of the middle. That is, most distributions are approximately **symmetrical.** (If you folded them in half, the two halves would look the same.)

Distributions that clearly are not symmetrical are called **skewed.** The stress ratings distribution is an example of a skewed distribution. A skewed distribution has one side that is long and spread out, somewhat like a tail. The side with *fewer* scores (the side that looks more like a tail) describes the direction of the skew. Thus a distribution with fewer scores left of the peak, like our stress ratings example, is *skewed to the left*. The other example we have examined in this chapter, the distributions of students' numbers of interactions in a week is *skewed to the right*. Figure 1–9 illustrates symmetrical and skewed distributions.

A distribution that is skewed to the right is also called *positively skewed*. A distribution skewed to the left is also called *negatively skewed*.

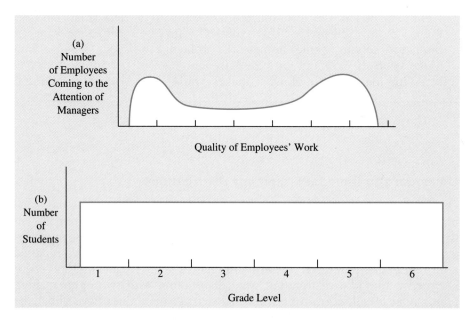

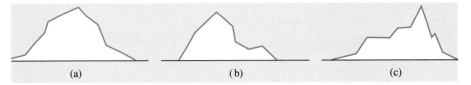

FIGURE 1–9
Examples of frequency polygons of distributions that are (a) approximately symmetrical, (b) skewed to the right (positively skewed), and (c) skewed to the left (negatively skewed).

Strongly skewed distributions come up in the social and behavioral sciences mainly when what is being measured has some lower or upper limit. For example, the number of social interactions in a week cannot be fewer than zero interactions. This kind of situation in which many scores pile up at the low end because it is impossible to have a lower score is called a **floor effect.**

An example of a skewed distribution caused by an upper limit is illustrated in Figure 1–10. This is a distribution of adults' scores on a multiplication table test. This distribution is highly skewed to the left. Most of the scores pile up at the right, the high end (a perfect score). This is an example of a **ceiling effect.** The stress example also shows a mild ceiling effect. This is because many students had high levels of stress, the maximum rating was 10, and people often do not like to use ratings right at the maximum.

floor effect

ceiling effect

Normal, Heavy-Tailed, and Light-Tailed Distributions

Social scientists also describe a distribution in terms of whether its tails are particularly heavy (thick, with many scores in them) or light (thin, with few scores in them). These are called **heavy-tailed distributions** and **light-tailed distributions** (This aspect of the shape of a distubution is also called *kurtosis*.) The standard of comparison is a bell-shaped curve. In social and behavioral science research and nature generally, distributions often are quite similar to this bell-shaped standard, called the **normal curve.** We will discuss this curve in some detail in later chapters. For now, however, the important thing is that the normal curve is a unimodal, symmetrical curve with average sort of tails—the sort of bell shape shown in Figure 1–11a. The stress-ratings example in this chapter is very roughly like a normal curve,

heavy-tailed distributions
light-tailed distributions

normal curve

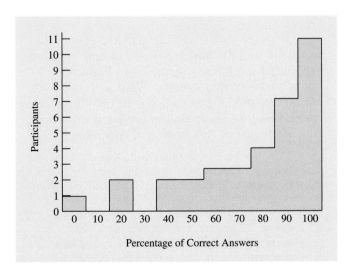

FIGURE 1–10
A distribution skewed to the left: fictional distribution of adults' scores on a multiplication table test.

BOX 1-2

Gender, Ethnicity, and Math Performance

From time to time, someone tries to argue that because some groups of people score better on math tests and make careers out of mathematics, this means that these groups have some genetic advantage in math (or statistics). Other groups are said or implied to be innately inferior at math. The issue comes up about gender and also racial and ethnic groups, and of course in arguments about overall intelligence as well as math. There's no evidence for such genetic differences that can't be refuted (A must-see article: Block, 1995). But the stereotypes persist.

The impact of these stereotypes has been well established in research by Steele and his colleagues (1997), who have done numerous studies on what they call "stereotype threat," which occurs when a negative stereotype about a group you belong to becomes relevant to you because of the situation you are in, like taking a math test, and provides an explanation for how you will behave. A typical experiment creating stereotype threat (Spencer, Steele, & Quinn, 1999) involved women taking a difficult math test. Half were told that men generally do better on the test and the other half that women generally do equally well. When told that women do worse, the women did indeed score substantially lower. In the other condition there was no difference. (In fact, in two separate studies men performed a little worse when they were told there was no gender difference, as if they had lost some of their confidence.)

The same results occur when African Americans are given parts of the Graduate Record Exam—they do fine on the test when they are told no racial differences in the scores have been found, and do worse when they are told such differences have been found (Steele, 1997).

These results certainly argue against there being any inherent differences in ability in these groups. But that is nothing new. Many lines of research indicate that prejudices, not genetics, are the probable cause of differences in test scores between groups. For example, the same difference of 15 I.Q. points between a dominant and minority group has been found all over the world, even when there is no genetic difference between the groups, and in cases where opportunities for a group have changed, as when they emigrate, differences have rapidly disappeared (Block, 1995).

If groups such as women and African Americans are not inherently inferior in any area of intellectual endeavor, but perform worse on tests, what might be the reasons? The usual explanation is that they have internalized the "superior" group's prejudices. Steele thinks the problem might not be so internal but may have to do with the situation. The stigmatized groups perform worse when they know that's what is expected—when they experience the threat of being stereotyped.

Of course in Steele's studies everyone tested had roughly the same initial educational background so that they knew the answers under the nonthreatening condition. Under the threatening condition, there is evidence that they try even harder. Too hard. And become anxious. Just as often, however, members of groups expected to do poorly simply stop caring about how they do. They disidentify with the whole goal of doing well in math, for example. They avoid the subject or take easy classes and just shrug off any low grades.

What Can You Do for Yourself?

So, do you feel you belong to a group that is expected to do worse at math? (This includes white males who feel they are among the "math dumbbells.") What can you do to get out from under the shadow of "stereotype threat" as you take this course?

First, care about learning statistics. Don't discount it to save your self-esteem and separate yourself from the rest of the class. Fight for your right to know this subject. What a triumph for those who hold the prejudice if you give up. Consider these words from the former president of the Mathematics Association of America:

> The paradox of our times is that as mathematics becomes increasingly powerful, only the powerful seem to benefit from it. The ability to think mathematically—broadly interpreted—is absolutely crucial to advancement in virtually every career. Confidence in dealing with data, skepticism in analyzing arguments, persistence in penetrating complex problems, and literacy in

communicating about technical matters are the enabling arts offered by the new mathematical sciences. (Steen, 1987, p. xviii)

Second, once you care about succeeding at statistics, realize you are going to be affected by stereotype threat. Think of it as a stereotype-induced form of test anxiety and work on it that way—see Box 1.1.

Third, in yourself, root out the effects of that stereotype as much as you can. It takes some effort. That's why we are spending time on it here. Research on stereotypes shows that they can be activated without our awareness (Fiske, 1998) even when we are otherwise low in prejudice or a member of the stereotyped group. To keep from being prejudiced about ourselves or others, we have to consciously resist stereotypes. So, to avoid unconsciously handicapping yourself in this course, as those in Steele's experiments probably did, you must make an active effort; you must consciously dismantle the stereotype and think about its falsehood.

Here are some points to think about.

- Women: Every bit of evidence for thinking that men are genetically better at math can and has been well disputed. For example, yes, the very top performers tend to be male, but the differences are slight, and the lowest performers are not more likely to be female, as would probably be the case if there were a genetic difference. Tobias (1982) cites numerous studies providing nongenetic explanations for why women might not make it to the very top in math. For example, in a study of students identified by a math talent search, it was found that few parents arranged for their daughters to be coached before the talent exams. Sons were almost invariably coached. In another study, parents of mathematically gifted girls were not even aware of their daughters' abilities, whereas parents of boys invariably were. In general, girls tend to avoid higher math classes, according to Tobias, because parents, peers, and even teachers often advise them against pursuing too much math. So even though women are earning more PhDs in math than ever before, it is not surprising that math is the field with the highest dropout rate for women.

- We checked the grades in our own introductory statistics classes and simply found no reliable difference for gender.
- Persons of color: Keep in mind that only 7 percent of the genetic variation in humans is between races (Block, 1995). Mostly, we are all the same.
- Associate with people who have a positive attitude about you and your group. Watch for subtle signs of prejudice and reject it. For example, Steele found that the grades of African-Americans in a large midwestern university rose substantially when they were enrolled in a transition-to-college program emphasizing that they were the cream of the crop and much was expected of them, while African American students at the same school who were enrolled in a "remedial program for minorities" received considerable attention, but their grades improved very little and many more of them dropped out of school. Steele argues that the very idea of a remedial program exposed those students to a subtle stereotype threat.
- Work hard during this course. If you are stuck get help. If you work at it, you can do it. This is not about genetics. Think about a study cited by Tobias (1995) comparing students in Asia and the United States on an international mathematics test. The U.S. students were thoroughly outperformed, but more important was why: Interviews revealed that Asian students saw math as an ability fairly equally distributed among people and thought that differences in performance were due to hard work. Contrarily, U.S. students thought some people are just born better at math, so hard work matters little.

In short, our culture's belief that "math just comes naturally to some people" is false and harmful. It especially harms students who hear it early in their career with numbers and believe it explains their difficulties, when their real problem is due to gender or racial stereotypes or difficulty with English. But once you vow to undo the harm done to you, you can overcome effects of prejudice. Doing well in this course may even be more satisfying for you than for others. And it will certainly be a fine thing that you have modeled that achievement for others in your group.

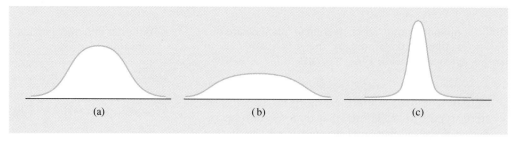

FIGURE 1–11
Examples of (a) normal, (b) heavy-tailed, and (c) light-tailed distributions.

except that it is somewhat skewed to the left and has a secondary high point. In our experience, most distributions that result from social and behavioral science research are actually closer to the normal curve than this example.

Figures 1–11b and 1–11c show examples of heavy-tailed and light-tailed distributions. Heavy-tailed distributions usually also have a low central peak compared to the normal curve. This is because in a heavy-tailed distribution more of the scores are at the two tails, so there are fewer left for the middle. An extreme case of a heavy-tailed distribution would be a rectangular distribution. In contrast, a light-tailed distribution usually has a high, narrow peak compared to a normal curve because fewer scores are in the two tails.

Frequency Tables, Histograms, and Frequency Polygons in Research Articles

Frequency tables, histograms, and frequency polygons are used by researchers mainly as a step in more elaborate statistical procedures. They usually are not included in research articles. The most common of these in research articles are frequency tables showing the frequencies and percentages of different categories of responses. For example, Anthony Nownes (2000), a political scientist, conducted a survey of representatives of interest groups who were registered as lobbyists of three U.S. state legislatures. One of the issues he studied was whether interest groups are in competition with each other. Table 1-5 (Nownes' Table 1) shows the results for one such

TABLE 1–5
Competition for Members and Other Resources

Answer	Question: How much competition does this group face from other groups with similar goals for members andother resources?	
	Percentage	*Number*
No competition	20	118
Some competition	58	342
A lot of competition	22	131
Total	100	591

NOTE: There were no statistically significant differences between states.For full results of significance tests, contact the author.

From "Policy Conflict and the Structure of Interest Communities" by Anthony J. Nownes, *American Politics Quarterly,* Vol. 28, No. 3, July 2000, p. 316, copyright © 2000. Reprinted by permission of Sage Publications Inc.

question. Notice that most respondents indicated a moderate amount of competition. (There are only three levels for this variable. However, if you were to make a histogram of it, you would see that it is unimodal and roughly symmetrical.)

Summary

1. Social scientists use descriptive statistics to describe—to summarize and make understandable—a group of numbers from a research study.
2. A frequency table organizes the numbers into a table in which each of the possible values is listed from highest to lowest, along with its frequency (number of scores that have that value, and percentage.)
3. When there is a large number of different values, a grouped frequency table will be more useful. It is like an ordinary frequency table except that the frequencies are given for intervals that include a range of values.
4. Most variables in the social and behaviorial sciences are numeric with approximately equal intervals. However, some numeric variables are rank-order (where the values are ranks), and some variables are not numeric at all, but are nominal (where the values are categories).
5. The pattern of frequencies in a distribution can be illustrated with a histogram, a kind of bar graph in which the height of each bar is the frequency for a particular value and there are no spaces between the bars. An alternative is a frequency polygon, in which a line connects dots, the height of each of which is the frequency for a particular value.
6. The general shape of the histogram or frequency polygon can be unimodal (having a single peak), bimodal, multimodal (including bimodal), or rectangular (having no peak); it can be symmetrical or skewed (having a long tail) to the right or the left; and compared to the bell-shaped normal curve, it can be light tailed or heavy tailed.
7. Frequency tables rarely appear in research articles. When they do, they often involve frequencies (and percentages) for various categories of a nominal variable. Histograms and frequency polygons almost never appear in articles, though the shapes of distributions (normal, skewed, and so on) occasionally are described in words.

Key Terms

bimodal distribution
ceiling effect
descriptive statistics
equal-interval variable
floor effect
frequency distribution
frequency polygon
frequency table
grouped frequency table

heavy-tailed distribution
histogram
inferential statistics
interval
light-tailed distribution
multimodal distribution
nominal variable
normal curve
numeric variable

rank-order variable
rectangular distribution
score
skewed distribution
symmetrical distribution
unimodal distribution
value
variable

Practice Problems

These problems involve tabulation and making graphs. Most real-life statistics problems are done on a computer. Even if you have a computer with appropriate software, do these by hand to ingrain the method in your mind.

For practice in using a computer to solve statistics problems, refer to the computer section of each chapter of the Student's Study Guide and Computer Workbook *that accompanies this text.*

All data are fictional.

Answers to selected problems are given at the back of the book.

1. Suppose that 50 students were asked how many hours they had studied last weekend and they responded as follows:

11, 2, 0, 13, 5, 7, 1, 8, 12, 11, 7, 8, 9, 10, 7, 4, 6, 10, 4, 7, 8, 6, 7, 10, 7, 3, 11, 18, 2, 9, 7, 3, 8, 7, 3, 13, 9, 8, 7, 7, 10, 4, 15, 3, 5, 6, 9, 7, 10, 6

(a) Make a frequency table (including percentages); (b) make a frequency polygon based on the frequency table; and (c) describe the shape of the distribution.

2. Here are the number of children in each of 30 classrooms in a particular elementary school.

24, 20, 35, 25, 25, 22, 26, 28, 38, 15, 25, 21, 24, 25, 25, 24, 25, 20, 32, 25, 22, 26, 26, 28, 24, 22, 26, 21, 25, 24

(a) Make a frequency table (including percentages); (b) make a histogram based on the frequency table; and (c) describe the shape of the distribution.

3. Draw an example of each of the following distributions: (a) symmetrical, (b) rectangular, and (c) skewed to the right.

4. Explain to a person who has never had a course in statistics what is meant by (a) a symmetrical, unimodal distribution and (b) a negatively skewed unimodal distribution. (Be sure to include in your first answer an explanation of what is meant by a distribution.)

5. Select a book and page of your choice (but be sure the page has at least 30 lines) and write down the full title, author, and so forth, along with the page number. Make a list of the number of words in each line; then use that list to do the following: (a) Make a frequency table; (b) make a histogram; (c) make a frequency polygon; and (d) describe the general shape of the distribution.

6. Give an example of something having these distribution shapes: (a) bimodal, (b) approximately rectangular, and (c) positively skewed. Do not use an example given in this book or in class.

The Mean, Variance, Standard Deviation, and *Z* Scores

2

CHAPTER OUTLINE

As we noted in Chapter 1, the purpose of descriptive statistics is to make a group of scores understandable. We looked at some ways of getting that understanding through tables and graphs. In this chapter, we consider the main statistical techniques for describing a group of scores with numbers. These numbers are the mean, the variance, the standard deviation, and Z scores. The mean is the average score. The variance and standard deviation are about the amount of variation in the scores. A Z score describes a particular score in terms of how much that score varies from the average.

Before beginning this chapter, you should be sure you are comfortable with the key terms of **variable, score,** and **value** that we considered in Chapter 1. It is also helpful, though not absolutely necessary, to have developed a solid understanding from Chapter 1 of frequency tables, histograms and frequency polygons.

The Mean

mean (M)

Usually, the best single number for describing a group of scores is the ordinary average, the sum of all the scores divided by the number of scores. In statistics, this is called the **mean (M).** Suppose that a political scientist does a study on experience in elected office. As part of this research, the political scientist finds out the number of years served by mayors of the 10 largest cities in a particular region. The numbers of years served were as follows:

7, 8, 8, 7, 3, 1, 6, 9, 3, 8

The mean of these 10 scores is 6 (the sum of 60 years served divided by 10 mayors). That is, on the average, these 10 mayors had served 6 years in office. The information for the 10 mayors is thus summarized by this single number, 6.

Many students find it helpful to visualize the mean as a kind of balancing point for the distribution of scores. Try it by visualizing a board balanced over a log, like a rudimentary teeter-totter. On the board, imagine piles of blocks set along the board according to their values, one for each score in the distribution. (This is a little like a histogram made of blocks.) The mean would be the point on the board where the weight of the blocks on each side would balance exactly. Figure 2–1 illustrates this for our 10 mayors.

Some other examples are shown in Figure 2–2. Note that there need not even be a block right at the balance point. That is, the mean doesn't have to be a value actually in the distribution. The mean is the average of the values, the balance point. Also notice that the blocks can be very spread out or very

FIGURE 2–1
Mean of the numbers of years in office for 10 mayors, illustrated using blocks on a board balanced on a log.

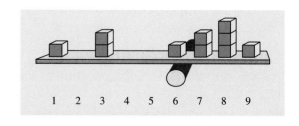

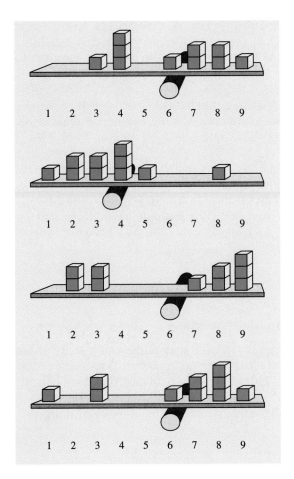

close together and that they don't have to be spread out evenly. In any of these examples, you can mark a balance point. (By the way, this analogy to blocks on a board, in reality, would work out precisely only if the board had no weight of its own.)

Formula for the Mean and Statistical Symbols

The rule for computing the mean is to add up all the scores and divide by the number of scores. This can be stated as the following formula:

$$M = \frac{\Sigma X}{N} \tag{2–1}$$

M is a symbol for the mean. An alternative symbol $\overline{X}$, sometimes called "*X*-bar," is also used. But *M* is most commonly used in research publications. In fact, you should know that there is not a general agreement for most of the symbols used in statistics. (In this book we generally use the symbols most widely found in research publications, but we now and then use a slightly less-common symbol when we think it will make your learning easier.)

Σ, the capital Greek letter "sigma," is the symbol for "sum of." It means "add up all the numbers" for whatever follows. It is the most common special arithmetic symbol used in statistics.

Σ

X stands for the scores in the distribution of the variable *X*. We could have picked any letter. However, if there is only one variable, it usually is called *X*. In later chapters we use formulas with more than one variable. In those formulas, we use a second letter along with *X* (usually *Y*) or subscripts (such as X_1 and X_2.).

ΣX means "the sum of *X*." That is, this tells you to add up all the scores in the distribution of the variable *X*. Suppose *X* is the number of years in office in our example of 10 mayors: ΣX would be 60, the sum of $7 + 8 + 8 + 7 + 3 + 1 + 6 + 9 + 3 + 8$.

N stands for number—the number of scores in a distribution. In our example, there are 10 scores. Thus, *N* equals 10.

Overall, the formula says to divide the sum of all the scores for the variable *X* by the total number of scores, *N*. In our example, this tells us that we divide 60 by 10. Put in terms of the formula,

$$M = \frac{\Sigma X}{N} = \frac{60}{10} = 6$$

Additional Examples of Computing the Mean

Consider the examples from Chapter 1. The first example was a study of the stress level of 151 students in their first week taking a statistics course (Aron et al., 1995). The 151 stress level ratings are shown on page 3 and are laid out as a frequency table in Table 1–1. The mean of the 151 stress-level ratings is figured by adding up all the ratings and dividing by the number of ratings.

FIGURE 2–3
Analogy of blocks on a board balanced on a fulcrum illustrating the mean for 151 statistics students' ratings of their stress level. (Data from Aron et al., 1995)

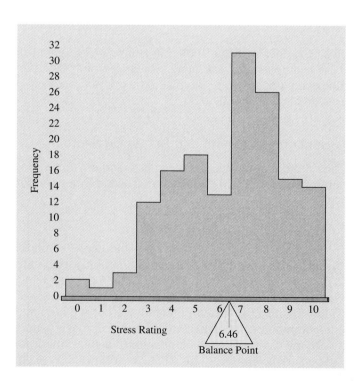

$$M = \frac{\Sigma X}{N} = \frac{975}{151} = 6.46$$

This tells you that the average rating on the 10-point stress scale was 6.46. This is clearly higher than the middle of that scale. You can also see this on a graph. Think again of the histogram as a pile of blocks on a board and the mean of 6.46 as the point where the board balances on a fulcrum. (See Figure 2–3.) This single number much simplifies the information in the 151 stress scores.

Similarly, consider the other main example from Chapter 1, the study in which 94 college students, for a full week, recorded every social interaction of 10 minutes or longer (McLaughlin-Volpe et al., 2001). The actual numbers of interactions for the students are listed on page 5. In Chapter 1, we organized the original scores into a frequency table (see Table 1-2). We can now take those same 94 scores, add them up, and divide by 94 to compute the mean:

$$M = \frac{\Sigma X}{N} = \frac{1,635}{94} = 17.40$$

This is illustrated in Figure 2–4.

This tells us that during this week these studies had an average of 17.4 social interactions.

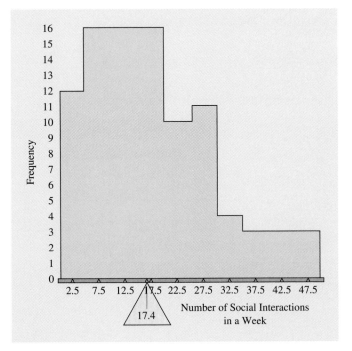

FIGURE 2–4
Analogy of blocks on a board balanced on a fulcrum illustrating the mean for number of social interactions during a week for 94 college students. (Data from McLaughlin et al. 2001)

FIGURE 2–5
Illustration of the mode as the high point in a distribution's histogram, using the fictional example of the number of years in office served by 10 mayors.

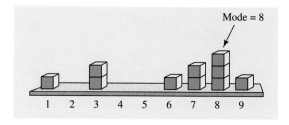

Other Measures of the Typical or Representative Value of a Group of Scores

mode

The mean is only one of several ways of describing the typical or representative value in a group of scores. One alternative is the **mode.** The mode is the most common single number in a distribution. In our mayors' example, the mode is 8 because there are three mayors with 8 years served in office and no other number of years served in office with as many mayors. Another way to think of the mode is that it is the value with the largest frequency in a frequency table, the high point or peak of a distribution's frequency polygon or histogram (as shown in Figure 2–5).

In a perfectly symmetrical unimodal distribution, the mode is the same as the mean. However, what happens when the mode and the mean are not the same? In that situation the mode is usually not a very good representative value for scores in the distribution. Also, the mode can be a particularly poor

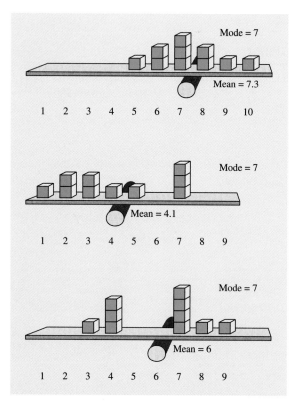

FIGURE 2–6
Illustration of the effect on the mean and on the mode of changing some scores, using the fictional example of the number of years in office served by 10 mayors.

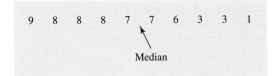

FIGURE 2–7
Illustration of the median as the middle score when scores are lined up from highest to lowest, using the fictional example of the number of years in office served by 10 mayors.

representative value because it is not reflective of many aspects of the distribution. For example, you can change some of the scores in a distribution without affecting the mode—but this is not true of the mean, which is affected by any changes in the distribution (see Figure 2-6). For these and other reasons, researchers use the mode only in very special situations.

Another alternative to the mean is the **median.** If you line up all the scores from highest to lowest, the middle score is the median. As shown in Figure 2–7, if you line up the numbers of years in office from highest to lowest, the fifth and sixth scores (the two middle ones), are both 7s. Either way, the median is 7 years.

median

When you have an even number of scores, the median can be between two different numbers. In that situation, you use the average of the two.

Sometimes the median is better than the mean as a typical or representative value for a group of scores. This happens when there are a few extreme scores that would strongly affect the mean but would not affect the median. For example, suppose that among the 100 families on a banana plantation in Central America, 99 families have an annual income of $100 and 1 family (the owner's) has an annual income of $90,100. The mean family income on this plantation would be $1,000 (99 × 100 = 9,900; 9,900 + 90,100 = 100,000; 100,000/100 = 1,000). That is, no family has an income even close to $1,000, so this number is completely misleading. The median income in this example would be $100—an income much more typical of whomever you would meet if you walked up to someone randomly on the plantation.

As this example illustrates, social scientists use the median as a descriptive statistic mainly in situations where there are a few extreme scores that would make the mean unrepresentative of most of the scores An extreme score like this is called an **outlier.**

outlier

The Variance and the Standard Deviation

Researchers also want to know how spread out a distribution is. For example, suppose you were asked, "How old are the students in your statistics class?" At a city-based university with many returning and part-time students, the mean age might be 38. You could answer, "The average age of the students in my class is 38." However, this would not tell the whole story. You could, for example, have a mean of 38 because every student in the class was exactly 38 years old. Or, you could have a mean of 38 because exactly half the class was 18 and the other half was 58. These are two quite different situations.

The general principle is that distributions with the same mean can have very different amounts of spread around the mean; also, distributions with different means can have the same amount of spread around the mean, To illustrate this, Figure 2–8a shows three different frequency distributions with

FIGURE 2–8
Examples of distributions with (a) the same mean but different amounts of spread and (b) different means but the same amount of spread.

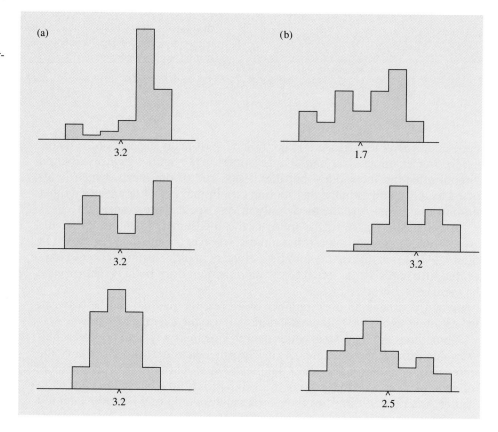

the same mean but different amounts of spread around the mean and Figure 2-8b shows three different frequency distributions with different means but the same amount of spread.

The Variance

variance (SD^2)

The **variance (SD^2)** of a group of scores tells you how spread out the scores are around the mean.[1] To be precise, the variance is the average of each score's squared difference from the mean. Here are the steps to figure the variance:

deviation score

1. **Subtract the mean from each score; this gives each score's deviation score.** The **deviation score** is how far away the actual score is from the mean.

squared deviation score
sum of squared deviations

2. **Square each of these deviation scores.** (Multiply each by itself.) This gives each score's **squared deviation score.**

3. **Add up the squared deviation scores.** This total is called the **sum of squared deviations.**

---

[1]There is also another way to describe the spread of a group of scores. You can just subtract—take the highest score minus the lowest score. This is called the *range* of a group of scores. However, the range is rarely used by researchers because it is a very crude way of describing the spread. It is crude because it does not take into account how clumped together the scores are within the range.

4. Divide the sum of squared deviations by the number of squared deviations. (That is, divide the sum of squared deviations by the number of scores). This gives the average of the squared deviations, called the variance.

This procedure may seem a bit awkward or hard to remember at first; but it works quite well. Suppose one distribution is more spread out than another. The more spread-out distribution has a larger variance because being spread makes the deviation scores bigger. If the deviation scores are bigger, the squared deviation scores also are bigger; thus the average of the squared deviation scores (the variance) is bigger. In the example of the class in which everyone was exactly 38 years old, the variance would be exactly 0. That is, there would be no variance. (In terms of the numbers, each person's deviation score would be 38 − 38 = 0; 0 squared is 0. The average of a bunch of zeros is 0.) By contrast, the class of half 18-year-olds and half 58-year-olds would have a rather large variance of 400. (The 18-year-olds would each have deviation scores of 18 − 38 = −20. The 58-year-olds would have deviation scores of 58 − 38 = 20. All the squared deviation scores, which are −20 squared or 20 squared, would come out to 400. The average of all 400s is 400.)

The variance is extremely important in many statistical procedures you will learn about later. However, the variance is rarely used as a descriptive statistic. This is because the variance is based on *squared* deviation scores, which do not give a very easy-to-understand sense of how spread out the actual, nonsquared scores are. For example, it is clear that a class with a variance of 400 has a more spread-out distribution than one whose variance is 10. However, the number 400 does not give an obvious insight into the actual variation among the ages, none of which are anywhere near 400.

The Standard Deviation

The most widely used way of *describing* the spread of a group of scores is the **standard deviation (SD).** The standard deviation is the positive square root of the variance: To find the standard deviation, you first figure the variance and then take its square root.

standard deviation (SD)

The variance is about squared deviations from the mean. Therefore, its square root, the standard deviation, is about direct, ordinary, not-squared deviations from the mean. *Roughly speaking, the standard deviation is the average amount that scores differ from the mean.*

For example, consider a class where the ages have a standard deviation of 20 years. This would tell you that the ages are spread out, on the average, about 20 years in each direction from the mean. Knowing the standard deviation gives you a general sense of the degree of spread.

The standard deviation is not exactly the average amount that scores differ from the mean. To be precise, the standard deviation is the square root of the average of the scores' squared deviations from the mean. This squaring, averaging, and then taking the square root gives a slightly different result from simply averaging the scores' deviations from the mean. Still, the result of this approach has technical advantages to outweigh this slight disadvantage of giving only an approximate description of the average variation from the mean.

Formulas for the Variance and the Standard Deviation

We have seen that the variance is the average squared deviation from the mean. In symbols, this is how it looks:

$$SD^2 = \frac{\Sigma(X-M)^2}{N}$$

(2–2)

SD^2 is the symbol for the variance. (In Chapter 8 you learn another symbol, S^2. This other symbol is for a slightly different kind of variance.) SD is short for *standard deviation*. The symbol SD^2 emphasizes that the variance is the standard deviation squared.

The top part of the formula is the sum of squared deviations. X is for each score and M is the mean. Thus, $X - M$ is the score minus the mean, the deviation score. The exponent, 2, tells you to square each deviation score. Finally, the sum sign (Σ) tells you to add together all these squared deviation scores. The bottom part of the formula tells you to divide the sum of squared deviation scores by N, the number of scores.

The standard deviation is the square root of the variance. So, if you already know the variance, the formula is

$$SD = \sqrt{SD^2}$$

(2–3)

Example of Figuring the Variance and the Standard Deviation

Table 2–1 shows the figuring for the variance and standard deviation for our example of mayors. (The table assumes we already have figured out the mean to be 6 years in office.) Usually, it is easiest to do your figuring using a calculator, especially one with a square root key.

TABLE 2–1
Figuring of Variance and Standard Deviation in the Example of Number of Years Served by 10 Mayors

Score (Number of Years Served)	−	Mean score (Mean Number of Years Served)	=	Deviation score	Squared Deviation score
7		6		1	1
8		6		2	4
8		6		2	4
7		6		1	1
3		6		−3	9
1		6		−5	25
6		6		0	0
9		6		3	9
3		6		−3	9
8		6		2	4
				Σ: 0	66

$$\text{Variance} = SD^2 = \frac{\Sigma(X-M)^2}{N} = \frac{66}{10} = 6.6$$

$$\text{Standard deviation} = SD = \sqrt{SD^2} = \sqrt{6.6} = 2.57$$

Additional Example of Figuring the Variance and the Standard Deviation

Table 2–2 shows the arithmetic for figuring the variance and standard deviation for the example of students' numbers of social interactions during a week. (To save space, the table shows only the first few and last few scores.)

   Roughly speaking, this result indicates that a student's number of social interactions in a week varies from the mean by an average of 11.49 interactions. This can also be shown on a histogram (Figure 2–9).

Computational and Definitional Formulas

In actual research situations, social and behavioral scientists must often figure the variance and the standard deviation for distributions with a great many scores, often involving decimals or large numbers. This can make the whole process quite time-consuming, even with a calculator. To deal with this problem, over the years researchers developed a number of shortcut formulas to simplify the figuring. A shortcut formula of this type is called a **computational formula.** The computational formula for the variance is

computational formula

$$SD^2 = \frac{\Sigma X^2 - (\Sigma X)^2 / N}{N} \qquad (2\text{--}4)$$

Note that ΣX^2 means that you square each score and then take the sum of these squared scores. However, $(\Sigma X)^2$ means that you first add up all the scores and then take the square of this sum. This formula is easier to use if

TABLE 2–2
Computation of Variance and Standard Deviation for Number of Social Interactions during a Week for 94 College Students (Showing Only First Few and Last Few Participants)

Number of Interactions	−	Mean Number of Interactons	=	Deviation Score	Squared Deviation Score
48		17.40		30.60	936.36
15		17.40		−2.40	5.76
33		17.40		15.60	243.36
3		17.40		−14.40	207.36
21		17.40		3.60	12.96
.		.		.	.
.		.		.	.
.		.		.	.
35		17.40		17.60	309.76
9		17.40		−8.40	70.56
30		17.40		12.60	158.76
8		17.40		−9.40	88.36
26		17.40		8.60	73.96
			Σ:	0.00	12,406.44

$$\text{Variance} = SD^2 = \frac{\Sigma(X - M)^2}{N} = \frac{12,406.44}{94} = 131.98$$

$$\text{Standard deviation} = \sqrt{SD^2} = \sqrt{131.98} = 11.49$$

Note: Data from McLaughlin-Volpe et al. 2001

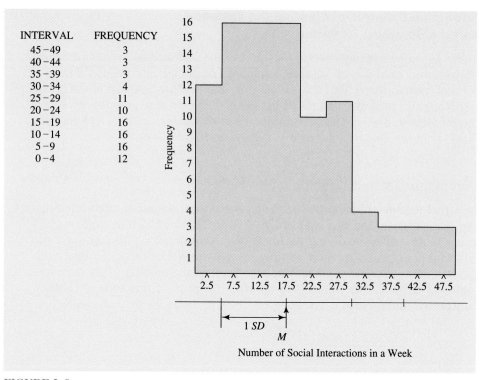

INTERVAL	FREQUENCY
45–49	3
40–44	3
35–39	3
30–34	4
25–29	11
20–24	10
15–19	16
10–14	16
5–9	16
0–4	12

FIGURE 2–9
Graphic description of the standard deviation as the distance along the base of a histogram, using example of number of social interactions in a week. (Data from McLaughlin-Volpe et al., 2001)

you are computing the variance for a lot of numbers by hand because you do not have to first find the deviation score for each raw score.

However, these days computational formulas are mainly of historical interest. They are used by researchers only when computers are not readily available to do the figuring. In fact, even many hand calculators are set up so that you need only enter the scores and press a button or two to get the variance and the standard deviation.

In this book, we give a few computational formulas (mainly in footnotes), just so you will have them if you someday do a research project with a lot of numbers and you don't have access to a computer with statistical software. However, we recommend *not* using the computational formulas when you are learning statistics. The problem is that the computational formulas tend to make it harder to understand the meaning of what you are figuring. It is much better to use the regular formulas we give when doing the practice problems. Using these formulas helps strengthen your understanding of what the figuring *means*. These usual formulas we give are called **definitional formulas.**

definitional formula

The Variance as the Sum of Squared Deviations Divided by N – 1

Researchers often use a slightly different kind of variance. We have defined the variance as the average of the squared deviation scores. Using that definition, you divide the sum of squared deviation scores by the number of scores. But you learn in Chapter 8 that for many purposes it is better to define the variance as the sum of squared deviation scores *divided by 1 less than the number of scores*. That is, for those purposes, the variance is the sum of squared deviations divided by $N - 1$. (As you learn in Chapter 8, you use this $N - 1$ approach when you have scores from a particular group of people and you want to estimate what the variance would be for the larger group of people these individuals represent.)

The variances and standard deviations given in research articles are often figured using the $N - 1$ approach. Also, when calculators or computers give the variance or the standard deviation automatically, they may be figured in this way. The approach you are learning in this chapter of dividing by N is entirely correct for our purposes here (which is describing the variation in a particular group of scores). It is also entirely correct for the material covered in the rest of this chapter (Z scores of the kind we are using), and for the material in Chapters 3 through 7. We mention this $N - 1$ approach now only so you will not be confused when you read about variance or standard deviation in other places or if your calculator or a computer program gives a surprising result. To keep things simple, we wait to discuss the $N - 1$ approach until it is needed, starting in Chapter 8.

Z Scores

So far in this chapter you have learned about describing a group of scores in terms of its mean and variation. In this section, you learn how to describe a particular score in terms of where it fits into the overall group of scores. That is, you learn to describe a score in terms of whether it is above or below the average and how much it is above or below the average.

Z scores have many practical uses. They also are part of many of the statistical procedures you learn later in this book. It is important that you become very familiar with them.

Suppose that you were told that a particular mayor, the Honorable Julia Hernandez, has served in this office in her town for 9 years. Now, suppose we did not know anything about the number of years served in office by other mayors in the region. In that case, it would be hard to tell whether this mayor had served a lot or a few years in relation to other mayors in her region. However, suppose we do know that for the 10 mayors in her region, the mean is 6 and the standard deviation is 2.57. With this knowledge, it is clear that Ms. Hernandez has served an above-average number of years. It is also clear that the amount she has served more than the average (3 years in office more than average) was a bit more than the amount mayors in her region typically vary from the average. This is all illustrated in Figure 2–10.

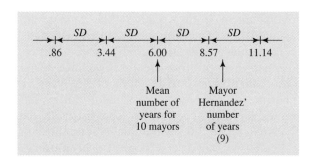

FIGURE 2–10
Relation of the number of years in office served by a particular mayor (Ms. Hernandez) to the overall distribution of number of years in office served by all mayors in a particular (fictional) region.

BOX 2-1

The Psychology of Statistics and the Tyranny of the Mean

Looking in the social science research journals, you would think that statistical methods are their sole tool and language, but there have also been rebellions against the reign of statistics. We are most familiar with this issue in psychology where one of the most unexpected oppositions came from the leader of behaviorism, the school of psychology most dedicated to keeping the field strictly scientific.

Behaviorism opposed the study of inner states because inner events are impossible to observe objectively. (Today most research psychologists claim to measure inner events indirectly but objectively.) Behaviorism's most famous advocate, B. F. Skinner, was quite opposed to statistics. Skinner even said, "I would much rather see a graduate student in psychology taking a course in physical chemistry than in statistics. And I would include [before statistics] other sciences, even poetry, music, and art" (Evans, 1976, p. 93).

Skinner was constantly pointing to the information lost by averaging the results of a number of cases. For instance, Skinner (1956) cited the example of three overeating mice—one naturally obese, one poisoned with gold, and one whose hypothalamus had been altered. Each had a different curve for learning to press a bar for food. If these learning curves had been summed or merged statistically, the result would have represented no actual eating habits of any real mouse at all. As Skinner said, "These three individual curves contain more information than could

probably ever be generated with measures requiring statistical treatment, yet they will be viewed with suspicion by many psychologists because they are single cases" (p. 232).

A different voice of caution was raised by another school of psychology, humanistic psychology, which began in the 1950s as a "third force" in reaction to Freudian psychoanalysis and behaviorism. The point of humanistic psychology was that human consciousness should be studied intact, as a whole, as it is experienced by individuals. Although statistics can be usefully applied to ascertain the mathematical relationships between phenomena, including events in consciousness, human conscious experience can never be fully explained by reducing it to numbers (any more than it can be reduced to words). Each individual's experience is unique.

This viewpoint existed in psychology even before humanistic psychology. In clinical psychology and the study of personality, voices have always been raised in favor of the in-depth study of one person instead of or as well as the averaging of persons. The philosophical underpinnings of the in-depth study of individuals can be found in phenomenology, which began in Europe after World War I (Husserl, 1970). This viewpoint has been important throughout the social sciences, not just in psychology.

Today, the rebellion is led in psychology by qualitative research methodologies (e.g., Mc-Cracken, 1988), an approach which is much

What Is a Z Score?

Z score

A **Z score** is the number of standard deviations the actual score is above the mean (if it is positive) or below the mean (if it is negative). The standard deviation now becomes a kind of yardstick, a unit of measure in its own right. In our mayoral example, Ms. Hernandez, who has served 9 years in office, has a Z score of +1.17 because her years in office are 1.17 standard deviations above the mean (a little more than 1 standard deviation of 2.57 years in office above the mean). Another mayor, the Honorable Samuel Phillips has served 6 years in office. He has a Z score of 0 because his score is exactly the mean. That is, his number of years in office is 0 standard deviations above or below the mean. What about a mayor who had served only 1 year in office?

more prominent in other social and behavioral sciences. The qualitative research methods were developed mainly in anthropology and typically involve long interviews or observations of a few individuals. The highly skilled researcher decides, as the event is taking place, what is important to remember, record, and pursue through more questions or observations. The mind of the researcher is the main tool because, according to this approach, only that mind can find the important relationships among the many categories of events arising in the respondent's speech.

Many who favor qualitative methods argue for a blend: First, discover the important categories through a qualitative approach. Then, determine their incidence in the larger population through quantitative methods. Too often, these advocates would argue, quantitative researchers jump to conclusions about a phenomenon without first exploring the human experience of it through free-response interviews or observations.

Finally, Carl Jung, founder of Jungian psychology, sometimes spoke of the "statistical mood" and its effect on a person's feeling of uniqueness. The Jungian analyst Marie Louise von Franz (1979) wrote about Jung's thoughts on this subject: When we walk down a street and observe the hundreds of blank faces and begin to feel diminished, or even so overwhelmed by overpopulation that we are glad that humans don't live forever, this is the statistical mood. We feel how much we are just part of the crowd, ordinary. Yet von Franz points out that if some catastrophe were to happen, each person would respond uniquely. There is at least as much irregularity to life as ordinariness. As she puts it,

The fact that this table does not levitate, but remains where it is, is only because the billions and billions and billions of electrons which constitute the table tend statistically to behave like that. But each electron in itself could do something else. (pp. IV–17)

Likewise, when we are in love, we feel that the other person is unique and wonderful. Yet in a statistical mood, we realize that the other person is ordinary, like many others.

Jung did not cherish individual uniqueness just to be romantic about it, however. He held that the important contributions to culture tend to come from people thinking at least a little independently or creatively, and their independence is damaged by this statistical mood.

Further, von Franz argues that a statistical mood is damaging to love and life. "An act of loyalty is required towards one's own feelings" (pp. IV–18). Feeling "makes your life and your relationships and deeds feel unique and gives them a definite value" (pp. IV–19). In particular, feeling the importance of our single action makes immoral acts—war and killing, for example—less possible. We cannot count the dead as numbers but must treat them as persons with emotions and purposes, like ourselves.

In short, there have been many who have questioned an exclusively statistical view of our subject matters, and their voices should be considered too as you proceed with your study of what has become the predominant, but not exclusive, means of doing behavioral and social science.

That mayor has served 5 years less than average. This would be nearly 2 standard deviations below the mean (a Z score of –1.95). In terms of years in office, this mayor would be about twice as far below average as mayors in this region typically vary from the average.

Z Scores as a Scale

Figure 2–11 shows, for our mayoral example, a scale of Z scores lined up against a scale of **raw scores.** A raw score is an ordinary score, as opposed to a Z score. The two scales are something like a ruler with inches lined up on one side and centimeters on the other.

raw score

FIGURE 2–11
Scales of Z scores and r aw scores in the mayoral example.

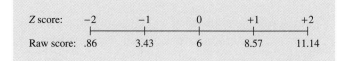

Z score:	−2	−1	0	+1	+2
Raw score:	.86	3.43	6	8.57	11.14

Additional Examples

Suppose that a developmental specialist observed 3-year-old Peter in a standardized laboratory situation playing with other children of the same age. During the observation, the specialist counted the number of times Peter spoke to the other children. The result, over several observations, is that Peter spoke to other children about 8 times per hour of play. Without any standard of comparison, it would be hard to draw any conclusions from this. Suppose, however, that it was known from previous research that under similar conditions the mean number of times children speak is 12, with a standard deviation of 4. Clearly, Peter spoke less often than other children in general, but not extremely less often. Peter would have a Z score of −1. (That is $M = 12$ and $SD = 4$; thus a score of 8 is 1 SD below M.) Suppose Ian was observed speaking to other children 20 times in an hour. Ian would clearly be unusually talkative, with a Z score of +2. Ian would speak not merely more than the average but more by twice as much as children tend to vary from the average! (See Figure 2–12.)

Z Scores as Giving a Generalized Standard of Comparison

Another advantage of Z scores is that scores on completely different variables can be made into Z scores and compared. With Z scores, the mean is always 0 and the standard deviation is always 1. Suppose the same children in our example were also measured on a test of language skill. In this situation, we could directly compare the Z scores on language skill to the Z scores on speaking to other children. Let's say Peter had a score of 100 on the language skill test. If the mean on that test was 82 and the standard deviation was 6, then Peter is much better than average at language skill, with a Z score of +3. Thus, it seems unlikely that Peter's less than usual amount of speaking to other children is due to poorer-than-usual language skill. (See Figure 2–13.)

Notice in this latest example that by using Z scores, we can directly compare the results of both the specialist's observation of the amount of talking and the language skill test. This is almost as wonderful as being able to compare apples and oranges!

Converting a number to a Z score is a bit like converting the words for measurement in various obscure languages into one language that everyone

FIGURE 2–12
Number of times each hour that two children spoke, expressed as raw scores and Z scores (fictional data).

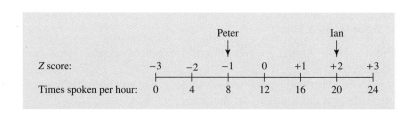

Z score:	−3	−2	−1	0	+1	+2	+3
Times spoken per hour:	0	4	8	12	16	20	24

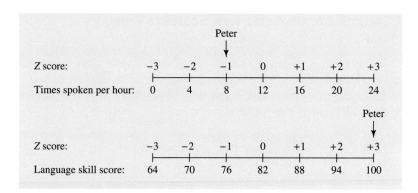

FIGURE 2–13
Scales of *Z* scores and raw scores for number of times spoken per hour and language skill, showing the first child's score on each (fictional data).

can understand—inches, cubits, and zinqles (we made that last one up), for example, into centimeters. It is a very valuable tool.

Changing a Raw Score into a *Z* Score

As we have seen, a *Z* score is the number of standard deviations the raw score falls above (or, if negative, below) its mean. To figure a *Z* score, subtract the mean from the raw score, giving the deviation score. Then, divide the deviation score by the standard deviation. In symbols, the formula is

$$Z = \frac{X - M}{SD} \tag{2-5}$$

For example, using the formula for the child who scored 100 on the language test,

$$Z = \frac{X - M}{SD} = \frac{100 - 82}{6} = \frac{18}{6} = 3$$

Changing a *Z* Score to a Raw Score

To change a *Z* score back to a raw score, the process is reversed: You multiply the *Z* score by the standard deviation and then add the mean. The formula is

$$X = (Z)(SD) + M \tag{2-6}$$

(Remember that when two symbols, or two parentheses, are next to each other in a formula, you are supposed to multiply them. If we used "X" to mean multiply in a formula like this, it might be confused with the *X* meaning the score.)

For example, if a child has a *Z* score of −1.5 on the language ability test, then the child is 1.5 standard deviations below the mean. Because a standard deviation in this example is 6 raw score points, the child is 9 raw score points below the mean. The mean is 82, so 9 points below this is 73. Using the formula,

$$X = (Z)(SD) + M = (-1.5)(6) + 82 = -9 + 82 = 73$$

Additional Examples of Changing Raw Scores to Z Scores and Vice Versa

Consider the stress ratings example. The mean of that distribution was 6.46, and the standard deviation was 2.30. Figure 2–14 shows the raw score and Z score scales. If a student's stress raw score was 9, the student is well above the mean. Specifically, using the formula,

$$Z = \frac{X - M}{SD} = \frac{9 - 6.46}{2.3} = \frac{2.54}{2.30} = 1.10$$

In comparison, a student with a Z score of –2.81 has a stress raw score well below the mean. Using the formula, the raw stress score is computed as

$$X = (Z)(SD) + M = (-2.81)(2.30) + 6.46 = -6.46 + 6.46 = 0$$

Let's also consider some examples from the study of students' numbers of social interactions in a week (McLaughlin-Volpe et al., 2001). The mean was 17.4 and the standard deviation was 11.49. A student who had 17 interactions in a week had a deviation score of –.4 (that is 17 – 17.4 = –.4). The Z score is then –.03 (that is, –.4/11.49 = –.03). This number of interactions is just below the mean. Similarly, a student who has 36 social interactions in a week has a deviation score of 18.6 (that is, 36 – 17.4 = 18.6). The Z score is 1.62 (that is, 18.6/11.49 = 1.62). This student is 1.62 standard deviations above the mean in terms of social interactions in a week.

To go the other way, suppose that you knew that a student's Z score was .57. This student's raw score would be the Z score times the standard deviation, plus the mean: (.57)(11.49) + 17.4 = 23.95 (rounded off, this person had 24 social interactions). These relationships are illustrated in Figure 2–15.

The Mean, Variance, Standard Deviation, and Z Scores As Used in Research Articles

The mean and the standard deviation (and occasionally, the variance) are commonly reported in research articles. Sometimes the mean and standard deviation are included in the text of an article. For example, our fictional political scientist, in a research article about the mayors of this region, would write, "At the time of the study, the mean number of years in office for the 10 mayors in this region was 6.0 (SD = 2.57)."

More commonly, however, means and standard deviations are given in tables, especially if there are different groups studied, or several variables are involved. For example, Goidel and Langley (1995) studied the positivity and negativity of newspaper accounts of economic events in the period just

---

FIGURE 2–14

Raw score and Z score scales for 151 statistics students' ratings of their stress levels (data from Aron et al., 1995), showing the scores of two sample individuals.

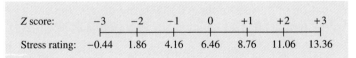

Z score:	–3	–2	–1	0	+1	+2	+3
Stress rating:	–0.44	1.86	4.16	6.46	8.76	11.06	13.36

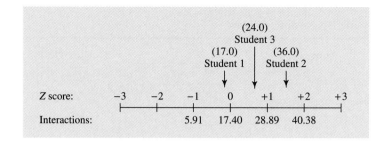

FIGURE 2–15
Raw score and Z score scales for 94 students' number of social interactions in a week showing scores of three sample students (Data from McLaughlin-Volpe et al., 2001).

before the 1992 U.S. Presidential election. As part of their report, they included a table showing the monthly means and standard deviations for numbers of front-page articles on economic news in the *New York Times* for the 23 months preceding the election. (See Table 2–3.) (In addition to the mean and standard deviation, their table also gives the number of articles in the month with the fewest articles and the number of articles in the month with the most articles.) After giving this table, Goidel and Langley commented as follows:

> As can be seen in Table 1 [our Table 2–3], during the average month, we would expect roughly six front-page articles devoted to the economy. In addition, we would expect one or two of these articles to have a positive tone and one or two of the articles to have a negative tone (and two or three of the articles to be neutral). Also worth noting in Table 1 is that there is considerable variation regarding the total number of articles within any given month as well as the general tone of these articles. (p. 318)

Table 2-4 (reproduced from Norcross et al., 1996) is a particularly interesting example. It does not give standard deviations, but it does give both means and medians. For example, in 1992 the mean number of applicants to doctoral counseling psychology programs was 120.2, but the median was only 110. This suggests that there were some programs with very high numbers of applicants that skewed the distribution. In fact, you can see from the table that in almost every case, and for both applications and enrollments, the means are typically higher than the medians. (You may also be struck by just how competitive it is to get into doctoral programs in many areas of psychology. It is our experience that one of the factors that makes a lot of difference is doing well in statistics courses!)

TABLE 2–3
Descriptive Statistics for News Coverage Variables Aggregated by Month, *New York Times Index,* **January 1981–November 1992.**

	Mean	Standard Deviation	Range	Total
Total Front-Page Articles	5.84	4.10	0–22	835
Positive Front-Page Articles	1.64	1.33	0–6	261
Negative Front-Page Articles	1.83	1.92	0–11	234

Source: *New York Times Index.*
Note: From "Media Coverage of the Economy and Aggregate Economic Evaluations" by Robert K. Goidel and Ronald E. Langley, *Political Research Quarterly,* Vol. 48, #2, June 1995. Reprinted by permission of the University of Utah, Copyright Holder.

TABLE 2–4
Application and Enrollment Statistics by Area and Year: Doctoral Programs

Program	Applications N of programs 1973[a]	1979[a]	1992	Applications M 1973[a]	1979[a]	1992	Applications Mdn 1973[a]	1979[a]	1992	Enrollments M 1992	Enrollments Mdn 1992
Clinical	105	130	225	314.4	252.6	191.1	290	234	168	12.0	8
Cognitive			47			24.6			22	2.6	2
Community	4	2	5	90.5		24.4	60		23	3.2	2
Counseling	29	43	62	133.4	90.9	120.2	120	84	110	7.3	6
Developmental	56	72	97	54.1	38.9	27.6	41	30	24	2.8	2
Educational	23	28	30	67.8	39.7	20.0	34	26	12	6.0	4
Experimental and general	118	127	78	56.2	33.2	31.3	42	25	26	4.4	3
Health			7			40.7			30	4.4	5
Industrial/organizational	20	25	49	39.9	54.7	66.2	37	48	70	4.9	4
Personality	23	15	10	42.5	24.7	12.3	33	17	6	1.0	1
Perception/psychophysics			15			8.3			6	1.4	1
Physiological/biopsychology	40	43	76	33.2	29.3	20.0	29	24	20	3.9	2
School	30	39	56	78.5	54.0	31.3	53	34	32	5.4	5
Social	58	72	59	46.7	30.9	47.1	40	24	37	3.3	3
Other	47	37	273	61.6	74.1	26.6	27	25	15	3.3	2
Total	566	645	1,089	106.1	85.2	69.4			31	5.6	4

Note. The academic years correspond to the 1975–1976, 1981–1982, and 1994 editions of *Graduate Study in Psychology,* respectively.
[a]Data are from Stoup and Benjamin (1982).
From J. C. Norcross, J. M. Hanych, & R. D. Terranova, tab. 7. "Graduate study in psychology: 1992–1993" *American Psychologist,* 51, 631–643. Copyright © 1996 by The American Psychological Association. Reprinted with permission of the authors and the American Psychological Association.

Summary

1. The mean is the ordinary average—the sum of the scores divided by the number of scores. In symbols, $M = \Sigma X/N$.
2. Some less commonly used ways of describing the typical value of a group of scores are the mode (the most common single value) and the median (the value of the middle score if all the scores were lined up from highest to lowest).
3. The variation among a group of scores can be described by the variance—the average of the squared deviation of each score from the mean. In symbols, $SD^2 = \Sigma (X - M)^2/N$.
4. The standard deviation is the square root of the variance. In symbols, $SD = \sqrt{SD^2}$. It can be best understood as, approximately, the average amount that scores differ from the mean.
5. A Z score is the number of standard deviations a raw score is above or below the mean. Among other uses, with Z scores you can compare scores on variables that have different scales.
6. Means and standard deviations are often given in research articles in the text or in tables. Z scores rarely are reported in research articles.

Key Terms

computational formula	mode	standard deviation (SD)
definitional formula	N	sum of squared deviations
deviation score	outlier	variance (SD^2)
mean (M)	raw score	Z score
median	squared deviation score	Σ

Practice Problems

These problems involve figuring (with the help of a calculator). Most real-life statistics problems are done on a computer. Even if you have a computer and statistical software, do these problems by hand to ingrain the method in your mind.

For practice in using a computer to solve statistics problems, refer to the computer section of each chapter of the Student's Study Guide and Computer Workbook *that accompanies this text.*

All data are fictional.

Answers to selected problems are given at the back of the book.

1. For each group of scores below, determine the following: (a) mean, (b) median, (c) variance, and (d) standard deviation. Be sure to show your work.

Set A: 32, 28, 24, 28, 28, 31, 35, 29, 26
Set B: 6, 1, 4, 2, 3, 4, 6, 6

2. The temperature in Montreal on December 26 of a particular year was measured, in degrees Celsius, at 10 random times. The results were –5, –4, –1, –1, 0, –8, –5, –9, –13, and –24. Describe the typical temperature and the amount of variation to a person who has never had a course in statistics. Give three ways of describing the typical temperature and two ways of describing its variation, explaining the differences and how you figured each. (You will learn more if you try to write your own answer first, before reading our answer.)

3. A researcher interested in political behavior measured the square footage of the desks in the official office of four U.S. governors and of four chief executive officers (CEOs) of major U.S. corporations. The figures for the governors were 44, 36, 52, and 40 square feet. The figures for the CEOs were 32, 60, 48, and 36 square feet. Figure the mean and the standard deviation for the governors and for the CEOs, and explain what you have done to a person who has never had a course in statistics. Also, note the ways in which the means and standard deviations differ, and speculate on the possible meaning of these differences, presuming that they are representative of U.S. governors and large U.S. corporations' CEOs in general.

4. A study involves measuring the number of days absent from work for 216 employees of a large company during the preceding year. As part of the results, the researcher reports, "The number of days absent during the preceding year ($M = 9.21$; $SD = 7.34$) was . . ." Explain the material in parentheses to a person who has never had a course in statistics.

5. Six months after a divorce, the former wife and husband each take a test that measures divorce adjustment. The wife's score is 63, and the husband's score is 59. Overall, the mean score for divorced women on this test is 60 ($SD = 6$); the mean score for divorced men is 55 ($SD = 4$). Which of the two has adjusted better to the divorce in relation to other divorced people of their own gender? Explain your answer to a person who has never had a course in statistics.

6. A person scores 81 on a test of verbal ability and 6.4 on a test of math ability. For the verbal ability test, the mean for people in general is 50 and the standard deviation is 20. For the math ability test, the mean for people in general is 0 and the standard deviation is 5. Which is this person's stronger ability, verbal or math? Explain your answer to a person who has never had a course in statistics.

3

Correlation and Prediction

Agroup of 113 married people in the small college town of Santa Cruz, California, responded to a questionnaire in the local newspaper about their marriage. (This was part of a larger study reported by Aron et al., 2000). Consider one of the findings: The more these respondents engaged in exciting activities with their partner, the more satisfied they reported being in their marriage.

Figure 3–1 is a graph of the results for these 113 people. The vertical axis is for scores on the standard measure of marital satisfaction used in this study. (This marital satisfaction questionnaire included items such as, "In general how often do you think that things between you and your partner are going well?") The horizontal axis is for responses to the question, "How exciting are the things you do together with your partner?", answered on a scale from 1—"Not exciting at all" to 5—"Extremely exciting." Each person's score is shown as a dot. The overall pattern is that the dots go from the lower left to the upper right. That is, lower scores on one variable more often go with lower scores on the other variable, and higher with higher. Even though the pattern is far from one to one, you can see a general trend.

The pattern of high scores on one variable going with high scores on the other variable, low scores going with low scores, and moderate with moderate, is an example of a **correlation.** There are countless examples of correlations: Among college students, there is a correlation between high school grades and college grades. In children, there is a correlation between age and coordination skills; among students, there is a correlation between amount of time studying and amount learned; in the marketplace, between price and quality—that higher prices go with higher quality and lower with lower.

correlation

This chapter explores the nature of correlation, including the relation correlation to causality, how it is described graphically, different types of correlations, how to compute the correlation coefficient (which tells you the degree of correlation), and how you can use correlation to predict the level of one variable from knowledge of a person's score on another correlated variable (such as predicting college grades from high school grades). In

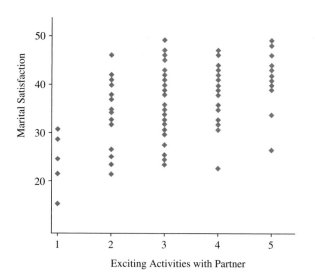

FIGURE 3–1
Scatter diagram showing the correlation for 113 married individuals between doing exciting activities with their partner and their marital satisfaction. (Data from Aron et al., 2000)

considering correlation and prediction, we move from the descriptive statistics for a single variable (Chapters 1 and 2) to the relationship between two or more variables.

Before beginning this chapter, you should have mastered the material in Chapter 2 on mean, standard deviation, and Z scores.

Causality and Correlation

Suppose two variables are correlated so that high scores on one go with high scores on the other, and lows on one go with lows on the other. We normally assume when two scores are correlated like this that there is a reason. However, the **direction of causality** (just what is causing what) cannot be figured out from the fact that the two variables are correlated. In the example we just considered, it could be that doing exciting activities together causes the partners to be more satisfied with their relationship. But it could also be that people who are more satisfied with their relationship choose to do more exciting activities together. It could also be that something like having less pressure (versus more pressure) at work makes people happier in their marriage and also gives them more time and energy to do exciting activities with their partner.

direction of causality

The principle is that for any correlation between variables X and Y, there are at least three possible directions of causality: X could be causing Y, Y could be causing X, or some third factor could be causing both X and Y. It is also possible (and often likely) that there is more than one direction of causality making two variables correlated.

Sometimes we can rule out one or more of these directions based on additional knowledge of the situation. For example, the correlation between high school grades and college grades cannot be due to college grades causing high school grades—causality doesn't go backwards in time. However, we still do not know whether the high school grades somehow caused the college grades (for example, by giving the students greater confidence), or some third factor, such as a tendency to study hard, makes for good grades in both high school and college.

longitudinal study

In the social and behavioral sciences, one major strategy to rule out at least one direction of causality is to do studies where people are measured at two different points in time. This is called a **longitudinal study.** (For example, we might measure a couple's level of exciting activities at one time and then examine the quality of their marriage a year later.)

true experiment

Another major strategy is to conduct a **true experiment** in which participants are randomly assigned (say, by flipping a coin) to experience different levels of variable X and then are measured on variable Y. For example, Aron et al. (2000) followed up their survey studies with a series of true experiments. Married couples came to their laboratory, spent 10 minutes doing a structured activity together, and then filled out a marital satisfaction questionnaire. What made this a true experiment is that half of the couples were randomly assigned (by flipping a coin) to do an activity that was exciting and the other half an activity that was pleasant but not particularly exciting. The finding was that when those who had done the exciting activities filled out the marital satisfaction questionnaires, they reported substantially higher levels of marital satisfaction than did those who had done the pleasant but not exciting activities. As a result of this experiment, we can be confident that at least under these kinds of conditions, there is a direction of causality from the activities to marital satisfaction.

The main point to remember from all this is that just knowing that two variables are correlated, by itself, does not tell you anything about the direction of causality between them. *Understanding this principle is perhaps the single most important indication of sophistication in understanding social and behavioral science research!*

Graphing Correlations: The Scatter Diagram

Figure 3–1, showing the correlation between exciting activities and marital satisfaction, is an example of a **scatter diagram** (also called a *scatterplot*). A scatter diagram shows you at a glance the degree and pattern of relation of the two variables.

scatter diagram

How to Make a Scatter Diagram

There are three steps to making a scatter diagram:

1. Draw the axes, and decide which variable should go on which axis. Often, it doesn't matter which variable goes on which axis. But if you think of one variable as predicting the other, then the one that is doing the predicting goes on the horizontal axis, the variable that is being predicted on the vertical axis. (In a true experiment, we would diagram the variable that is the cause on the horizontal axis and the one that is the effect on the vertical axis.) We will have more to say about prediction later in the chapter. In Figure 3–1, we put exciting activities on the horizontal axis and marital satisfaction on the vertical axis because in the context of the study, we were working from a theory that exciting activities is a cause of marital satisfaction. Yet since this was a strictly correlational study, and we were not really planning to use these results to make predictions, it would also have been correct to put the axes the other way.

2. Determine the range of values to use for each variable and mark them on the axes. Your numbers should go upward on each axis, starting from where the axes meet. Ordinarily, begin with the lowest value your measure can possibly have (usually 0), and continue to the highest value your measure can possibly have. When there is no obvious or reasonable lowest or highest possible value, begin or end at a value that is as high or low as people ordinarily score in the group of people of interest for your study.

In Figure 3–1, the horizontal axis starts at 1 and goes to 5, because the scale that participants used to answer the question has a lowest possible score of 1 and a highest possible score of 5. The vertical axis goes from 10 to 60, the lowest and highest possible scores on the marital satisfaction scale used. (It had 10 items, each answered on a 1-to-6 scale).

3. Mark a dot for the pair of scores for each person. Find the place on the horizontal axis for that person's score on the horizontal axis variable. Then move up to the height on the vertical axis for the person's score on that variable, then mark a clear dot. (If there are two persons with the same scores, you can either put the number 2 in that place or locate a second dot as near as possible to the first—touching, if possible—but making it clear that there are, in fact, two dots in the one place.)

TABLE 3–1
Hours Slept Last Night and Happy Mood Example (Fictional Data)

Hours Slept	Happy Mood
7	4
9	5
8	3
9	7
8	4
6	1
8	3
7	2
10	6
8	5

An Example

Suppose a researcher is studying the relation of sleep to mood. As an initial test, the researcher asks 10 students in her seminar how many hours sleep they had last night and then to rate how happy they feel at the moment on a scale from 0—"Not at all happy" to 8—"Extremely happy." (In practice, a much larger group should be used for this kind of research, but we will use just 10 participants for simplicity in teaching.) Let's suppose that the results were those shown in Table 3–1.

1. Draw the axes, and decide which variable should go on which axis. Because sleep comes before mood, it makes most sense to think of sleep as the predictor. (However, it is certainly possible that people who are in general in a good mood are able to get more sleep.) Thus, we put hours

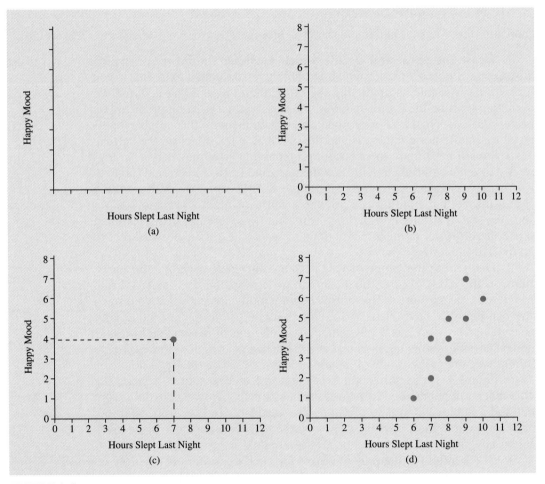

FIGURE 3–2
How to make a scatter diagram. (a) The axes are set up—the predictor variable (Hours Slept Last Night) on the horizontal axis, the other (Happy Mood) on the vertical axis. (b) The range of values has been marked on the axes. (c) A dot has been placed for the pair of scores for the first student. (d) A dot has been placed for the pair of scores for all 10 students.

slept on the horizontal axis and happy mood on the vertical axis. (See Figure 3–2a.)

2. **Determine the range of values to use for each variable and mark them on the axes.** For the horizontal axis, the minimum amount of sleep possible is 0 hours. We do not know the maximum possible, but let us assume that students rarely sleep more than 12 hours. The vertical axis goes from 0 to 8, the limits of the questionnaire in this example. (See Figure 3–2b.)

3. **Mark a dot for the pair of scores for each person.** For the first student, the number of hours slept last night was 7. Move across to 7 on the horizontal axis. Then, move up to the point across from the 4 (the mood rating for the first student) on the vertical axis. Place a dot at this point. (See Figure 3–2c.) Do the same for each of the other nine students. The result should look like Figure 3–2d.

Patterns of Correlation

Linear and Curvilinear Correlations

In each of the examples we have looked at so far, the pattern in the scatter diagram roughly approximates a straight line. Thus, it is an example of a **linear correlation.** For example, in the scatter diagram of Figure 3–1, you could draw a line showing the general trend of the dots, as we have done in Figure 3–3. Similarly, you could draw such a line in our second example, as shown in Figure 3–4. Notice that the scores do not all fall right on the line—far from it in fact—but that the line does describe their general tendency.

Sometimes, however, the general relationship between two variables does not follow a straight line at all, but instead follows the more complex pattern of a **curvilinear correlation.** For example, it is known that up to a point, more physiological arousal makes you do better on almost any kind of task (such as on a math test). Beyond that point, still greater physiological arousal makes you do worse. That is, going from being nearly asleep to a moderate level of arousal makes you more effective. Beyond that moderate

linear correlation

curvilinear correlation

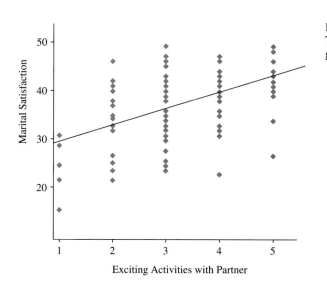

FIGURE 3–3
The scatter diagram of Figure 3–1 with a line drawn in to show the general trend. (Data from Aron et al., 2000)

FIGURE 3–4
The scatter diagram of Figure 3–2d with a line drawn in to show the general trend.

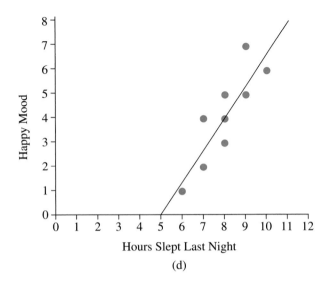

(d)

level, further increases in arousal may make you too "keyed up" to do well. This particular curvilinear pattern is illustrated in Figure 3–5. Notice that you could not draw a straight line to describe this pattern.

The usual way of figuring the degree of correlation (which is the one you learn in this chapter) gives the degree of *linear* correlation. If the true pattern of association is curvilinear, computing the correlation in the usual way could show little or no correlation. Thus, it is really quite important to look at scatter diagrams to unearth these richer relationships rather than automatically carrying out correlations in the usual way, assuming that the only relationship is a straight line.

No Correlation

no correlation

It is also possible for two variables to be completely unrelated to each other. For example, if you were to do a study of income and shoe size, your results might appear as shown in Figure 3–6. The dots are spread everywhere, and there is no line, straight or otherwise, that is any reasonable representation of a trend. There is simply **no correlation.**

FIGURE 3–5
Example of a curvilinear relationship: task performance and arousal.

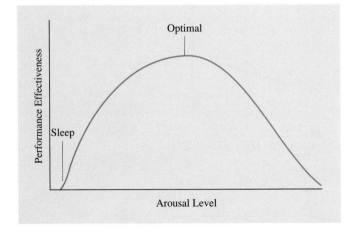

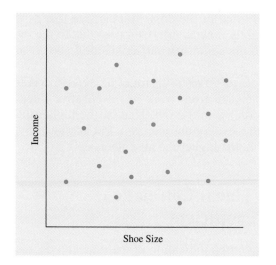

FIGURE 3–6
Two variables with no association with each other: income and shoe size.

Positive and Negative Linear Correlations

In the examples of linear correlations, we have considered so far, such as exciting activities and marital satisfaction or hours slept and positive mood, high scores go with high scores, lows with lows, and mediums with mediums. This situation is called a **positive correlation.** (One reason these examples of linear correlations are called "positive" is that in geometry, the slope of a line that describes the pattern is positive when it goes up and to the right on a graph like this. Notice that in Figures 3–3 and 3–4 the lines go up and to the right.)

    Sometimes, however, the relationship between the variables is not positive. Instead, high scores go with low scores and lows with highs. This is called a **negative correlation.** For example, in the newspaper survey, the researchers also asked participants to indicate how bored they were with their relationship and their partner. Not surprisingly, they found that the more bored a person was, the *lower* was his or her marital satisfaction. That is, in this situation, low scores on one variable go with high scores on the other. This pattern is shown in the scatter diagram in Figure 3–7. We put a line in

positive correlation

negative correlation

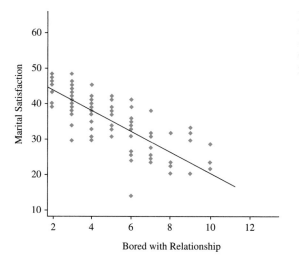

FIGURE 3–7
Scatter diagram with the line drawn in to show the general trend for negative correlation between two variables: Greater boredom with the relationship goes with lower marital satisfaction. (Data from Aron et al., 2000)

the figure to emphasize the general trend of the dots. You can see that as it goes from left to right, it slopes slightly downward. (Compare this to the result for the relation of exciting activities and marital satisfaction shown in Figure 3–3, which slopes upward.)

Another study (Mirvis & Lawler, 1977) also illustrates a negative correlation. That study found that absenteeism from work had a negative linear correlation with "intrinsic satisfaction" with the job. That is, the higher the level of job satisfaction, the lower the level of absenteeism. Put another way, the lower the level of job satisfaction, the higher the absenteeism.

Computing the Degree of Linear Correlation: The Pearson Correlation Coefficient

Looking at a scatter diagram gives a rough indication of the type and degree of relationship between two variables. It is obviously not a very precise approach. What we need is a number that gives the precise degree of correlation.

Degree of Correlation

What we mean by the *degree of correlation* is how much there is a clear pattern of some particular relationship between the two variables. For example, we saw that a positive linear correlation is that in which high scores go with highs, mediums with mediums, lows with lows. The degree of such a correlation, then, is how much highs go with highs, and so on. Similarly, the degree of negative linear correlation is how much highs on one variable go with lows on the other, and so forth. In terms of a scatter diagram, a high degree of linear correlation means that the dots all fall very close to a straight line (the line sloping up or down depending on whether the linear correlation is positive or negative). A perfect linear correlation means all the dots fall exactly on the straight line.

Figuring the Degree of Linear Correlation

The first thing we need in order to figure the degree of correlation is some way of gauging what a high score is and what a low score is—and how high a high is and how low a low. This means comparing scores on different variables in a consistent way. This kind of problem of comparing apples and oranges, as we saw in Chapter 2, can be solved by using Z scores.

To review, a Z score is the number of standard deviations a score is from the mean. Whatever the scale on which you have measured something, if you convert your raw scores to Z scores, a raw score that is high (that is, above the mean of the other scores on that variable) will always have a positive Z score, and a raw score that is low (below the mean) will always have a negative Z score. Further, regardless of the particular measure used, Z scores give a standard indication of just how high or low each score is. A Z score of 1 is always exactly 1 standard deviation above the mean, and a Z score of 2 is twice as many standard deviations above the mean. Z scores on one variable are directly comparable to Z scores on another variable.

There is an additional reason why Z scores are used when we figure the degree of correlation. It has to do with what happens if you multiply a score on one variable times a score on the other variable. When using Z scores, this is called a **cross-product of Z scores.** If you multiply a high Z score by a high Z score, you will always get a positive cross-product because no matter what the scale, scores above the mean become positive Z scores, and a positive times a positive is a positive. Further—and here is where it gets interesting—if you multiply a low Z score by a low Z score, you also always will get a positive cross-product because no matter what the scale, scores below the mean become negative Z scores, and a negative times a negative gives a positive.

cross-product of Z scores

If highs on one variable go with highs on the other and lows on the one go with lows on the other, the cross-products of Z scores always will be positive. Considering a whole distribution of scores, suppose you take each person's Z score on one variable and multiply it by that person's Z score on the other variable. The result of doing this when highs go with highs and lows with lows is that the multiplication for each person will come out positive. If you sum up these cross-products of Z scores for all the people in the study, which are all positive, you will end up with a big positive number.

On the other hand, with a negative correlation, highs go with lows and lows with highs. In terms of Z scores, this would mean positives with negatives and negatives with positives. Multiplied out, that gives all negative cross-products. If you add all these negative cross-products together, you get a large negative number.

Finally, suppose there is no linear correlation. In this case, for some people highs on one variable would go with highs on the other variable (and some lows would go with lows), making positive cross-products. For others, highs on one variable would go with lows on the other variable (and some lows would go with highs), making negative cross-products. Adding up these cross-products for all the people in the study would result in the positive cross-products and the negative cross-products canceling each other out, giving a number around 0.

In each situation, we changed all the scores to Z scores, multiplied the two Z scores for each person times each other, and added up these cross-products. The result is you get a large positive number if there is a positive correlation, a large negative number if there is a negative correlation, and a number near 0 if there is no linear correlation.

However, you are still left with the problem of figuring the *degree* of a positive or negative correlation. Obviously, the larger the number, the bigger the correlation. But how large is large, and how large is not very large? You cannot judge from the sum of the cross-products alone, which increases rapidly just by adding the cross-products of more persons together. (That is, a study with 100 people would have a bigger sum of cross-products than the same study with only 25 people.)

The solution is to divide this sum of the cross-products by the number of people in the study. That is, you compute the *average of the cross-products of Z scores.* It turns out that this average can never be more than +1, which would be a positive linear **perfect correlation.** Its minimum is −1, which would be a negative linear perfect correlation. In the case of no linear correlation, the average of the cross-products of Z scores is 0.

perfect correlation

For a positive linear correlation that is not perfect, which is the usual situation, the average of the cross-products of Z scores is between 0 and +1. To put it another way, if the general trend of the dots is upward and to the right, but they do not fall exactly on a single straight line, this number is between 0 and +1. The same rule holds for negative correlations: They fall between 0 and −1.

The Correlation Coefficient

correlation coefficient (*r*)

The average of the cross-products of *Z* scores thus serves as an excellent way of figuring the degree of linear correlation. It is called the **correlation coefficient (*r*).** It also is called the *Pearson correlation coefficient* (or the *Pearson product-moment correlation coefficient*, to be very traditional). It is named after Karl Pearson (whom you meet in Box 11–1). Pearson, along with Francis Galton (see Box 3–1), played a major role in developing the correlation

---

BOX 3–1

Galton: Gentleman Genius

Francis Galton is credited with inventing the correlation coefficient. (Karl Pearson and others worked out the formulas, but Pearson was a student of Galton and gave Galton all the credit.) As you may be sensing, statistics at this time was a tight little British club. (In fact, most of science was an only slightly larger club. Galton also was influenced greatly by his own cousin, Charles Darwin.)

Of the members of this club, Galton was a typical, eccentric, independently wealthy gentleman scientist. Aside from his work in statistics, he possessed a medical degree, had explored "darkest Africa," invented glasses for reading underwater, experimented with stereoscopic maps, dabbled in meteorology and anthropology, and wrote a paper about receiving intelligible signals from the stars.

Above all, Galton was a compulsive counter. Some of his counts are rather infamous. Once while attending a lecture, he counted the fidgets of an audience per minute, looking for variations with the boringness of the subject matter. While twice having his picture painted, he counted the artist's brush strokes per hour, concluding that each portrait required an average of 20,000 strokes. While walking the streets of various towns in the British Isles, he classified the beauty of the female inhabitants by fingering a recording device in his pocket to register "good," "medium," or "bad."

Galton's consuming interest, however, was the counting of geniuses, criminals, and other types in families. He wanted to understand how each type was produced so that science could improve the human race by encouraging governments to enforce eugenics—selective breeding for intelligence, proper moral behavior, and other qualities—to be determined, of course, by the eugenicists. (Eugenics has since been generally discredited.) The concept of correlation came directly from his first simple efforts in this area, the study of the relation of the height of children to their parents.

At first, Galton's method of exactly measuring the tendency for "one thing to go with another" seemed almost the same as proving the cause of something. For example, if it could be shown mathematically that most of the brightest people came from a few highborn British families and most of the least intelligent people came from poor families, that would prove that intelligence was caused by the inheritance of certain genes (provided that you were prejudiced enough to overlook the differences in educational opportunities). The same study might prove more convincingly that if you were a member of one of those better British families, history would make you a prime example of how easy it is to misinterpret the meaning of a correlation.

References: Peters (1987); Tankard (1984).

coefficient. The correlation coefficient is abbreviated by the letter *r,* which is short for *regression,* a concept closely related to correlation. (We discuss regression later in the chapter.) Figure 3–8 shows scatter diagrams and the correlation coefficients for several examples.

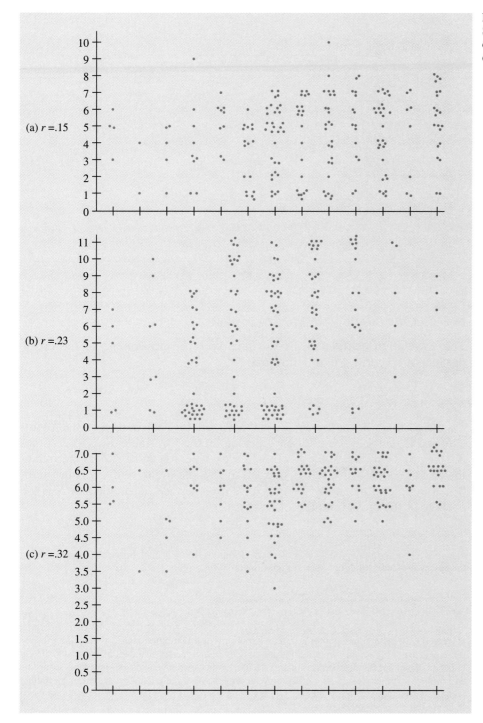

FIGURE 3–8
Scatter diagrams and correlation coefficients for fictional studies with different correlations.

FIGURE 3–8 (*cont.*)

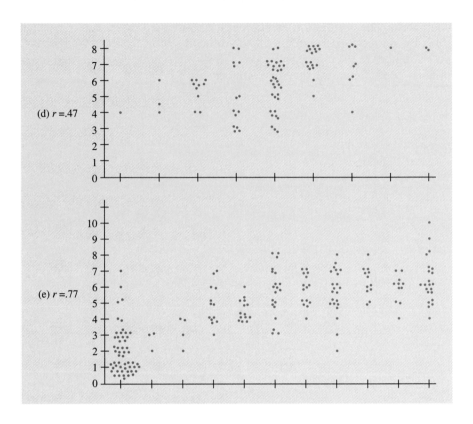

(d) $r = .47$

(e) $r = .77$

Formula for the Correlation Coefficient

The correlation coefficient, as we have seen, is the average of the cross-product of Z scores. Put as a formula,

$$r = \frac{\Sigma\ Z_X Z_Y}{N} \tag{3–1}$$

r is the correlation coefficient. Z_X is the Z score for each person on the X variable and Z_Y is the Z score for each person on the Y variable. $Z_X Z_Y$ is Z_X times Z_Y (the cross-product of the Z scores) for each person and $\Sigma Z_X Z_Y$ is the sum of the cross-products of Z scores over all the people in the study. N is the number of people in the study. Putting it all together, $\Sigma Z_X Z_Y$ divided by N is the average of the cross-products of Z scores.[1]

---

[1]There is also a "computational" version of this formula, which is mathematically equivalent and thus gives the same result but does not require you to first figure out Z scores:

$$r = \frac{N\Sigma(XY) - \Sigma X \Sigma Y}{\sqrt{[N\Sigma X^2 - (\Sigma X)^2]}\ \sqrt{[N\Sigma Y^2 - (\Sigma Y)^2]}} \tag{3–2}$$

However, as we noted in Chapter 2, researchers rarely use computational formulas like this any more because most actual computations are done by computer. As a student learning statistics, it is better to use the definitional formula (3-1). This is because when solving problems using the definitional formula you are strengthening your understanding of what the correlation coefficient means. In all examples in this chapter, we use the definitional formula and we urge you to use it in doing the chapter exercises.

Steps for Computing the Correlation Coefficient

Here are the four steps for computing the correlation coefficient.

1. **Convert all scores to Z scores.** This requires figuring the mean and the standard deviation of each variable, then figuring the Z score for each raw score. (Figure Z scores using the method you learned in Chapter 2.)
2. **Figure the cross-product of the Z scores for each person.** That is, for each person, multiply the Z score for one variable times the Z score for the other variable.
3. **Sum the cross-products of the Z scores.**
4. **Divide by the number of people in the study.**

An Example

Let us try these steps with the sleep and mood example.

1. **Convert all scores to Z scores.** Starting with the number of hours slept last night, the mean is 8 (sum of 80 divided by 10 students), and the standard deviation is 1.10 (sum of squared deviations, 12, divided by 10 students, for a variance of 1.2, the square root of which is 1.10). For the first student, then, a number of hours slept of 9 is 1 hour above the mean of 8, and 1 divided by 1.10 is .91. Thus the first score is .91 standard deviations above the mean, or a Z score of .91. We figured the rest of the Z scores in the same way and show them in the appropriate columns in Table 3–2.
2. **Figure the cross-product of the Z scores for each person.** For the first student, multiply .91 times .58. This gives .53. The cross-products for all the students are shown in the last column of Table 3–2.
3. **Sum the cross-products of the Z scores.** Adding up all the cross-products of Z scores, as shown in Table 3–2, gives a sum of 8.41.
4. **Divide by the number of people in the study.** Dividing 8.41 by 10 (the number of students in the study) gives a result of .841, which rounded off to .84. This is the correlation coefficient.

TABLE 3–2
Figuring the Correlation Coefficient for the Sleep and Mood Study (Fictional Data)

Number of Hours Slept (X)				Happy Mood (Y)				Cross-Products
Deviation		Dev Squared		Deviation		Dev Squared		
X	$X–M$	$(X–M)^2$	Z_X	Y	$Y–M$	$(Y–M)^2$	Z_Y	$Z_X Z_Y$
9	1	1	.91	5	1	1	.58	.53
8	0	0	.00	3	−1	1	−.58	.00
9	1	1	.91	7	3	9	1.73	1.58
8	0	0	.00	4	0	0	.00	.00
6	−2	4	−1.82	1	−3	9	−1.73	3.15
8	0	0	.00	3	−1	1	−.58	.00
7	−1	1	−.91	2	−2	4	−1.16	1.05
10	2	4	1.82	6	2	4	1.16	2.10
8	0	0	.00	5	1	1	.58	.00
$\Sigma = 80$		$\Sigma(X − M)^2 = 12$		$\Sigma = 40$		$\Sigma(Y − M)^2 = 30$		$\Sigma Z_X Z_Y = 8.41$
$M = 8$		$SD^2 = 1.20$		$M = 4$		$SD^2 = 3.00$		$r = .84$
		$SD = 1.10$				$SD = 1.73$		

In terms of the correlation coefficient formula,

$$r = \frac{\Sigma \ Z_X Z_Y}{N} = \frac{8.41}{10} = .841$$

Because this correlation coefficient is positive and near 1, the highest possible value, this is a very strong positive linear correlation.

An Example of Graphing and Computing a Correlation

In this example, we put together the steps of making a scatter diagram and computing the correlation coefficient.

Suppose that an educational researcher had the average class size and average achievement test score from the five elementary schools in a particular small school district, as shown in Table 3–3. (Again, it would be very rare in actual research practice to do a study or figure a correlation with only five cases. We have kept the numbers low here to make it easier for you to follow the steps of the example.) The question he then asks is, what is the relationship between these two variables?

The first thing he must do is to make a scatter diagram. This requires three steps.

1. Draw the axes, and decide which variable should go on which axis. Because it seems more reasonable to think of class size as affecting achievement test scores rather than the other way around, we will draw the axes with class size along the bottom.

2. Determine the range of values to use for each variable and mark them on the axes. We will assume that the achievement test scores go from 0 to 100. Class size has to be at least 1 and in this example we guessed that it would be unlikely to be more than 50.

3. Mark a dot for the pair of scores for each person. (In this example, of course, we have schools instead of persons.) The completed scatter diagram is shown in Figure 3–9.

In any correlation problem, before figuring the correlation coefficient, it is a good idea to look at the scatter diagram to be sure that the pattern is roughly a straight line. In this example, it is. It is also wise to make a rough estimate of the direction and degree of correlation. This serves as a check against making a major mistake in figuring. In this example, the basic pattern is one in which the dots go down and to the right fairly consistently. This suggests a

TABLE 3–3
Average Class Size and Achievement Test Scores in Five Elementary Schools (Fictional Data)

Elementary School	Class Size	Achievement Test Score
Main Street	25	80
Casat	14	98
Harland	33	50
Shady Grove	28	82
Jefferson	20	90

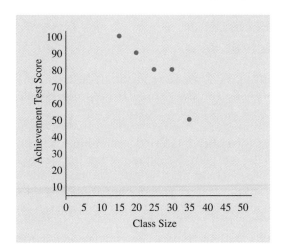

FIGURE 3–9
The last step in making a scatter diagram for the scores in Table 3–3. A dot has been placed for each pair of scores for each of the five schools.

strong negative correlation. Now we can proceed to figure the correlation co-efficient, following the usual steps.

1. **Convert all scores to Z scores.** The mean for class size is 24, and the standard deviation is 6.54. The Z score for the first class size, of 25, is .15. That is, $(25 - 24)/6.54 = 0.15$. All of the Z scores are shown in the appropriate columns of Table 3–4.

2. **Figure the cross-product of the Z scores for each person.** The first cross product is .15 times 0, which is 0. The second is –1.53 times 1.10, which equals –1.68. All of the cross-products of Z scores are shown in the rightmost column of Table 3–4.

3. **Sum the cross-products of the Z scores.** The total is –4.52.

4. **Divide by the number of people in the study.** The sum –4.52 divided by 5 is –.90; that is, $r = -.90$.

Note that a correlation coefficient of –.90 agrees well with our original estimate of a strong negative correlation.

TABLE 3–4
Figuring the Correlation Coefficient for Average Class Size and Achievement Test Scores in Five Elementary Schools (Fictional Data)

School	Class Size		Achievement Test Score		Cross-Product
	X	Z_X	Y	Z_Y	$Z_X Z_Y$
Main Street	25	.15	80	.00	.00
Casat	14	–1.53	98	1.10	–1.68
Harland	33	1.38	50	–1.84	–2.53
Shady Grove	28	.61	82	.12	.08
Jefferson	20	–.61	90	.61	–.38
Σ:	120		400		–4.52
M:	24		80		$r = -.90$
$SD = \sqrt{214/5} = 6.54$			$\sqrt{1,328/5} = 16.30$		

Testing the Statistical Significance of the Correlation Coefficient

The correlation coefficient, by itself, is a descriptive statistic. It describes the degree and direction of linear correlation in the particular group of people studied. However, when doing research, we often are more interested in a particular group of scores as representing some larger group that we have not studied directly. For example, the researcher interested in the link of sleep and mood tested only 10 individuals, but with the intention that they would tell her something about the link of sleep and mood for people more generally. (In practice, one would want a much larger group than 10 for this purpose. We have used small groups in our examples to make them easier to follow.)

The problem, however, is that by studying only some of the people in the larger group you want to know about, it is possible to pick by chance just those people where highs happen to go with highs and lows with lows, even though, had we studied all the people in the larger population, there might really be no correlation.

We say that a correlation is *significant* if it is unlikely that we could have gotten a correlation this big if, in fact, the overall group had no correlation. Specifically, we figure out whether that likelihood of no correlation in the larger population is less than some small degree of probability (p), such as 5 percent or 1 percent. If it is that small, we say that the correlation is "statistically significant" with "$p < .05$" or "$p < .01$."

statistical significance

The method and logic of figuring **statistical significance** is the main focus of this book starting with Chapter 4, and we would be jumping ahead if we were to try to explain it fully now. However, by the time you have completed the later chapters, the details will be quite clear. (The needed information is in the appendix to this chapter, but we suggest that you leave this appendix until you have completed Chapter 8.) We mention this now only so that you will have a general idea of what is meant if you see mentions of statistical significance, $p < .05$, or some such phrase, when reading a research article that reports correlation coefficients.

Prediction

One important use of correlations is to help in making predictions. A college admissions officer might want to use an applicant's score on one variable, such as the applicant's SAT score, to predict what the applicant's score would be on another variable, such as the applicant's likely college grade point average (GPA). Similarly, a personnel manager might want to use the score on a job application examination to predict whether the applicant will be successful on the job; a parole officer might want to use the number of rule violations to predict whether a prisoner will commit a crime if released; a public health official might want to use tomorrow's expected high temperature to predict the number of people likely to have heat-related health problems; and so forth. In each situation, if there is a high correlation between the variable used as the basis for the prediction, such as SAT scores, and the variable whose value is being predicted, such as college grades, then the prediction will be more accurate. If there is no correlation, then there is no basis for prediction.

Predictor (X) and Criterion (Y) Variables

With correlation it did not matter much which variable was which. But with regression we have to decide which variable is being predicted from and which variable is being predicted to. The variable being predicted from is called the **predictor variable**. The variable being predicted to is called the **criterion variable**. In equations the predictor variable is usually labeled X, the criterion variable, Y. That is, X predicts Y. In the example we just considered, SAT scores would be the predictor variable or X and college grades would be the criterion variable or Y.

predictor variable
criterion variable

Prediction Using Z Scores

It is easier to learn about prediction if we first consider prediction using Z scores. (We will get to prediction using ordinary scores shortly.) The **prediction model,** or formula, that we use to make predictions with Z scores is as follows: A person's predicted Z score on the criterion variable is found by multiplying a particular number, called a **regression coefficient,** times that person's Z score on the predictor variable. That is, a person's predicted Z score on the criterion variable is the regression coefficient times the person's Z score on the predictor variable.

prediction model

regression coefficient

Because we are working with Z scores, which are also called standard scores, the regression coefficient is called a **standardized regression coefficient;** it is symbolized by the Greek letter "beta" (β)**.** In symbols,

standardized regression coefficient (b)

$$\text{Predicted } Z_Y = (\beta)(Z_X) \tag{3-3}$$

In this formula, predicted Z_Y is the predicted value of the Z score for the particular person's score on the criterion variable Y. (The predicted value of a score often is written with a hat symbol. Thus $\hat{Z}_Y$ means Predicted Z_Y.) β is the standardized regression coefficient. Z_X is the known Z score for the particular person's score on the predictor variable X. Thus, $(\beta)(Z_X)$ means multiplying the standardized regression coefficient times the person's Z score on the predictor variable.

For example, suppose that at your school the beta for predicting college GPA at graduation from SAT at admission is .3. A person applying to your school has an SAT score that is 2 standard deviations above the mean (that is, a Z score of +2). The predicted Z score for this person's GPA would be .3 times 2, which is .6. That is, this person's predicted Z score for their college GPA is .6 standard deviations above the mean. In symbols,

$$\text{Predicted } Z_Y = (\beta)(Z_X) = (.3)(2) = .6$$

It can be proved mathematically (using methods that are beyond the level of this book) that when predicting using Z scores, the best number to use for beta is the correlation coefficient. That is, when predicting one variable from another using Z scores, $\beta = r$.

An Example

Consider again the sleep and mood example. In this example, the correlation between hours slept and happy mood was .84. Thus $\beta = .84$ and the model for predicting a person's Z score for happy mood is to multiply .84 times the person's Z score for the number of hours slept the night before. Suppose you were thinking about staying up so late one night so that you would get only 5 hours sleep. This would be a Z score of -2.73 on numbers of hours slept—that is, nearly three standard deviations less sleep than the mean. (We changed 5 hours to a Z score using the procedure you learned in Chapter 2 for converting raw scores to Z scores: $Z = (X - M)/SD$.) We could then predict your Z score on happy mood the next day by multiplying .84 times -2.73, which comes out to -2.29. This means that based on the results of our little study, if you sleep only 5 hours tonight, tomorrow we would expect you to have a happy mood that is more than 2 standard deviations below the mean (that is, you would be very unhappy). In terms of the formula,

$$\text{Predicted } Z_Y = (\beta)(Z_X) = (.84)(-2.73) = -2.29$$

By contrast, if you planned to get 9 hours sleep, the model would predict that tomorrow you would have a Z score for happy mood of .84 times .91 (the Z score when the number of hours slept is 9), which is $+.76$. You would be a bit happier than the average. That is,

$$\text{Predicted } Z_Y = (\beta)(Z_X) = (.84)(.91) = .76.$$

(Incidentally, it is not a good idea to make predictions that involve values of the predictor variable very far from those in the original study. For example, you should not conclude that sleeping 20 hours would make you extremely happy the next day!)

Why Prediction Is Also Called Regression

Statisticians usually refer to prediction of the kind we are doing as *regression*. The term comes from the fact that when there is less than a perfect correlation between two variables, the criterion variable Z score is some fraction (the value of r) of the predictor variable Z score. As a result, the criterion variable Z score is closer to its mean. (That is, it regresses or returns toward a Z of 0.)

For example, in the sleep and mood example, the student who slept 5 hours the night before has a Z score for hours slept of -2.73, but the predicted happy mood level is -2.29, a number closer to the mean Z score of 0.

Prediction Using Raw Scores

Based on what you have learned, you can now also make predictions involving raw scores as follows:

1. Convert the person's raw score on the predictor variable to a Z score.

TABLE 3–5
Summary, Using Formulas, of Steps for Making Raw Score Predictions with Raw-to-Z and Z-to-Raw Conversions, with an Example

Step	Formula	Example
1	$Z_X = (X - M_X)/SD_X$	$Z_X = (9-8)/1.10 = .91$
2	Predicted $Z_Y = (\beta)(Z_X)$	Predicted $Z_Y = (.84)(.91) = .76$
3	Predicted $Y = (SD_Y)(\text{Predicted } Z_Y) + M_Y$	Predicted $Y = (.76)(1.73) + 4 = 5.31$

   2. **Multiply beta (the correlation coefficient) times the person's predictor variable Z score to get the person's predicted Z score on the criterion variable.**
   3. **Convert the person's predicted Z score on the criterion variable to a raw score.**[2]

For example, in the sleep and mood study, when we wanted to predict your mood the next day if you sleep 5 hours tonight, we first converted 5 to a Z score (–2.73). This was Step 1. We then found the predicted mood Z score by multiplying beta times this Z score (.84 times –2.73 gave a predicted mood Z score of –2.29). This was Step 2. Step 3 (which we did not do earlier) is to convert this predicted mood Z score of –2.29 to a mood raw score. Using the formula from Chapter 2 for converting a Z score to a raw score, this comes out to a mood raw score of .04. That is, $(-2.29)(1.73) + 4 = -3.96 + 4 = .04$. In other words, using the regression procedure for the model based on the little study of ten students, we would predict that if you sleep only 5 hours tonight, tomorrow you will rate your happy mood as about a zero!

   These steps are laid out in Table 3–5 for the other example prediction we made (for the situation in which you sleep 9 hours tonight).

   In using these steps, be careful when changing raw scores to Z scores and Z scores to raw scores to use the mean and standard deviation for the correct variable. In Step 1, you are working only with the score, mean, and standard deviation for the predictor variable (X). In Step 3, you are working only with the score, mean, and standard deviation for the criterion variable (Y).

---

[2]In practice, if you are going to make predictions for many different people, you would use a *raw-score prediction formula* that allows you to just plug in a particular person's raw score on the predictor variable and then solve directly to get the person's predicted raw score on the criterion variable. What the raw score prediction formula amounts to is taking the usual Z-score prediction formula, but substituting for the Z scores the formula for getting a Z score from a raw score. If you know the mean and standard deviation for both variables and the correlation coefficient, this whole thing can then be reduced algebraically to give the raw-score prediction formula. This raw-score prediction formula is of the form predicted $Y = a + (b)(X)$, where a is called the *regression constant* (because this number that is added into the prediction does not change regardless of the value of X) and b is called the *raw-score regression coefficient* (because it is the number multiplied by the raw-score value of X and then added to a to get the predicted value of Y). You will sometimes see these terms referred to in research reports. However, since the logic of regression and its relation to correlation is most directly appreciated from the Z-score prediction formula, that is our emphasis in this introductory text.

Multiple Regression and Correlation

So far we have predicted a person's score on a criterion variable using the person's score on a single predictor variable. What if you also could use additional predictor variables? For example, in predicting happy mood, all we had to work with was the number of hours slept the night before. Suppose that we also knew about how well you slept or how many dreams you had. This added information might allow us to make a much more accurate prediction of mood.

multiple correlation
multiple regression

The association between a criterion variable and two or more predictor variables is called **multiple correlation.** Making predictions in this situation is called **multiple regression.**

We will explore these topics only very briefly because the details are beyond the level of an introductory book. However, since multiple regression and correlation are frequently used in research articles in the social and behavioral sciences, it will be useful for you to have a general understanding of them.

In multiple regression, each predictor variable has its own regression coefficient. The predicted Z score of the criterion variable is found by multiplying the Z score for each predictor variable times its beta (standardized regression coefficient) and then adding up the results. For example, the Z-score multiple regression formula with three predictor variables follows:

$$\text{Predicted } Z_Y = (\beta_1)(Z_{X_1}) + (\beta_2)(Z_{X_2}) + (\beta_3)(Z_{X_3})$$

$$(3\text{--}4)$$

β_1 is the standardized regression coefficient for the first predictor variable. Similarly, β_2 and β_3 are the standardized regression coefficients for the second and third predictor variables. Z_{X1} is the Z score for the first predictor variable. Similarly, Z_{X2} and Z_{X3} are the Z scores for the second and third predictor variables. $(\beta_1)(Z_{X1})$ means multiplying β_1 times Z_{X1}; and so forth.

For example, in the sleep and mood study, a multiple regression model for predicting happy mood (Y) using the predictor variables of number of hours slept, which we could now call X_1 and also a rating of how well you slept (X_2) and number of dreams during the night (X_3) might turn out to be as follows:

$$\text{Predicted } Z_Y = (.53)(Z_{X1}) + (.28)(Z_{X2}) + (.03)(Z_{X3})$$

Suppose that you were asked to predict the mood of a student who had a Z score of -1.82 for number of hours slept, a Z score of 2.34 for how well she slept, and a Z score of .94 for number of dreams during the night. That is, the student did not sleep very long, slept very well, and had a few more dreams than average. You would figure your predicted Z score for happy mood by multiplying .53 times the number of hours slept Z score, .28 times the how well slept Z score, and .03 times the number of dreams Z score, then adding up the results:

$$\text{Predicted } Z_Y = (.53)(-1.82) + (.28)(2.34) + (.03)(.94)$$
$$= -.96 \qquad + .66 \qquad + .03 \qquad = -.27$$

So under these conditions, you would predict a happy mood Z score of $-.27$, which means a mood about one-quarter of a standard deviation below the mean. You can see that how well the student slept partially offset getting fewer hours sleep. Given the very low β for dreams in this model, the number of dreams would in general make very little difference in mood the next day no matter how many or how few.

In multiple regression, the overall correlation between the criterion variable and all the predictor or predictor variables is called the **multiple correlation coefficient** and is symbolized as capital **R.**

There is one particularly important difference between multiple regression and prediction when using only one predictor variable. In ordinary correlation, $\beta = r$. But in multiple regression, the beta for a predictor variable is not the same as the ordinary correlation coefficient (r) of that predictor variable with the criterion variable. Usually, the beta will be lower (closer to 0) than r. The reason is that usually part of what makes any one predictor variable successful in predicting the criterion variable will overlap with what makes the other predictor variables successful in predicting the criterion variable. In multiple regression, beta is related to the unique, distinctive contribution of the variable, excluding any overlap with other predictor variables.

Consider the sleep and mood example. When we were predicting mood using just the number of hours slept, beta was the same as the correlation coefficient of .84. Now, in our example with the multiple regression model, beta for number of hours slept is only .53. It is less because part of what makes number of hours slept predict mood overlaps with what makes sleeping well predict mood (people who sleep more hours usually sleep well). Because of this overlap among the predictor variables, the multiple correlation (R) is usually smaller than the sum of the individual rs of each predictor variable with the criterion variable.

multiple correlation coefficient (R)

The Correlation Coefficient and the Proportion of Variance Accounted for

A correlation coefficient tells you the strength of a linear relationship. Bigger rs (values farther from 0) mean a higher degree of correlation. That is, an r of .4 is a stronger correlation than an r of .2. However, an r of .4 is *more than* twice as strong as an r of .2. To compare correlations with each other, you have to square each correlation (that is, you use r^2 instead of r). The correlation squared is called the **proportion of variance accounted for (r^2).**[3]

For example, a correlation of .2 is equivalent to an r^2 of .04, and a correlation of .4 is equivalent to an r^2 of .16. A correlation of .2 actually means a

proportion of variance accounted for (r^2)

[3]The reason r^2 is called proportion of variance accounted for can be understood as follows: Suppose you used the prediction formula to predict each person's score on Y. Unless the correlation between X and Y was perfect (1.0), the variance of those predicted Y scores would be smaller than the variance of the original Y scores. There is less variance in the predicted Y scores because these predicted scores are on the average closer to the mean than are the original scores. (We discussed this in this section on why prediction is called regression.) However, the more accurate the prediction, the more the predicted scores are like the actual scores. Thus, the more accurate the prediction, the closer the variance of the predicted scores is to the variance of the actual scores. Now suppose you divide the variance of the predicted Y scores by the variance of the original Y scores. The result of this division is the proportion of variance in the actual scores "accounted for" by the variance in the predicted scores. This proportion turns out (for reasons beyond what we can cover in this book) to be r^2.

relationship between X and Y that is only one-quarter as strong as a correlation of .4.

This all works the same way in multiple regression. In multiple regression, the proportion of variance in the criterion variable accounted for by all the predictor variables taken together is the multiple correlation squared, R^2.

Correlation and Prediction as Described in Research Articles

Scatter diagrams are occasionally reported in research articles. For example, Yvette Sheline and her colleagues (1999) were interested in testing a theory that depression causes chemical changes that result in injury to the hippocampus, a region of the brain involved in memory. In their study, 24 depressed psychotherapy patients completed questionnaires, which the researchers used to figure the number of days each participant had been depressed during his or her life. Participants in this study then completed a brain-scan session to allow the researchers to measure the size of their hippocampus. Their results are shown in Figure 3–10. Note that, as predicted, there was a clear linear negative trend. (They also show a squared correlation of .36—the square root of this is a large r of .60.) Thus, this graph suggests that the more days depressed, the smaller the hippocampus. In light of our discussion earlier regarding causality and correlation, it is important to emphasize that it is possible that something about having a smaller hippocampus causes depression, or that some other factor, such as general life stress causes both depression and decrease in hypothalamus size. (Also, you should know that although this result is very consistent, even those with the most days depressed still had plenty of hippocampus remaining.)

Research articles usually give correlation coefficients either in the text of research articles or in tables. (Sometimes the "significance level," such as $p < .05$, will also be reported.) The result we started the chapter with would be described as follows: There was a positive correlation ($r = 51$) between excitement of activities done with partner and marital satisfaction.

Tables of correlations are very common when several variables are involved. Usually, the table is set up so that each variable is listed both at the top and at the left side; the correlation of each pair of variables is shown inside the table. This kind of table is called a **correlation matrix.**

correlation matrix

FIGURE 3–10

Correlation between duration of depression and hippocampal volume. The Pearson correlation between cumulative lifetime total days of major depression was derived from the Diagnostic Interview for Genetic Studies using the Post Life Charting Method (Post et al., 1988) and the total hippocampal gray matter volumes. (From "Depression Duration But Not Age Predicts Hippocampal Volume Loss in Medically Healthy Women with Recurrent Major Depression" by Yvette I. Sheline, Milan Sanghav, et al., *The Journal of Neuroscience,* June 15, 1999, 19(12), p. 5039. Copyright 1999 by the Society for Neuroscience. Reprinted by permission.)

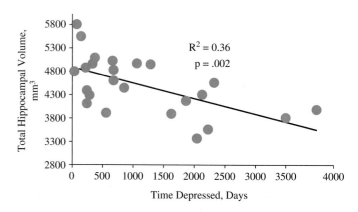

TABLE 3–6
Intercorrelations Between Measures of Victimization

Measure	1	2	3	4	5
1. Peer (Schwartz et al., 1997)	—	.80**	.21*	.26**	.34**
2. Peer (Perry et al., 1988)		—	.32**	.21*	.22**
3. Self-report			—	.34**	.07
4. Diary				—	.08
5. Observe					—

$* p < .05.$ $** p < .01.$

Table 2 from "An Empirical Comparison of Methods of Sampling Aggression and Victimization in School Settings," by A. D. Pellegrini and Mara Bartini, *Journal of Educational Psychology,* June 2000. Vol. 92. No. 2. Copyright © 2000 by The American Psychological Association. Reprinted with permission.

Table 3–6 is from a study by Pellegrini and Bartini (2000) of bullying and victimization among 367 middle school students. Victimization was measured in several ways in the study, including two kinds of ratings by peers (fellow students), an overall self-report questionnaire, a monthly diary completed by the students about their experiences of bullying and aggression in the last 24 hours, and direct observations by the research team watching the students at breaks between classes, lunch, and so forth. Notice that the correlation of a variable with itself is not given (a short line is put in instead in this example). Also, notice that only the upper right triangle of the table is filled in. This is because the lower left triangle would contain exactly the same information. That is, a correlation between two variables is the same whichever way you consider it. For example, if it were shown, the correlation of .08 between Diary (4) and Observe (5) would be exactly the same for the correlation of Observe with Diary.

In terms of what the table tells you, you can see that there is very strong agreement between the two kinds of peer reports ($r = .80$). However, correlations of peer reports with self reports have only moderate correlations of .21 and .32. Direct observation by the research team correlates moderately with peer reports (.34 and .22) but hardly at all with self-report or diary measures (.07 and .08). This suggests that the extent to which fellow students see a student as being victimized corresponds moderately well with how outside observers see it, but that the extent to which students see themselves as victimized does not well correspond to how outside observers see the situation.

When prediction models are given in research articles, they are usually for multiple regression. Multiple regression is quite common in the social and behavioral sciences. Consider a study by Jehn and Shah (1997) on performance of three-person groups on physical and decision-making tasks together in a laboratory situation. The researchers videotaped the interactions and analyzed the tapes for various aspects of group interaction. Table 3–7 shows the regression coefficients for predicting task performance from various interaction qualities. You can see that positive communication and planning had relatively small (and negative) betas, while commitment, monitoring, and cooperation were much more important unique predictors of performance. Also notice (from the bottom of the table) that the overall correlation of the five predictors with performance had an R of .55. This is substantial. On the other hand, it means that less than a third of the overall variance in performance (that is, $R^2 = .30$) was predicted by these five variables. The table also includes the unstandardized (labeled with a capital B

TABLE 3–7
Summary of Regression Analysis for Variables Predicting Performance

Variable	B	$SE\ B$	β
Positive Communication	0.288	.228	−.127*
Planning	0.062	.055	−.190*
Commitment	1.340	.134	−.432*
Monitoring	1.210	.049	−.449*
Cooperation	0.780	.154	−.376*

Note. $N = 106$, $R = .55$.

*p < .01.

Data from K. A. Jehn, and P. P. Shah, lab. 4, "Interpersonal relationships and task performance: An examination of process in friendship and acquaintance groups." *Journal of Personality and Social Psychology, 72,* 775–790, April, 1997. Copyright © 1997 by the American Psychological Association. Reprinted by permission.

here) and standardized regression coefficients. Finally, for each B, it gives what is called its standard error ($SE\ B$). These have to do with the accuracy of estimation of these coefficients in the population in general. You will have a better understanding of these after Chapter 6.

Summary

1. When two variables are associated in a clear pattern, for example, when high scores on one consistently go with high scores on the other, and lows on one go with lows on the other, the two variables are correlated.
2. If two variables, X and Y, are correlated, this could be because X is causing Y, Y is causing X, or a third factor is causing both X and Y.
3. A scatter diagram shows the relation between two variables. The lowest to highest possible values of the one variable (the predictor variable, if they are distinguishable) are marked on the horizontal axis, and the lowest to highest possible values of the other variable are marked on the vertical axis. Each individual pair of scores is shown as a dot.
4. When the dots in the scatter diagram generally follow a straight line, this is called a linear correlation. In a curvilinear correlation, the dots follow a line other than a simple straight line. No correlation exists when the dots do not follow any kind of line. In a positive linear correlation, the line goes upward to the right (so that low scores go with lows and highs with highs). In a negative linear correlation, the line goes downward to the right (so that low scores go with highs and highs with lows).
5. The correlation coefficient (r) gives the degree of linear correlation. It is the average of the cross-products of Z scores. The correlation coefficient is highly positive when there is a strong positive linear correlation. This is because positive Z scores are multiplied by positive, and negative Z scores by negative. The correlation coefficient is highly negative when there is a strong negative linear correlation.

This is because positive Z scores are multiplied by negative and negative Z scores by positive. The coefficient is 0 when there is no linear correlation. This is because positive Z scores are sometimes multiplied by positive and sometimes by negative Z scores and negative Z scores are sometimes multiplied by negative and sometimes by positive. Thus, positive and negative cross-products cancel each other out.

6. The maximum positive value of r is +1. $r = +1$ when there is a perfect positive linear correlation. The maximum negative value of r is −1. $r = -1$ when there is a perfect negative linear correlation.

7. A correlation usually is based on scores from a particular group that is intended to represent some larger group. When statistical procedures (to be taught later in this book) make it unlikely that there is no correlation in the larger group, we say that the correlation is statistically significant.

8. Prediction (or regression) makes predictions about scores on a criterion variable based on scores on a predictor variable. The best model for predicting a person's Z score on the criterion variable is to multiply a number called the standardized regression coefficient (beta) times the person's Z score on the predictor variable. The best number to use for the standardized regression coefficient in this situation is the correlation coefficient.

9. Predictions with raw scores can be made by converting the person's score on the predictor variable to a Z score, multiplying it by beta, and then converting the resulting predicted Z score on the criterion variable to a raw score.

10. In multiple regression, a criterion variable is predicted using two or more predictor variables. In a multiple regression model, each predictor variable is multiplied by its own regression coefficient (beta), and the results are added up to make the prediction. However, because the predictor variables overlap in their influence on the criterion variable, each of the regression coefficients generally is smaller than the variable's correlation coefficient with the criterion variable. The multiple correlation coefficient (R) describes the overall degree of association between the criterion variable and the predictor variables taken together.

11. Comparisons of the degree of linear correlation are considered most accurate in terms of the correlation coefficient squared (r^2 or R^2), the proportion of variance accounted for.

12. Correlational results are usually presented in research articles either in the text with the value of r (and sometimes the significance level) or in a special table (a correlation matrix) showing the correlations among several variables. Multiple correlation results typically report betas and overall R (or R^2), as well as other statistics.

Key Terms

correlation
correlation coefficient (r)
correlation matrix
criterion variable

cross-product of Z scores
curvilinear correlation
direction of causality
linear correlation

longitudinal study
multiple correlation
multiple correlation
  coefficient (R)

multiple regression
negative correlation
no correlation
perfect correlation
positive correlation

prediction model
predictor variable
proportion of variance
    accounted for (r^2)
regression coefficient

scatter diagram
standardized regression
    coefficient (β)
statistical significance
true experiment

Practice Problems

These problems involve computation. Most real-life statistics problems are done on a computer. But do these problems by hand (with the help of a calculator) to ingrain the method in your mind. Answers to selected problems are given at the back of this book.

For practice using a computer to solve statistics problems, refer to the computer section of each chapter of the Student's Study Guide and Computer Workbook *that accompanies this text.*

All data are fictional unless an actual citation is given.

For Problems 1 through 4, do the following: (a) Make a scatter diagram of the raw scores; (b) describe in words the general pattern of association, if any; (c) figure the correlation coefficient; (d) explain the logic of what you have done, writing as if you were speaking to someone who has never had a statistics course (but who does understand the mean, standard deviation, and Z scores); (e) give three logically possible directions of causality, saying for each whether it was a reasonable direction in light of the variables involved (and why); (f) make raw score predictions on the criterion variable for persons with Z scores on the predictor variable of –2, –1, 0, +1, and +2; and (g) give the proportion of variance accounted for (R^2).

1. An instructor asked five students how many hours they had studied for an exam. (For part f, assume that hours studied is the predictor variable.) Here are the number of hours studied and the students' grades:

Hours Studied	Test Grade
0	52
10	95
6	83
8	71
6	64

2. Four young children were monitored closely over several weeks to measure how much they watched violent television programs and their amount of violent behavior toward their playmates. (For part (f), assume that hours watching violent television is the predictor variable.) The results were as follows:

Child's Code Number	Weekly Viewing of Violent TV (hours)	Number of Violent or Aggressive Acts Toward Playmates
G3368	14	9
R8904	8	6
C9890	6	1
L8722	12	8

3. The Louvre Museum is interested in the relation of the age of a painting to public interest in it. The number of people stopping to look at each of 10 randomly selected paintings is observed over a week. (For part (f), assume that age is the predictor variable.) The results are as shown:

Painting Title	Approximate Age (Years)		Number of People Stopping to Look	
	(M = 253.4, SD = 152.74)		(M = 88.2, SD = 29.13)	
	X	Z_X	Y	Z_Y
The Entombment	465	1.39	68	–.69
Mys Mar Ste Catherine	515	1.71	71	–.59
The Bathers	240	–.09	123	1.19
The Toilette	107	–.96	112	.82
Portrait of Castiglione	376	.80	48	–1.38
Charles I of England	355	.67	84	–.14
Crispin and Scapin	140	–.75	66	–.76
Nude in the Sun	115	–.91	148	2.05
The Balcony	122	–.86	71	–.59
The Circus	99	–1.01	91	.10

4. A schoolteacher thought that he had observed that students who dressed more neatly were generally better students. To test this idea, the teacher had a friend rate each of the students for neatness of dress. Following are the ratings for neatness, along with each student's score on a standardized school achievement test. (For part (f) assume that neatness is the predictor variable.)

Child	Score on Neatness Rating (M = 19.6, SD = 3.07)		Score on Achievement Test (M = 63.1, SD = 4.70)	
	X	Z_x	Y	Z_y
Janet	18	–.52	60	–.66
Gareth	24	1.43	58	–1.09
Grove	14	–1.82	70	1.47
Kevin	19	–.20	58	–1.09
Joshua	20	.13	66	.62
Nicole	23	1.11	68	1.04
Susan	20	.13	65	.40
Drew	22	.78	68	1.04
Marie	15	–1.50	56	–1.51
Chad	21	.46	62	–.23

5. Gable and Lutz (2000) studied 65 3-to-10-year-old children and their parents. One of their results was: "Parental control of child eating showed a negative association with children's participation in extracurricular activities ($r = .34$; $p < .01$). " Another result was: "Parents who held less appropriate beliefs about children's nutrition reported that their children watched more hours of television per day ($r = .36$; $p < .01$)." (Both quotes from page 296.) Explain these results as if you were writing to a person who has never had a course in statistics. Be sure to comment on possible directions of causality for each result.

6. Gunn and her colleagues (2000) studied reading in a group of Hispanic and non-Hispanic third graders. As part of this study, they did an analysis predicting reading comprehension (called "passage comprehension") from three more specific measures of reading ability: Letter-word Identification ("ability to read irregular words"), Word Attack ("ability to use phonic and structural analysis"), and Oral Reading Fluency ("correct words per minute"). The results are shown in Table 3–8 (their Table 9). Explain the results as if you were writing to a person who understands correlation but has never learned anything about regression or multiple regression analysis. (Ignore the columns for t, p, F, and p. These have to do with statistical significance.)

7. Based on Table 3–8 (from Gunn et al. 2000), determine the regression equation (for Z scores), and then calculate the predicted Passage Comprehension Score for each of the following third graders (figures are Z scores):

Third Grader	Letter-Word Identification	Word Attack	Oral Reading Fluency
A	1	1	1
B	0	0	0
C	–1	–1	–1
D	1	0	0
E	0	1	0
F	0	0	1
G	3	1	1
H	1	3	1
I	3	1	3

TABLE 3–8
Multiple Regression Predicting Comprehension From Decoding Skill and Oral Reading Fluency

Variable	Beta	t	p	R^2	F	p
Passage Comprehension raw score						
Letter-Word Identification	–.227	–2.78	.006			
Word Attack	.299	3.75	.001			
Oral Reading Fluency—Correct words per minute	.671	9.97	.001			
				.534	57.70	.001

Table 9 from "The Efficacy of Supplemental Instruction in Decoding Skills for Hispanic and Non-Hispanic Students in Early Elementary School" by Barbara Gunn, Anthony Biglan, Keith Smolkowski and Dennis Ary as appeared in *The Journal of Special Education*, February 2000. Reprinted by permission.

Chapter Appendix: Hypothesis Tests and Power for the Correlation Coefficient

This material is for students who have already completed at least through Chapter 8 and are now returning to this chapter.

Significance of a Correlation Coefficient

Hypothesis testing of a correlation coefficient follows the usual five-step process. However, there are three important points to note. First, usually the null hypothesis is that the correlation in a population like that observed is no different from a population in which the true correlation is zero. Second, if the data meet assumptions (explained in the next paragraph), the comparison distribution is a t distribution with degrees of freedom equal to the number of people minus 2. Third, you figure the correlation coefficient's score on that t distribution using the formula

$$t = \frac{(r)\,(\sqrt{[N-2]})}{\sqrt{(1-r^2)}}$$

(3–5)

Also, note that significance tests of a correlation, like a t test, can be either one-tailed or two-tailed. A one-tailed test means that the researcher has predicted the sign (positive or negative) of the correlation.

Assumptions for the significance test of a correlation coefficient are that both variables should be normally distributed, and the distribution of each variable at each point of the other variable should have about equal variance. However, as with the t test and analysis of variance (Chapter 10), moderate violations of these assumptions are not fatal.

An Example

Here is an example using the sleep and mood study example. Let's suppose that the researchers predicted a positive correlation between number of employees supervised and stress, to be tested at the .05 level.

   1. **Restate the question as a research hypothesis and a null hypothesis about the populations.** There are two populations:

   Population 1: People like those in this study
   Population 2: People for whom there is no correlation between number of hours slept the night before and mood the next day.

The null hypothesis is that the two populations have the same correlation. The research hypothesis is that Population 1 has a higher correlation than Population 2. (That is, the prediction is for a population correlation greater than 0.)
   2. **Determine the characteristics of the comparison distribution.** Assuming that we meet the assumptions (in practice, it would be hard to tell with only 10 people in the study), the comparison distribution is a t distribution with $df = 8$. (That is, $df = N - 2 = 10 - 2 = 8$.)
   3. **Determine the cutoff sample score on the comparison distribution at which the null hypothesis should be rejected.** The t table (Table A–2 in Appendix A) shows that for a one-tailed test at the .05 level, with 8 degrees of freedom, you need a t of at least 1.860.
   4. **Determine your sample's score on the comparison distribution.** We computed a correlation of $r = .84$. Applying the formula to find the equivalent t, we get

$$t = \frac{(r)\left(\sqrt{N-2}\right)}{\sqrt{1-r^2}} = \frac{(.84)\left(\sqrt{8}\right)}{\sqrt{1-.71}} = \frac{(.84)(2.83)}{\sqrt{.29}} = \frac{2.38}{.54} = 4.41$$

   5. **Decide whether to reject the null hypothesis.** The t score of 4.41 for our sample correlation is more extreme than the minimum needed t score of

TABLE 3–9
Approximate Power of Studies Using the Correlation Coefficient (r) for Testing Hypotheses at the .05 Level of Significance

		Effect Size		
		Small (r = .10)	*Medium* (r = .30)	*Large* (r = .50)
Two-tailed				
Total *N:*	10	.06	.13	.33
	20	.07	.25	.64
	30	.08	.37	.83
	40	.09	.48	.92
	50	.11	.57	.97
	100	.17	.86	a
One-tailed				
Total *N:*	10	.08	.22	.46
	20	.11	.37	.75
	30	.13	.50	.90
	40	.15	.60	.96
	50	.17	.69	.98
	100	.26	.92	a

[a]Nearly 1.00.

1.860. Thus, we can reject the null hypothesis and the research hypothesis is supported.

Effect Size and Power

The correlation coefficient itself is a measure of effect size. Cohen's (1988) conventions for the correlation coefficient are .10 for a small effect size, .30 for a medium effect size, and .50 for a large effect size. Table 3–9 gives approximate power. Table 3–10 gives minimum sample size for 80-percent power. (More complete tables are provided in Cohen, 1988, pp. 84–95, 101–102.)

TABLE 3–10
Approximate Number of Participants Needed for 80-percent Power for a Study Using the Correlation Coefficient (r) for Testing a Hypothesis at the .05 Significance Level

	Effect Size		
	Small (r = .10)	*Medium* (r = .30)	*Large* (r = .50)
Two-tailed	783	85	28
One-tailed	617	68	22

4

Some Key Ingredients for Inferential Statistics:
The Normal Curve, Probability, and Population Versus Sample

Ordinarily, social and behavioral scientists do a research study to test some theoretical principle or the effectiveness of some practical procedure. For example, an educational researcher might compare reading speeds of students taught with two different methods to examine a theory of teaching. A sociologist might examine the effectiveness of a program of neighborhood meetings intended to promote water conservation. Such studies are conducted with a particular group of research participants. But the researchers use inferential statistics to make more general conclusions about the theoretical principle or procedure being studied. These conclusions go beyond the particular group of research participants studied.

This chapter and Chapters 5, 6, and 7 introduce inferential statistics. In this chapter, we consider three topics: the normal curve, probability, and population versus sample. This is a comparatively short chapter, preparing the way for the next ones, which are more demanding. Before beginning this chapter you should have mastered the material in Chapter 1 on the shapes of distributions and the material in Chapter 2 on mean, standard deviation, and Z scores.

The Normal Distribution

We noted in Chapter 1 that the graphs of many of the distributions of variables that social scientists study (as well as many other distributions in nature) follow a unimodal, roughly symmetrical, bell-shaped distribution. These bell-shaped histograms or frequency polygons approximate a precise and important mathematical distribution called the **normal distribution** or, more simply, the **normal curve.** An example of the normal curve is shown in Figure 4–1.

normal distribution
normal curve

Why the Normal Curve Is So Common in Nature

Take, for example, the number of different letters a particular person can remember accurately on various testings (with different random letters each time). On some testings, the number of letters remembered may be high, on others low, and on most somewhere in between. That is, the number of different letters a person can recall on various testings probably approximately follows a normal curve. Suppose that the person has a basic ability to recall, say, seven letters in this kind of memory task. Nevertheless, on any particular testing, the actual number recalled will be affected by various influences (noisiness of the room, the person's mood at the moment, a combination of random letters unwittingly confused with a familiar name, and so on).

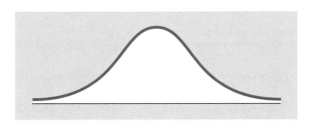

FIGURE 4–1
A normal curve.

These various influences add up to make the person do better than seven on some testings and worse than seven on others; however, if the particular combination of such influences that come up at any testing is essentially random, on most testings positive and negative influences should cancel out. The chances of all the negative influences happening to come together on a testing when none of the positive influences show up is not very good. Thus, in general, the person remembers a middle amount, an amount in which all the opposing influences cancel each other out. Very high or very low scores are much less common.

This creates a unimodal distribution—most of the scores near the middle and fewer at the extremes. It also creates a distribution that is symmetrical, because the number of letters recalled is as likely to be above as below the middle. Being a unimodal symmetrical curve does not guarantee that it will be a normal curve; it could be too flat or too peaked. However, it can be shown mathematically that in the long run, if the influences are truly random and the number of different influences being combined is large, a precise normal curve results. Mathematical statisticians call this principle the *central limit theorem*. We have more to say about this principle in Chapter 6.

The Normal Curve and the Percentage of Scores between the Mean and 1 and 2 Standard Deviations from the Mean

The shape of the normal curve is standard. Thus, there is a known percentage of scores above or below any particular point. For example, exactly 50% of the scores is below the mean because in any symmetrical distribution, half the scores are below the mean. More interestingly, as shown in Figure 4–2, approximately 34% of the scores is always between the mean and 1 standard deviation from the mean. (Notice, incidentally, that in Figure 4–2 the 1 standard deviation point on the normal curve is at the place the curve starts going more out than down.)

Consider IQ scores. On many widely used intelligence tests, the mean IQ is 100, the standard deviation is 16, and the distribution of IQs is roughly normal (see Figure 4–3). Knowing about the normal curve and the percentages of scores between the mean and 1 standard deviation above the mean allows us to know that about 34% of people have IQs between 100, the mean, and 116, the IQ score 1 standard deviation above the mean. Similarly, because the normal curve is symmetrical, about 34% of people have IQs between 100 and 84 (the score 1 standard deviation below the mean), and 68% (34% + 34%) have IQs between 84 and 116.

FIGURE 4–2
Normal curve with approximate percentages of scores between the mean and 1 and 2 standard deviations above and below the mean.

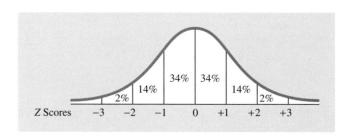

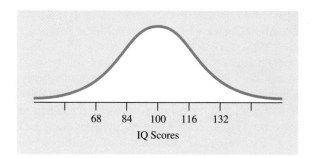

FIGURE 4–3
Distribution of IQ scores on many standard intelligence tests
(with $M = 100$ and $SD = 16$).

As you can also see from looking at the normal curve, there are many fewer scores between 1 and 2 standard deviations from the mean than there are between the mean and 1 standard deviation from the mean. It turns out that about 14% of the scores is between 1 and 2 standard deviations above the mean (see Figure 4–2). (Because the normal curve is symmetrical, about 14% of the scores is between 1 and 2 standard deviations below the mean.) Thus, about 14% of people have IQs between 116 (1 standard deviation above the mean) and 132 (2 standard deviations above the mean).

If you can remember the 50%, 34%, and 14% figures, you will have a good sense of the percentage of scores above and below a score if you know its number of standard deviations from the mean. You can also reverse this approach and figure out a person's number of standard deviations from the mean from a percentage. Suppose a laboratory test showed that a particular archaeological sample of ceramics was in the top 2% of all the samples in the excavation for containing iron, and it is known that the distribution of iron in such samples is roughly normal. In this situation, the sample must have a level of iron that is at least 2 standard deviations above the mean level of iron. This is because of the 50% of the scores above the mean. There is 34% between the mean and 1 *SD* and another 14% between 1 and 2 *SD*s above the mean, leaving a remainder of 2% that is 2 *SD*s above the mean. Remember from Chapter 2 that a *Z* score is the number of standard deviations a score is above or below the mean—which is just what we are talking about here. Thus, if you knew the mean and the standard deviation of the iron concentrations in the samples, you could figure out the raw score (the actual level of iron in this sample) that is equivalent to being two *SD*s above the mean, using the ordinary method for converting *Z* scores (in this case, a *Z* score of +2) to raw scores, and vice versa, that you learned in Chapter 2:

$$X = (Z)(SD) + M \quad \text{and} \quad Z = (X - M) / SD$$

The Normal Curve Table and *Z* Scores

The 50%, 34%, and 14% figures are useful, practical rules for getting a sense of where a particular score stands in relation to others in the group of interest. However, in many research and applied situations, we need more precise information. Because the normal curve is mathematically exact, it is possible to compute the exact percentage of scores between any two points on the normal curve, not just those in which a score happens to be right at 1 or 2 standard deviations from the mean. That is, it is possible to figure the exact percentage of scores between any two Z scores. For example, exactly 68.59% of scores have a Z score between +.62 and –1.68; exactly 2.81% of scores have a Z score between +.79 and +.89, and so forth.

You can figure these percentages using the calculus formula for the normal curve, which you can look up in a mathematical statistics text. However, you can also do this much more simply. Statisticians have worked out tables for the normal curve that give the percentage of scores between the mean (a Z score of 0) and any other Z score. If you want to know the percentage of scores between the mean and a Z score of .62, you just look up .62 in the table, and it tells you that 23.24% of the scores, in a perfect normal distribution, fall between the mean and this Z score.

normal curve table

We have included such a **normal curve table** in Appendix A (Table A–1). As you can see, the first column in the table lists the Z score, and the column next to it gives the percentage of scores between the mean and that Z score. Notice also that the table repeats these two columns several times on the page, so be sure to look across only one column. Also, notice that the table lists only positive Z scores. It is unnecessary to list the negative Z scores because the normal curve is perfectly symmetrical; thus, the percentage of scores between the mean and, say, a Z of +2.38 is exactly the same as the percentage of scores between the mean and a Z of –2.38.

In our example, you would find .62 in the "Z" column and then, right next to it in the "% Mean to Z" column, you would find 23.24.

You also can reverse the process and use the table to find the Z score for a particular percentage of scores. For example, suppose you were told that Janice's creativity score was in the top 10% of ninth-grade students. Assuming that creativity scores follow a normal curve, you could figure out her Z score as follows: First, you would reason that if she is in the top 10%, then 40% of students have scores between her score and the mean. (There are 50% above the mean and she is in the top 10% of scores overall, which leaves 40%.) Then, you would look at the "% Mean to Z" column of the table until you found a percentage that was very close to 40%. In this case, the closest you could come would be 39.97%. Finally, you would look at the "Z" column to the left of this percentage. In this case, the Z score for 39.97% is 1.28. Thus, Janice's Z score for her level of creativity (as measured on this test) is 1.28. If you know the mean and standard deviation for ninth-grade students' creativity scores, you can figure out Janice's actual raw score on the test by changing this Z score of 1.28 to a raw score using the usual method of changing Z scores to raw scores.

Figuring the Percentages of Scores From Raw Scores and Z Scores Using a Normal Curve Table

Here are the four steps for figuring percentage of scores.

1. **If you are beginning with a raw score, first convert it to a Z score.**
2. **Draw a picture of the normal curve, where the Z score falls on it, and shade in the area for which you are finding the percentage.** (When marking where the Z score falls on the normal curve, be sure to put it in the right place above or below the mean according to whether it is a positive or negative Z score.)

3. **Make a rough estimate of the shaded area's percentage based on the 50%-34%-14% percentages.** You don't need to be very exact—it is enough just to estimate a range in which the shaded area has to fall, figuring it is between two particular whole Z scores.

4. **Find the exact percentage using the normal curve table.** Look up the Z score in the "Z" column of Table A–1 and find the percentage in the "% Mean to Z" column next to it. If you want the percent of scores between the mean and this Z score, this would be your final answer.

However, often you will need to add 50% to this percentage (if the Z score is positive and you want the total percent below this Z score, or if the Z score is negative and you want the total percent above this Z score). Other times you will have to subtract this percentage from 50% (if the Z score is positive and you want the percent higher than it, or if the Z score is negative and you want the percent lower than it).

Don't try to memorize rules about adding or subtracting the 50%. It is much easier to make a picture for the problem and reason out whether the percentage you have from the table is correct as is, or if you need to add or subtract 50%.

5. **Check that your exact percentage is similar to your rough estimate (from Step 3).**

Two Examples

Here are two examples using IQ scores where $M = 100$ and $SD = 16$.

Example 1: If a person has an IQ of 125, what percentage of people have higher IQs?

1. **If you are beginning with a raw score, first convert it to a Z score.** Using the usual formula, $Z = (125–100)/16 = +1.56$.

2. **Draw a picture of the normal curve, where the Z score falls on it, and shade in the area for which you are finding the percentage.** This is shown in Figure 4–4.

3. **Make a rough estimate of the shaded area's percentage based on the 50%-34%-14% percentages.** If the shaded area started at a Z score of 1, it would include 16%. If it started at a Z score of 2, it would include only 2%. So with a Z score of 1.56, it has to be somewhere between 16% and 2%.

4. **Find the exact percentage using the normal curve table.** In the table, 1.56 in the "Z" column goes with 44.06 in the "% mean to Z" column. Thus, 44.06% of people have IQ scores between the mean IQ and an IQ of 125 (Z score of +1.56). Because 50% of people are above the mean on any

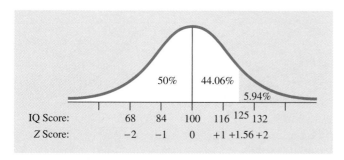

FIGURE 4–4
Distribution of IQ scores showing percentage of scores above an IQ score of 125 (the shaded area).

normal curve and 44.06% of the people above the mean are below this person's IQ, that leaves 5.94% above this person's score (that is, 50%–44.06% = 5.94%). This is the answer to our problem.

5. **Check that your exact percentage is within the range of your rough estimate.** 5.94% is within the 16%-to-2% range we estimated.

Example 2: Suppose a person has an IQ of 95. What is the percentage of people with IQs lower than this person?

1. **If you are beginning with a raw score, first convert it to a Z score.** $Z = (95–100)/16 = –.31$.

2. **Draw a picture of the normal curve, where the Z score falls on it, and shade in the area for which you are finding the percentage.** This is shown in Figure 4–5.

3. **Make a rough estimate of the shaded area's percentage based on the 50%-34%-14% percentages.** We know that 50% of the curve is below the mean. So the shaded area has to be less than 50%. We also can figure that 16% of the curve is below a Z score of –1. (This is because 34% is between 0 and –1, leaving 16% below –1.) Thus, our Z score of –.31 has to have between 50% and 16% at the scores below it.

4. **Find the exact percentage using the normal curve table.** The table shows that 12.17% of scores are between the mean and a Z score of .31. The percentage below a Z score of –.31 is the total of 50% below the mean, less the 12.17% between the mean and –.31, leaving 37.83% (that is, 50% – 12.17% = 37.83%).

5. **Check that your exact percentage is similar to your rough estimate.** 37.83% is within the 50%-to-36% range.

Figuring Z Scores and Raw Scores From Percentages Using the Normal Curve Table

Going from a percentage to a Z score or raw score is similar to going from a Z score or raw score to a percentage. However, you use just the reverse procedure for the part of figuring the exact percentage. Also, any necessary conversion between a Z score and raw score is done at the end. Here are the steps.

1. **Draw a picture of the normal curve, roughly where the percentage falls on it, and shade in the approximate area for that percentage using the 50%-34%-14% percentages.**

FIGURE 4–5
Distribution of IQ scores showing percentage of scores below an IQ score of 95 (the shaded area).

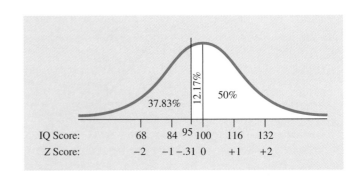

2. **Make a rough estimate of the Z score where the shaded area starts.**

3. **Find the exact Z score using the normal curve table.** Looking at your picture, figure out the percentage between the mean and where the shading starts or ends. For example, if your percentage is the top 8%, then the percentage from the mean to where that shading starts is 42%. If your percentage is the bottom 35%, then the percentage from where the shading starts is 15%. If your percentage is the top 83%, then the percentage from the mean to where the shading stops is 33%.

Once you have the percentage from the mean to where the shading starts or stops, look up the closest number you can find to it in the "% Mean to Z" column of the normal curve table and find the Z score in the "Z" column next to it. That Z will be your answer—except it may be negative. The best way to tell if it is positive or negative is by looking at your picture.

4. **Check that your exact Z score is similar to your rough estimate.**

5. **If you want to find a raw score, convert to it from the Z score.**

Three Examples

Once again, we will use IQ for our examples, where $M = 100$ and $SD = 16$.

Example 1: What IQ score would a person need to be in the top 5%?

1. **Draw a picture of the normal curve, roughly where the percentage falls on it, and shade in the approximate area for that percentage using the 50%-34%-14% percentages.** We wanted the top 5%. Thus, the shading has to begin above 1 *SD* (there are 16% of scores above 1 *SD*). However, it cannot start above 2 *SD* because there are only 2% of scores above 2 *SD*. But 5% is a lot closer to 2% than to 16%. Thus, you would draw in the shading as starting a small ways to the left of the 2 *SD* point. This is shown in Figure 4–6.

2. **Make a rough estimate of the Z score where the shaded area starts.** The Z score has to be between +1 and +2.

3. **Find the exact Z score using the normal curve table.** Since 50% of people have IQs above the mean, at least 45% have IQs between this person and the mean (that is, 50% − 5% = 45%). Looking in the "% Mean to Z" column of the normal curve table, the closest figure to 45% is 44.95% (or you could use 45.05%). This goes with a Z score of 1.64 in the "Z" column.

4. **Check that your exact percentage is similar to your rough estimate.** +1.64 is between +1 and +2.

5. **If you want to find a raw score, convert to it from the Z score.** Using the formula from Chapter 2, $X = 100 + (1.64)(16) = 126.24$.

In sum, to be in the top 5%, a person would need an IQ of at least 126.24.

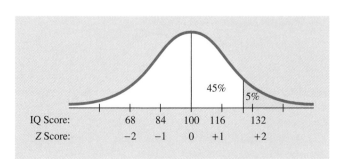

FIGURE 4–6
Finding the Z score corresponding to the top 5% of IQ scores (shaded area).

Example 2: What IQ score would a person need to be in the lowest 1%?

1. Draw a picture of the normal curve, roughly where the percentage falls on it, and shade in the approximate area for that percentage using the 50%-34%-14% percentages. You want the bottom 1%. Thus, the shading has to begin below (to the left of) –2 *SD* (there are 2% of scores below –2 *SD*). Thus, you would draw in the shading as starting to the left (below) the 2 *SD* point. This is shown in Figure 4–7.

2. Make a rough estimate of the Z score where the shaded area starts. The Z score has to be below –2.

3. Find the exact Z score using the normal curve table. Being in the bottom 1% means that at least 49% of people have IQs between this IQ and the mean (that is, 50%–1% = 49%). In the normal curve table, 49% in the "% Mean to Z" column (or as close as you can get, which is 49.01%) goes with a Z score of 2.33. Because we are below the mean, this becomes –2.33.

4. Check that your exact percentage is similar to your rough estimate. As we estimated, –2.33 is below –2.

5. If you want to find a raw score, convert to it from the Z score. X = 100 + (–2.33)(16) = 62.72.

In sum, a person in the bottom 1% on IQ has a score that is 62.72 or below.

Example 3: What range of IQ scores includes the 95% of people in the middle range of IQ scores?

This kind of problem, of finding the middle percentage, may seem odd. However, it is actually a very common type of situation in some procedures you learn about in later chapters.

When dealing with this kind of problem, the best way to think of it is in terms of finding the particular scores that go with the upper and lower ends of this percentage. Thus, in this example, you are really trying to find the points where the bottom 2.5% ends and the top 2.5% begins.

1. Draw a picture of the normal curve, roughly where the percentage falls on it, and shade in the approximate area for that percentage using the 50%-34%-14% percentages. Let's begin with the point where the top 2.5% begins. This has to be higher than 1 *SD* (there are 16% of scores higher than 1 *SD*). However, it can not start above 2 *SD* because there are only 2% of scores above 2 *SD*. But 2.5% is very close to 2%. Thus, you would figure that the top 2.5 % starts just to the left of the 2 *SD* point. Similarly, the point where the bottom 2.5% comes in would be just to the right of –2 *SD*. The result of all this is that we will shade in the area starting just above –2 *SD* and continuing up to just below +2 *SD*. This is shown in Figure 4–8.

FIGURE 4–7
Finding the Z score corresponding to the bottom 1% of IQ scores (shaded area).

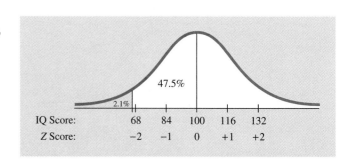

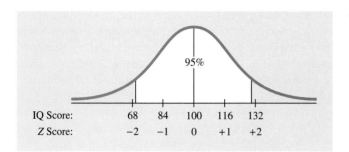

2. Make a rough estimate of the Z score or raw score where the shaded area starts. You can see from the picture that the Z score for the upper limit of the shaded area has to be between +1 and +2, but quite close to +2. Similarly, the lower limit of the shaded area has to be between –1 and –2, but quite close to –2.

3. Find the exact Z score using the normal curve table. Being in the top 2.5% means that at least 47.5% of people have IQs between this IQ and the mean (that is, 50% – 2.5% = 47.5%). In the normal curve table, 47.5% in the "% Mean to Z" column goes with a Z score of 1.96. The normal curve is entirely symmetrical. Thus, the **Z** score for the bottom 2.5% should be –1.96.

4. Check that your exact percentage is similar to your rough estimate. As we estimated, 1.96 is between 1 and 2 and is very close to 2 and –1.96 is between –1 and –2 and very close to –2.

5. If you want to find a raw score, convert to it from the Z score. For the high end, $X = 100 + (1.96)(16) = 131.36$. For the low end, $X = 100 + (-1.96)(16) = 68.64$.

In conclusion: the middle 95% of IQ scores run from 68.64 to 131.36.

Probability

Probability is very important in science. In particular, probability is very important in inferential statistics, the methods social and behavioral scientists use to go from results of research studies to conclusions about theories or applied procedures.

Probability has been studied for centuries by mathematicians and philosophers. Yet even today, the topic is full of controversy. Fortunately, however, you need to know only a few key ideas to understand and carry out the inferential statistical procedures you learn in this book.[1] These few key points are not very difficult—indeed, some students find them obvious.

In statistics, we usually define **probability (p)** as "the expected relative frequency of a particular outcome." An **outcome** is the result of an

probability (p)
outcome

---

[1]There are, of course, many probability topics that are not related to statistics and other topics related to statistics that are not important for the kinds of statistics used in the social and behavioral sciences. For example, computing joint and conditional probabilities, which is covered in many statistics books, is not covered here because it is rarely seen in published research in the social and behavioral sciences and is not necessary for an intuitive grasp of the logic of the major inferential statistical methods covered in this book.

expected relative frequency

long-run relative-frequency interpretation of probability

experiment (or just about any situation in which the result is not known in advance, such as a coin coming up heads or it raining tomorrow). Frequency is how many times something happens. The relative frequency is the number of times something happens relative to the number of times it could have happened. That is, relative frequency is the proportion of times it happens. (A coin might come up heads 8 times out of 12 flips, for a relative frequency of 8/12, or 2/3.) **Expected relative frequency** is what you expect to get in the long run, if you repeated the experiment many times. (In the case of a coin, in the long run you expect to get 1/2 heads.) This is called the **long-run relative-frequency interpretation of probability.**

Figuring Probabilities

Probabilities are usually figured as the proportion of successful outcomes—the number of possible successful outcomes divided by the number of *all* possible outcomes. That is,

$$\text{Probability} = \frac{\text{Possible successful outcomes}}{\text{All possible outcomes}}$$

Consider the probability of getting heads when flipping a coin. There is one possible successful outcome (getting heads) out of two possible outcomes (getting heads or getting tails). This makes a probability of 1/2, or .5. In a throw of a single die, the probability of a 2 (or any other particular side of the die) is 1/6, or .17. This is because there is one possible successful outcome out of six possible outcomes of any kind. The probability of throwing a die and getting a number 3 or lower is 3/6, or .5. There are three possible successful outcomes (a 1, a 2, or a 3) out of six possible outcomes.

Now consider a slightly more complicated example. Suppose a class has 200 people in it, and 30 are seniors. If you were to pick someone from the class at random, the probability of picking a senior would be 30/200, or .15. This is because there are 30 possible successful outcomes (getting a senior) out of 200 possible outcomes.

Range of Probabilities

Probabilities are proportions (the number of successful outcomes to the total number of possible outcomes). A proportion cannot be less than 0 or greater than 1. In terms of percentages, proportions range from 0% to 100%. Something that has no chance of happening has a probability of 0, and something that is certain to happen has a probability of 1.

Probabilities Expressed as Symbols

Probability usually is symbolized by the letter p. The actual probability number is usually given as a decimal, though sometimes fractions or percentages are used. A 50-50 chance is usually written as $p = .5$, but it could also be written as $p = 1/2$ or $p = 50\%$. It is also common to see a probability written as being "less than" some number using the less than sign. For example, "$p < .05$" means "the probability is less than .05."

Probability and the Normal Distribution

Until now we have discussed probabilities of specific events that might or might not happen. We also can talk about a range of events that might or might not happen. The throw of a die coming out 3 or lower is an example (it includes the range 1, 2, and 3). Another example is the probability of selecting someone on a city street who is between the ages of 30 and 40.

If you think of probability in terms of proportion of scores, probability fits in well with frequency distributions (see Chapter 1). In the frequency distribution shown in Figure 4–9, 10 of the total of 50 people scored 7 or higher. If you were selecting people from this group of 50 at random, there would be 10 chances (possible successful outcomes) out of 50 (all possible outcomes) of selecting one that was 7 or higher, so $p = 10/50 = .2$.

You can also think of the normal distribution as a probability distribution. With a normal curve, the proportion of scores between any two Z scores is known. As we are seeing, the proportion of scores between any two Z scores is the same as the probability of selecting a score between those two Z scores. For example, the probability of a score being between the mean and a Z score of +1 (1 standard deviation above the mean) is about 34%; that is, $p = .34$.

What we are saying may have been obvious all along. In a sense, it is merely a technical point that the normal curve can be seen as either a frequency distribution or a probability distribution. We mention this only so that you will not be confused when we refer later to the probability of a score coming from a particular portion of the normal curve.

Sample and Population

We are going to introduce you to some important ideas by thinking of beans. Suppose you are cooking a pot of beans and taste a spoonful to see if they are done. In this example, the pot of beans is a **population,** the entire set of things of interest. The spoonful is a **sample,** the part of the population about which you actually have information. This is illustrated in Figure 4–10a. Figures 4–10b and 4–10c are other ways of illustrating the relation of a sample to a population.

population
sample

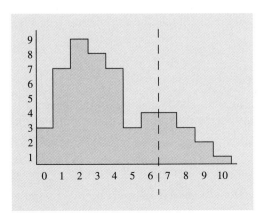

FIGURE 4–9
Frequency distribution (shown as a histogram) of 50 people in which $p = .2$ (10/50) of randomly selecting a person with a score of 7 or higher.

FIGURE 4–10
Populations and samples: In (a), the entire pot of beans is the population, and the spoonful is a sample. In (b), the entire larger circle is the population, and the circle within it is the sample. In (c), the frequency histogram is of the population and the particular shaded scores together make up the sample.

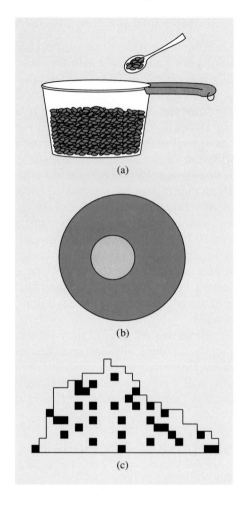

In social and behavioral science research, we typically study samples not of beans but of individuals to make inferences about some larger group. A sample might consist of 50 Canadian women who participate in a particular experiment, whereas the population might be intended to be all Canadian women. In an opinion survey, 1,000 people might be selected from the voting-age population and asked for whom they plan to vote. The opinions of these 1,000 people are the sample. The opinions of the larger voting public, to which the pollsters hope to apply their results, is the population (see Figure 4–11).[2]

Why Samples Are Studied Instead of Populations

If a researcher wants to draw conclusions about a population, the results would be most accurate if the researcher could study the entire population, rather than a subgroup from that population. However, in most research situ-

---

[2]Strictly speaking, population and sample refer to scores (numbers or measurements), not to the people who have those scores. In the first example, the sample is really the *scores* of the 50 Canadian women, not the 50 women themselves, and the population is really what the *scores* would be if all Canadian women were tested.

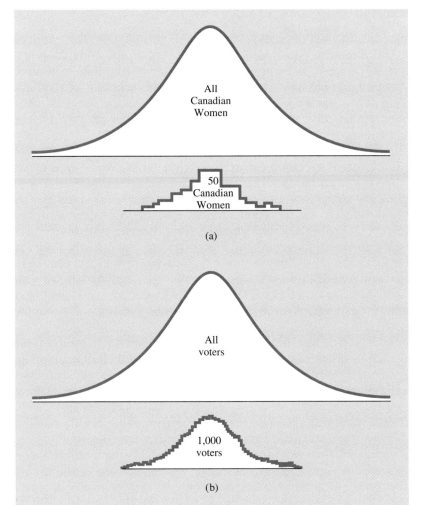

FIGURE 4–11
Additional examples of populations and samples. In (a), the population is the scores of all Canadian women, and a sample consists of the scores of the 50 particular Canadian women studied. In (b), the population is the voting preferences of the entire voting-age population, and a sample consists of the voting preferences of the 1,000 voting-age people who were surveyed.

ations this is not practical. More important, the whole point of research is usually to be able to make generalizations or predictions about events beyond our reach. We would not call it research if you tested three particular cars to see which gets better gas mileage—unless you hoped to say something about the gas mileage of those models of cars in general. In other words, a researcher might do an experiment on the effect of a particular method of teaching geography using 40 students as participants in the experiment. The purpose of the experiment is not to find out how these particular 40 students respond to the experimental condition but rather to discover something about what works best in general when teaching geography.

The strategy in almost all social and behavioral science research is to study a sample of individuals who are believed to be representative of the general population (or of some particular population of interest). The sample is what is studied, and the population is an unknown that researchers draw conclusions about on the basis of the sample. Most of what you learn in the rest of this book is about the important work of drawing conclusions about populations based on information from samples.

Methods of Sampling

random selection

Usually, the ideal method of picking out a sample to study is called **random selection.** The researcher starts with a complete list of the population and randomly selects some of them to study. An example of a random method of selection would be to put each name on a table-tennis ball, put all the balls into a big hopper, shake it up, and have a blindfolded person select as many as are needed. (In practice, most researchers use a computer-generated list of random numbers.)

haphazard selection

It is important not to confuse truly random selection with what might be called **haphazard selection,** for example, just taking whoever is available or happens to be first on a list. When using haphazard selection, it is surprisingly easy to accidentally pick a group of people to study that is really quite different from the population as a whole. Consider a survey of attitudes about your statistics instructor. Suppose you give your questionnaire only to other students sitting near you in class. Such a survey would be affected by all the things that influence where students choose to sit, some of which have to do with just what you are studying—how much they like the instructor or the class. (Similarly, asking students who sit near you would result in opinions more like your own than a truly random sample would.)

Unfortunately, it is often impossible to study a truly random sample. One problem is that we do not usually have a complete list of the full population. Another problem is that not everyone a researcher approaches agrees to participate in the study. Yet another problem is the cost and difficulty of tracking down people who live in remote places. For these and other reasons as well, social and behavioral scientists use various approximations to truly random samples that are more practical. However, researchers are consistently careful to rule out, as much as possible in advance, any systematic influence on who gets selected. Once the study has begun, researchers are constantly on the alert for any ways in which the sample may be systematically different from the population. For example, in much experimental research in education and psychology, it is common to use volunteer college students as the participants in the study. This is done for practical reasons and because often the topics studied in these experiments (for example, how short-term memory works) are thought to be relatively consistent across different types of people. Yet even in these cases, researchers avoid, for example, selecting people with a special interest in their research topic. Such researchers are also very aware that their results may not apply beyond college students, volunteers, people from their region, and so forth.

Statistical Terminology for Samples and Populations

population parameters

The mean, variance, and standard deviation of a population are called **population parameters.** A population parameter usually is unknown and can only be estimated from what you know about a sample from that population. You do not taste all the beans, just the spoonful. "The beans are done" is an inference about the whole pot.

In this book, when referring to the population mean, standard deviation, or variance, even in formulas, we use the word *Population* (or the abbrevi-

BOX 4-1

Surveys, Polls, and 1948's Costly "Free Sample"

It is time to make you a more informed reader of polls in the media. Usually the results of properly done public polls will be accompanied, somewhere in fine print, by a statement like "From a telephone poll of 1,000 American adults taken on June 4 and 5. Sampling error 63%." What does all this mean?

The Gallup poll is a good example (Gallup, 1972), and there is no better place to begin than 1948, when all three of the major polling organizations—Gallup, Crossley (for Hearst papers), and Roper (for *Fortune*)—wrongly predicted Thomas Dewey's victory over Harry Truman for the U.S. presidency. Yet Gallup's prediction was based on 50,000 interviews and Roper's on 15,000. By contrast, to predict George Bush's 1988 victory Gallup used only 4,089. Since 1952, the pollsters have never used more than 8,144, but with very small error and no outright mistakes. What has changed?

The method used before 1948, and never repeated since, was called "quota sampling." Interviewers were assigned a fixed number of persons to interview, with strict quotas to fill in all the categories that seemed important, such as residence, sex, age, race, and economic status. Within these specifics, however, they were free to interview whomever they liked. Republicans generally tended to be easier to interview: They were more likely to have telephones and permanent addresses and to live in better houses and better neighborhoods. This slight bias had not mattered prior to 1948. Democrats had been winning for years anyway. In 1948, the election was very close, and the Republican bias produced the embarrassing mistake that changed survey methods forever.

Since 1948, all survey organizations have used what is called a "probability method." Simple random sampling is the purest case of the probability method, but simple random sampling for a survey about a U.S. presidential election would require drawing names from a list of all the eligible voters in the nation—a lot of people. Each person selected would have to be found, in diversely scattered locales. So instead, "multistage cluster sampling" is used. The United States is divided into seven size-of-community groupings, from large cities to rural open country; these groupings are divided into seven geographic regions (New England, Middle Atlantic, and so on), after which smaller equal-sized groups are zoned, and then city blocks are drawn from the zones, with the probability of selection being proportional to the size of the population or number of dwelling units. Finally, an interviewer is given a randomly selected starting point on the map and is required to follow a given direction, take households in sequence, and ask for the youngest man 18 or older or, if no man is at home, the oldest woman 18 or older. (This has been found to compensate best for the tendencies for young men, and then all men, and then older women, in that order, to be not at home and hence underrepresented.)

Actually, telephoning is often the favored method for polling today. Phone surveys cost about one-third of door-to-door polls. Since most persons now own phones, this method is less biased than in Truman's time. Phoning also allows computers randomly to dial phone numbers and, unlike telephone directories, this method calls unlisted numbers.

Whether the survey is by telephone or face to face, there will be about 35% nonrespondents after three attempts. This creates yet another bias, reckoned with through questions about how much time a person spends at home, so that a slight extra weight can be given to the responses of those reached but usually at home less, to make up for those missed entirely.

Now you know quite a bit about opinion polls, but we have left two important questions unanswered: Why are only about 1,000 included in a poll meant to describe all U.S. adults, and what does the term *sampling error* mean? For these answers, you must wait for Chapter 6 (Box 6–1).

sample statistics

ated *Pop*)[3] before the *M, SD*^{2}, or *SD*. The mean, variance, and standard deviation you figure for the scores in a sample are called **sample statistics.** A sample statistic is figured from known information. Sample statistics are what we have been calculating all along. Sample statistics use the symbols we have been using all along: *M, SD*^{2} and *SD*.

Normal Curves, Probabilities, Samples, and Populations in Research Articles

The topics covered in this chapter are basic for understanding what comes next. These topics are rarely mentioned directly in research articles (except articles about methods or statistics). Sometimes you will see the normal curve mentioned, usually when a researcher is describing the pattern of scores on a particular variable. (We say more about this and give some examples from published articles in Chapter 11, where we consider circumstances in which the scores do not follow a normal curve.)

Probability is also rarely discussed directly, except in relation to statistical significance, a topic we mentioned briefly in Chapter 3. In almost any article you look at, the Results section will be strewn with descriptions of various methods associated with statistical significance, followed by something like "*p* < .05" or "*p* < .01." The *p* refers to probability, but the probability of what? That is the main topic of our discussion of statistical significance in Chapter 5.

Finally, you will sometimes see a brief mention of the method of selecting the sample from the population. For example, Altman, Levine, Howard, and Hamilton (1997) carried out a telephone survey of the attitudes of the U.S. adult public towards tobacco farmers. In the Methods section of their article, they explained that their respondents were "randomly selected from a nationwide list of telephone numbers" (p. 117). Thus, Altman et al. specified both the listing they used for the population (the nationwide list of phone numbers) and the method they used (random selection) to pick out their sample from this listing.

Summary

1. The scores on many variables in social science research approximately follow a bell-shaped, symmetrical, unimodal distribution called the normal curve. Because the shape of this curve follows an exact mathematical formula, there is a specific percentage of scores between any two points on a normal curve.
2. A useful working rule for normal curves is that 50% of the scores are above the mean, 34% between the mean and 1 standard deviation above the mean, and 14% between 1 and 2 standard deviations above the mean.

[3]In statistics writing, it is common to use Greek letters to refer to population parameters. For example, the population mean is μ and the population standard deviation is σ. However, we have not used these symbols in this text, wanting to make it easier for students to grasp the formulas without also having to deal with Greek letters.

3. A normal curve table gives the percentage of scores between the mean and any particular positive Z score. Using this table, and knowing that the curve is symmetrical and that 50% of the scores are above the mean, you can figure the percentage of scores above or below any particular Z score. You can also use the table to figure the Z score for the point where a particular percentage of scores begins or ends.

4. Most social scientists consider the probability of an event to be its expected relative frequency. Probability usually is figured as the proportion of successful outcomes to total possible outcomes. It is symbolized by p and has a range from 0 (event is impossible) to 1 (event is certain). The normal distribution provides a way to know the probabilities of scores' being within particular ranges of values.

5. A sample is an individual or group that is studied—usually as representative of a larger group or population that cannot be studied in its entirety. Ideally, the sample is selected from a population using a strictly random procedure. The mean, variance, and so forth of a sample are called sample statistics. When of a population, they are called population parameters.

6. Research articles rarely discuss normal curves (except briefly when the variable being studied seems not to follow a normal curve) or probability (except in relation to statistical significance). However, procedures of sampling, particularly when the study is a survey, are sometimes described, and the representativeness of a sample when random sampling could not be used may be discussed.

Key Terms

expected relative frequency
haphazard selection
long-run relative-frequency interpretation of probability
normal curve
normal curve table
normal distribution
outcome
population
population parameters
probability (p)
random selection
sample
sample statistics

Practice Problems

These problems involve computation. Most real-life statistics problems are done on a computer. Even if you have a computer and statistics software, do these problems by hand (with the help of a calculator) to ingrain the method in your mind.

For practice in using a computer to solve statistics problems, refer to the computer section of each chapter of the Student's Study Guide and Computer Workbook *that accompanies this text.*

All data are fictional.

Answers to selected problems are given at the back of the book.

1. Suppose that a researcher found that the people living in a particular city have a mean score of 40 and a standard deviation of 5 on a measure of concern about the environment. Assume that their concern scores are normally distributed. Approximately what percentage of people in this city have a score (a) above 40, (b) above 45, (c) above 30, (d) above 35, (e) below 40, (f) below 45, (g) below 30, (h) below 35? What is the minimum score a person has to have to be in the top (i) 2%, (j) 16%, (k) 50%, (l) 84%, (m) 98%? (Use the 50%-34%-14% approximations for this problem.)

2. Suppose that the scores of architects on a particular creativity test are normally distributed. What percentage of architects have Z scores (a) above .10, (b) below .10, (c) above .20, (d) below .20, (e) above 1.10, (f) below 1.10, (g) above –.10, (h) below –.10?

3. Assuming a normal curve, (a) if a person is in the top 10% of the country on mathematics ability, what is that person's Z score? (b) If the person was in the top 1%, what would be the Z score?

4. Consider a test of coordination that has a normal distribution, a mean of 50, and a standard deviation of 10. How high a score would a person need to be in the top 5%? Explain your answer to someone who has never had a course in statistics.

5. The following numbers of employees in a company received special assistance from the personnel department last year:

Drug/alcohol	10
Family crisis counseling	20
Other	20
Total	50

If you were to select a score at random from the records for last year, what is the probability that it would be in each of the following categories? (a) drug/alcohol, (b) family, (c) drug/alcohol or family, (d) any category except "Other," (e) any of the three categories.

6. A research article about the level of self-esteem of Australian high school students emphasizes that it surveyed a "random sample" of the country's high school students. Explain to a person who has never had a course in statistics what this means and why it is important.

5

Introduction to Hypothesis Testing

hypothesis testing

Iɴ Chapter 4, you learned about the normal curve, probability, and the difference between a sample and a population. In this chapter, we introduce the crucial topic of **hypothesis testing.** Hypothesis testing is a systematic procedure for deciding whether the results of a research study, which examines a sample, supports a particular theory or practical innovation, which applies to a population. Hypothesis testing is the central theme in all the remaining chapters of this book, as it is in most social and behavioral science research.

We should warn you at this point that many students find the most difficult part of the course to be mastering the basic logic of this chapter and the next. This chapter in particular requires some mental gymnastics, and even if you follow everything the first time through, you will be wise to review it thoroughly. Hypothesis testing involves a group of ideas that make little sense covered separately, so in this chapter you learn a fairly large number of ideas all at once. However, a benefit of this is that once you understand the material in this chapter and the two that follow, your mind will be used to this sort of thing, and the rest of the course should seem easier.

At the same time, we have kept this introduction as simple as possible, putting off what we could for later chapters. For example, real-life social and behavioral science research almost always involves samples of many individuals. However, to simplify how much you have to learn at one time, all of the examples in this chapter are about studies in which the sample is a single individual. To do this, we had to create some odd examples. Just remember that you are building a foundation that will, by Chapter 8, prepare you to understand hypothesis testing as it is actually carried out.

The material in this chapter builds upon what you learned in Chapter 4 and the chapters it is based upon, particularly the material in Chapter 2 on mean, standard deviation, and Z scores. We strongly urge you not to proceed to this chapter until you are confident you have mastered this earlier material.

A Hypothesis-Testing Example

Here is your first necessarily odd example that we made up to keep this introduction to hypothesis testing as straightforward as possible. A large research project has been going on for several years. In this project, new babies are given a special vitamin and then the research team follows their development during the first two years of life. So far, the vitamin has not speeded up the development of babies. The ages at which these and all other babies start to walk is shown in Figure 5–1. Notice that the mean is 14 months, the standard deviation is 3 months, and the ages follow a normal curve. Looking at the distribution, you can see that less than 2% start walking before 8 months of age; these are the babies who are 2 standard deviations below the mean. (This fictional distribution actually is close to the true distribution researchers have found for European babies, although that true distribution is slightly skewed to the right [Hindley, Filliozat, Klackenberg, Nicolet-Meister, & Sand, 1966.])

One of the researchers working on the project has an idea. Based on some new theories, she reasons that if the vitamin the babies are taking could be more highly refined, the effect of the vitamin would be dramatically greater: Babies taking the highly purified version should start walking much

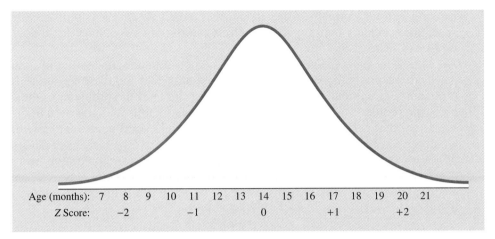

FIGURE 5–1
Distribution of when babies begin to walk (fictional data).

earlier than other babies. (We will assume that the purification process could not possibly make the vitamin harmful.) However, refining the vitamin in this way is extremely expensive for each dose, so the research team decides to try the procedure with just enough highly purified doses for only one baby. A newborn in the project is then randomly selected to take the highly purified version of the vitamin, and its progress is followed over the first two years. What kind of result should lead the researchers to conclude that the highly purified vitamin allows babies to walk earlier?

This is an example of a hypothesis-testing problem. The researchers want to draw a general conclusion about whether the purified vitamin allows babies in general to walk earlier. The conclusion about babies in general, however, will be based on results of studying only a sample. (In this strange example, the sample is of a single baby.)

The Core Logic of Hypothesis Testing

There is a standard way to approach a hypothesis-testing problem like this one. The researcher uses the following reasoning. Ordinarily, the chance of a baby's starting to walk at age 8 months or earlier would be less than 2%. Thus, walking at 8 months or earlier is highly unlikely. But what if the randomly selected baby in our study does start walking by 8 months? If that happens, we will be able to *reject* the idea that the specially purified vitamin has *no* effect. If we reject the idea that the specially purified vitamin has no effect, then we must also *accept* the idea that the specially purified vitamin *does* have an effect. (The logic of this example is central to everything else we do in the book. You may want to read this paragraph again.)

The researchers first spelled out what would have to happen for them to conclude that the special purification procedure makes a difference. Having laid this out in advance, the researchers can then go on to carry out their study. In this example, carrying out the study means giving the specially purified vitamin to a randomly selected baby and watching to see how early that baby walks. Suppose the result of the study shows that the baby starts walking before 8 months. They would then conclude that it is unlikely the specially purified vitamin makes no difference and thus conclude that it does make a difference.

This kind of opposite-of-what-you-predict, roundabout reasoning is at the heart of inferential statistics. It is something like a double negative. It turns out that without such a tortuous way of going at the problem, in most cases the problem simply cannot be solved at all. In almost all research in the social and behavioral sciences, whether involving experiments, surveys, or whatever, we base our conclusions on this question: What is the probability of getting our research results if the opposite of what we are predicting were true? That is, we are usually predicting an effect of some kind. However, we decide on whether there *is* such an effect by seeing if it is unlikely that there is *not* such an effect.

The Hypothesis-Testing Process

Let's look at our example, going over each step in some detail. Along the way, we cover the special terminology of hypothesis testing. Most important, we introduce you to a five-step process you will use for the rest of this book.

Step 1: Restate the Question as a Research Hypothesis and a Null Hypothesis about the Populations

First, note that the researchers are interested in the effects on babies in general (not just this particular baby). Thus, it will be useful to restate the question in terms of populations. That is, for purposes of analyzing the present situation, we can think of babies as falling into two groups:

> **Population 1:** Babies who take the specially purified vitamin
> **Population 2:** Babies who do not take the specially purified vitamin

Population 1 are those who receive the experimental treatment. In our example, there is only one real-life baby in Population 1. Yet this one baby represents an as-yet-unborn future group of many babies to whom the researchers want to apply their results. Population 2 is a kind of baseline of what is known.

The prediction of the research team is that Population 1 babies (those who take the specially purified vitamin) will on the average walk earlier than Population 2 babies (those who do not take the specially purified vitamin). This prediction is based on the researchers' theory of how these vitamins work. A prediction like this about the difference between populations is called a **research hypothesis.**

research hypothesis

The opposite of the research hypothesis is that the populations are not different in the way predicted. Under this scenario, Population 1 babies (those who take the specially purified vitamin) will on the average *not* walk earlier than Population 2 babies (those who do not take the specially purified vitamin). This prediction is that there is no difference in when Population 1 and Population 2 babies start walking: They start at the same time. A statement like this, about a lack of difference between populations, is the crucial opposite of the research hypothesis. It is called a **null hypothesis.** The null

null hypothesis

hypothesis has this name because it states the situation in which there is no difference (the difference is null) between populations.[1]

The research hypothesis and the null hypothesis are complete opposites. If one is true, the other cannot be true. This oppositeness and the direct focus on the null hypothesis is completely central to the hypothesis-testing logic. For this reason the research hypothesis, which is ultimately our real interest, is sometimes called the *alternative hypothesis*. (Also note that you will sometimes see the research hypothesis abbreviated as H_1 and the null hypothesis abbreviated as H_0.)

Step 2: Determine the Characteristics of the Comparison Distribution

The next step is to consider how the results of studying a sample might help us make the choice between the research hypothesis and the null hypothesis. Thus, the question we ask now is this: Given a particular sample result (in this case, the age at which our randomly selected baby who gets the specially purified vitamin starts to walk), what is the probability we could have gotten that result if the null hypothesis were true?

To answer this question, we have to know about the situation if the null hypothesis were true. That is, we need to know the details of the population distribution from which the sample would be coming if the null hypothesis were true. If we know the distribution of the population from which our sample would be coming, and we know it is a normal curve, we are in a good position: We can directly determine the probability of having gotten any particular score from that distribution using the normal curve table.

How can we know the details of the distribution from which our sample would be coming if the null hypothesis is true? It is possible to know because *if the null hypothesis is true, both populations are the same*. We usually know about one of the populations (Population 2). Thus, if the null hypothesis is true and both populations are the same, we also know about the other population (Population 1). In our example, if the null hypothesis is true, both populations follow a normal curve and have a mean of 14 months and a standard deviation of 3 months (see Figure 5–1).

In this book, the distribution for the situation in which the null hypothesis is true—the distribution to which you will compare your actual sample—we call the **comparison distribution.**[2] We call it the comparison distribution because in the hypothesis-testing process, you compare your actual sample score to this distribution. You are comparing in the sense of figuring out the probability of getting a score as extreme as your sample's score on this comparison distribution. In the present example, the comparison distribution is the same as the distribution of scores in Population 2, the population in which the experimental procedure has not been applied.

comparison distribution

---

[1]We have oversimplified a bit here. Because the research hypothesis is that one population will walk earlier than the other, its opposite is that the other group will either walk at the same time or walk later. That is, the opposite of the research hypothesis includes both no difference and a difference in the direction opposite to that predicted. We discuss this issue in some detail later in the chapter.
[2]The comparison distribution is also sometimes called a "statistical model." In most cases, it is also called a "sampling distribution," a distribution of a characteristic of samples—an idea we discuss in Chapter 6.

Step 3: Determine the Cutoff Sample Score on the Comparison Distribution at which the Null Hypothesis Should Be Rejected

cutoff sample score

Ideally, well before conducting the study, researchers set a target against which they will judge their result—how extreme a score their sample would need to have in order to draw a confident conclusion. Specifically, they determine the score the sample would need to have to make them decide against the null hypothesis—how extreme it would have to be for it to be too unlikely that they could get such an extreme score if the null hypothesis were true. This is called the **cutoff sample score.** (The cutoff sample score is also known as the *critical value.*)

Consider our purified vitamin example in which the null hypothesis is that it doesn't matter whether a baby is fed the specially purified vitamin. The researchers might decide that if the null hypothesis were true, a randomly selected baby walking by 8 months would be very unlikely. Assuming a normal distribution being 2 standard deviations below the mean (walking at 8 months) could occur less than 2% of the time. Thus, based on the comparison distribution, the researchers set their cutoff sample score even before doing the study. What they are doing is deciding in advance that *if* the result of their study is a baby who walks before 8 months, they will reject the null hypothesis. Moreover, if they reject the null hypothesis, they are left with the research hypothesis. We would then say that the "research hypothesis is supported."

On the other hand, what if the baby does not start walking until after 8 months? If that happens, they will not be able to reject the null hypothesis. Note however, that in this situation they will *not* be able to say "the null hypothesis is supported." Not rejecting the null hypothesis leaves a situation that is ambiguous. No conclusions can be drawn except perhaps that more research is needed. We have more to say about this later.

When setting in advance how extreme a score has to be to reject the null hypothesis, researchers do not generally use an actual number of units on the direct scale of measurement (such as months). Instead, they decide how extreme a score needs to be in terms of a probability and the Z score that goes with that probability.[3] In our purified vitamin example, the researchers might decide that if a result were less likely than 2% (the probability), they would reject the null hypothesis. Being in the bottom 2% on a normal curve means having a Z score of about -2 or lower. Thus, the researchers would set -2 as their Z score cutoff point on the comparison distribution for deciding that a result is extreme enough to reject the null hypothesis.

Suppose that the researchers are even more cautious about too easily rejecting the null hypothesis. They might decide that they will reject the null hypothesis only if they get a result that could occur by chance only 1% of the time or less. They could then figure out the Z score cutoff for 1%. Using the normal curve table, to have a score in the lower 1% of a normal curve, you

---

[3]These days, when hypothesis testing is usually done on the computer, researchers need only decide in advance on the probability. This is because the computer prints out the exact probability of getting your result if the null hypothesis were true. Thus, the researcher need only check the printed-out probability to see if it is less than the probability level set in advance. However, in order to *understand* what these probability levels mean, you need to learn the entire process, including how to figure the Z score for a particular probability.

need a Z score of −2.33 or less. (In our example, a Z score of −2.33 means 7 months.) In Figure 5–2, we have shaded the 1% of the comparison distribution in which a sample would be considered so extreme that the possibility that it came from a distribution like this would be rejected.

In general, social and behavioral science researchers use a cutoff on the comparison distribution with a probability of 5% that a score will be at least that extreme. That is, researchers reject the null hypothesis if the probability of getting a result this extreme (if the null hypothesis were true) is less than 5%. This probability is usually written as "$p < .05$." However, in some areas of research, or when researchers want to be especially cautious, they use a cutoff of 1% ($p < .01$) or even .1% ($p < .001$).

These are called **conventional levels of significance.** They are described as the *.05 significance level* or the *.01 significance level*. (We discuss in more detail in Chapter 7 the issues in deciding on the significance level to use.) When a sample score is so extreme that researchers reject the null hypothesis, the result is said to be **statistically significant.**

conventional levels of significance

statistically significant

Step 4: Determine Your Sample's Score on the Comparison Distribution

The next step is to carry out the study and get the actual result for your sample. The researcher figures out the Z score for the sample's raw score based on the mean and standard deviation of the comparison distribution.

Assume that the researchers did the study and the baby who was given the specially purified vitamin started walking at 6 months. The mean of the comparison distribution to which we are comparing these results is 14 months and the standard deviation is 3 months. Thus a baby who walks at 6 months is 8 months below the mean, which puts this baby 2 2/3 standard deviations below the mean. The Z score for this sample baby on the comparison distribution is thus −2.67. Figure 5–3 shows the score of our sample baby on the comparison distribution.

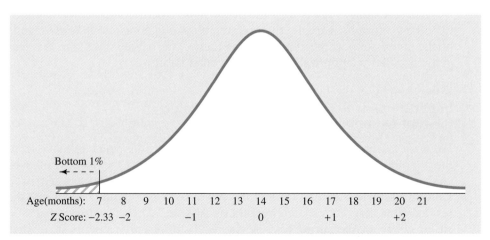

FIGURE 5–2
Distribution of when babies begin to walk, with bottom 1% indicated (fictional data).

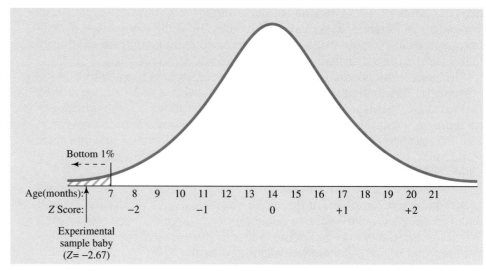

FIGURE 5–3
Distribution of when babies begin to walk, indicating both the bottom 1% and the single baby that is the sample studied (fictional data).

Step 5: Decide Whether to Reject the Null Hypothesis

To decide whether to reject the null hypothesis, you compare the cutoff Z score to reject the null hypothesis to the actual sample's Z score. In our example, suppose the researchers had determined that they would reject the null hypothesis if the Z score of the sample came out more extreme than -2. The actual result was -2.67. This is more extreme than -2. Thus, they would reject the null hypothesis.

Or suppose the researchers had used the more conservative 1% significance level? The needed Z score to reject the null hypothesis would then have been -2.33. But, again, the actual Z for the randomly selected baby was -2.67. Thus, even with this more conservative cutoff, they would still reject the null hypothesis. This situation is shown in Figure 5–3.

If a researcher rejects the null hypothesis, what remains is the research hypothesis. In this example, the research team can conclude that the results of the study support the research hypothesis that babies who take the specially purified vitamin walk earlier than other babies.

Implications of Rejecting or Failing to Reject the Null Hypothesis

We want to emphasize two points about the conclusions you can make from the hypothesis-testing process. First, suppose you reject the null hypothesis, so that your results support the research hypothesis (as in our example). You would still not say that the result "proves" the research hypothesis or that the results show that the research hypothesis is "true." Such conclusions are too strong. They are too strong because the results of research studies are always based on probabilities. In this case, they are based on the probability being low of getting your result if the null hypothesis is true. "Proven" and "true" are okay in logic and mathematics, but to use these words in conclusions from scientific research is thoroughly unprofessional. (It is okay to use "true" when speaking hypothetically—for example, "*if* this hypothesis *were* true, then . . ."—but not when speaking of conclusions about an actual result.)

Second, as we briefly noted earlier, when a result is not extreme enough to reject the null hypothesis, you do not say that the result "supports the null hypothesis." A result that is not strong enough for us to reject the null hypothesis means only that the study was inconclusive. The results may not be extreme enough to reject the null hypothesis, but the null hypothesis might still be false (and the research hypothesis true). Suppose that in our example the specially purified vitamin had only a slight but still real effect. In that case, we would not expect to find any single baby given the purified vitamin to be walking a lot earlier than other babies. Thus, we would not be able to reject the null hypothesis, even though it is false.

Showing that the null hypothesis is true would mean showing that there is absolutely no difference between the populations. It is always possible that there is a difference between the populations but that the difference is much smaller than what the particular study was able to detect. Therefore, when a result is not extreme enough to reject the null hypothesis, researchers generally say only that the results are "inconclusive." Sometimes, however, if studies have been done using large numbers and accurate measuring procedures, evidence may build up in support of the approximate accuracy of a particular null hypothesis. (We have more to say on this issue in Chapter 7. Also see Box 5–1.)

Summary of the Steps of Hypothesis Testing

Here is a summary of the five steps of hypothesis testing:

1. Restate the question as a research hypothesis and a null hypothesis about the populations.
2. Determine the characteristics of the comparison distribution.
3. Determine the cutoff sample score on the comparison distribution at which the null hypothesis should be rejected.
4. Determine your sample's score on the comparison distribution.
5. Decide whether to reject the null hypothesis.

One-Tailed and Two-Tailed Hypothesis Tests

In the baby-walking example, the research hypothesis was about a situation in which the researchers cared about only one direction of the result. The researchers wanted to know whether babies given the specially purified vitamin would walk *earlier* than other babies. The researchers in this study were really not even imagining that giving the specially purified vitamins could cause babies to start walking later.

Directional Hypotheses and One-Tailed Tests

The baby-walking study was an example of a **directional hypothesis.** The researchers were focusing on a specific direction of the effect. It is important to notice that when a researcher makes a directional hypothesis, the null

directional hypothesis

BOX 5–1

To Be or Not to Be—But Can Not Being Be? The Problem of Whether and When to Accept the Null Hypothesis

The null hypothesis states that there is no difference between populations represented by different groups or experimental conditions. As we have seen, the usual rule in statistics is that a study cannot find the null hypothesis to be true. A study can only tell you that you cannot reject the null hypothesis. That is, a study that fails to reject the null hypothesis is simply uninformative. Such studies tend not to be published, obviously. However, much work could be avoided if people knew what interventions, measures, or experiments had not worked. Indeed, Greenwald (1975) reports that sometimes ideas have been assumed too long to be true just because a few studies found them true, while many more, unreported, had not.

However, Frick (1995) has pointed out a more serious problem with being rigidly uninterested in the null hypothesis: Sometimes it may be true that one thing has no effect on another. This does not mean that there would be a zero relationship of no correlation or no difference at all—a result almost impossible to obtain in many situations. It would only mean that it was so small that it probably represented no real or at least no important relationship or difference.

The problem is knowing when to conclude that the null hypothesis (or something close to it) might be true. Frick (1995) gives three criteria. First, the null hypothesis should seem possible. Second, the results in the study should be consistent with the null hypothesis and not easily interpreted any other way. There should be no other obvious way to interpret them. Third, and most important, the researcher has to have made a strong effort to find the effect that he or she wants to conclude is not there. Among other things, this means studying a large sample and having very thorough and sensitive measurement. If the study is an experiment, the experimenter should have tried to produce the difference by using a strong manipulation and rigorous conditions of testing.

Frick points out that all of this leaves a subjective element to the acceptance of the null hypothesis: Who decides when a researcher's effort was strong enough? Subjective judgments are a part of science, like it or not. For example, reviewers of articles have to decide if a topic is important enough to be worth the space in their journal. Further, the null hypothesis is being accepted all the time anyway. (For example, many social scientists accept the null hypothesis about the effect of extrasensory perception.) It is better to discuss our basis for accepting the null hypothesis than just to accept it.

What are we to make of all this? It is clear that just failing to reject the null hypothesis is not the same as supporting it. However, Frick reminds us that there are situations in which the evidence ought to convince us that something like the null hypothesis is likely to be the case.

hypothesis is also, in a sense, directional. Suppose the research hypothesis is that taking the specially purified vitamin will make babies walk earlier. In that case, the null hypothesis is that the specially purified vitamin will either have no effect or make babies walk later. Thus, in Figure 5–2, for the null hypothesis to be rejected, the sample had to have a score in the bottom 1%—the lower extreme or tail of the comparison distribution. (A score at the other tail would be considered the same as a score in the middle for purposes of rejecting the null hypothesis.) For this reason, a test of a directional hypothesis is called a **one-tailed test.**

In this example, the prediction was that the baby would walk early—a prediction in the direction of a low score on months before walking. Thus,

one-tailed test

the cutoff region was at the low end (left side) of the comparison distribution. In other research situations with a directional hypothesis, it is quite common for the cutoff to be at the high end (right side) of the comparison distribution That is, in these situations, the researchers would be predicting that the experimental procedure will produce a high score.

Nondirectional Hypotheses and Two-Tailed Tests

Sometimes a research hypothesis is simply that an experimental procedure will have an effect, without specifying whether it will produce a very high score or a very low score. For example, a researcher may be interested in the impact of a new social-skills program on worker productivity. It is possible that the program will improve productivity by making the working environment more pleasant. However, it is also possible that it will hurt productivity by encouraging people to socialize instead of work. The research hypothesis would be simply that the skills program changes the level of productivity. The null hypothesis would be that the program does not affect productivity one way or the other.

Whenever a hypothesis predicts an effect but does not predict the direction of that effect, it is called a **nondirectional hypothesis.** To test the significance of a nondirectional hypothesis, you must take into account the possibility that a score could be extreme at either tail of the comparison distribution. Thus, this is called a **two-tailed test.**

nondirectional hypothesis

two-tailed test

Determining Cutoff Points With Two-Tailed Tests

There is a special complication in a two-tailed test. You have to divide up the significance percentage between the two tails. For example, with a 5% significance level, you would reject a null hypothesis only if the sample was so extreme that it was in either the top 2 1/2% or the bottom 2 1/2%. In this way, the overall chance of the null hypothesis's being true is kept at a total of 5%.

Note that a two-tailed test makes the cutoff Z scores for the 5% level +1.96 and −1.96. For a one-tailed test at the 5% level, the cutoff was not so extreme—only +1.64 or −1.64, but only one side of the distribution was considered. These situations are illustrated in Figure 5–4a.

Using the 1% significance level, a two-tailed test (.5% at each tail) has cutoffs of +2.58 and −2.58, while a one-tailed test's cutoff is either +2.33 or −2.33. These situations are illustrated in Figure 5–4b.

When to Use One-Tailed or Two-Tailed Tests

If the researcher decides in advance to use a one-tailed test, then the sample's score will not need to be so extreme to be significant as it would need with a two-tailed test. Yet there is a price: With a one-tailed test, if the result is extreme in the direction opposite to what was predicted, no matter how extreme, the result cannot be considered significant.

In principle, you plan to use a one-tailed test when you have a clearly directional hypothesis and a two-tailed test when you have a clearly nondirectional hypothesis. In practice, it is not so simple. Even when a theory clearly

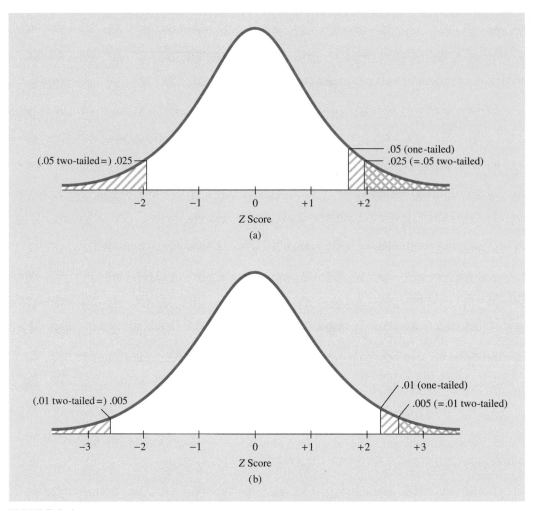

FIGURE 5–4
Significance level cutoffs for one- and two-tailed tests: (a) .05 significance level; (b) .01 significance level. (The one-tailed tests in these examples assume the prediction was for a high score. You could instead have a one-tailed test where the prediction is for the lower, left tail.)

predicts a particular result, the actual result may come out just the opposite of what we expected. Sometimes this opposite result may be even more interesting than what we had predicted. By using one-tailed tests, we risk having to ignore possibly important results.

Thus, social scientists disagree about whether one-tailed tests should be used, even when there is a clearly directional hypothesis. To be safe, many researchers use two-tailed tests even when their theories make clearly directional hypotheses. In fact, in most research articles, unless the researcher specifically notes that a one-tailed test was used, it is usually assumed that it was a two-tailed test.

Given this disagreement, it is fortunate that in most actual studies, the final conclusion is not really affected by whether a one- or two-tailed test is used. It is our experience that the majority of the time research results are either so extreme that they will be significant by any reasonable standard or so far from extreme that they would not be significant no matter what procedure was used.

What happens when a result gives less certain conclusions? The researcher's decision about one- or two-tailed tests takes on added importance. In this situation the researcher attempts to use the approach that will give the most accurate and noncontroversial conclusion. The idea is to let nature—and not a researcher's decisions—determine the conclusion as much as possible. Further, whenever a result is less than completely clear one way or the other, most researchers will not be comfortable drawing strong conclusions until more research is done.

An Example of Hypothesis Testing Using a Two-Tailed Test

Here is another fictional example, this time using a two-tailed test. A researcher is interested in the effect of going through a natural disaster on the attitude of police chiefs about the goodness of the people in their city. The researchers believe that after a disaster, the police chief is likely to have a more positive attitude about the people of the city (because the chief will have seen many acts of heroism and helping of neighbors after the event). However, it is also possible that a disaster will lead to police chiefs having more negative attitudes, because there may be cases of looting and other dishonest behavior after the disaster. Thus, the researchers will make a nondirectional hypothesis.

Let us assume that there is considerable previous research on the attitudes of police chiefs about the goodness of the people in their cities and that on a standard questionnaire, the mean attitude rating is 69.5 with a standard deviation of 14.1, and the attitude scores follow a normal curve. Let us also assume that a major earthquake has just occurred in an isolated city and shortly afterwards the researcher is able to give the standard questionnaire to the police chief of that city.

The hypothesis-testing procedure is then carried out as follows:

1. Restate the question as a research hypothesis and a null hypothesis about the populations. There are two populations of interest:

Population 1: Police chiefs whose city has just been through a disaster
Population 2: Police chiefs in general

The research hypothesis is that police chiefs whose city has just been through a disaster (Population 1) score differently from police chiefs in general (Population 2) on their attitude toward the goodness of the people of their city. The opposite of the research hypothesis, the null hypothesis, is that police chiefs whose city has just been through a disaster have the same attitude as police chiefs in general. (That is, the null hypothesis is that the attitudes of Populations 1 and 2 are the same.)

2. Determine the characteristics of the comparison distribution. If the null hypothesis is true, the distributions for Populations 1 and 2 will be the same. We know the distribution of Population 2, so it can serve as our comparison distribution. As noted, it is normally distributed with $M = 69.5$ and $SD = 14.1$.

3. Determine the cutoff sample score on the comparison distribution at which the null hypothesis should be rejected. The researcher selects the 5% significance level. The researcher has made a nondirectional hypothesis and will therefore use a two-tailed test. Thus, the researcher will reject the null hypothesis only if the police chief's attitude score is in either the top or bottom 2 1/2% of the comparison distribution. In terms of Z scores, these cutoffs are +1.96 and –1.96 (see Figure 5–5).

4. Determine your sample's score on the comparison distribution. The police chief who went through the earthquake took the standard attitude questionnaire and had a score of 41. This corresponds to a Z score on the comparison distribution of –2.02. (That is, $Z = [41 – 69.5]/14.1 = –2.02$.)

5. Decide whether to reject the null hypothesis. A Z score of –2.02 is slightly more extreme than the Z score of –1.96, which is where the lower 2 1/2% of the comparison distribution begins. This is a result so extreme that it is unlikely to have occurred if this police chief were from a population no different than Population 2. Therefore, the researcher rejects the null hypothesis. This result supports the research hypothesis that going through a disaster does indeed change police chiefs' attitudes toward their city. In this case, the results would mean that the effect is one of making the chief less positive about the city's people. (Remember, however, that this is a fictional study.)

Hypothesis Tests as Reported in Research Articles

In general, hypothesis testing is reported in research articles as part of one of the specific statistical procedures you learn in later chapters. For each result of interest, the researcher usually first notes whether the result was "statistically significant." Next, the researcher usually gives a symbol based on the specific technique used in determining the probabilities, such as a "t" or an

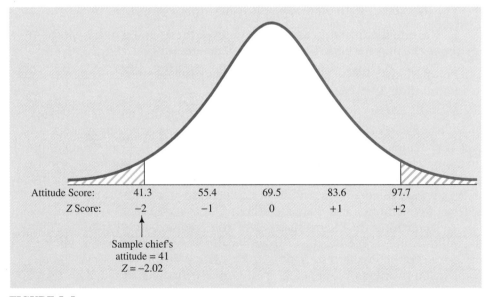

FIGURE 5–5
Distribution of attitudes of police chiefs toward goodness of people in their cities with upper and lower 2 1/2% shaded and showing the sample police chief whose city has just been through a disaster (fictional data).

"*F*" (these procedures are covered in Chapters 8–12). Finally, there will be an indication of the significance level, such as "*p* < .05" or "*p* < .01." For example, Reber and Kotovsky (1997), in a study of problem solving, described one of their results comparing a specific group of participants within their overall control condition as follows: "This group took an average of 179 moves to solve the puzzle, whereas the rest of the control participants took an average of 74 moves, $t(19) = 3.31$, $p < .01$" (p. 183).

When the researchers write "*p* < .01," they mean that the probability of their results being as extreme as they were if the null hypothesis were true is less than .01 (1%). If the result were close but did not reach the significance level chosen, it may be reported anyway as a "near significant trend," with "*p* < .10," for example. If the result were not significant, sometimes the actual *p* level will be given (for example, "*p* = .27"), or the abbreviation *ns,* for "not significant," will be used. In addition, if a one-tailed test were used, that usually will be noted. Again, when reading research articles, assume a two-tailed test if nothing is said otherwise.

Even though a researcher has chosen a significance level in advance, such as .05, results that meet more rigorous standards may be noted as such. (You are supposed to be impressed.) Thus, in the same article you may see results in which some are noted as "*p* < .05," others as "*p* < .01," and still others as "*p* < .001," for example.

Finally, in many cases the results of hypothesis testing are shown simply as asterisks in a table of results, in which a result with an asterisk is significant and one without one is not.

In all of these examples, researchers may not make the research hypothesis or the null hypothesis explicit or describe any of the other steps of the process in any detail. It usually is assumed that the reader understands all of this very well.

Summary

1. Hypothesis testing considers the probability that the result of a study could have been obtained even if the experimental treatment had no effect. If this probability is low, the scenario is rejected and the theory from which the treatment or comparison was proposed is supported.
2. The expectation of an effect is the research hypothesis, and the hypothetical situation in which there is no effect is the null hypothesis.
3. When a result would be extremely unlikely if the null hypothesis were true, the null hypothesis is said to be rejected and the research hypothesis supported. If the results are not that extreme, the study is inconclusive.
4. Social and behavioral scientists in most fields consider a result too extreme if it is less likely than 5%, though a more stringent 1%, or even .1%, cutoff is sometimes used. These percentages may apply to the probability of the result's being extreme in a predicted direction, a directional or one-tailed test, or to the probability of its being extreme in either direction, a nondirectional or two-tailed test.
5. The hypothesis-testing process involves five steps:
   (1) Restate the question as a research hypothesis and a null hypothesis about the populations.

(2) Determine the characteristics of the comparison distribution.
(3) Determine the cutoff sample score on the comparison distribution at which the null hypothesis should be rejected.
(4) Determine your sample's score on the comparison distribution.
(5) Decide whether to reject the null hypothesis.

6. Research articles typically report the results of hypothesis testing by noting that a result was or was not significant and giving the probability level cutoff (usually 5% or 1%) at which the decision was made.

Key Terms

comparison distribution
conventional levels of significance ($p < .05$, $p < .01$)
cutoff sample score

directional hypothesis
hypothesis testing
nondirectional hypothesis
null hypothesis

one-tailed test
research hypothesis
statistically significant
two-tailed test

Practice Problems

These problems involve computation. Most real-life statistics problems are done on a computer. Even if you have a computer and statistics software, do these problems by hand (with the help of a calculator) to ingrain the method in your mind.

For practice in using a computer to solve statistics problems, refer to the computer section of each chapter of the Student's Study Guide and Computer Workbook *that accompanies this text.*

All data are fictional (unless an actual citation is given).

Answers to selected problems are given at the back of the book.

1. Define the following terms in your own words: (a) research hypothesis, (b) null hypothesis, (c) hypothesis testing procedure, (d) comparison distribution, (e) .05 significance level, (f) one-tailed test.

2. For each of the following, (a) indicate what two populations are being compared, (b) state the research hypothesis, (c) state the null hypothesis, and (d) say whether you should use a one-tailed or two-tailed test and why.

(i) Do Canadian children whose parents are librarians do better than Canadian children in general on reading ability?

(ii) Is the level of income for residents of a particular city different from the level of income for people in the region?

(iii) Do people who have experienced an earthquake have more or less self-confidence than the general population?

(iv) Based on anthropological reports in which the status of women is scored on a 10-point scale, the mean and standard deviation across many cultures are known. A new culture is found in which there is an unusual family arrangement. The status of women is also rated in this culture. Do cultures with this kind of unusual family arrangement provide higher status to women than cultures in general?

3. Based on the information given for each of the following studies, decide whether to reject the null hypothesis. In each case, give the Z-score cutoff (or cutoffs) on the comparison distribution at which the null hypothesis should be rejected, the Z score on the comparison distribution for the sample score, and the conclusion. Assume that all populations are normally distributed.

Study	Population M	Population SD	Sample Score	p	Tails of Test
A	10	2	14	.05	1 (high predicted)
B	10	2	14	.05	2
C	10	2	14	.01	1 (high predicted)
D	10	2	14	.01	2
E	10	4	14	.05	1 (high predicted)
F	10	1	14	.01	2
G	10	2	16	.01	2
H	12	2	16	.01	2
I	12	2	8	.05	1 (low predicted)

4. A researcher interested in the senses of taste and smell has carried out extensive studies in which university students are given each of 20 different foods (apricot, chocolate, cherry, coffee, garlic, and so on). She adminis-

ters each food by dropping a liquid on the tongue. Over the entire student population at her university, the mean number of these 20 foods that students can identify correctly is 14, with a standard deviation of 4. (Let us assume that all the students at this college are tested as a part of a medical screening at the start of each year.) The researcher wants to know whether people's accuracy on this test has more to do with smell or with taste. Thus, she sets up special procedures that keep the person from being able to use the sense of smell during the test. The researcher then tries the procedure on one randomly selected student. This student is able to identify only 5 correctly. Using the .05 significance level, what should the researcher conclude? Solve this problem explicitly using all five steps of hypothesis testing. Then explain your answer to someone who has never had a course in statistics.

5. A nursing researcher working with people who have undergone a particular type of major surgery proposed that people will recover from the operation more quickly if friends and family are in the room with them for the first 48 hours after the operation. It is known (in this fictional example) that time to recover is normally distributed with a mean of 12 days and a standard deviation of 5 days. The procedure is tried with a randomly selected patient, and this patient recovers in 18 days. Using the .01 significance level, what should the researcher conclude? Solve this problem explicitly using all five steps of hypothesis testing. Then explain your answer to someone who is familiar with mean, standard deviation, Z scores, and the normal curve, but doesn't know anything else about statistics or hypothesis testing.

6. Pecukonis (1990), as part of a larger study, measured ego development (a measure of overall maturity) and ability to empathize with others among a group of 24 aggressive adolescent girls in a residential treatment center. The girls were divided into high- and low-ego development groups, and the empathy ("cognitive empathy") scores of these two groups were compared. In his Results section, Pecukonis reported, "The average score on cognitive empathy for subjects scoring high on ego development was 22.1 as compared with 16.3 for low scorers, . . . $p < .005$" (p. 68). Explain this result to a person who has never had a course in statistics. (Focus on the meaning of this result in terms of the general logic of hypothesis testing and statistical significance.)

6

Hypothesis Tests with Means of Samples

I N Chapter 5, we introduced the basic logic of hypothesis testing. We used as examples studies in which the sample was a single individual. As we noted, however, in actual practice, social and behavioral science research almost always involves samples of many individuals. In this chapter, we build on what you have learned so far and consider hypothesis testing involving a sample of more than one. Mainly this requires examining in some detail what we call a distribution of means.

It is important that you understand Chapter 5 quite solidly before going on to this chapter.

The Distribution of Means

Hypothesis testing in the usual research situation, where you are studying a sample of many individuals, is exactly the same as you learned in Chapter 5—with an important exception. When you have more than one person in your sample, there is a special problem with Step 2, determining the characteristics of the comparison distribution. The problem is that the score you care about in your sample is the mean of the group of scores. The comparison distributions we have been considering so far have been distributions of populations of individuals (such as the population of ages when individual babies start walking). Comparing the mean of a sample of, say, 50 people to a distribution of a population of individual scores is a mismatch—like comparing apples to oranges. Instead, when you are interested in the mean of a sample of 50, you need a comparison distribution that is a distribution of means of samples of 50 scores. Such a comparison distribution we call a **distribution of means.**

distribution of means

A distribution of means is a distribution of the means of each of a very large number of samples of the same size, with each sample randomly taken from the same population of individuals.[1] The distribution of means is the proper comparison distribution when there is more than one person in a sample. Thus, in most research situations, determining the characteristics of a distribution of means is necessary for Step 2 of the hypothesis-testing procedure (determining the characteristics of the comparison distribution).

Building a Distribution of Means

To help you understand the idea of a distribution of means, we will consider how you could build up such a distribution from an ordinary population distribution of individuals. Suppose our population of individuals was of the grade levels of the 90,000 elementary and junior high school children in a particular region. Suppose further (to keep the example simple) that there are exactly 10,000 children at each grade level, from first through ninth grade.

[1]Statisticians also call this distribution of means a "sampling distribution of the mean." In this book, however, we use the term "distribution of means" to make it clear that we are discussing populations, not samples or distributions of samples.

FIGURE 6–1
Distribution of grade levels among 90,000 school children (fictional data).

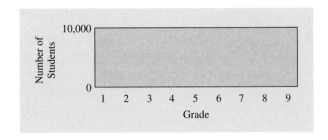

This population distribution would be rectangular, with a mean of 5, a variance of 6.67, and a standard deviation of 2.58 (see Figure 6–1).

Next, suppose you wrote each child's grade level on a table tennis ball and put all 90,000 plastic balls into a giant tub. The tub would contain 10,000 balls with a 1 on them, 10,000 with a 2 on them, and so forth. Stir up the balls in the tub, and then take two of them out. You have taken a random sample of two balls. Suppose one ball has a 2 on it and the other has a 9 on it. The mean grade level of this sample of two children's grade level is 5.5, the average of 2 and 9. Now you put the balls back, mix up all the balls, and select two balls again. Maybe this time you get two 4s, making the mean of your second sample 4. Then you try again; this time you get a 2 and a 7, making your mean 4.5. So far you have three means: 5.5, 4, and 4.5.

These three numbers (each a mean of a sample of grade levels of two school children) can be thought of as a small distribution in its own right. The mean of this little distribution of three numbers is 4.67 (the sum of 5.5, 4, and 4.5 divided by 3). The variance of this distribution is .39 (the variance of 5.5, 4, and 4.5). The standard deviation is .62 (the square root of .39). A histogram of this distribution of three means is shown in Figure 6–2.

If you continued the process, the histogram of means would continue to grow. An example after 10 samples, each of two randomly drawn balls, is shown in Figure 6–3a. Figure 6–3b shows the histogram of the distribution of means after 20 samples, each of two randomly drawn balls. After 100 such samples, the histogram of the distribution of the means might look like that in Figure 6–3c; after 1,000, like Figure 6–3d. (We actually made the histograms shown in Figure 6–3 using a computer to make the random selections, instead of using 90,000 table tennis balls and a giant tub.)

In practice, researchers almost never take many different samples from a population. It is quite a lot of work to come up with a single sample and study the people in that sample. Fortunately, however, as you will soon see,

FIGURE 6–2
Distribution of the means of three samples, each of two school children randomly taken from a population of 90,000 school children (fictional data).

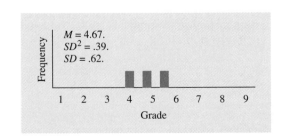

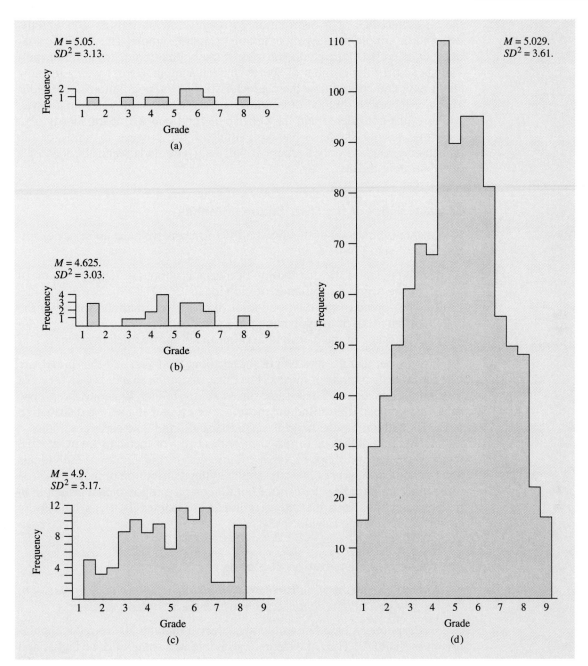

FIGURE 6–3

Distributions of the means of samples, each of two randomly drawn balls, from a population of 90,000 balls, consisting of 10,000 with each of the numbers from 1 through 9. Numbers of sample means in each distribution shown are (a) 10 sample means, (b) 20 sample means, (c) 100 sample means, and (d) 1,000 sample means. (Actual sampling simulated by computer.)

the characteristics of a distribution of means can be figured out directly, using some simple rules, without taking even one sample. The only information you need is (a) the characteristics of the population distribution of individuals and (b) the number of scores in each sample. (Don't worry for now about how you could know the characteristics of the population of individuals.) The laborious method of building up a distribution of means in the way we have just considered and the concise method you will learn shortly give the same result. We have had you think of the process in terms of the painstaking method only because it will help you understand the idea of a distribution of means.

Characteristics of the Distribution of Means

Notice three things about the distribution of means we built up in our example, as shown in Figure 6-3d.

1. The mean of the distribution of means is about the same as the mean of the original population of individuals (5).
2. The spread of the distribution of means is less than the spread of the distribution of the population of individuals.
3. The shape of the distribution of means is approximately normal.

It turns out that the first two of these, about the mean and the spread, are true for all distributions of means. The third, about the shape, is true for most distributions of means. These three observations, in fact, illustrate three basic rules that you can use to find the mean, variance, and shape of a distribution of means without having to write on plastic balls and take endless samples.

As we noted earlier, to use these rules, all you need to know are the mean, variance, and shape of the distribution of the population of individuals and the number of scores in each sample in the distribution of means. (These three rules are based on the *central limit theorem,* a fundamental principle in mathematical statistics that we mentioned in Chapter 4.) Let's look more closely at these three rules.

The Mean of a Distribution of Means

mean of a distribution of means

> **Rule 1:** The **mean of a distribution of means** is the same as the mean of the population of individuals from which the samples are taken.

Each sample is based on randomly selected individuals from the population of individuals. Thus, the mean of a sample will sometimes be higher and sometimes be lower than the mean of the whole population of individuals. However, because the selection process is random and because we are taking a very large number of samples, eventually the high means and the low means perfectly balance each other out.

Determining the Variance of a Distribution of Means

As in our example in Figure 6-3, a distribution of means will be less spread out than the population of individuals from which the samples are taken. The reason is as follows: Any one score, even an extreme score, has some chance of being selected in a random sample. The chance is less of two extreme scores being selected in the same random sample. Further, for a randomly selected sample to have an extreme sample mean, the two extreme scores would have to be extreme in the same direction (both very high or both very low). For this reason, having more scores in each sample has a moderating effect on the means of such samples. In any one sample, the extremes tend to be balanced out by middle scores or by extremes in the opposite direction. This makes each sample mean tend toward the middle and away from extreme values. With fewer extreme means, the variance of the means is less.

Consider our example. There were plenty of 1s and 9s in the population, making a fair amount of spread. That is, a ninth of the time, if you were taking samples of single scores, you would get a 1, and a ninth of the time you would get a 9. If you are taking samples of two at a time, you would get a sample with a mean of 1 (that is, in which both balls were 1s) or a mean of 9 (both balls 9s) much less often. Getting two balls that average out to a middle value such as 5 is much more likely. (This is because several combinations could give this result—a 1 and a 9, a 2 and an 8, a 3 and a 7, a 4 and a 6, or two 5s.)

The more individuals in each sample, the less spread out will be the means of those samples. This is because with several scores in each sample, it is even rarer for extremes in any particular sample not to be balanced out by middle scores or extremes in the other direction. In terms of the plastic balls in our example, we rarely got a mean of 1 when taking samples of two balls at a time. If we were taking three balls at a time, getting a sample with a mean of 1 (all three balls would have to be 1s) is even less likely. Getting middle values for the means becomes more likely.

Using samples of two balls at a time, the variance of the distribution of means came out to about 3.33. This is half of the variance of the population of individuals, which was 6.67. If we had built up a distribution of means using samples of three balls each, the variance of the distribution of means would have been 2.22. This would be one-third of the variance of the population of individuals. Had we randomly selected five balls for each sample, the variance of the distribution of means would have been one-fifth of the variance of the population of individuals.

These examples follow a general rule:

> ***Rule 2:*** *The **variance of a distribution of means** is the variance of the distribution of the population of individuals divided by the number of individuals in each of the samples.*

variance of a distribution of means

This rule holds in all situations and can be proven mathematically.

Formula for the Variance of a Distribution of Means

Stated as a formula, here is the rule for determining the variance of the distribution of means:

$$\text{Population } SD^2{}_M = \frac{\text{Population } SD^2}{N}$$

(6–1)

In this formula, Population $SD^2{}_M$ is the variance of the distribution of means. Population SD^2 is the variance of the population of individuals. N is the number of individuals in each sample.

In our example, the variance of the population of individual children's grade levels was 6.67, and there were two school children's grade levels in each sample. Thus,

$$\text{Population } SD^2_M = \frac{\text{Population } SD^2}{N} = \frac{6.67}{2} = 3.34$$

To use a different example, suppose a population had a variance of 400 and you wanted to know the variance of a distribution of means of 25 individuals each:

$$\text{Population } SD^2_M = \frac{\text{Population } SD^2}{N} = \frac{400}{25} = 16$$

The Standard Deviation of a Distribution of Means

standard deviation of a distribution of means

*Rule 2 (continued): The **standard deviation of a distribution of means** is the square root of the variance of the distribution of means.*

Stated as a formula,

$$\text{Population } SD_M = \sqrt{\text{Population } SD^2_M}$$

(6–2)

In this formula, Population SD_M is the standard deviation of the distribution of means.

standard error

The standard deviation of the distribution of means is sometimes called by a special name of its own, the *standard error of the mean,* or the **standard error,** for short. This name represents the degree to which particular means of samples are typically "in error" as estimates of the mean of the population of individuals. That is, the standard error of the mean tells you how much the particular means in the distribution of means typically deviate from the mean of the population. We will have more to say about this idea in the discussion of confidence intervals at the end of the chapter.

The Shape of a Distribution of Means

Whatever the shape of the distribution of the population of individuals, the distribution of means tends to be unimodal and symmetrical. In the grade-level example, the population distribution was rectangular. (It had an equal

shape of the distribution of means

number at each grade level.) However, the **shape of the distribution of means** was roughly that of a bell—unimodal and symmetrical. Had we taken many more than 1,000 samples, the shape would have been even more clearly unimodal and symmetrical.

A distribution of means tends to be unimodal because of the same process of extremes balancing each other out that we noted in the discussion of the variance: Middle scores for means are more likely, and extreme means are less likely. A distribution of means tends to be symmetrical because lack of symmetry (skew) is caused by extremes. With fewer extremes, there is less asymmetry. In our grade-level example, the distribution of means we built up also came out so clearly symmetrical because the population distribution of individual grade levels was symmetrical. Had the population distribution of individuals been skewed to one side, the distribution of means would have still been skewed, but not as much.

The more individuals in each sample, the closer the distribution of means will be to a normal curve. In fact, with samples of 30 or more individuals, even with a nonnormal population of individuals, the approximation of the distribution of means to a normal curve is very close and the percentages in the normal curve table will be extremely accurate.[2]

Finally, whenever the population distribution of individuals is normal, the distribution of means will be normal, regardless of the number of individuals in each sample.

Taking all this into account:

Rule 3: *The shape of a distribution of means is approximately normal if either (a) each sample is of 30 or more individuals, or (b) the distribution of the population of individuals is normal.*

(Even when both conditions are not met, the distribution of means will still tend to be unimodal and roughly symmetrical. And all of this occurs for much the same reason as we discussed in Chapter 4 when considering why things in nature in general tend to follow a normal curve, a logic we said is based on what is called the *central limit theorem.*)

Summary of the Rules for Determining the Characteristics of a Distribution of Means

Here are the three rules:

1. **The mean of a distribution of means is the same as the mean of the distribution of the population of individuals.**
2. **The variance of a distribution of means is the variance of the distribution of the population of individuals divided by the number of individuals in each sample. Its standard deviation is the square root of its variance.**
3. **The shape of a distribution of means is approximately normal if either (a) each sample is of 30 or more individuals, or (b) the distribution of the population of individuals is normal.**

These principles are shown graphically in Figure 6–4.

Example of Finding the Characteristics of a Distribution of Means

Consider the population of scores of students who have taken the Graduate Record Examinations (GRE). Suppose the distribution is approximately normal with a mean of 500 and a standard deviation of 100. What will be the characteristics of the distribution of means of samples of 50 students?

1. The mean of the population of individuals is 500. Thus, the mean of the distribution of means is also 500.

---

[2]We have ignored the fact that a normal curve is a smooth theoretical distribution. In most real-life examples, scores fall at specific intervals, such as a child being in a particular grade and not in a fraction of a grade. So one difference between our example distribution of means and a normal curve is that the normal curve is smooth. However, in social and behavioral science research, even when our measurements are at specific intervals, we usually assume that the underlying thing being measured is continuous.

FIGURE 6–4
Relation of a distribution of means (lower curve) to the distribution of the population of individuals (upper curve).

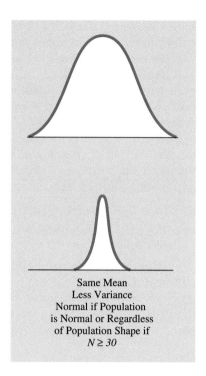

Same Mean
Less Variance
Normal if Population
is Normal or Regardless
of Population Shape if
$N \geq 30$

2. The standard deviation of the population of individuals is 100. Thus, the variance of the population of individuals is 10,000. The variance of the distribution of means is 10,000 divided by 50 (the size of each sample). This comes out to 200. In terms of the formula,

$$\text{Population } SD^2_M = \frac{\text{Population } SD^2}{N} = \frac{10,000}{50} = 200$$

The standard deviation of the distribution of means is the square root of the variance of the distribution of means: $\sqrt{200} = 14.14$.

3. The shape of the distribution of means will be normal. Both of our requirements are met: (a) each sample is well over 30; and (b) the population distribution of individuals is normal. (It would have been enough even if only one of these requirements had been met.)

Review of the Three Kinds of Distributions

We have considered three different kinds of distributions: (a) the distribution of a population of individuals, (b) the distribution of a particular sample of individuals taken from that population, and (c) the distribution of means. Figure 6–5 illustrates these three kinds of distributions and Table 6–1 describes the comparisons.

Hypothesis Testing with a Distribution of Means

Now we are ready to turn to hypothesis testing when there is more than one individual in a study's sample.

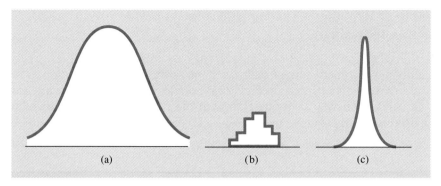

FIGURE 6–5
Three kinds of distributions: (a) the distribution of a population of individuals, (b) the distribution of a particular sample taken from that population, and (c) the distribution of means.

The Distribution of Means as the Comparison Distribution in Hypothesis Testing

In the usual situation in the social and behavioral sciences, a researcher studies a sample of more than one person. In this situation, the distribution of means is the comparison distribution. It is the distribution whose characteristics need to be determined in Step 2 of the hypothesis-testing process. The distribution of means is the distribution to which you compare your sample's mean to see how likely it is that you could have selected such a sample if the null hypothesis were true.

TABLE 6–1
Comparison of Three Types of Distributions

	Population's Distribution	A Particular Sample's Distribution	Distribution of Means
Content	Scores of all individuals in the population	Scores of the individuals in a single sample	Means of samples randomly taken from the population
Shape	Could be any shape; often normal	Could be any shape	Approximately normal if samples have ≥ 30 individuals each or if population is normal
Mean	Population M	$M = \Sigma X/N$ figured from scores of those in the sample	Population M_M = Population M
Variance	Population SD^2	$SD^2 = \Sigma (X-M)^2/N$	Population SD^2_M = Population SD^2/N
Standard Deviation	Population SD	$SD = \sqrt{SD^2}$	Population SD_M = $\sqrt{\text{Population } SD^2_M}$

Example of Hypothesis Testing with a Sample of More Than One Individual

A (fictional) team of educational researchers are interested in the effects of instructions on timed school achievement tests. These educational researchers have a theory that predicts that people will do better on a test if they are told to answer each question with the first response that comes to mind. To test this theory, the researchers give a standard school achievement

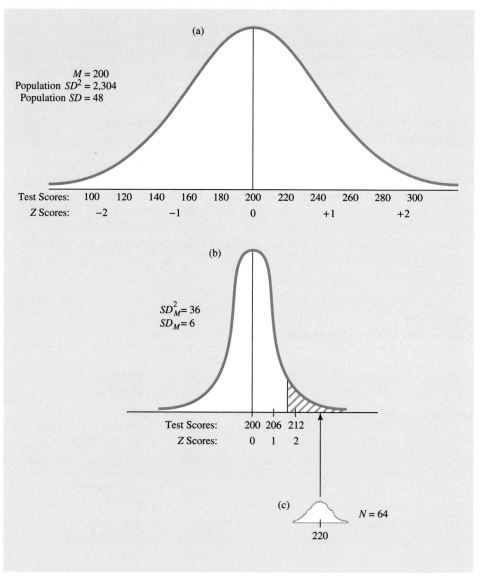

(a)

$M = 200$
Population $SD^2 = 2,304$
Population $SD = 48$

Test Scores: 100 120 140 160 180 200 220 240 260 280 300
Z Scores: −2 −1 0 +1 +2

(b)

$SD^2_M = 36$
$SD_M = 6$

Test Scores: 200 206 212
Z Scores: 0 1 2

(c) $N = 64$

220

FIGURE 6–6
For the fictional study of performance on a standard school achievement test, (a) the distribution of the population of individuals, (b) the distribution of means (the comparison distribution), and (c) the sample's distribution. The shaded area in the distribution of means is the rejection region—the area in which the null hypothesis will be rejected if the study's sample's mean turns out to be in that area.

test to 64 randomly selected fifth-grade school children. They give the test in the usual way, except that they add to the instructions an additional sentence. This additional sentence says to answer each question with the first response that comes to mind.

When given in the usual way, the test is known to have a mean of 200, a standard deviation of 48, and an approximately normal distribution. This distribution is shown in Figure 6–6a.

Let's follow the steps of hypothesis testing for this example.

1. Restate the question as a research hypothesis and a null hypothesis about the populations. The two populations are these:

Population 1: Fifth graders who get the special instructions
Population 2: Fifth graders who do not get the special instructions

The research hypothesis is that the population of fifth graders who takes the test with the special instructions will have a higher average score than the population of fifth graders who takes the test in the normal way. The null hypothesis is that Population 1's scores will not on the average be higher than Population 2's. (Note that these are directional hypotheses.)

2. Determine the characteristics of the comparison distribution. The study will give us a mean of a sample of 64 individuals (fifth graders in this case). Thus, the comparison distribution has to be the distribution of means for samples of 64 individuals each. This comparison distribution of means will have a mean of 200 (the same as the population mean). Its variance will be the population variance divided by the number of individuals in the sample. The population variance is 2,304 (the population standard deviation of 48 squared); the sample size is 64. Thus, the variance of the distribution of means will be 2,304/64, or 36. The standard deviation of the distribution of means is the square root of 36, or 6. Finally, because there are more than 30 individuals in the sample, the shape of the distribution of means will be approximately normal. Figure 6–6b shows this distribution of means.

3. Determine the cutoff sample score on the comparison distribution at which the null hypothesis should be rejected. Let's assume the researchers decide to use the standard 5% significance level. The researchers in this study have made a clear directional prediction. Also, they are not really interested in any effect in the opposite direction. If the special instructions do not improve test scores, they would not be used in the future. Any possible results showing a negative effect are irrelevant. Hence, the researchers will use a one-tailed test. Thus, they will reject the null hypothesis if the sample's mean turns out to be in the top 5% of the comparison distribution. The comparison distribution (the distribution of means) is a normal curve. Thus, the top 5% can be found from the normal curve table to start at a Z score of +1.64. This top 5% is shown as the shaded area in Figure 6–6b.

4. Determine your sample's score on the comparison distribution. Let's suppose the result of the study is that the 64 fifth graders given the special instructions had a mean of 220. (This sample's distribution is shown in Figure 6–6c.) This is 3.33 standard deviations above the mean of the distribution of means.

5. Decide whether to reject the null hypothesis. We set the minimum Z score to reject the null hypothesis at +1.64. The Z score of the sample is +3.33. Thus, the educational researchers can reject the null hypothesis and conclude that the research hypothesis is supported. To put this another way, the result is statistically significant at the $p < .05$ level. You can see this in Figure 6–6b. Note how extreme the sample's mean is on the distribution of means (the distribution that would apply if the null hypothesis were true).

The final conclusion would be that among people like those studied, the special instructions do improve test scores.

Estimation and Confidence Intervals

Hypothesis testing is our main focus in this book. However, there is another kind of statistical question related to the distribution of means that is sometimes important in the social and behavioral sciences. This other kind of question is estimating an unknown population mean based on the scores in a sample. This is important, for example, in survey research. For instance, suppose 1,000 randomly selected adults from a given region are polled on their attitude toward immigrants. The researchers will then want to use that information to estimate the attitudes of the entire population of adults in the region.

Point Estimates and Interval Estimates

The best estimate of the population mean is the sample mean. In the study of fifth graders who recieved the special instructions, the mean score for the sample of 64 fifth graders was 220. Thus, 220 is the best estimate of the mean for the unknown population of fifth graders who might ever receive the special instructions.

point estimate

interval estimate

In this example, we are estimating the specific value of the population mean. Whenever we estimate a specific value of a population parameter, this is called a **point estimate.** You also can estimate the *range* of possible means that are likely to include the population mean. For example, you might estimate that the true population mean for fifth graders who get the special instructions is between 200 and 240. This is called an **interval estimate.**

Principle and Terminology of Confidence Intervals

confidence interval

confidence limits

The wider the interval estimate, the more certain you can be that it will include the true population mean. In our fifth-grader example, you might be quite sure that the true population mean is somewhere between 100 and 340. You would be taking quite a chance of being wrong if you estimated from our sample of 64 that the true mean for the entire population is somewhere between 219 and 221.

In general, you want an interval that is wide enough to be quite sure it includes the population mean. This is called a **confidence interval.** If you want to be 95% sure, you want the *95% confidence interval.* The 95% confidence interval in the fifth-grader example is from 208.24 to 231.76. (You will learn shortly how to figure this yourself.) What the 95% confidence interval tells you is that, based on the sample studied, you can be 95% sure that the true population mean is somewhere between 208.24 and 231.76. The upper and lower ends of the confidence interval are called **confidence limits.** In this example, the confidence limits are 208.24 and 231.76.

Logic and Computation of Finding Confidence Limits

Confidence limits are about the population mean. Thus, you figure them based on the distribution of means. What you want to know are the points at which the middle 95% of means begin and end on this distribution. Thus, you need to find the cutoff points for the bottom 2.5% and the top 2.5%. (This leaves a total of 95% in the middle.)

Let's start with the lower limit. As usual, it is easiest to think in terms of Z scores. The Z score for the bottom 2.5% on a normal curve is -1.96. (You would find this from the normal curve table.) The example has a mean of 220 and a standard deviation of the distribution of means of 6. Thus, on this distribution of means, a Z score of -1.96 is 208.24. (That is, we converted the Z score of -1.96 to the raw score of 208.24 using the usual procedure for converting a Z score to a raw score.)

Figuring the upper limit works the same way. The Z score for the top 2.5% is $+1.96$. This comes out to a raw score of 231.76.

For the *99% confidence interval*, you would need to figure the scores that go with the top and bottom .5% (leaving 99% in between).

Steps for Figuring Confidence Limits

Here are three steps for figuring confidence limits. These steps assume that the distribution of means is approximately a normal distribution.

1. **Determine the characteristics of the distribution of means.**
2. **Use the normal curve table to find the Z scores that go with the upper and lower percentage you want**. For a 95% confidence interval, this is the Z score that goes with the top and bottom 2.5%. For a 99% confidence interval, this is the Z score for the top and bottom .5%.
3. **Convert these Z scores to raw scores on your distribution of means.** These are the upper and lower confidence limits.

Confidence Intervals and Hypothesis Testing

You can also use confidence intervals as a way to do hypothesis testing. If the confidence interval does not include the mean of the null hypothesis distribution, the result is significant. This is because the confidence interval says there is a 95% (or 99%) chance that the true population mean falls in a particular range. If this 95% range does not include the Population 2 mean, then there is less than a 5% chance that this sample could have come from Population 2.

Most social and behavioral science research uses ordinary hypothesis testing. However, sometimes you will see the confidence-interval method used instead. Sometimes you will see both.

Hypothesis Tests about Means of Samples and Confidence Intervals as Described in Research Articles

As we have noted several times, research in which there is a known population mean and standard deviation is rare in social and behavioral science research. We have asked you to learn about this situation mainly as a building

BOX 6-1

More about Polls: Sampling Errors and Errors in Thinking about Samples

If you think back to Box 4–1 on surveys and the Gallup poll, you will recall that we left two important questions unanswered about fine print with the results of a poll, saying something like "From a telephone poll of 1,000 American adults taken on June 4 and 5. Sampling error 63%." First, you might wonder how such small numbers like 1,000 (but rarely much less) can be used to predict the opinion of the entire U.S. public. Second, after plowing through this chapter, you may wonder what a "sampling error" means when a sample is not randomly sampled but rather selected by the complicated probability used for polls.

Regarding sample size, you know from this chapter that large sample sizes, like 1,000, greatly reduce the standard deviation of the distribution of means. That is, the curve becomes very high and narrow, gathered all around the population mean. The mean of any sample of that size is very close to being the population mean.

Still, you might persist in an intuitive feeling that the number required to represent all of the huge U.S. public might need to be larger than just 1,000. However, if you think about it, when a sample is only a small part of a very large population, the sample's absolute size is the only determiner of accuracy. This absolute size determines the impact of the random errors of measurement and selection. What remains important is reducing bias or systematic error, which can be done only by careful planning.

As for the term *sampling error,* when simple random sampling is not used, sampling error is not quite the same as the standard deviation of a distribution of means, or the confidence interval based on it, as described in this chapter. Instead, the sampling error for polls is worked out according to past experience with the sampling procedures used. It is expressed in tables for different sample sizes (usually below 1,000, because that is where error increases dramatically).

So now you understand opinion polls even better. The number of people polled is not very important (provided that it is at least 1,000 or so). What matters very much, however, is the method of sampling and estimating error, which will not be reported even in the fine print in the detail necessary to judge whether the results are reliable. The reputation of the organization doing the survey is probably the best criterion. If the sampling and error-estimating approach is not revealed, be cautious.

Z test

block for understanding hypothesis testing in common research situations. In the rare situation in which research with a known population distribution is conducted, it is often described as a **Z test,** because it is the Z score that is checked against the normal curve.

Here is an example. As part of a larger study, Wiseman (1997) gave a loneliness test to a group of college students in Israel. As a first step in examining the results, Wiseman checked that the average score on the loneliness test was not different from a known population distribution based on a large U.S. study of university students that had been conducted earlier by Russell et al. (1980). Wiseman reported:

> . . . [T]he mean loneliness scores of the current Israeli sample were similar to those of Russell et al.'s (1980) university sample for both males (Israeli: $M = 38.74$, $SD = 9.30$; Russell: $M = 37.06$, $SD = 10.91$; $z = 1.09$, NS) and females (Israeli: $M = 36.39$, $SD = 8.87$; Russell: $M = 36.06$, $SD = 10.11$; $z = .25$, NS). (p. 291)

In this example, the researcher gives the standard deviation for both the sample studied (the Israeli group) and the population (the data from Russell). However, in the steps of computing each Z (the sample's score on the distribution of means), they would have used the standard deviation only for the population. Notice also that the researcher took the nonsignificance of the difference as support for the sample means being "similar" to the population means. However, the researcher was very careful not to claim that these results showed there was no difference.

Of the topics we have covered in this chapter, the one you are most likely to see discussed in a research article is the standard deviation of the distribution of means, used as an indication of the amount of variation that might be expected among means of samples of a given size from this population. In this context, it is usually called the *standard error,* abbreviated *SE.* Often the lines that go above and below the tops of the bars in a bar graph are for the standard error. For example, Lee et al. (2000) tested a theory of the role of distinctiveness in face perception. In their study, participants indicated whether or not they recognized each of 48 faces of male celebrities when they were shown rapidly on a computer screen. A third of the faces were shown in a "Caricature" form, in which facial features were electronically modified so that distinctive features were slightly exaggerated; a third were shown in "Veridical" form, in which the faces were not modified at all; and a third were shown in "Anticaricature" form, in which facial features were modified to be slightly more like the average of the celebrities' faces. The average percent correct across their participants is shown in Figure 6-7 (reproduced from their Figure 2), which includes error bars.

Confidence intervals are sometimes reported in research articles, especially in surveys. A researcher might explain that the average number of overtime hours worked in a particular industry is 3.7 with a 95% confidence interval of 2.5 to 4.9. This would tell you that the true average number of overtime hours is probably somewhere between 2.5 and 4.9, which may be accurate enough for most purposes. For example, Anderson et al. (2000) report that "Responses from the NHIS [National Health Interview Survey] indicate that by 1995, 39.7% of adults (95% CI = 38.8%, 40.5%) had been tested at least once . . ." (p. 1090). "CI" refers to confidence interval.

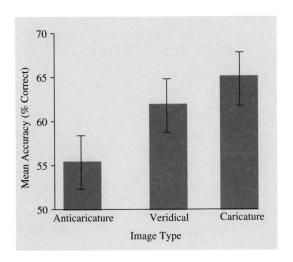

FIGURE 6–7
Identification accuracy as a function of image type. Standard error bars are shown. (From "Caricature Effects, Distinctiveness, and Identification: Testing the Face-Space Framework" by Kieran Lee, Graham Byatt, and Gillian Rhodes. *Psychological Science,* Vol. 11, September, 2000, p. 381. Reprinted by permission of Blackwell Publishers Journals.)

Summary

1. When studying a sample of more than one individual, the comparison distribution in the hypothesis-testing process is a distribution of means. It can be thought of as describing what the result would be of (a) taking a very large number of samples, each of the same number of scores taken randomly from the population of individuals, and then (b) making a distribution of the means of these samples.
2. The distribution of means has the same mean as the population of individuals. However, it has a smaller variance because the means of samples are less likely to be extreme than individual scores. (In any one sample, extreme scores are likely to be balanced by middle scores or extremes in the other direction.) Specifically, the variance of the distribution of means is the variance of the population of individuals divided by the number of individuals in each sample. Its standard deviation is the square root of its variance. The shape of the distribution of means approximates a normal curve if either (a) the samples are each of 30 or more individuals or (b) the population of individuals is normally distributed.
3. Hypothesis tests involving a single sample of more than one individual and a known population are done in the same way as the hypothesis tests of Chapter 5 (where the studies were of a single individual compared to population of individual scores). The main exception is that the comparison distribution is now a distribution of means.
4. The best point estimate for the population mean is the sample mean. You can make an interval estimate of the population mean based on the distribution of means. The 95% confidence interval will be the middle 95% of the distribution of means.
5. The kind of hypothesis test described in this chapter is rarely used in research practice. (You have learned it as a stepping stone.) The standard deviation of the distribution of means, often called the standard error *(SE)*, is sometimes used to describe the expected variability of means, particularly in bar graphs in which the standard error may be shown as the length of a line above and below the top of each bar. Confidence intervals are sometimes reported in research articles, particularly when describing results of surveys.

Key Terms

confidence interval
confidence limits
distribution of means
interval estimate
mean of a distribution of means

point estimate
shape of a distribution of means
standard deviation of a distribution of means (Population SD_M)

standard error *(SE)*
variance of a distribution of means (Population SD^2M)
Z test

Practice Problems

These problems involve computation. Most real-life statistics problems are done on a computer. Even if you have a computer and statistics software, do these problems by hand (with the help of a calculator) to ingrain the method in your mind.

For practice in using a computer to solve statistics problems, refer to the computer section of each chapter of the Student's Study Guide and Computer Workbook *that accompanies this text.*

All data are fictional.

Answers to selected problems are given at the back of this book.

1. Explain why the standard deviation of a distribution of means is generally smaller than the standard deviation of the distribution of the population of individuals.

2. A population of individuals has a standard deviation of 10. What is the standard deviation of the distribution of means for samples of size (a) 2, (b) 3, (c) 4, (d) 5, (e) 10, (f) 20, (g) 100?

3. For (a)–(g) in Problem 2, compute the 95% confidence interval (that is, the upper and lower confidence limit). Assume that in each case the researcher's sample has a mean of 100 and that the population of individuals is known to follow a normal curve.

4. A particular population of individuals has a mean of 40, has a standard deviation of 6, and follows a normal curve. For each of the following samples, indicate whether it would be less likely than 5% to be randomly selected from this population: (a) a sample of 10 with a mean of 44, (b) a sample of 1 with a mean of 48, (c) a sample of 81 with a mean of 42, (d) a sample of 16 with a mean of 42. For each part, show how you arrived at your answer and include a diagram of the distributions involved. (Use one-tailed tests throughout.)

5. Twenty-five women between the ages of 70 and 80 were randomly selected from the general population of women their age to take part in a special program to decrease reaction time. After the course, the women had an average reaction time of 1.5 seconds. Assume that the mean reaction time for the general population of women of this age group is 1.8, with a standard deviation of .5 seconds. (Also assume that the population is approximately normal.) What should you conclude about the effectiveness of the course? (a) Carry out the steps of hypothesis testing (use the .01 level). (b) Compute the 99% confidence interval. (c) Explain your answer to someone who is familiar with the general logic of hypothesis testing, the normal curve, Z scores, and probability, but who is not familiar with the idea of a distribution of means or confidence intervals.

6. A large number of people have seen a particular film of an automobile collision between a moving car and a stopped car. Each person then filled out a questionnaire about how likely it was that the driver of the moving car was at fault, on a scale from *not at fault* = 0 and *completely at fault* = 10. The distribution of ratings under ordinary conditions is known and turns out to be normally distributed with a mean of 5.5 and a standard deviation of .8. Sixteen randomly selected individuals are tested under conditions in which the wording of the question is changed so that instead of calling them just Car A and Car B, the question asks, "How likely is it that the driver of the car that crashed into the other was at fault?" Using this instruction (which uses the words "crashed into"), these 16 individuals gave a mean at-fault rating of 5.9. Using the 5% significance level, did the changed instructions significantly increase the rating of being at fault? (a) Carry out the steps of hypothesis testing. (b) Compute the 95% confidence interval. (c) Explain your answer to someone who has never taken statistics.

7. A researcher is interested in whether North Americans are able to identify emotions correctly in people from other cultures. It is known that, using a particular method of measurement, the accuracy ratings of adult North Americans in general are normally distributed with a mean of 82 and a variance of 20. This distribution is based on ratings made of emotions expressed by other North Americans. In this study, however, the researcher arranges to test 50 adult North Americans rating emotions of individuals from Indonesia. The mean accuracy for these 50 individuals was 78. Using the .05 level, what should the researcher conclude? (a) Carry out the steps of hypothesis testing. (b) Compute the 95% confidence interval. (c) Explain your answer to a person who understands hypothesis testing with a sample of a single individual but knows nothing about a distribution of means or how to do hypothesis testing involving a sample of more than a single individual.

8. Cut up 100 small slips of paper, and write each number from 0 to 9 on 10 slips each. Put the 100 slips in a large bowl and mix them up. Now take out a slip, write down on a separate sheet of paper the number on it, and put it back. Do this 20 times. Make a histogram, and figure the mean and the variance of the result. You should get an approximately rectangular distribution. Then take two slips out, figure out their mean, write it down, and put the slips back. Repeat this process about 20 times. Make a histogram, and figure the mean and the variance of this distribution of means. The variance should be about half of the variance of the distribution of samples of one slip each. Finally, repeat the process again, this time taking three slips at a time. This distribution of means of three slips each should have a variance of about a third of the distribution of samples of one slip each. Also note that as the sample size increases, your distributions are getting closer to normal. (Had you begun with a normally distributed distribution of slips, your distributions of means would have been fairly close to normal regardless of the number in each sample.)

7

Making Sense of Statistical Significance:
Decision Error, Statistical Power, and Effect Size

Statistical significance is extremely important in social and behavioral science research, but it can also be misused. Sophisticated researchers and readers of research understand that there is more to the story of a research result than $p < .05$ or *ns*. This chapter helps you become sophisticated about significance.

Gaining this sophistication means learning about three closely interrelated issues: decision error, statistical power, and effect size. This chapter builds very directly on Chapters 5 and 6. We do not recommend embarking on this chapter until you have a strong grasp of the key material in those chapters, especially hypothesis testing and the distribution of means.

Decision Errors

The kind of error we consider here is about how, in spite of doing all your figuring correctly, your conclusions from hypothesis testing can still be incorrect. It is *not* about making mistakes in calculations or even about using the wrong procedures. That is, **decision errors** are a situation in which the right procedures lead to the wrong decisions.

decision errors

Decision errors are possible in hypothesis testing because we are making decisions about populations based on information in samples. The whole hypothesis-testing process is based on probabilities. The hypothesis-testing process is set up to make the probability of decision errors as small as possible. For example, we decide to reject the null hypothesis only if a sample's mean is so extreme that there is a very small probability (say, less than 5%) that we could have gotten such an extreme sample if the null hypothesis were true. Yet a very small probability is not the same as a zero probability! Thus, in spite of our best intentions, decision errors are always possible.

There are two kinds of decision errors in hypothesis testing: Type I error and Type II error.

Type I Error

You make a **Type I error** when you reject the null hypothesis when in fact the null hypothesis is true. Or to put it in terms of the research hypothesis, you make a Type I error when you conclude that the study supports the research hypothesis when in reality the research hypothesis is false.

Type I error

Suppose you carried out a study in which you had set the significance-level cutoff at a very lenient probability level, such as 20%. This would mean that it would not take a very extreme result to reject the null hypothesis. If you did many studies like this, you would often (about 20% of the time) be deciding to consider the research hypothesis supported when you should not. That is, you would have a 20% chance of making a Type I error.

Even when you set the probability at .05 or .01, you can still make a Type I error sometimes (to be precise, 5% or 1% of the time). Consider the example from the last chapter on giving special instructions intended to make fifth graders perform better on a standard achievement test. Suppose the special instructions in reality make no difference whatsoever. However, in randomly picking a sample of fifth graders to study, the researchers might just happen to pick a group of fifth graders to be in the study who would do unusually well on the test no matter what kind of instructions you gave them. Randomly selecting a sample like this is unlikely because in general a random sample, especially one of 64 individuals, will have a mean that is close to the population mean. However, such extreme samples are possible, and should this happen, the researchers would reject the null hypothesis and conclude that the special instructions do make a difference. Their decision to reject the null hypothesis would be wrong—a Type I error. Of course the researchers could not know they had made a decision error of this kind. What reassures researchers is that they know from the logic of hypothesis testing that the probability of making such a decision error is kept low (less than 5% if you use the .05 significance level).

Still, the fact that Type I errors can happen at all is of serious concern to social scientists, who might construct entire theories and research programs, not to mention practical applications, based on a conclusion from hypothesis testing that is in fact mistaken. It is because these errors are of such serious concern that they are called Type I.

As we have noted, researchers cannot tell when they have made a Type I error. However, they can try to carry out studies so that the chance of making a Type I error is as small as possible.

What is the chance of making a Type I error? It is the same as the significance level we set. If we set the significance level at $p < .05$, we are saying we will reject the null hypothesis if there is less than a 5% (.05) chance that we could have gotten our result if the null hypothesis were true. When rejecting the null hypothesis in this way, we are allowing up to 5% chance that we got our results even though the null hypothesis was actually true. That is, we are allowing a 5% chance of a Type I error. (You will sometimes see the significance level, the chance of making a Type I error, referred to as *alpha,* the Greek letter α.)

Again, the significance level is the same as the chance of making a Type I error. Thus, the lower probability we set for the significance level, the smaller the chance of a Type I error. Researchers who do not want to take a lot of risk set the significance level lower than .05, such as $p < .001$. In this way the result of a study has to be very extreme in order for the hypothesis testing process to reject the null hypothesis.

Using a .001 significance level is like buying insurance against making a Type I error. However, as when buying insurance, the better the protection, the higher the cost. There is a cost in setting the significance level at too extreme a level. We turn to that cost next.

Type II Error

If you set a very stringent significance level, such as .001, you run a different kind of risk. With a very stringent significance level, you can carry out a study in which in reality the research hypothesis is true, but the result does not come out extreme enough to reject the null hypothesis. Thus, the decision error you would make is in *not* rejecting the null hypothesis when in fact the null hypothesis is false. To put this in terms of the research hypothesis, you make this kind of decision error when the hypothesis testing procedure leads you to decide that the results of the study are inconclusive when in reality the research hypothesis is true. This is called a **Type II error.**

Type II error

Consider again our fifth-grader example. Suppose that, in truth, giving the special instructions *does* make fifth graders do better on the test. However, in conducting your particular study, the results are not strong enough to allow you to reject the null hypothesis. Perhaps the random sample that you selected to try out the new instructions happened to include mainly fifth graders who do very poorly on this kind of test regardless of the instructions given. As we have seen, even though the special instructions might help them do better than they would have otherwise, their scores may still not be much higher than the average of all fifth graders. The results would not be significant. Having decided not to reject the null hypothesis, and thus refusing to draw a conclusion, would be a Type II error.

Type II errors especially concern social scientists interested in practical applications, because a Type II error could mean that a valuable practical procedure is not used.

As with a Type I error, we cannot know when we have made a Type II error, but we can try to conduct our studies so as to reduce the probability of making one. One way of buying insurance against a Type II error is to set a very lenient significance level, such as $p < .10$ or even $p < .20$. In this way, even if a study results in only a very small effect, the results have a good chance of being significant. There is a cost to this insurance policy too.

Relation of Type I and Type II Errors

When it comes to setting significance levels, protecting against one kind of decision error increases the chance of making the other. The insurance policy against Type I error (setting a significance level, of say, .001) has that cost that you increase the chance of making a Type II error. (This is because with a stringent significance level like .001, even if the research hypothesis is true, the results have to be quite strong to be extreme enough to reject the null hypothesis.) The insurance policy against Type II error (setting a significance level, of say, .20) has the cost that you increase the chance of making a Type I error. (This is because with a level of significance like .20, even if the null hypothesis is true, it is fairly easy to get a significant result just by accidentally getting a sample that is higher or lower than the general population before doing the study.)

The trade-off between these two conflicting concerns usually is worked out by compromise—thus the standard 5% and 1% significance levels.

Summary of Possible Outcomes of Hypothesis Testing

The entire issue of possible correct and mistaken conclusions in hypothesis testing is diagrammed in Table 7–1. Along the top of this table are the two possibilities about whether the null hypothesis or the research hypothesis is really true. (You never actually know this.) Along the side is whether, after hypothesis testing, you decide that the research hypothesis is supported (reject the null hypothesis) or decide that the results are inconclusive (do not reject the null hypothesis). Table 7–1 shows that there are two ways to be correct and two ways to be in error in any hypothesis-testing situation. We will have more to say about these possibilities after we consider the topic of statistical power.

TABLE 7-1
Possible Correct and Incorrect Decisions in Hypothesis Testing

		Real Situation (in practice, unknown)	
		Null Hypothesis True	*Research Hypothesis True*
Conclusion Using Hypothesis-testing Procedure	*Research hypothesis supported (reject null hypothesis)*	Error (Type I)	Correct decision
	Study is inconclusive (do not reject null hypothesis)	Correct decision	Error (Type II)

Statistical Power

statistical power

Power is the ability to achieve your goals. A goal of a researcher conducting a study is to get a significant result—but only *if* the research hypothesis really is true. The **statistical power** of a research study is the probability that the study will produce a statistically significant result if the research hypothesis is true.

Notice that the power of an experiment is about the situation *if* the research hypothesis is true. If the research hypothesis is false, we do not want to get significant results. (That would be a Type I error.)

Now you may ask, "If the research hypothesis is true, won't the experiment automatically give a significant result?" The answer is no. The particular sample that happens to be selected from the population may not turn out to be extreme enough to reject the null hypothesis.

As you will learn in this chapter, statistical power is important for several reasons. For example, computing power when planning a study helps you figure out how many participants you need. Also, understanding power is extremely important when you read a research article, particularly for making sense of results that are not significant or results that are statistically but not practically significant.

An Example

Consider again our example of the effects of giving special instructions to fifth graders taking a standard achievement test. In the hypothesis-testing process for this example, we compared two populations:

Population 1: Fifth graders receiving special instructions
Population 2: Fifth graders not receiving special instructions

The research hypothesis was that Population 1 would score higher than Population 2.

The top distribution of means in Figure 7–1 shows a situation in which this research hypothesis is true. The bottom of the figure shows the distribution for Population 2.

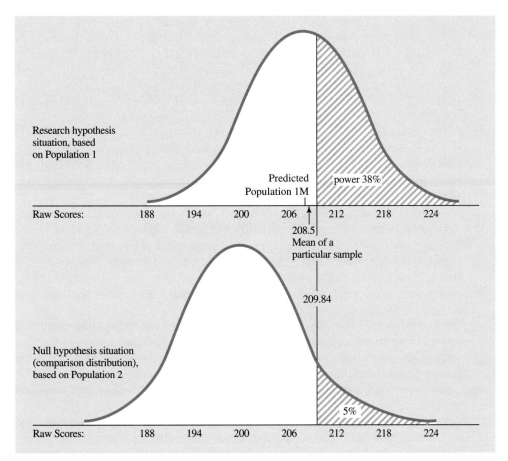

FIGURE 7–1
Distributions of mean test scores of 64 fifth graders from a fictional study of fifth graders taking a standard achievement test. The lower distribution of means is based on a known distribution of individual test scores of fifth graders who do not receive any special instructions (Population 2). The upper distribution of means is based on a predicted distribution of individual test scores of fifth graders who receive the special instructions (Population 1). The researchers predict a mean of 208 for this population. Shaded sections of both distributions are the area in which the null hypothesis will be rejected. Power = 38%.

The bottom distribution is also the comparison distribution, the distribution of means that you would expect for both populations if the null hypothesis were true. The shaded part of the right tail of this bottom distribution is the area where you would reject the null hypothesis if, as a result of your study, the mean of your sample was in this area. The shaded rejection area begins at 209.84 (a Z score of 1.64), taking up 5% of this comparison distribution.

The top curve is the distribution of means that the researchers *predict* for the population receiving special instructions (Population 1). In the last chapter, we never talked about this distribution. This was partly because this population is quite imaginary—*unless* the research hypothesis is true. If the null hypothesis is true, the distribution for Population 1 is the same as the distribution based on Population 2. The Population 1 distribution would not be set off to the right.

However, to learn about power, we now consider the situation in which the research hypothesis is true. In this situation, for this example, the mean of Population 1 is farther to the right than the mean of Population 2. Specifically, the upper distribution of means (for predicted Population 1) is shown with a mean of 208. The comparison distribution's mean is only 200. This is to show that the population receiving the special instructions (Population 1) is predicted to have, on the average, scores that are eight points higher.

Now, suppose the researchers carry out the study. They give the special instructions to a randomly selected group of 64 fifth graders and find their mean score on the test. Remember, if the research hypothesis is true, the mean of their group of 64 students is from a distribution like the upper distribution of means.

In this example, however, this upper distribution of means (from the researchers' prediction about Population 1) is only slightly to the right of the comparison distribution. That is, the researchers are predicting that the special instructions will produce only a small increase in scores (8 points). Thus the upper, predicted distribution is only a small distance to the right of the lower, comparison distribution. What this picture tells us is that most of the means from this upper distribution will not be far enough to the right on the lower distribution to reject the null hypothesis. That is, less than half of the upper distribution is shaded. Put another way, if the research hypothesis is true, the sample we study is in effect a random sample from the distribution shown here based on Population 1. However, there is less than a 50-50 chance that such a random sample from this population will be in the shaded area.

For example, suppose the particular sample of 64 fifth graders studied had a mean of 208.5, as shown by the arrow under this distribution in the figure. However, you need a mean of at least 209.84 to reject the null hypothesis. Thus, the result of this experiment would not be statistically significant. It would not be significant even though we are assuming here the research hypothesis really is true. That is, we would have made a Type II error.

It is entirely possible that the researchers might happen to select a sample from Population 1 with a mean far enough to the right (that is, with a high enough mean test score) to be in the area. However, given the way we have set up the example, there is a better-than-even chance that the study will *not* turn out significant, *even though we know the research hypothesis is true.* (Of course, once again, the researcher would not know this.) When a study like the one in this example has only a small chance of being significant even if the research hypothesis is true, we say the study has low power.

Suppose, on the other hand, the situation was one in which we expected an upper curve far to the right of the lower curve, so that almost any sample taken from the upper curve would be in the shaded rejection area in the lower curve. In that situation, the study would have high power.

Figuring Statistical Power

The statistical power of a study can be calculated. In a situation like the fifth-grader-testing example, calculating power involves figuring out the area of the shaded portion of the upper distribution in Figure 7–1. However, the computations are somewhat laborious. Further, the calculations become quite complex once we consider, starting in the next chapter, more realistic hypothesis-testing situations. Thus, instead of calculating power themselves, researchers usually find the power of a study using special charts called **power tables.** (Such tables have been prepared by Cohen, 1988, and Kraemer & Thiemann, 1987, among others.) In the following chapters, with each method you learn, we will provide basic power tables and discuss how to use them.

power tables

Thus, you will not be learning to calculate power in this book. However, it is very important that you understand what power is about. It is especially important to understand the factors that affect the power of a study and how to use power when planning a study and when making sense of a study you read.

What Determines the Power of a Study

The statistical power of a study depends on two main factors: The first is how big an effect the research hypothesis predicts. This first factor of effect size involves both how far apart the means are predicted to be and how much variance is expected in the population. The second main factor is how many participants are in the sample studied. Power also is affected by (a) the significance level chosen, (b) whether a one- or two-tailed test is used, and (c) the kind of hypothesis-testing procedure used.

Effect Size

Figure 7–1 shows the situation in which the researchers predicted that those who got the special instructions (Population 1, the top curve) would have a mean score eight points higher than fifth graders in general (Population 2, the bottom curve). Figure 7–2 shows the same study for a situation in which the researchers predicted that those who got the special instructions would have a mean 16 points higher than fifth graders in general. Compare Figure 7–2 to Figure 7–1. You are more likely to get a significant result in the situation shown in Figure 7–2. This is because there is more overlap of the top curve with the shaded area on the comparison distribution. In fact, it turns out that the probability of getting a significant result (the power) for the situation in Figure 7–1 is only 38%. However, for the situation in Figure 7–2, the power is 85%. In any study, the bigger the difference we expect between the means of the two populations, the more power in the study.

Figure 7–3 shows two distributions of means based on the same example. However, this time we have changed the example so that the variance is much smaller. In this example, the standard deviation in the distribution of means is exactly half of what it was in Figure 7–1. In this example, the predicted mean is the 208 from our original example, but both curves are much narrower. Therefore, there is much more overlap between the upper curve and the shaded rejection area on the lower curve (the comparison distribution). The result is that the power is much higher (85%) than in the Figure 7–1 situation (where, again, it was only 38%).

Overall, these examples illustrate the general principle that the less overlap between the two distributions, the more likely that a study will give a

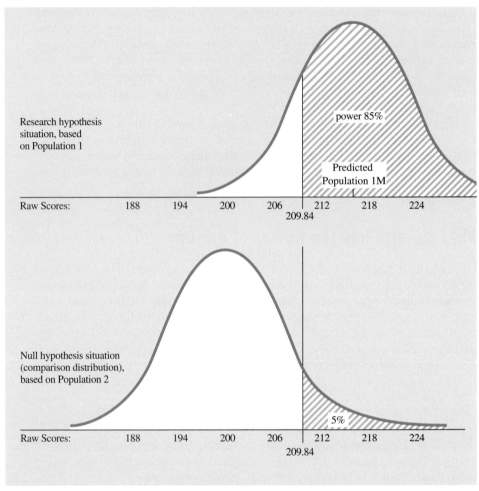

FIGURE 7–2
Distributions of means of test scores of 64 fifth graders based on predicted (upper) and known (lower) distributions of populations of individuals. (From a fictional study of fifth graders taking a standard achievement test.) Scores are shown on both distributions for the significance cutoff on the lower distribution (the significance cutoff is based on $p < .05$, one-tailed). In this example, the predicted mean of the upper distribution is 216. Power = 85%.

significant result. (Don't get confused here. Power is greater when there is *less* overlap between the two distributions. This is precisely because less overlap between the distributions overall creates *more* overlap between the top, predicted distribution and the *rejection area* of the bottom, comparison distribution.) Two distributions might have little overlap overall either because there is a large difference between their means (as in Figure 7–2) or because they have so little variance that even with a small mean difference they do not overlap much (as in Figure 7–3). This principle is summarized more generally in Figure 7–4.

    The extent to which the two populations overall do not overlap is called the **effect size** because it is the extent to which the experimental procedure has an *effect* of separating the two populations. That is, the larger the difference expected between the two population means, the greater the effect size;

effect size

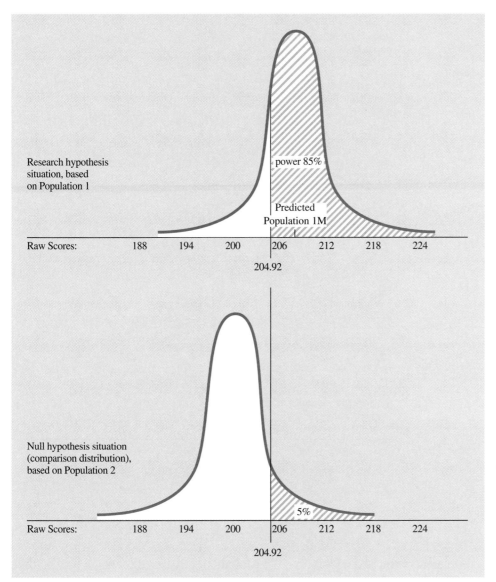

FIGURE 7–3
Distributions of means of test scores of 64 fifth graders based on predicted (upper) and known (lower) distributions of populations of individuals. (From a fictional study of fifth graders taking a standard achievement test.) Scores are shown on both distributions for the significance cutoff on the lower distribution (the significance cutoff is based on $p < .05$, one-tailed). In this example, the population standard deviation is half as large as that shown in the original example in Figure 7–1. Power = 85%.

and the smaller the variance within the two populations, the greater the effect size. The greater the effect size, the greater the power.

Figuring Effect Size

To determine the power of a study you are planning, you first need to figure your predicted effect size. The predicted effect size is based on two numbers. The first number is the researcher's prediction of the difference between the

FIGURE 7–4
The predicted and comparison distributions of means might have little overlap (and thus the study would have high power) because either (a) the two means are very different or (b) the variance is very small.

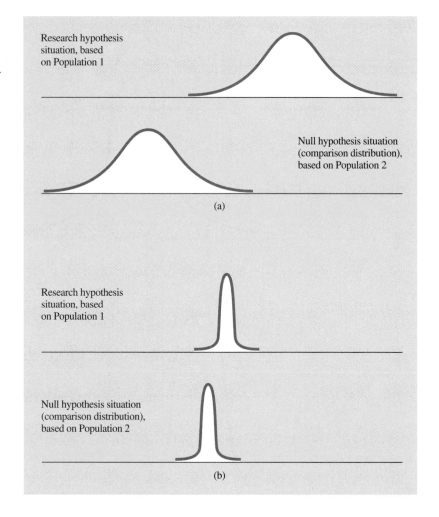

Research hypothesis situation, based on Population 1

Null hypothesis situation (comparison distribution), based on Population 2

(a)

Research hypothesis situation, based on Population 1

Null hypothesis situation (comparison distribution), based on Population 2

(b)

means of the two populations. This prediction is based on some precise theory, on previous experience with research of this kind, or on what would be the smallest difference that would be useful. The second number is the population standard deviation. In the situations we have considered so far, the standard deviation (or the variance) is known in advance.

Here is the rule for calculating effect size: Divide the predicted difference between the means by the population standard deviation.[1] Stated as a formula,

$$\text{Effect Size} = \frac{\text{Population 1 } M \ - \ \text{Population 2 } M}{\text{Population } SD}$$

(7–1)

[1]This procedure gives a measure of effect size called "Cohen's *d*." It is the preferred method for the kind of hypothesis testing you have learned so far. (In later chapters, you learn of other measures of effect size that are appropriate to other hypothesis-testing situations.)

Notice that when figuring effect size you don't use the standard deviation of the distribution of means. Instead, you use the standard deviation of the population of individuals. Also notice that you are concerned with only one population's *SD*. This is because in hypothesis testing you usually assume that both populations have the same standard deviation. (We will say more about this in later chapters.)

Consider the fifth-grader example in Figure 7–1 with which we began. The difference between the two population means is 8 and the standard deviation of the populations of individuals is 48. Thus, the effect size is 8/48, or .17. In terms of the formula,

$$\text{Effect Size} = \frac{\text{Population 1 } M - \text{Population 2 } M}{\text{Population } SD} = \frac{208 - 200}{48} = \frac{8}{48} = .17$$

Now consider the next example (from Figure 7–2), where the mean difference is 16 test points and the population standard deviation is still 48. The effect size is doubled: 16/48, or .33. When we use a mean difference of 8 with a population standard deviation of 24 (the example of Figure 7–3), the effect size is 8/24, which also happens to be .33.

A More General Importance of Effect Size

Effect size, as we have seen, is the difference between means divided by the population standard deviation. This division by the population standard deviation standardizes the difference between means, in the same way that a *Z* score gives a standard for comparison to other scores, even scores on different scales. Especially by using the standard deviation of the population of individuals, we bypass the variation from study to study of different sample sizes, making comparison even easier and effect size even more of a standard.

Knowing the effect size of a study lets you compare results with effect sizes found in other studies, even when the other studies have different sample sizes. Equally important, knowing the effect size lets you compare studies using different measures, even if those measures have different means and variances.

Also, within a particular study, our general knowledge of what is a small or a large effect size helps you evaluate the overall importance of a result. For example, a result may be statistically significant but not very large. Or a result that is not statistically significant (perhaps due to a small sample) may have just as large an effect size as another study (perhaps one with a larger sample) where the result was significant. Knowing the effect sizes of the studies helps us make better sense of such results. We examine both of these important implications of effect size in later sections of this chapter.

An important development in statistics in recent years is a procedure called **meta-analysis.** This procedure combines results from different studies, even results using different methods of measurement. When combining results, the crucial thing combined is the effect sizes. As an example, a sociologist might be interested in the effects of cross-race friendships on prejudice, a topic on which there has been a large number of surveys. Using

meta-analysis

meta-analysis, the sociologist could combine the results of these surveys. This would provide an overall effect size. It also would tell how effect size differs for studies done in different countries or about prejudice towards different ethnic groups. (For an example of such a study, see Pettigrew & Meertens, 1995). For another example of meta-analysis, see Box 7–1, "Effect Sizes for Relaxation and Meditation: A Restful Meta-Analysis."

BOX 7–1

Effect Sizes for Relaxation and Meditation: A Restful Meta-Analysis

In the 1970s and 1980s, the results of research on meditation and relaxation were the subject of considerable controversy. Eppley et al. (1989) decided to look at the issue systematically by conducting a meta-analysis of the effects of various relaxation techniques on trait anxiety (that is, ongoing anxiety as opposed to a temporary state). Eppley and colleagues chose trait anxiety for their meta-analysis because it is a definite problem related to many other mental health issues, yet in itself is fairly consistent from test to test with the same measure and from one measure to another measure of it.

Following the usual procedure, the researchers culled the scientific literature for studies—not only research journals but also books and unpublished doctoral dissertations. Finding all the relevant research is one of the most difficult parts of meta-analysis.

To find the "bottom line," Eppley et al. compared effect sizes for each of the four main methods of meditation and relaxation that have been studied in systematic research. The result was that the average effect size for the 35 Transcendental Meditation (TM) studies was .70 (meaning an average difference of .70 standard deviation in anxiety scores between those who practiced this meditation procedure versus those in the control groups). This effect size was significantly larger than the average effect size of .28 for the 44 studies on all other types of meditation, the average effect size of .38 for the 30 "progressive relaxation" (a widely used method by clinical psychologists), and the average effect size of .40 for the 37 studies on other forms of relaxation.

However, the meta-analysis had really just begun. There were many subvariables of interest. For example, looking at different populations of research participants, they discovered that people who were screened to be highly anxious contributed more to the effect size, and prison populations and younger subjects seemed to gain more from TM. There was no impact on effect size of the skill of the instructors, expectations of the subjects, whether subjects had volunteered or been randomly assigned to conditions, experimenter bias (the TM results were actually stronger when any apparently pro-TM researchers' data were eliminated), the various measures of anxiety, and the research designs.

The researchers thought that one clue to TM's high performance might be that techniques involving concentration produced a significantly smaller effect, whereas TM makes a point of teaching an "effortless, spontaneous" method. Also, TM uses Sanskrit mantras (special sounds) said to come from a very old tradition and selected for each student by the instructor. Results were lower for methods employing randomly selected Sanskrit sounds or personally selected English words.

Whatever the reasons, the authors concluded that there are "grounds for optimism that at least some current treatment procedures can effectively reduce trait anxiety" (p. 973). So if you are prone to worry about little matters like statistics exams, consider these results.

Effect Size Conventions

It's hard to know how big an effect size to expect before you do a study. If you knew, you would not need to do the study. Jacob Cohen (1988), a researcher who did a great deal of work in developing the statistics of power, has helped solve this problem. Cohen came up with some **effect size conventions** based on the effects observed in many actual studies. These conventions at least tell a researcher what to consider as a small, medium, and large effect. If the researcher believes a particular study should have a medium effect, the researcher now has a specific number that Cohen said is typical of medium effects. The researcher can then use that number to compute power (or to look it up on a table).

effect size conventions

Recall that we figured effect size as the predicted difference between the means of the two populations, divided by the population standard deviation. Cohen recommended that for the kind of situation we are considering in this chapter, we should think of a "small effect size" as about .2. Cohen noted that with an effect size of .2, the populations of individuals have an overlap of about 85%. This small effect size of .2 is, for example, the average difference in height between 15- and 16-year-old girls (see Figure 7–5a), which is about a half-inch difference with a standard deviation of about 2.1 inches. (When

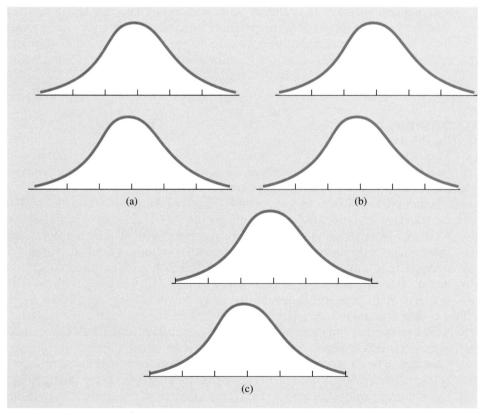

FIGURE 7–5
Comparisons of pairs of population distributions of individuals showing Cohen's conventions for effect size: (a) small effect size (.2), (b) medium effect size (.5), (c) large effect size (.8).

TABLE 7–2
Summary of Cohen's Effect Size Conventions for Mean Differences

Verbal Description	Effect Size
Small	.2
Medium	.5
Large	.8

we speak of percentage overlap in these examples, we are referring to the overlap of the populations of individuals. The amount of overlap of the distributions of means will be less, depending on the sample size.)

Cohen considered a medium effect size to be .5, which means an overlap of about 67%. This is about the average difference in heights between 14- and 18-year-old girls (see Figure 7–5b). Finally, Cohen defined a large effect size as .8. This is only about 53% overlap. It is about the average difference in height between 13- and 18-year-old girls (see Figure 7–5c). These three effect sizes are summarized in Table 7–2.

Consider another example. As we noted earlier in the book, many IQ tests have a standard deviation of 16 points. An experimental procedure with a small effect size would be an increase of 3.2 IQ points. (A difference of 3.2 IQ points between the mean of the population who goes through the experimental procedure and the population that does not, divided by the population standard deviation of 16, gives an effect size of .2.) An experimental procedure with a medium effect size would increase IQ by 8 points. An experimental procedure with a large effect size would increase IQ by 12.8 points.

Cohen's effect size conventions are important to researchers because in many research situations it is hard to know in advance how big an effect size to predict. (If you can't predict the effect size, you can't even look up the power on a table.) Sometimes researchers can base their predictions of effect size on previous research or theory. Also, sometimes there is a smallest effect size that would matter for some practical purpose. However, in many situations, researchers are studying something for the first time, and they can only make the vaguest guess about the amount of effect they expect. Cohen's conventions help researchers turn that vague guess into a number.

Sample Size

The other major influence on power, besides effect size, is the number of people in the sample that is studied, the sample size. Basically, the more people there are in the study, the more power.

Sample size affects power because the larger the sample size, the smaller the standard deviation of the distribution of means. If these distributions have a smaller standard deviation, they are narrower. And if they are narrower, there is less overlap between them. Figure 7–6 shows the situation for our fifth-grader example if the study included 100 fifth graders instead of the 64 in the original example. The power now is 51%. (It was 38% with 64 fifth graders.) With 500 participants in the study, power is 98% (see Figure 7–7).

Don't get mixed up. The distributions of means can be narrow (and thus have less overlap and more power) for two very different reasons. One reason is that the populations of individuals may have small standard deviations. This reason has to do with effect size. The other reason is that the sample size is large. This reason is completely separate from the first reason. Sample size has nothing to do with effect size. Both effect size and sample size influence power. However, as we will see shortly, these two different influences on power lead to completely different kinds of practical steps for increasing power when planning a study.

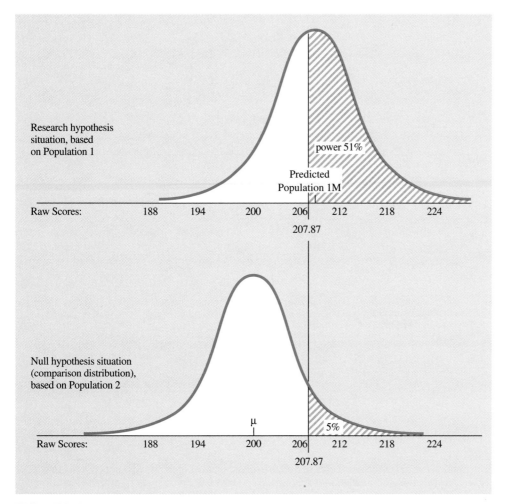

Raw Scores: 188   194   200   206   212   218   224

FIGURE 7–6
Distributions of means of test scores of 100 fifth graders based on predicted (upper) and known (lower) distributions of populations of individuals. (From a fictional study of fifth graders taking a standard achievement test.) Scores are shown on both distributions for the significance cutoff on the lower distribution (the significance cutoff is based on $p < .05$, one-tailed). Power = 51%. Compare this example to the original example (in Figure 7–1) in which the sample size was 64 (and power was 38%).

Figuring the Needed Sample Size for a Given Level of Power

When planning a study, the main reason researchers figure power is to help decide how many people to include in the study. Sample size has an important influence on power. Thus, a researcher wants to be sure to have enough people in the study for the study to have fairly high power. Suppose the researchers in our example were planning their study, with their predicted effect size from the original situation where they predicted an effect size of .17—it turns out that they would need 222 fifth graders to have 80% power. To help researchers come up with figures like this, statisticians have prepared special tables. These tables tell you how many participants you need in a

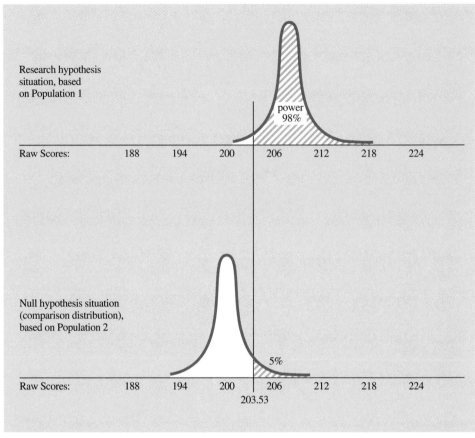

FIGURE 7–7
Distributions of means of test scores of 500 fifth graders based on predicted (upper) and known (lower) distributions of populations of individuals. (From a fictional study of fifth graders taking a standard achievement test.) Scores are shown on both distributions for the significance cutoff on the lower distribution (the significance cutoff is based on $p < .05$, one-tailed). Power = 98%. Compare this example to the original example in Figure 7–1 in which the sample size was 64 and the example in Figure 7–6 in which the sample size was 100.

study to have a high level of power, given a certain effect size. We will provide simplified versions of such tables for each of the main hypothesis-testing procedures you learn in upcoming chapters.

Other Influences on Power

Three other factors (besides effect size and sample size) affect power:

1. Significance level. Less extreme significance levels (such as .10 or .20) mean more power. More extreme significance levels (.01 or .001) mean less power. Less extreme significance levels result in more power because the shaded rejection area on the lower curve is bigger. Thus, more of the area in the upper curve is shaded. More extreme significance levels result in less power because the shaded rejection region on the lower curve is smaller.

Suppose in our original version of the fifth-grader example, we had instead used the .01 significance level. The power would have dropped from 38% to only 16% (see Figure 7–8).

2.   **One- versus two-tailed tests.** Using a two-tailed test makes it harder to get significance on any one tail. Thus, keeping everything else the same, power is less with a two-tailed test than with a one-tailed test.

Suppose in our fifth-grader testing example we had used a two-tailed test instead of a one-tailed test (but still using the 5% level overall). As shown in Figure 7–9, power would be only 26% (compared to 38% in the original one-tailed version shown in Figure 7–1).

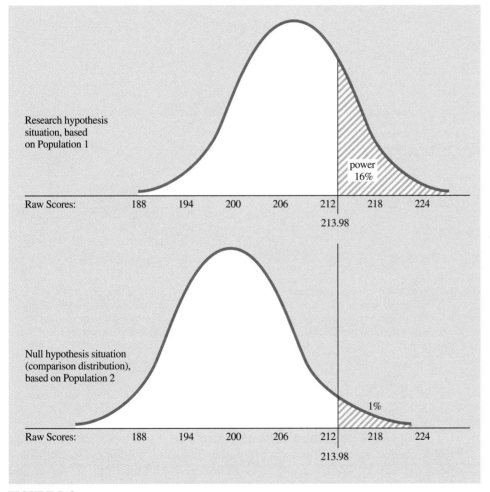

FIGURE 7–8

Distributions of means of test scores of 64 fifth graders based on predicted (upper) and known (lower) distributions of populations of individuals. (From a fictional study of fifth graders taking a standard achievement test.) Scores are shown on both distributions for the significance cutoff on the lower distribution. The significance cutoff is based on $p < .01$, one-tailed. Power = 16%. Compare this example to the original example (in Figure 7–1) in which the significance cutoff was $p < .05$.

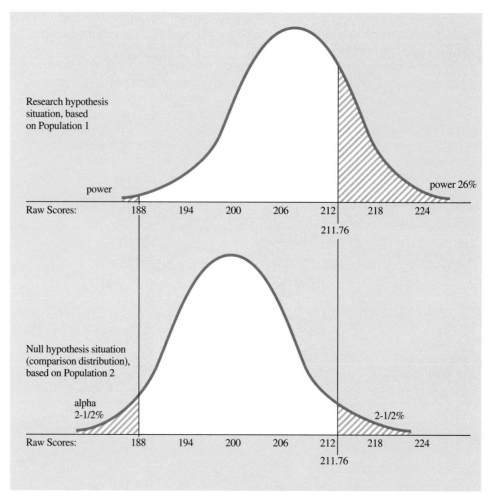

FIGURE 7–9
Distributions of means of test scores of 64 fifth graders based on predicted (upper) and known (lower) distributions of populations of individuals. (From a fictional study of fifth graders taking a standard achievement test.) Scores are shown on both distributions for the significance cutoff on the lower distribution. The significance cutoff is based on $p < .05$, two-tailed. Power = 26%. Compare this example to the original example (in Figure 7–1) in which the significance test was one-tailed.

    3. Type of hypothesis-testing procedure. Sometimes the researcher has a choice of more than one hypothesis-testing procedure to use for a particular study. We have not considered any such situations so far in this book but we will do so in Chapter 11.

Summary of Influences on Power

Table 7–3 summarizes the effects of various factors on the power of a study.

TABLE 7–3
Influences on Power

Feature of the Study	Increases Power	Decreases Power
Effect size	Large	Small
Effect size combines the following two features:		
Predicted difference between population means	Large Differences	Small Differences
Population standard deviation	Small Population SD	Large Population SD
Sample size (N)	Large N	Small N
Significance level	Lenient (Such as .10)	Stringent (Such as .01)
One-tailed versus two-tailed test	One-tailed	Two-tailed
Type of hypothesis-testing procedure used	Varies	Varies

Role of Power When Planning a Study

Figuring out power is very important when planning a study. If you do a study in which the power is low, even if the research hypothesis is true, this study will probably not give statistically significant results. Thus, the time and expense of carrying out the study would probably not be worthwhile. So when the power of a planned study is found to be low, researchers look for practical ways to increase the power to an acceptable level.

What is an acceptable level of power? A widely used rule is that a study should have 80% power to be worth conducting (see Cohen, 1988). Obviously, the more power the better. However, the costs of greater power, such as studying more people, often make even 80% power beyond your reach.

How can you increase the power of a planned study? In principle, you can increase the power of a planned study by changing any of the factors summarized in Table 7–3. Let's consider each.

1. Increase the effect size by increasing the predicted difference between population means. You can't just arbitrarily predict a bigger difference. There has to be a basis for your prediction. Thus, to increase the predicted difference your method in carrying out the study must make it reasonable to expect a bigger difference. Consider again our example of the experiment about the impact of special instructions on fifth graders' test scores. One way to increase the expected mean difference would be to make the instructions more elaborate, spending more time explaining them, perhaps allowing time for practice, and so forth. A disadvantage of this approach of increasing the impact of the experimental procedure is that it can be difficult or costly. Another disadvantage is that you may have to use an experimental procedure that is not like the one to which you want the results of your study to apply.

2. Increase effect size by decreasing the population standard deviation. You can decrease the population standard deviation in a planned study in at least two ways. One way is to use a population that has less variation within it than the one originally planned. With the fifth-grade testing example, you might only use fifth graders in a particular suburban school system. The disadvantage is that your results will then apply only to the more limited population.

Another way to decrease the population standard deviation is to use conditions of testing that are more standardized and measures that are more precise. For example, testing in a controlled laboratory setting usually makes for smaller overall variation among scores in results (meaning a smaller standard deviation). Similarly, using tests with very clear wording and clear procedures for marking answers also reduces variation. When practical, this is an excellent way to increase power, but often the study is already as rigorous as it can be.

3. **Increase the sample size.** The most straightforward way to increase power in a study is to study more people. Of course, if you are studying astronauts who have walked on the moon, there is a limit to how many are available. In most practical cases, sample size is the main way to modify a study to bring it up to sufficient power.

4. **Use a less-stringent level of significance.** Ordinarily, the level of significance you use should be the least stringent that reasonably protects against Type I error. Normally, this will be .05. It is rare that much can be done to improve power in this way.

5. **Use a one-tailed test.** Whether you use a one- or a two-tailed test depends on the logic of the hypothesis being studied. As with significance level, it is rare that you have much of a choice about this factor.

6. **Use a more sensitive hypothesis-testing procedure.** This is fine if alternatives are available. We consider some options of this kind in Chapter 11. Usually, however, the researcher begins with the most sensitive method available, so little more can be done.

Table 7–4 summarizes some practical ways to increase the power of a planned experiment.

Importance of Power in Judging the Results of a Study

Understanding statistical power and what affects it is very important in drawing conclusions from the results of research.

Role of Power When a Result Is Significant: Statistical Significance versus Practical Significance

You have learned that a study with a larger effect size is more likely to come out significant. It also is possible for a study with a very small effect size to come out significant. This is likely to happen when a study has high power due to other factors, especially a large sample size. Consider a study in which among all students who take the Scholastic Aptitude Test (SAT) in a particular year, a sample of 10,000 whose first name begins with a particular letter are randomly selected. Suppose that their mean SAT verbal score is 504,

TABLE 7–4
Summary of Practical Ways of Increasing the Power of a Planned Study

Feature of the Study	Practical Way of Raising Power	Disadvantages
Predicted difference between population means	Increase the intensity of the experimental procedure.	May not be practical or may distort the study's meaning.
Standard deviation	Use a less diverse population.	May not be available; decreases generalizability.
	Use standardized, controlled circumstances of testing or more precise measurement.	Not always practical.
Sample size	Use a larger sample size.	Not always practical; can be costly.
Significance level	Use a more lenient level of significance (such as .10).	Raises the probability of a Type I error.
One-tailed versus two-tailed test	Use a one-tailed test.	May not be appropriate to the logic of the study.
Type of hypothesis-testing procedure	Use a more sensitive procedure.	None may be available or appropriate.

compared to the overall population's mean SAT verbal score of 500 ($SD = 100$). This result would be significant at the .001 level. Its effect size is a tiny .04. That is, the significance test tells us that there is a real difference—that the population of students whose first name begins with this letter have higher SAT scores than the general population of students. At the same time, the difference is not very important. The effect size (or just looking at the mean difference) makes it clear that this difference is not very important. The distributions of the two populations overlap so much that it would be of little use to know what letter any particular person's first name begins with.

The message here is that in judging a study's results, there are two questions. First, is the result statistically significant? If it is, you can consider there to be a real effect. The next question is then, is the effect size large enough for the result to be useful or interesting? This second question is especially important if the study has any potential practical implications. (Sometimes, in a study testing purely theoretical issues, it may be enough just to be confident there is an effect at all in a particular direction.)

If the sample was small, you can assume that a statistically significant result is probably also practically significant. On the other hand, if the sample size is very large, you must consider the effect size directly, as it is quite possible that the effect size is too small to be useful.

The implications of what we just said may seem a bit of a paradox. Most people assume that the more participants in the study, the more important its results. In a sense, just the reverse is true. All other things being equal, if a study with only a few people manages to be significant, that significance must be due to a large effect size. A study with a large number of people in it that is statistically significant may or may not have a large effect size.

Notice that it is not a good idea to compare the significance level of two studies to see which has the more important result. A study with a small number of participants that is significant at the .05 level might well have a larger effect size than a study with a large number of participants that is significant at the .01 level.

However, the most important lesson from all this is that the word "significant" in "statistically significant" has a very special meaning. It means that you can be pretty confident that there is some real effect. Yet it does *not* mean that the effect is significant in a practical sense, that it is important or noteworthy.

Role of Power When a Result Is Not Statistically Significant

We saw in Chapter 5 that a result that is not significant is inconclusive. Often, however, we really would like to conclude that there is little or no difference between the populations. Can we ever do that?

Consider the relation of power to a nonsignificant result. Suppose you carried out a study that had low power and did not get a significant result. In that situation, the result is entirely inconclusive. Not getting a significant result may have come about because the research hypothesis was false or because the study had too little power (for example, due to having very few participants).

On the other hand, suppose you carried out a study that had high power and you did not get a significant result. In this situation (where there is high power), a nonsignificant result is a fairly strong argument against the research hypothesis. This does not mean that all versions of the research hypothesis are false. For example, it is possible that the populations are only very slightly different (and power was figured assuming a large difference).

In sum, a nonsignificant result from a study with low power is truly inconclusive. However, a nonsignificant result from a study with high power does suggest that either the research hypothesis is false or that there is less of an effect than was predicted when figuring power.

Summary of the Role of Significance and Sample Size in Interpreting Research Results

Table 7–5 summarizes the role of significance and sample size in judging research results.

Decision Error, Power, and Effect Size as Discussed in Research Articles

You mainly think about decision error and power when planning research. (Power, for example, is often a major topic in proposals requesting funding for research and in thesis proposals.) As for research articles, power is sometimes mentioned in the final section of an article where the author discusses the meaning of the results or in discussions of results of other studies. Here, the emphasis tends to be on the meaning of null hypothesis results. Also, when power is discussed, it is common for power to be explained in some de-

TABLE 7–5
Role of Significance and Sample Size in Judging Experimental Results

Result Statistically Significant	Sample Size	Conclusion
Yes	Small	Important result
Yes	Large	Might or might not have practical importance
No	Small	Inconclusive
No	Large	Research hypothesis probably false

tail. This is because it has only been recently that most social and behavioral scientists have begun to be knowledgeable about power.

For example, Denenberg (1999), in discussing the basis for his own study, makes the following comments about a relevant previous study by Moody et al. (1997) that had not found significant results.

> [T]hey were confronted with the serious problem of having to accept the null hypothesis. . . . we can view this issue in terms of statistical power. . . . A minimal statistical power of .80 is required before one can consider the argument that the lack of significance may be interpreted as evidence that Ho [the null hypothesis] is true. To conduct a power analysis, it is necessary to specify an expected mean difference, the alpha level, and whether a one-tailed or two-tailed test will be used. Given a power requirement of .8, one can then determine the N necessary. Once these conditions are satisfied, if the experiment fails to find a significant difference, then one can make the following kind of a statement: "We have designed an experiment with a .8 probability of finding a significant difference, if such exists in the population. Because we failed to find a significant effect, we think it quite unlikely that one exists. Even if it does exist, its contribution would appear to be minimal."
>
> Moody et al. never discussed power, even though they interpreted negative findings as proof of the validity of the null hypothesis in all of their experiments. . . . Because the participants were split in this experiment, the ns were reduced to 10 per group. Under such conditions one would not expect to find a significant difference, unless the experimental variable was very powerful. In other words it is more difficult to reject the null hypothesis when working with small ns. The only meaningful conclusion that can be drawn from this study is that no meaningful interpretation can be made of the lack of findings. . . .

It is increasingly common (though still the exception) for articles to mention effect size. For example, Moorehouse and Tuber (2000) studied the effectiveness of an intervention program for "high-risk, multiproblem, inner-city, primarily African-American and Latino youth." The authors reported "Youth who received 5–30 hours of intervention ([the high dosage group], $n = 101$) were compared with those who received 1–4 hours (the low-dosage group, $n = 31$). . . . The difference between the groups in terms of reduction in [alcohol and drug] use was highly significant. A between-groups effect size of .68 was achieved for the high-dosage group when compared with the low-dosage group." (Their wording about the study is a bit confusing—they are using "dosage" here to mean the amount of intervention, not the amount of drugs anyone was taking!) The meaning of the .68 effect size is that the group getting 5–30 hours of intervention was .68 standard deviations higher in terms of reduction on their drug and alcohol use than the group getting only 1–4 hours of the intervention. This is a medium-to-large effect size.

Summary

1. There are two kinds of decision errors one can make in hypothesis testing. A Type I error occurs when a researcher rejects the null hypothesis, but the null hypothesis is actually true. A Type II error occurs when a researcher does not reject the null hypothesis, but the null hypothesis is actually false.

2. The statistical power of a study is the probability that it will produce a statistically significant result if the research hypothesis is true. Researchers usually look up the power of a study on special tables.

3. There are two main factors that affect power: effect size and sample size. Effect size takes into account the predicted difference between means (the greater the difference, the larger the effect size) and the population variance (the smaller this is, the larger the effect size). Effect size is the difference between population means divided by the population standard deviation. Effect size influences power because the greater the effect size the more overlap between the distributions of means of the predicted population and the rejection area of the distribution of means for the comparison population. Cohen's (1988) conventions for effect size consider a small effect to be .2, a medium effect to be .5, and a large effect to be .8. Effect size is important in its own right in interpreting results of studies. It is also used to compare and combine results of studies, as in meta-analysis, and to compare different results within a study.

4. The larger the sample size, the greater the power. This is because the larger the sample, the smaller the variance of the distribution of means, so for a given effect size there is less overlap between distributions (and thus more overlap between the distributions of means of the predicted population and the rejection area of the distribution of means for the comparison population).

5. Power also is affected by significance level (the more extreme, such as .01, the lower the power), by whether a one- or two-tailed test is used (with less power for a two-tailed test), and by the type of hypothesis-testing procedure used (in the rare situation where there is a choice of procedure).

6. Statistically significant results from a study with high power (such as one with a large sample size) may not have practical importance. Results that are not statistically significant from a low power study (such as one with a small sample size) make it possible that important, statistically significant results might show up if power were increased. It is not possible to "prove" the null hypothesis. But if a study has very high power, a nonsignificant finding may suggest that any true effect is extremely small.

7. Research articles sometimes include discussions of power, especially when discussing nonsignificant results. Mentions of effect size are increasingly common in research articles.

Key Terms

decision error	meta-analysis	Type I error
effect size	power tables	Type II error
effect size conventions	statistical power	

Practice Problems

All data are fictional. Answers to selected problems are given at the back of the book.

1. For each of the following studies, make a chart of the four possible correct and incorrect decisions, and explain what each would mean. (Each chart should be laid out like Table 7–1, but you should put into the boxes the actual result using the names of the variables involved in the study.)

(a) A study of whether increasing the amount of recess time improves schoolchildren's in-class behavior.

(b) A study of whether colorblind individuals can distinguish gray shades better than the population at large.

(c) A study of whether high school students who receive an acquired immune deficiency syndrome (AIDS) prevention program in their school are more likely to practice safe sex than high school students in general.

(d) A study whether individuals who have ever been in psychotherapy are more tolerant of other people's upsets than is the general population.

2. What is meant by the statistical power of an experiment? (Write your answer for a lay person.)

3. Here is information about several possible versions of a planned study, each involving a single sample. Figure the predicted effect size for each study:

	Population 2 M	SD	Predicted Population 1 M
(a)	90	4	91
(b)	90	4	92
(c)	90	4	94
(d)	90	4	86
(e)	90	2	91
(f)	90	1	91
(g)	90	2	92
(h)	90	2	94
(i)	90	2	86

4. You read a study in which the key result is significant ($p < .05$). You then look at the size of the sample. If the sample is very large (rather than very small), how should this affect your interpretation of (a) the probability that the null hypothesis is actually true and (b) the practical importance of the result?

5. You read a study in which the key result is not statistically significant. You then look at the size of the sample. If the sample is very large (rather than very small), how should this affect your judgment of (a) the probability that the null hypothesis is actually true and (b) the probability that the null hypothesis is actually false?

6. What is the effect of each of the following on the power of a planned study?

(a) A larger predicted difference between the means of the populations (where the researcher actually changes the procedures so that there is reason to predict a larger mean difference).

(b) A larger population standard deviation

(c) A larger sample size

(d) Using a more stringent significance level (e.g., .01 instead of .05)

(e) Using a two-tailed test instead of a one-tailed test

7. You are planning a study that you determine from a table as having quite low power. Name six things that you might do to increase power.

8 Introduction to the *t* Test

AT this point, you may think you know all about hypothesis testing. Here's a surprise: What you know so far will not help you much as a researcher. Why? The procedures for testing hypotheses described up to this point were, of course, absolutely necessary for what you will now learn. However, these procedures involved comparing a group of scores to a known population. In real research practice, you often compare two or more groups of scores to each other, without any direct information about populations. For example, you may have two scores for each of several people, such as a score on a test of attitudes toward the courts before and after having gone through a law suit. Or you might have one score per person for two groups of people, such as an experimental group and a control group in a study of the effect of a new method of training teachers.

These kinds of research situations are very common in social and behavioral science research, where usually the only information available is from the samples. Nothing is known about the populations that the samples are supposed to come from. In particular, the researcher does not know the variance of the populations involved, which is a crucial ingredient in Step 2 of the hypothesis-testing process (determining the characteristics of the comparison distribution).

In this chapter, we first examine the solution to the problem of not knowing the population variance by focusing on a special situation, the comparison of the mean of a single sample to a population with a known mean but an unknown variance. Then, having seen how to handle this problem of not knowing the population variance, we go on to consider the situation in which there is no known population at all—the situation in which all we have are two scores for each of a number of people.

The hypothesis-testing procedures you learn in this chapter, those in which the population variance is unknown, are examples of what are called **t tests.** The t test is sometimes called "Student's t" because its main principles were originally developed by William S. Gosset, who published his articles anonymously, using the name "Student" (see Box 8–1).

In order to understand this chapter, you will need to know well the material in Chapters 5, 6, and 7, especially the logic and procedures for hypothesis testing and the distribution of means.

t tests

The *t* Test for a Single Sample

Let's begin with the following situation. You conduct a study that gives you scores for a sample of individuals and you want to compare the mean of this sample to a population for which the mean is known but not the variance. Hypothesis testing in this situation is called a **t test for a single sample.** (It is also called a *one-sample t test*.)

t test for a single sample

The *t* test for a single sample works basically the same way as the procedure you learned in Chapter 6. In the studies we considered in Chapter 6, you had scores for a sample of individuals (such as a group of 64 fifth graders who had taken a standard test with special instructions) and you wanted to compare the mean of this sample to a population (such as fifth graders in general). However, in the studies we considered in Chapter 6, you knew both

BOX 8–1

William S. Gosset, alias "Student": Not a Mathematician, but a "Practical Man"

William S. Gosset graduated from Oxford in 1899 with a degree in mathematics and chemistry. It happened that in the same year the Guinness brewers in Dublin, Ireland, were seeking a few young scientists to take a first-ever scientific look at beer-making. Gosset took one of these jobs and soon had immersed himself in barley, hops, and vats of brew.

The problem was how to make beer less variable, and especially to find the cause of bad batches. A proper scientist would say, "Conduct experiments!" But a business such as a brewery could not afford to waste money on experiments involving large numbers of vats, some of which any brewer worth his hops knew would fail. So Gosset was forced to contemplate the probability of, say, a certain strain of barley producing terrible beer when the experiment could consist of only a few batches of each strain. Adding to the problem was that he had no idea of the variability of a given strain of barley—perhaps some fields of it were better than others. (Does this sound familiar? Poor Gosset, like today's researchers, had no idea of his population's variance.)

Gosset was up to the task. To his colleagues at the brewery, he was a professor of mathematics. To his statistical colleagues, mainly at the Biometric Laboratory at University College in London, he was a mere brewer. In short, Gosset was the sort of scientist who was not above applying his talents to real life.

In fact, he seemed to revel in real life: raising pears, fishing, golfing, building boats, skiing, cycling, and lawn bowling (after he broke his leg by driving his car, a two-seater Model T Ford that he called "The Flying Bedstead," into a lamppost). He especially reveled in simple tools that could be applied to anything and simple formulas that he could compute in his head. (A friend described him as an expert carpenter but claimed that Gosset did almost all of his finer woodwork with nothing but a penknife!)

Gosset discovered the *t* distribution and invented the *t* test—simplicity itself (compared to most statistics)—for situations when samples are small and the variability of the larger population is unknown. Most of his work was done on the backs of envelopes, with plenty of minor errors in arithmetic that he had to weed out later. Characteristically, he published his paper on his "brewery methods" only when editors of scientific journals demanded it. To this day, most statisticians call the *t* distribution "Student's *t*" because Gosset wrote under the anonymous name "Student" so that the Guinness brewery would not have to admit publicly that it sometimes brewed a bad batch!

References: Peters (1987); Stigler (1986); Tankard (1984).

the mean and variance of the general population to which you were going to compare your sample. In the situations we are now going to consider, everything is the same, but you don't know the population variance. This presents two important new wrinkles, having to do with the details of how you carry out two of the steps of the hypothesis testing process.

The first important new wrinkle is in Step 2. Because the population variance is not known, you must estimate it. So the first new wrinkle we consider is how to estimate an unknown population variance. The other important new wrinkle affects both Steps 2 and 3. When the population variance has to be estimated, the shape of the comparison distribution is not a normal curve. So the second new wrinkle we consider is the shape of the comparison distribution (for Step 2) and how to use a special table to find the cutoff (Step 3) on this slightly differently shaped distribution.

An Example

Suppose your college newspaper reports an informal survey showing that students at your college study an average of 2.5 hours each day. However, you think the students in *your* dormitory study much more than that. You randomly pick 16 students from your dormitory and ask them how much they study each day. (We will assume that they are all honest and accurate.) Your result is that these 16 students study an average of 3.2 hours per day. Should you conclude that students in general in your dormitory study more than the college average? Or should you conclude that your results are so close to the college average, that the small difference of .7 hours might well be due to your having accidentally picked 16 of the more studious residents of your dormitory?

Step 1 of the hypothesis-testing process is to restate the problem as hypotheses about populations.

There are two populations:

Population 1: The kind of students who live in your dormitory
Population 2: The kind of students at your college generally

The research hypothesis is that Population 1 students study more than Population 2 students; the null hypothesis is that Population 1 students do not study more than Population 2 students. So far the problem is no different from those in Chapter 6.

Step 2 is to determine the characteristics of the comparison distribution. Its mean will be 2.5, what the survey found for students at your college generally (Population 2).

The next part of Step 2 is finding the variance of the distribution of means. With the current example, you face a new kind of problem. Up to now in this book, you have always known the variance of the population of individuals. Using that variance, you then figured the variance of the distribution of means. However, in the present example, the variance of the number of hours studied for students at your college (the Population 2 students) was not reported in the newspaper article. So you email the paper. Unfortunately, the reporter did not calculate the variance, and the original survey results are no longer available. What to do?

Basic Principle of the *t* Test: Estimating the Population Variance from the Sample Scores

If you do not know the variance of the population of individuals, you can estimate it from what you do know—the scores of the people in your sample.

In the logic of hypothesis testing, the group of people we study is considered to be a random sample from a particular population. The variance of this sample ought to reflect the variance of that population. If the scores in the population have a lot of variation, then the scores in a sample randomly selected from that population should also have a lot of variation. If the population is very uniform, with very little variation, the scores in samples from that population should also not have much variation. Thus, it should be possible to use the variation among the scores in a sample to make an informed guess about the variation of the scores in the population. That is, we could

biased estimate

unbiased estimate of the population variance

figure the variance of the sample's scores and that should be similar to the variance of the scores in the population. (See Figure 8–1.)

There is, however, one small hitch. The variance of a sample will generally be slightly smaller than the variance of the population from which it is taken. For this reason, the variance of the sample is a **biased estimate** of the population variance. To oversimplify a little, the reason that a sample's variance tends to be smaller than the population's is that it is slightly less likely to include extreme scores.[1]

Fortunately, you can figure an **unbiased estimate of the population variance** by slightly changing the ordinary variance formula. The ordinary way to figure the variance is to take the sum of the squared deviation scores and divide this by the number of scores. In the changed procedure, you still take the sum of the squared deviation scores, but you divide this sum by the number of scores *minus 1*. Dividing by a slightly smaller number makes the result of the dividing (the variance) bigger.

It turns out that dividing by the number of scores minus one increases the resulting variance just enough to make it an unbiased estimate of the population variance. "Unbiased," incidentally, means that the estimate is equally likely to be too high as it is to be too low. It does *not* mean that your estimate will be exactly the true population variance.

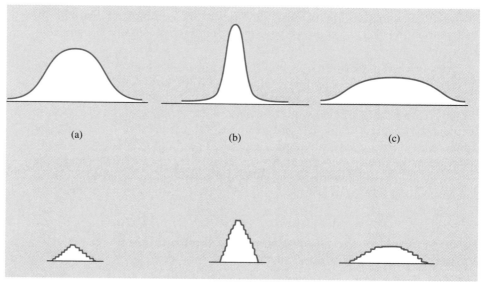

FIGURE 8–1
Variance in samples (lower distributions) and the populations they are taken from (upper distributions).

[1]Here is a more precise explanation. The variance is based on deviations from the mean, and hence a population's variance is based on deviations from its mean. However, when calculating the variance of a sample, the deviations are figured from the sample's mean. The sample's mean is the optimal balance point for its scores. Thus, the average squared deviations from it will be less than from any other number, such as the population's mean. One way to think of the correction for bias discussed in the next paragraph is that it exactly accounts for the degree to which a sample's mean tends to vary from the true population mean.

The symbol we will use for the unbiased estimate of the population variance is S^2. The formula is the usual variance formula, but with the division by $N-1$ instead of by N:

$$S^2 = \frac{\Sigma(X-M)^2}{N-1} \qquad (8\text{–}1)$$

Let's return to our example of hours spent studying and figure the estimated population variance from the sample's 16 scores. First, you figure the sum of squared deviation scores. (Subtract the mean from each of the scores, square those deviation scores, and add them.) Presume in our example that this comes out to 9.6. To get the estimated population variance, you divide this sum of squared deviation scores by the number of scores (16) minus 1. The result of 9.6 divided by 15 is .64. In terms of the formula,

$$S^2 = \frac{\Sigma(X-M)^2}{N-1} = \frac{9.6}{16-1} = \frac{9.6}{15} = .64$$

Degrees of Freedom

The number you divide by (sample size minus 1) to get the estimated population variance has a special name. It is called the **degrees of freedom (*df*).** It has this name because it is the number of scores in a sample that are "free to vary." The idea is that, when figuring the variance, you first have to know the mean. If you know the mean and all the scores in the sample but one, you can figure out the one you don't know with a little arithmetic. Thus, once you know the mean, one of the scores in the sample is not free to have any possible value. So the degrees of freedom is the number of scores minus 1. In terms of a formula,

degrees of freedom (*df*)

$$df = N-1 \qquad (8\text{–}2)$$

In our example, $df = 16 - 1 = 15$. (In some situations you learn about in later chapters, the degrees of freedom are figured a bit differently. This is because in those situations, the number of scores free to vary is different. For all the situations in this chapter, $df = N - 1$.) The formula for the estimated population variance is often written using df instead of $N - 1$.

$$S^2 = \frac{\Sigma(X-M)^2}{df} \qquad (8\text{–}3)$$

The Standard Deviation of the Distribution of Means

Once you have estimated the population variance, you can figure the standard deviation of the comparison distribution using the same procedures you learned in Chapter 6. As always, when we have a sample of more than one, the comparison distribution is a distribution of means. And the variance of a distribution of means is the variance of the population of individuals divided by the sample size. We have just estimated the variance of the population. Thus, you can estimate the variance of the distribution of means by dividing the estimated population variance by the sample size. The standard deviation of the distribution of means is the square root of its variance. Stated as formulas,

$$S_M^2 = \frac{S^2}{N}$$

(8–4)

$$S_M = \sqrt{S_M^2}$$

(8–5)

Note that with an estimated population variance, the symbols for the variance and standard deviation of the distribution of means use S instead of Population *SD*.

In our example, the sample size was 16 and the estimated population variance we just worked out was .64. The variance of the distribution of means, based on that estimate, will be .04. That is, .64 divided by 16 equals .04. The standard deviation is .2, the square root of .04. In terms of the formulas,

$$S_M^2 = \frac{S^2}{N} = \frac{.64}{16} = .04$$

$$S_M = \sqrt{S_M^2} = \sqrt{.04} = .2$$

Be careful. To find the variance of a distribution of means, you always divide the population variance by the sample size. This is true whether the population's variance is known or only estimated. In our example, you divided the population variance, which you had estimated, by 16. It is only when making the estimate of the population variance that you divide by the sample size minus 1. That is, the degrees of freedom are used only when estimating the variance of the population of individuals.

The Shape of the Comparison Distribution When Using an Estimated Population Variance: The *t* Distribution

In Chapter 6, you learned that when the population distribution follows a normal curve, the shape of the distribution of means will also be a normal curve. However, this changes when we do hypothesis testing using an estimated population variance. When we are using an estimated population variance, we have less true information and more room for error. The mathematical effect is that extreme means are slightly more likely than would be found in a distribution of means that was an exact normal curve. Further, the smaller your sample size, the bigger this tendency. This is because, with a smaller sample size, your estimate of the population variance is based on less information.

The result of all of this is that, when doing hypothesis testing using an estimated variance, your comparison distribution will not be a normal curve.

Instead, the comparison distribution will be a slightly different curve called a *t* distribution.

t distribution

Actually, there is a whole family of *t* distributions. They vary in shape according to the degrees of freedom in the sample used to estimate the population variance. However, for any particular degrees of freedom, there is only one *t* distribution.

Generally, *t* distributions look to the eye like a normal curve—bell-shaped, completely symmetrical, and unimodal. A *t* distribution differs subtly in having heavier tails (that is, slightly more scores at the extremes). Figure 8–2 shows the shape of a *t* distribution compared to a normal curve.

The subtle difference in shape affects how extreme a score you need to reject the null hypothesis. As always, to reject the null hypothesis, your sample mean has to be in an extreme section of the comparison distribution of means, such as the top 5%. However, if the comparison distribution of means has more extreme means than a normal curve would have, then the point where the top 5% begins has to be farther out on this comparison distribution. Thus, it takes a slightly more extreme sample mean to get a significant result when using a *t* distribution than when using a normal curve.

Just how much the *t* distribution differs from the normal curve depends on the degrees of freedom, the amount of information used in estimating the population variance. The *t* distribution differs most from a normal curve when the degrees of freedom are low (because the estimate of the population variance is based on a very small sample). For example, using the normal curve, you may recall that the cutoff is 1.64 for a one-tailed test at the .05 level. On a *t* distribution with 7 degrees of freedom (that is, with a sample size of 8), the cutoff is 1.895 for a one-tailed test at the .05 level. If the estimate is based on a larger sample, say, a sample of 25 (so that $df = 24$), the cutoff is 1.711, a cutoff much closer to that for the normal curve. If your sample size is infinite, the *t* distribution is the same as the normal curve. (Of course, if your sample size were infinite, it would include the entire population!) But even with sample sizes of 30 or more, the *t* distribution is nearly identical to a normal curve.

Shortly you will learn how to find the cutoff using a *t* distribution, but let's first return briefly to our example: how much students at your dormitory study each night. You finally have everything you need to complete Step 2 about the characteristics of the comparison distribution. We have already seen that the distribution of means in this example has a mean of 2.5 hours

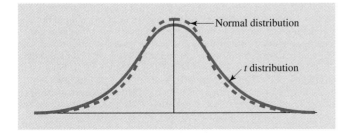

FIGURE 8–2
A *t* distribution (solid line) compared to the normal curve (dashed line).

t table

and a standard deviation of .2. You can now add that the shape of the comparison distribution will be a *t* distribution with 15 degrees of freedom.[2]

The Cutoff Sample Score for Rejecting the Null Hypothesis: Using the *t* Table

Step 3 of hypothesis testing is determining the cutoff for rejecting the null hypothesis. There is a different *t* distribution for any particular degrees of freedom. However, to avoid taking up pages and pages with tables for each different *t* distribution, you use a simplified table that gives only the crucial cutoff points. We have included such a ***t* table** in Appendix A (Table A–2).

In the hours-studied example, you have a one-tailed test. (You want to know whether students in your dormitory study *more* than students in general at your college study.) You will probably want to use the 5% significance level because the cost of a Type I error (mistakenly rejecting the null hypothesis) is not great. You have 16 people, making 15 degrees of freedom for your estimate of the population variance.

Table 8–1 shows a portion of a *t* table like Table A–2. Find the column for the .05 significance level for one-tailed tests and move down to the row

TABLE 8–1
Cutoff Scores for *t* Distributions with 1 through 17 Degrees of Freedom

	One-Tailed Tests			Two-Tailed Tests		
df	*.10*	*.05*	*.01*	*.10*	*.05*	*.01*
1	3.078	6.314	31.821	6.314	12.706	63.657
2	1.886	2.920	6.965	2.920	4.303	9.925
3	1.638	2.353	4.541	2.353	3.182	5.841
4	1.533	2.132	3.747	2.132	2.776	4.604
5	1.476	2.015	3.365	2.015	2.571	4.032
6	1.440	1.943	3.143	1.943	2.447	3.708
7	1.415	1.895	2.998	1.895	2.365	3.500
8	1.397	1.860	2.897	1.860	2.306	3.356
9	1.383	1.833	2.822	1.833	2.262	3.250
10	1.372	1.813	2.764	1.813	2.228	3.170
11	1.364	1.796	2.718	1.796	2.201	3.106
12	1.356	1.783	2.681	1.783	2.179	3.055
13	1.350	1.771	2.651	1.771	2.161	3.013
14	1.345	1.762	2.625	1.762	2.145	2.977
15	1.341	**1.753**	2.603	1.753	2.132	2.947
16	1.337	1.746	2.584	1.746	2.120	2.921
17	1.334	1.740	2.567	1.740	2.110	2.898

[2]Statisticians make a subtle distinction in this situation between the comparison distribution and the distribution of means. (We have avoided this distinction to simplify your learning of what is already fairly difficult.) The general procedure of hypothesis testing with means of samples as you learned it in Chapter 6 can be described as figuring a Z score for your sample's mean, and then comparing this Z score to a cutoff Z score from the normal curve table. Statisticians would say that when doing this, actually you are comparing your computed Z score to a distribution of Z scores, which is simply an ordinary normal curve. Similarly, with a *t* test, you will see shortly that we compute what is called a *t* score in the same way as a Z score, but using a standard deviation of the distribution of means based on an estimated population variance. The *t* score is then compared to a cutoff *t* score from a *t* distribution table. According to the formal statistical logic, you can think of this process as involving a comparison distribution of *t* scores, not of means.

for 15 degrees of freedom. The crucial cutoff is 1.753. This means that you will reject the null hypothesis if your sample's mean is 1.753 or more standard deviations above the mean on the comparison distribution. (If you were using a known variance, you would have found your cutoff from a normal curve table. The Z score needed to reject the null hypothesis based on the normal curve would have been 1.645.)

One other point about using the t table: In the full t table in Appendix A, there are rows for each degree of freedom from 1 through 30, then for 35, 40, 45, and so on, up to 100. Suppose your study has degrees of freedom between two values. To be safe, you should use the nearest degrees of freedom to yours that is given in the table that is less than yours. For example, in a study with 43 degrees of freedom, you would use the cutoff for $df = 40$.

The Sample Mean's Score on the Comparison Distribution: The t Score

Step 4 of hypothesis testing is figuring your sample mean's score on the comparison distribution. In Chapter 6, this meant finding the Z score on the comparison distribution—the number of standard deviations your sample's mean is from the mean on the comparison distribution. You do exactly the same thing when your comparison distribution is a t distribution. The only difference is that, instead of calling this a Z score, because it is for a t distribution, we call it a **t score.** In terms of a formula,

t score

$$t = \frac{M - \text{Population } M}{S_M}$$

(8–6)

In the example, your sample's mean of 3.2 is .7 hours from the mean of the distribution of means, which amounts to 3.5 standard deviations from the mean (.7 hours divided by the standard deviation of .2 hours). That is, the t score in the example is 3.5. In terms of the formula,

$$t = \frac{M - \text{Population } M}{S_M} = \frac{3.2 - 2.5}{.2} = \frac{.7}{.2} = 3.5$$

Deciding Whether to Reject the Null Hypothesis

Step 5 of hypothesis testing is deciding whether to reject the null hypothesis. This step is exactly the same with a t test as it was in those discussed in previous chapters. You compare the cutoff score from Step 3 with the sample's score on the comparison distribution from Step 4. In the example, the cutoff t score was 1.753 and the actual t score for our sample was 3.5. Conclusion: Reject the null hypothesis. The research hypothesis is supported that students in your dormitory study more than students in the college overall. Figure 8–3 illustrates the various distributions for this example.

FIGURE 8–3
Distributions involved in the hours-studied example.

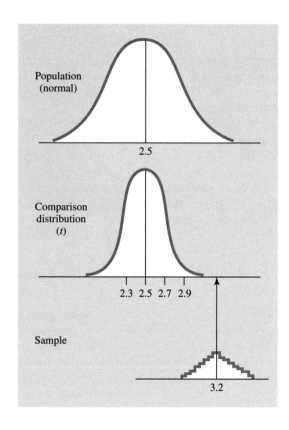

Summary of Hypothesis Testing When the Population Variance Is Not Known

Table 8–2 compares hypothesis testing procedure we have just considered (for a *t* test for a single sample) with the hypothesis testing procedure you learned in Chapter 6 (for a *Z* test for a single sample). That is, we are comparing the current situation in which you know the population's mean but not its variance to the Chapter 6 situation where you knew the population's mean *and* variance. Table 8–3 summarizes the steps of hypothesis testing for the *t*-test for a single sample.

The *t* Test for Dependent Means

The situation you just learned about occurs when you know the population mean but not its variance and where you have a single sample of scores. It turns out that in most research you do not even know the population's *mean*; plus, in most research situations, you usually have not one, but *two* sets of scores. These two things—not knowing the population mean and having two sets of scores--almost always go together. This situation is very common. It is in this section that, finally, we start to do the sort of hypothesis testing commonly done by social and behavioral scientists.

In particular, the rest of this chapter focuses on the important research situation where we have two scores from each person in your sample. This kind

TABLE 8–2
Hypothesis Testing with Single Sample Mean When Population Variance Is Unknown (*t* Test for a Single Sample) Compared to When Population Variance Is Known (Z Test for a Single Sample)

Step in Hypothesis Testing	Difference from When Population Variance Is Known
1. Restate the question as a research hypothesis and a null hypothesis about the populations.	No difference in method.
2. Determine the characteristics of the comparison distribution:	
Population mean	No difference in method.
Population variance	Estimate from the sample.
Standard deviation of the distribution of sample means	No difference in method (but based on estimated population variance).
Shape of the comparison distribution	Use the *t* distribution with $df = N - 1$.
3. Determine the significance cutoff.	Use the *t* table.
4. Determine your sample's score on the comparison distribution.	No difference in method (but called a *t* score).
5. Decide whether to reject the null hypothesis.	No difference in method.

of research situation is called a **repeated-measures design** (also known as a *within-subjects design*). A common example is when you measure the same people before and after some social or psychological intervention. For example, an organizational specialist might measure days missed from work for 80 workers before and after a new health-promotion program was introduced.

repeated measures design

TABLE 8–3
Steps for a *t*-Test for a Single Sample

1. Restate the question as a research hypothesis and a null hypothesis about the populations.
2. Determine the characteristics of the comparison distribution.
   a. The mean is the same as the known population mean.
   b. The standard deviation is computed as follows:
   i. Compute the estimated population variance:
   $$S^2 = \Sigma(X - M)^2 / (N - 1)$$
   ii. Compute the variance of the distribution of means:
   $$S_M^2 = S^2/N.$$
   iii. Compute the standard deviation: $S_M = \sqrt{S_M^2}$.
   c. The shape will be a *t* distribution with $N - 1$ degrees of freedom.
3. Determine the cutoff sample score on the comparison distribution at which the null hypothesis should be rejected.
   a. Determine the degrees of freedom, desired significance level, and number of tails in the test (one or two).
   b. Look up the appropriate cutoff in a *t* table.
4. Determine your sample's score on the comparison distribution: $t = (M - \text{Population } M) / S_M$
5. Decide whether to reject the null hypothesis: Compare the scores from Steps 3 and 4.

t test for dependent means

The hypothesis-testing procedure you use for a repeated-measures design where each person is measured twice is called a ***t* test for dependent means.** It has the name "dependent means" because the mean for each group of scores (for example, a group of "before" scores and a group of "after" scores) are dependent on each other in that they are both from the same people. (In Chapter 9, we consider the situation in which you compare scores from two different groups of people, a research design analyzed by a "*t* test for independent means.")

The *t* test for dependent means is also called a *t test for paired samples*, *t test for correlated means,* and *t test for matched samples.* Each of these names comes from this same idea that in this kind of *t* test we are comparing two sets of scores that are related to each other in a direct way, such as each person being tested before and after some procedure. (Compare this, for example, to the very different situation in which one group of people is tested before and a different group of people is tested after—or the even more common research situation in which you have a set of scores from one group of participants tested under one condition and from another set of participants tested under another condition. We will have more to say about this distinction later.)

You do a *t* test for dependent means in exactly the same way as a *t* test for a single sample, except that (a) you use something called difference scores and (b) you assume that the population mean is 0.

Difference Scores

difference scores

With a repeated-measures design, your sample includes two scores for each person instead of just one. The way you handle this is to make the two scores per person into one score per person! You do this magic by creating **difference scores:** For each person you subtract one score from the other.

Consider the health-promotion, absence-from-work example. The organizational specialist subtracts the number of days missed from work for the month after the program from the number of days missed during the month before the program. This gives an after-minus-before difference score for each employee. When the two scores are a "before" and an "after" score, we usually take the "after" score minus the "before" score to indicate the *change.*

Once you have the difference score for each person in the study, you do the rest of the hypothesis-testing with difference scores. That is, you treat the study as if there were a single sample of scores (scores that in this situation happen to be difference scores).[3]

Population of Difference Scores with a Mean of 0

So far in the research situations we have considered in this book, you have always known the mean of the population to which you compared your sample's mean. For example, in the college dormitory survey of hours

[3]You can also use a *t* test for dependent means when you have scores from pairs of people. You consider each pair as if it were one person and compute a difference score for each pair. For example, suppose you have 30 married couples and you are comparing ages of husbands and wives to see if husbands are consistently older than wives. You could compute for each couple a difference score of husband's age minus wife's age. The rest of the figuring would then be exactly the same as for an ordinary *t* test for dependent means. When the *t* test for dependent means is used in this way, it is sometimes called a *t test for matched pairs.*

studied, you knew the population mean was 2.5 hours. However, now we are using difference scores, and we usually don't know the mean of the population of difference scores.

Here is the solution. Ordinarily, the null hypothesis in a repeated-measures design is that there is no difference between the two groups of scores. For example, the null hypothesis in the health-promotion study is that absences from work will be the same before and after the health-promotion program is started. The research hypothesis of a difference is thus compared to a null hypothesis of no difference.

What does "no difference" mean? That is, what does it mean to say that in the population there is on the average no difference between the two scores for each person? It is the same as saying that the mean of the population of the difference scores is 0. In other words, saying that there is on the average no difference between the two scores is the same as saying that average of the difference scores is 0.

Therefore, when working with difference scores, we assume a null-hypothesis population of difference scores with a population mean of 0.

Example of a *t* Test for Dependent Means

Olthoff (1989) tested the communication quality of engaged couples 3 months before and again 3 months after marriage. One of the groups he studied was of 19 couples who received ordinary premarital counseling from their ministers. (To keep the example simple, we will focus only on this group and only on the husbands. The pattern of scores for the wives were similar, but somewhat more complicated.)

The scores for the 19 husbands are listed in the "Before" and "After" columns of Table 8–4, followed by the entire *t*-test analysis. The mean of the "before" scores was 116.316, and the mean of the "after" scores was 104.263. More important, however, we also have figured the difference scores. The mean of the difference scores is –12.05. That is, on the average, these husbands' communication quality decreased by about 12 points.

Is this decrease significant? In other words, how likely is it that this sample of change scores is a random sample from a population of change scores whose mean is 0? Let's carry out the hypothesis-testing procedure.

1. Restate the question as a research hypothesis and a null hypothesis about the populations. There are two populations:

Population 1: Husbands who receive ordinary premarital counseling
Population 2: Husbands whose communication quality does not change from before to after marriage

The research hypothesis is that Population 1 is different from Population 2. That is, the research hypothesis is that husbands who receive ordinary premarital counseling (such as the husbands Olthoff studied) *do* change in communication quality from before to after marriage. The null hypothesis is that the populations are the same. That is, the null hypothesis is that the husbands who receive ordinary premarital counseling do *not* change in their communication quality from before to after marriage.

Notice that we have no actual information about Population 2 husbands. The husbands in the study are a sample of Population 1 husbands. In fact, if the research hypothesis is correct, Population 2 husbands may not even really

TABLE 8–4
***t*-Test for Communication Quality Scores Before and After Marriage for 19 Husbands Who Received No Special Communication Training**

Husband	Communication Quality		Difference (After – Before)	Deviation of Differences from the Mean of Differences	Squared Deviation
	Before	*After*			
A	126	115	– 11	1.05	1.1
B	133	125	– 8	4.05	16.4
C	126	96	– 30	–17.95	322.2
D	115	115	0	12.05	145.2
E	108	119	11	23.05	531.3
F	109	82	– 27	–14.95	233.5
G	124	93	– 31	–18.95	359.1
H	98	109	11	23.05	531.3
I	95	72	– 23	–10.95	119.9
J	120	104	– 16	– 3.95	15.6
K	118	107	– 11	1.05	1.1
L	126	118	– 8	4.05	16.4
M	121	102	– 19	– 6.95	48.3
N	116	115	– 1	11.05	122.1
O	94	83	– 11	1.05	1.1
P	105	87	– 18	– 5.95	35.4
Q	123	121	– 2	10.05	101.0
R	125	100	– 25	–12.95	167.7
S	128	118	– 10	2.05	4.2
Σ:	2,210	1,981	–229		2,772.9

For difference scores:

$M = -229/19 = -12.05$.

Population $M = 0$ (assumed as a no-change baseline of comparison).

$S^2 = \Sigma(X - M)^2/df = 2{,}772.9/(19 - 1) = 154.05$.

$S_M^2 = S^2/N = 154.05/19 = 8.11$.

$S_M = \sqrt{S_M^2} = \sqrt{8.11} = 2.85$.

t with $df = 18$ needed for 5% level, two-tailed $= \pm 2.101$.

$t = (M - \text{Population } M)/S_M = (-12.05 - 0)/2.85 = -4.23$.

Decision: Reject the null hypothesis.

Note: Data from Olthoff (1989).

exist. For the purposes of hypothesis testing, we simply set up Population 2 as a kind of straw man comparison group. That is, we set up a comparison group for purposes of the analysis of husbands who, if measured before and after marriage, would show no change.

   2. Determine the characteristics of the comparison distribution. If the null hypothesis is true, the mean of the population of difference scores is 0. You can estimate the variance of the population of difference scores from the sample of difference scores. As shown in Table 8–4, the sum of squared deviations of the difference scores from the mean of the difference scores is 2,772.9. With 19 husbands in the study, there are 18 degrees of freedom. Dividing the sum of squared deviation scores by the degrees of freedom gives an estimated population variance of 154.05.

The distribution of means (from this population of difference scores) will have a mean of 0, the same as the population mean. Its variance will be the estimated population variance (154.05) divided by the sample size (19), which gives 8.11. The standard deviation is the square root of 8.11, which is 2.85. Because Olthoff was using an estimated population variance, the comparison distribution is a *t* distribution. The estimate of the population variance was based on 18 degrees of freedom, so this comparison distribution is a *t* distribution for 18 degrees of freedom.

3. Determine the cutoff sample score on the comparison distribution at which the null hypothesis should be rejected. Olthoff used a two-tailed test because there was no clear reason for predicting either an increase or a decrease in communication quality. Using the .05 significance level and 18 degrees of freedom, Table A–2 shows that to reject the null hypothesis you need a *t* score of +2.101 or above, or a *t* score of –2.101 or below.

4. Determine your sample's score on the comparison distribution. Olthoff's sample had a mean difference score of –12.05. That is, the mean was 12.05 points below the mean of 0 on the distribution of means. The standard deviation of the distribution of means was 2.85. Thus, the mean of the difference scores is 4.23 standard deviations below the mean of the distribution of means. So Olthoff's sample of difference scores has a *t* score of –4.23.

5. Decide whether to reject the null hypothesis. The *t* is –4.23 for the sample of difference scores is more extreme than the needed *t* of ±2.101. Thus, Olthoff could reject the null hypothesis. This suggests that the husbands are from a population in which husbands' communication quality is different after marriage from what it was before (it got lower).

Olthoff's actual study was more complex. You may be interested to know that he found that the wives also showed this decrease in communication quality after marriage. A group of similar engaged couples who were given special communication-skills training had no significant decline in marital communication quality after marriage (see Figure 8–4).

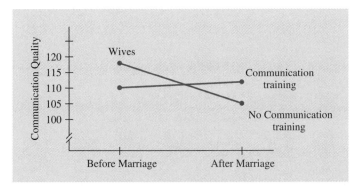

FIGURE 8–4
Communication skills of wives given premarital communications training and wives not given such training. (Based on Olthoff, 1989.)

Second Example of a _t_ Test for Dependent Means

Here is another example. A researcher is studying a theory that predicts that people feel more positively toward their government during a war. To test this idea, the researcher surveys a randomly selected group of nine people about their attitudes toward their government while their country is at war and then surveys them again a year after the war is over. (In a real study, the researcher would use a much larger sample. We have made the sample size small to keep the example simple.) The prediction was that people are more pro-government during the war.

The fictional results, along with all the calculations are shown in Table 8–5. The _t_ test is conducted as follows:

1. Restate the question as a research hypothesis and a null hypothesis about the populations. There are two populations:

Population 1: People in the country studied
Population 2: People who are not more pro-government during a war than they are one year after a war

The research hypothesis is that Population 1 is different from Population 2. That is, the research hypothesis is that people in the country studied _are_ more pro-government during a war than one year after. The null hypothesis is that Population 1 is the same as Population 2. That is, the null hypothesis is that people in the country studied are not more pro-government during a war than they are one year after a war.

TABLE 8–5
_t_ Test for a Study of Pro-Government Attitudes During versus One Year After a War (Fictional Data)

Survey Respondent	Conditions		Difference	Deviation	Squared Deviation
	During War	_1 Year After_			
1	18	12	6	6 − 2 = 4	16
2	21	21	0	−2	4
3	19	16	3	1	1
4	21	16	5	3	9
5	17	19	−2	−4	16
6	20	19	1	−1	1
7	18	16	2	0	0
8	16	17	−1	−3	9
9	20	16	4	2	4
Σ:	170	152	18	0	60

For difference scores:
   $M = 18/9 = 2.0$.

   Population $M = 0$ (assumed as a no-change baseline of comparison).
   $S^2 = \Sigma(X - M)^2/df = 60/(9 - 1) = 60/8 = 7.5$.
   $S_M^2 = S^2/N = 7.50/9 = .83$.
   $S_M = \sqrt{S_M^2} = \sqrt{.83} = .91$.
   t for $df = 8$ needed for 5% significance level, one-tailed = 1.860.
   $t = (M - \text{Population } M)/S_M = (2.00 - 0)/.91 = 2.20$.
   Decision: Reject the null hypothesis.

2. Determine the characteristics of the comparison distribution. If the null hypothesis is true, the mean of the population of difference scores is 0. What is the variance of this population of difference scores? Estimating from the sample of difference scores, it is the sum of the squared deviations of the difference scores, divided by the degrees of freedom. This is shown in Table 8–5 to be 7.5.

The mean of the comparison distribution is 0, the same as the null hypothesis population. The variance of the comparison distribution is .83 (the estimated population variance divided by the sample size). The standard deviation of the comparison distribution is the square root of this, .91. The comparison distribution is a *t* distribution for 8 degrees of freedom. It is a *t* distribution because we figured its variance based on an estimated population variance. It has 8 degrees of freedom because there were 8 degrees of freedom in the estimate of the population variance.

3. Determine the cutoff sample score on the comparison distribution at which the null hypothesis should be rejected. This is a one-tailed test because there was a reasonable basis for predicting the direction of the difference. Using the .05 significance level with 8 degrees of freedom, Table A–2 shows a cutoff *t* of 1.860.

4. Determine your sample's score on the comparison distribution. The sample's mean difference of 2 is 2.20 standard deviations (of .91 each) above the mean of 0 on the distribution of means.

5. Decide whether to reject the null hypothesis. The sample's *t* score of 2.20 is more extreme than the cutoff *t* of 1.860. You can reject the null hypothesis. People in the country studied have a more positive attitude toward their government in war time.

You may be interested to know that McLeod, Everland, and Signorielli (1994) did an actual study of this kind. They surveyed 167 people in the United States by telephone during the Persian Gulf War and then surveyed these same people again one year after the war. Their results, like the fictional example here, showed significantly greater pro-government attitudes during the war than after.

Summary of Steps for Conducting a *t* Test for Dependent Means

Table 8–6 summarizes the steps for carrying out a *t* test for dependent means.[4]

---

[4]The usual steps of carrying out a *t* test for dependent means can be somewhat combined into computational formulas for *S* and *t* based on difference scores. For purposes of learning the ideas, we strongly recommend that you use the regular procedures as we have discussed them in this chapter when doing the practice problems. In a real research situation, the computations are usually done by computer. However, if you ever have to do a *t* test for dependent means for an actual research study by hand (without a computer), you may find these formulas useful.

D in the formulas below is for difference score:

$$S = \sqrt{\frac{\Sigma D^2 - (\Sigma D)^2 / N}{N - 1}}$$

(8–7)

$$t = \frac{\Sigma D / N}{S / \sqrt{N}}$$

(8–8)

TABLE 8–6
Steps for Carrying out a _t_ Test for Dependent Means

1. Restate the question as a research hypothesis and a null hypothesis about the populations.
2. Determine the characteristics of the comparison distribution.
   (a) Make each person's two scores into a difference score. Do all the remaining steps using these difference scores.
   (b) Figure the mean of the difference scores.
   (c) Assume a population mean of 0.
   (d) Figure the estimated population variance of difference scores:
   $$S^2 = \sqrt{\Sigma(X - M)^2 / (N - 1)}.$$
   (e) Figure the variance of the distribution of means of difference scores:
   $$S_M^2 = S^2 / N.$$
   (f) Figure the standard deviation of the distribution of means of difference scores:
   $$S_M = \sqrt{S_M^2}.$$
   (g) The shape is a _t_ distribution with $df = N - 1$.
3. Determine the cutoff sample score on the comparison distribution at which the null hypothesis should be rejected.
   (a) Decide the significance level and whether to use a one-tailed or a two-tailed test.
   (b) Look up the appropriate cutoff in a _t_ table.
4. Determine your sample's score on the comparison distribution: $t = (M - \text{Population } M)/S_M$.
5. Decide whether to reject the null hypothesis: Compare the scores from Steps 3 and 4.

Assumptions of the _t_ Test

assumption

The underlying mathematics of the _t_ test assume that the population of individuals follows a normal curve. Such an assumption for a hypothesis-testing procedure is called an **assumption.** That is, a normal population distribution is one assumption of the _t_ test. The effect of this assumption is that if the population distribution is not normal, the comparison distribution will be some indeterminate shape other than a _t_ distribution—and thus the cutoffs on the _t_ table will be incorrect.

Unfortunately, when you do a _t_ test you don't know whether the population is normal. This is because when doing a _t_ test, usually all you have are the scores in your sample. Fortunately, however, as we saw in Chapter 4, distributions in the social and behavioral sciences quite often do approximate a normal curve. (This also applies to distributions of difference scores.) Also, statisticians have found that in practice, you get reasonably accurate results with _t_ tests even when the population is rather far from normal. The only very common situation in which using a _t_ test for dependent means is likely to give a seriously distorted result is when you are using a one-tailed test and the population is highly skewed (is very asymmetrical, with a much longer tail on one side than the other). If the sample of difference scores is highly skewed, this suggests that the population the sample comes from is also highly skewed (and therefore does not meet the assumption of following a normal curve).

Effect Size and Power for the *t* Test for Dependent Means

Effect Size

The estimated effect size for a study using a *t* test is the mean of the difference scores divided by the estimated variance of the population of difference scores. In terms of a formula,

$$\text{Estimated Effect Size} = M/S$$

$$(8\text{--}9)$$

M is the mean of the difference scores and *S* is the estimated standard deviation of the population of individual difference scores.

This is basically the same as the way you learned to figure effect size in Chapter 7, except that (a) we use the mean of the difference scores instead of the difference of the sample mean from the population mean, and (b) we use an estimated population standard deviation instead of a known population standard deviation.

The conventions for effect sizes are the same as you learned for the situation we considered in Chapter 7: A small effect size is .20, a medium effect size is .50, and a large effect size is .80.

For our first example of a *t* test for dependent means (the Olthoff study of husbands' change in communication quality), the mean of the difference scores was −12.05, and the estimated population standard deviation of the difference scores was 12.41 (that is, S^2 was 154.05; $\sqrt{S^2} = 12.41$). The effect size is −12.05 divided by 12.41, which is −.97. This is clearly a large effect. (The sign of the effect, in this case negative, only means that the large effect was a decrease.)

Power

Table 8–7 gives the approximate power at the .05 significance level for small, medium, and large effect sizes and one- or two-tailed tests.[5]

Suppose a researcher plans a study using the .05 significance level, two-tailed, with 20 participants. The predicted effect size is about .5 (a medium effect size). The table shows the study would have a power of .59. This means that, if the research hypothesis is in fact true and has a medium effect size, there is a 59% chance that this study will come out significant.

The power table (Table 8–7) is also useful when you are reading about a nonsignificant result in a published study. Suppose that a study using a *t* test for dependent means has a nonsignificant result. The study tested significance at the .05 level, was two-tailed, and had 10 participants. Should you conclude that there is in fact no difference at all in the populations? Probably

---

[5]More detailed tables, in terms of numbers of participants, levels of effect size, and significance levels, are provided by Cohen (1988, pp. 28–39). In these tables, effect size, which they label as *d,* is actually based on a *t* test for independent means (the situation we consider in Chapter 9). For a *t* test for dependent means, as you have learned to do in this chapter, first multiply your effect size by 1.4. The only other difference from our table is that Cohen uses the letter *a* (for "alpha level") to indicate significance level, along with a subscript of either 1 or 2, to indicate a one- or two-tailed test.

TABLE 8–7
Approximate Power for Studies Using the *t* Test for Dependent Means in Testing Hypotheses at the .05 Significance Level

Sample Size (N)	Effect Size		
	Small (.20)	*Medium (.50)*	*Large (.80)*
Two-tailed test			
10	.09	.32	.66
20	.14	.59	.93
30	.19	.77	.99
40	.24	.88	*
50	.29	.94	*
100	.55	*	*
One-tailed test			
10	.15	.46	.78
20	.22	.71	.96
30	.29	.86	*
40	.35	.93	*
50	.40	.97	*
100	.63	*	*

*Nearly 1.

not. Even assuming a medium effect size, Table 8–7 shows that there is only a 32% chance of getting a significant result in this study.

Consider another study that was not significant. This study also used the .05 significance level, one-tailed. This study had 100 research participants. Table 8–7 tells you that there would be a 63% chance of the study's coming out significant if there were even a true small effect size in the population. If there were a medium effect size in the population, the table indicates that there is almost a 100% chance that this study would have come out significant. In this study with 100 participants, we could conclude from the results of this study that in the population there is probably at most a small difference.

Planning Sample Size

Table 8–8 gives the approximate number of participants needed to have 80% power for a planned study. (Eighty percent is a common figure used by researchers for the minimum power to make a study worth doing.) The table gives the number of participants needed based on predicted small, medium, and large effect sizes, using one- and two-tailed tests, and for the .05 significance levels.[6] Suppose you plan a study in which you expect a large effect size and will use the .05 significance level, two-tailed. The table shows that for 80% power you would need only 14 participants. On the other hand, for 80% power in a study using the same significance level, also two-tailed,

---

[6]More detailed tables, giving needed numbers of participants for levels of power other than 80% (and also for effect sizes other than .20, .50, and .80 and for other significance levels) are provided in Cohen (1988, pp. 54–55). However, see footnote 5 in this chapter about using Cohen's tables for a *t* test for dependant means.

TABLE 8–8
Approximate Number of Participants Needed for 80% Power for the *t* Test for Dependent Means in Testing Hypotheses at the .05 Significance Level

	Effect Size		
	Small (.20)	*Medium (.50)*	*Large (.80)*
Two-tailed	196	33	14
One-tailed	156	26	12

but in which you expect only a small effect size, you would need 196 participants.

The Power of Studies Using *t* Test for Dependent Means

Studies using difference scores (that is, studies using a repeated-measures design) often have much larger effect sizes for the same amount of expected difference between means than have other kinds of research designs. That is, testing each of a group of participants twice (once under one condition and once under a different condition) usually gives more power than dividing the participants into two groups and testing each once (one group tested under one condition and the other tested under the other condition).

The reason repeated-measures designs have so much power is that the standard deviation of difference scores is quite low. (The standard deviation of difference scores is what you divide by to get the effect size when using difference scores.) In a repeated measures design, the only variation is in the difference scores. Variation among participants on each testing's scores are not part of the variation involved in the analysis because difference scores are all comparing participants to themselves. The effect of all this is that studies using difference scores often have quite large effect sizes (and thus high power) even with a small number of people in the study.

However, although it has advantages from the point of view of power, the kind of repeated-measures study discussed in this chapter often has disadvantages from the point of view of the meaning of the results. The main problem is that when you test a group of people twice, one testing often affects the other testing. For example, consider a study where people are tested before and after some experimental procedure. If you get a significant difference it could be due to the experimental procedure; however, it also could be due to the effect of having been tested before (or even just to time passing). The limitations of this kind of research are discussed in detail in research methods textbooks.

t Tests for Dependent Means As Described in Research Articles

Research articles usually describe *t* tests in a fairly standard format that includes the degrees of freedom, the *t* score, and the significance level. For example, "$t(24) = 2.80, p < .05$" tells you that the researcher used a *t* test with 24 degrees of freedom, found a *t* score of 2.80, and the result was significant at the .05 level. Whether a one- or two-tailed test was used may also be noted. (If not, assume that it was two-tailed.) Usually the means, and sometimes the standard deviations, are given for each testing. Rarely is the standard deviation of the difference scores reported.

Olthoff (1989) might have reported his result in the example we used in this way: "There was a significant decline in communication quality, dropping from 116.32 before marriage to 104.26 after marriage, $t(18) = 2.76$, $p < .05$, two-tailed." Here is how McLeod et al. (1994) reported some of their results:

> Confidence in the president declined from 2.57 (out of a possible 3) to 2.17 ($t[165] = 4.32$, $p < .001$). The decline in confidence in people running Congress was even steeper, falling from 2.23 during the war to 1.74 one year later ($t[165] = 5.26$, $p < .001$).

Results of *t* tests are sometimes given in tables. For example, Table 8–9 reproduces the table from the McLeod et al. (1994) article. As you can see, the same pattern of pro-government (and also pro-war) attitudes was consistent over almost all the questions asked. Notice, incidentally, the method of using stars to indicate the level of significance. This is a common procedure; in fact, sometimes the *t* value itself is not given, just the stars (with the note at the bottom as to the exact *p* levels to which they refer).

Table 8–9
***t*-Tests for Differences between Time 1 and 2 Responses**

	During War Mean	1-Year Later Mean	*T*-Value
War-related attitude scales (Maximum = 5.0)			
War is justified	3.41	3.11	2.11*
War is correct option	3.61	3.44	2.47**
Institutional confidence variables (Maximum = 3.0)			
Confidence in president	2.57	2.17	4.32***
Confidence in Congress	2.23	1.74	5.26***
Confidence in military	2.83	2.69	1.64*
Confidence in TV	2.16	2.18	−0.24
Confidence in newspapers	2.39	2.34	0.36
Media roles variables (Maximum = 7.0)			
Providing information	6.10	6.42	−2.38**
Explaining significance	5.60	5.71	−0.83
Building solidarity	5.58	5.01	3.26***
Reducing tension	5.07	4.47	3.18***
Restrictive attitude scales (Maximum = 3.0)			
Anti-war gore	2.39	2.12	3.59***
Anti-protest	2.95	2.77	3.38***

$N = 167$
*$p < .05$ **$p < .01$ ***$p < .001$

Note: From "Conflict and Public Opinion: Rallying Effects of the Persian Gulf War" by McLeod et al., *Journalism Quarterly,* 71: 20–31, 1994. Copyright © 1994 by the Association for Education in Journalism and Mass Communication. Reprinted by permission.

Summary

1. The standard five steps of hypothesis testing are used when the variance of the population is not known. However, in this situation you must estimate the population variance from the scores in the sample, using a formula that divides the sum of squared deviation scores by the degrees of freedom ($df = N - 1$). Also, when the variance is not known, the comparison distribution of means is a t distribution (with cutoffs given in a t table). A t distribution has slightly heavier tails than a normal curve (just how much heavier depends on how few degrees of freedom). Finally, in this situation the number of standard deviations from the mean that a sample's mean is on the t distribution is called a t score.

2. You use a t test for dependent means in studies where each participant has two scores, such as a "before" score and an "after" score. In this t test, you first figure a difference score for each participant, then carry out the usual 5 steps of hypothesis testing with the modifications described in the paragraph above and making Population 2 a population of difference scores with a mean of 0 (no difference).

3. An assumption of the t test is that the population distribution is a normal curve. However, even when it is not, the t test is usually fairly accurate.

4. The effect size of a study using a t test for dependent means is the mean of the difference scores divided by the standard deviation of the difference scores. Power and needed sample size for 80% power can be looked up in special tables. The power of studies using difference scores is usually much higher than that of studies using other designs with the same number of participants.

5. t tests are reported in research articles using a standard format. For example, "$t(24) = 2.80, p < .05$."

Key Terms

assumption	t distribution	t test for a single sample
biased estimate	t score	t test for dependent means
degrees of freedom (df)	t table	unbiased estimate of the population
difference scores	t test	variance (S^2)
repeated-measures design		

Practice Problems

These problems involve figuring. Most real-life statistics problems are done on a computer. Even if you have a computer and statistics software, do these practice problems by hand (with the help of a calculator) to ingrain the method in your mind.

For practice in using a computer to solve statistics problems, refer to the computer section of each chapter of the Student's Study Guide and Computer Workbook *that accompanies this text.*

All data are fictional.
Answers to selected problems are given at the back of the book.

1. In each of the following studies, a single sample's mean is being compared to a population with a known mean but an unknown variance. For each study, decide whether the result is significant. (Be sure to show all of your calculations.)

	Sample Size (N)	Population Mean	Estimated Population Variance (S²)	Sample Mean (M)	Tails	Significance Level
(a)	64	12.40	9.00	11.00	1 (low predicted)	.05
(b)	49	1,006.35	317.91	1,009.72	2	.01
(c)	400	52.00	7.02	52.41	1 (high predicted)	.01

2. Suppose a candidate running for sheriff claims that she will reduce the average speed of emergency response to less than 30 minutes. (30 minutes is thought to be the average response time with the current sheriff.) There are no past records, so the actual standard deviation of such response times cannot be determined. Thanks to this campaign, she is elected sheriff, and careful records are now kept. The response times for the first month are 26, 30, 28, 29, 25, 28, 32, 35, 24, and 23 min.

Using the .05 significance level, did she keep her promise? (a) Go through the five steps of hypothesis testing. (b) Illustrate your answer with a histogram of the sample's scores and sketches of the population distribution and the distribution of means, showing the *t* score and cutoff points for significance. (c) Explain your answer to someone who has never taken a course in statistics.

3. For each of the following studies using difference scores, decide whether the mean difference is significantly greater than 0. Also figure the estimated effect size (be sure to show all of your calculations).

	Number of Difference Scores in Sample	Mean of Difference Scores in Sample	Estimated Population Variance of Difference Scores	Tails	Significance Level
(a)	20	1.7	8.29	1 (high predicted)	.05
(b)	164	2.3	414.53	2	.05
(c)	15	−2.2	4.00	1 (low predicted)	.01

4. A program to decrease littering was carried out in four cities in California's Central Valley starting in August 2000. The amount of litter in the streets (average pounds of litter collected per block per day) was measured during the July before the program was started and then the next July, after the program had been in effect for a year. The results were as follows:

City	July 2000	July 2001
Fresno	9	2
Merced	10	4
Bakersfield	8	9
Stockton	9	1

Using the 1% level of significance, was there a significant decrease in the amount of litter? (a) Go through the five steps of hypothesis testing. (b) Illustrate your answer with a histogram of the sample's difference scores and sketches of the population distribution (of difference scores) and the distribution of means (of difference scores), showing the *t* score and cutoff points for significance. (c) Explain your answer to someone who understands mean, standard deviation, and variance, but knows nothing else about statistics.

5. Five people who were convicted of speeding were ordered by the court to attend a workshop. A special device put into their cars kept records of their speeds for 2 weeks before and after the workshop. The maximum speeds for each person during the two weeks before and the two weeks after the workshop follow:

Person	Before	After
L. B.	65	58
J. K.	62	65
R. C.	60	56
R. T.	70	66
J. M.	68	60

Using the .05 significance level, should we conclude that people are likely to drive more slowly after such a workshop? (a) Go through the five steps of hypothesis testing. (b) Give the estimated effect size of your result. (c) Illustrate your answer with a histogram of the sample's difference scores and sketches of the population distribution (of difference scores) and the distribution of means (of difference scores), showing the *t* score and cutoff points for significance. (d) Explain your answer to someone who is familiar with hypothesis testing with known populations, but has never learned anything about *t* tests.

6. What is the power of each of the following studies (based on the .05 significance level)?

	Effect Size	N	Tails
(a)	Small	20	1
(b)	Medium	20	1
(c)	Medium	30	1
(d)	Medium	30	2
(e)	Large	30	2

7. For each of the following planned studies, how many participants would you need to have 80% power (based on the .05 significance level)?

	Expected Effect Size	Tails
(a)	Small	1
(b)	Small	2
(c)	Medium	1
(d)	Medium	2
(e)	Large	1
(f)	Large	2

8. A study compared union activity of employees in 10 plants during two different decades. The researchers reported "a significant increase in union activity, $t(9) = 3.28$, $p < .01$." Explain this result to a person who has never had a course in statistics. Be sure to use sketches of the distributions in your answer.

9

The *t* Test
for Independent Means

T HIS chapter examines hypothesis testing in the very common situation of comparing two samples, such as an experimental group and a control group. This is a *t* test situation because you don't know the population variances so they must be estimated. This time it is called a *t* **test for independent means** because we are comparing the means of two entirely separate groups of people whose scores are independent of each other. This is in contrast to the *t* test for dependent means, considered in the last chapter, in which there were two groups of scores, but both were for the same people (such as the same people measured before and after a health-promotion educational program).

t test for independent means

You should be thoroughly comfortable with the material in Chapter 8, particularly the basic logic and procedures of the *t* test, before going on to the material in this chapter.

Basic Strategy of the *t* Test for Independent Means: The Distribution of Differences Between Means

The *t* test for independent means works in the same way as the hypothesis testing you have already learned, with one main exception: The key result of the study is a difference between the means of the two samples. Thus, the comparison distribution is a **distribution of differences between means**.

distribution of differences between means

What Is in a Distribution of Differences between Means?

This special distribution is, in a sense, two steps removed from the populations of individuals: First, there is a distribution of means from each population of individuals. Second, there is a distribution of differences between pairs of means, one of each pair from each of these distributions of means.

Think of this distribution of differences between means as being built up as follows: (a) Randomly select one mean from the distribution of means for Population 1, (b) randomly select one mean from the distribution of means for Population 2, and (c) subtract. (That is, take the mean from the first distribution of means minus the mean from the second distribution of means.) This gives a difference score between the two selected means. Then repeat the process. This creates a second difference, a difference between the two newly selected means. Repeating this process a large number of times creates a distribution of differences between means.

Illustration of the Overall Logic of the *t* Test for Independent Means

Figure 9–1 diagrams the entire logical construction involved in a distribution of differences between means. At the top are the two population distributions. We do not know the characteristics of these population distributions. But we do know that if the null hypothesis is true, the two population means are the same. That is, the null hypothesis is that Population M_1 = Population M_2. We also can estimate the variance of these populations, based on the sample information (these estimated variances will be S_1^2 and S_2^2).

FIGURE 9–1
The steps in creating a distribution of differences between means.

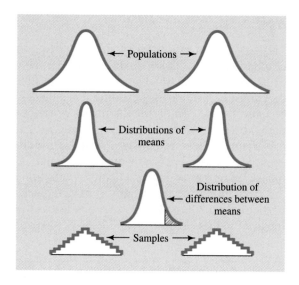

Below each population distribution is the distribution of means for that population. Using the estimated population variance and knowing the size of each sample, you can figure the variance of each distribution of means in the usual way. (It is the variance of its parent population divided by the size of the sample.)

Below these two distributions of means, and built from them, is the crucial distribution of differences between means. This distribution's variance is ultimately based on estimated population variances. Thus, we can think of it as a *t* distribution. The goal of a *t* test for independent means is to decide whether the difference between the means of our two actual samples is a more extreme difference than the cutoff difference on this distribution of differences.

The two actual samples are shown (as little histograms) at the bottom. Remember, this whole procedure is really a kind of complicated castle in the air. It exists only in our minds to help us make decisions based on the results of an actual experiment. The only concrete reality in all of this is the actual scores in the two samples. The population variances are estimated on the basis of these sample scores. The variances of the two distributions of means are based entirely on these estimated population variances (and the sample sizes). And, as you will see shortly, the characteristics of the distribution of differences between means is based on these two distributions of means.

Still, the procedure is a powerful one. It has the power of mathematics and logic behind it. It helps you develop general knowledge based on the specifics of a particular study.

With this overview of the basic logic, we now turn to five key details: (a) the mean of the distribution of differences between means, (b) the estimated population variance, (c) the variance and standard deviation of the distribution of differences between means, (d) the shape of the distribution of differences between means, and (e) the *t* score for the difference between the particular two means being compared.

Mean of the Distribution of Differences Between Means

In a *t* test for independent means, two populations are being considered—for example, one population from which an experimental group is taken and one population from which a control group is taken. In practice, a researcher does not know the mean of either population. The researcher does know that if the null hypothesis is true, these two populations have equal means. Also, if these two populations have equal means, the two distributions of means will have equal means. (This is because each distribution of means has the same mean as its parent population of individuals.) Finally, if you take random samples from two distributions with equal means, the differences between the means of these random samples, in the long run, should balance out to 0. The result of all this is the following: Whatever the specifics of the study, the researcher knows that if the null hypothesis is true, the distribution of differences between means has a mean of 0.

Estimating the Population Variance

In Chapter 8, you learned to estimate the population variance using the scores in your sample. It is the sum of squared deviation scores divided by the degrees of freedom (the number in the sample minus 1).

To carry out a *t* test for independent means, it has to be reasonable to assume that the populations the two samples come from have the same variance. (If the null hypothesis is true, they also have the same mean. However, whether or not the null hypothesis is true, you must be able to assume the two populations have the same variance.) Therefore, when we estimate the population variance from the scores in either sample, we are getting two separate estimates of what should be the same number. In practice, the two estimates will almost never be exactly identical. Since they are both supposed to be estimating the same thing, the best solution is to average the two estimates to get the best single overall estimate. This is called the **pooled estimate of the population variance (S^2_{Pooled}).**

In making this average, however, we also have to take into account the fact that the two samples may not be the same size. If one sample is larger than the other, the estimate it provides is likely to be more accurate (because it is based on more information). If both samples are exactly the same size, we can just take an ordinary average of our two estimates. On the other hand, when they are not the same size, we need to make some adjustment in our averaging to give more weight to the larger sample. We need a **weighted average,** an average weighted by the amount of information each sample provides.

Also, to be precise, the amount of information each sample provides is not its number of scores, but its degrees of freedom (its number of scores minus 1). Thus, when you create a weighted average, it has to be based on the degrees of freedom each sample provides. The procedure to find the weighted average is to figure out what proportion of the total degrees of freedom each sample contributes, and multiply that proportion times the population variance estimate from that sample. Finally, you add up the two results and that is your weighted, pooled estimate. Here is this principle stated as a formula:

$$S^2_{\text{Pooled}} = \frac{df_1}{df_{\text{Total}}}(S^2_1) + \frac{df_2}{df_{\text{Total}}}(S^2_2)$$

(9–1)

In this formula, S^2_{Pooled} is the pooled estimate of the population variance. df_1 is the degrees of freedom for Population 1, and df_2 is the degrees of

pooled estimate of the population variance (S^2_{Pooled})

weighted average

freedom for Population 2. (Remember each sample's *df* is its number of scores minus 1.) df_{Total} is the total degrees of freedom ($df_{Total} = df_1 + df_2$). S_1^2 is the estimate of the population variance based on the scores in the sample from Population 1; S_2^2 is the estimate based on the scores in the sample from Population 2.

Consider a study in which the population variance estimate based on an experimental group of 11 participants is 60 and the population variance estimate based on a control group of 31 participants is 80. The estimate from the experimental group is based on 10 degrees of freedom (11 participants minus 1), and the estimate from the control group is based on 30 degrees of freedom (31 minus 1). The total information on which the estimate is based is the total degrees of freedom—in this example, 40 (10+30). Thus, the experimental group provides one quarter of the information (10/40 = 1/4), and the control group provides three quarters of the information (30/40 = 3/4). The population variance estimate from the experimental group of 60 is then multiplied by 1/4, making 15. The population variance estimate from the control group of 80 is multiplied by 3/4, making 60. Adding the two together gives an overall estimate of 15 plus 60, or 75. Using the formula,

$$S_{Pooled}^2 = \frac{df_1}{df_{Total}}(S_1^2) + \frac{df_2}{df_{Total}}(S_2^2) = \frac{10}{40}(60) + \frac{30}{40}(80)$$

$$= \frac{1}{4}(60) + \frac{3}{4}(80) = 15 + 60 = 75$$

notice that this procedure does not give the same result as ordinary averaging (without weighting). Ordinary averaging would give an estimate of 70 (that is, [60 + 80] / 2 = 70). Our weighted, pooled estimate of 75 is closer to the estimate based on the control group alone than to the estimate based on the experimental group alone. This is as it should be, because the control group estimate in this example was based on more information.

Figuring the Variance of Each of the Two Distributions of Means

The pooled estimate of the population variance is the best estimate for both populations. (Remember, to do a *t* test for independent means, you have to be able to assume that the two populations have the same variance.) However, even though the two populations have the same variance, the distributions of means taken from them do not usually have the same variance. That is because the variance of a distribution of means is the population variance divided by the sample size. So even though the population variance is the same for the two populations, if the two samples have different sample sizes, then the two distributions of means will have different variances. In terms of formulas:

$$S_{M_1}^2 = \frac{S_{Pooled}^2}{N_1}$$

(9–2)

$$S_{M_2}^2 = \frac{S_{Pooled}^2}{N_2} \qquad\qquad (9\text{--}3)$$

Consider again the example of the study in which there were 11 in the experimental group and 31 in the control group. In that example, we found that the pooled estimate of the population variance is 75. So for the experimental group, the variance of the distribution of means would be 75/11, which is 6.82. For the control group, the variance would be 75/31, which is 2.42. (Remember that when figuring estimated variances you divide by the degrees of freedom. But when figuring the variance of a distribution of means, which does not involve any additional estimation, you divide by the actual number in the sample.) In terms of formulas:

$$S_{M1}^2 = \frac{S_{Pooled}^2}{N_1} = \frac{75}{11} = 6.82$$

$$S_{M2}^2 = \frac{S_{Pooled}^2}{N_2} = \frac{75}{31} = 2.42$$

Variance and Standard Deviation of the Distribution of Differences between Means

The **variance of the distribution of differences between means** $(S_{Difference}^2)$ is the variance of Population 1's distribution of means plus the variance of Population 2's distribution of means. (This is because in a difference between two numbers, the variation in each contributes to the overall variation in their difference. It is like subtracting a moving number from a moving target.) Stated as a formula,

variance of the distribution of differences between means $(S_{Difference}^2)$

$$S_{Difference}^2 = S_{M_1}^2 + S_{M_2}^2 \qquad\qquad (9\text{--}4)$$

The **standard deviation of the distribution of differences between means** $(S_{Difference})$ is the square root of the variance:

standard deviation of the distribution of differences between means $(S_{Difference})$

$$S_{Difference} = \sqrt{S_{Difference}^2} \qquad\qquad (9\text{--}5)$$

Consider again the example study with 11 in the experimental group and 31 in the control group. We found that the variance of the distribution of means for the experimental group was 6.82 and the variance of the distribution of means for the control group was 2.42. The variance of the distribution of the difference between means would thus be 6.82 plus 2.42, which is 9.24. This makes the standard deviation of this distribution the square root of 9.24, which is 3.04. In terms of formulas:

$$S_{Difference}^2 = S_{M_1}^2 + S_{M_2}^2 = 6.82 + 2.42 = 9.24$$

$$S_{\text{Difference}} = \sqrt{S^2_{\text{Difference}}} = \sqrt{9.24} = 3.04$$

Shape of the Distribution of Differences between Means

The distribution of differences between means is based on estimated population variances. Thus, the distribution of differences between means (our comparison distribution) is a *t* distribution. The variance of this distribution is figured based on population variance estimates from two samples. Therefore, the degrees of freedom for this *t* distribution are the sum of the degrees of freedom of the two samples ($df_{\text{Total}} = df_1 + df_2$).

In our example with an experimental group of 11 and a control group of 31, we saw earlier that the total degrees of freedom is 40 (11 − 1 = 10; 31 − 1 = 30; 10 + 30 = 40). To determine the *t* score needed for significance, you look up the cutoff point in the *t* table in the row with 40 degrees of freedom. Suppose you were conducting a one-tailed test using the .05 significance level. The *t* table in Appendix A shows that with 40 degrees of freedom, for a result to be significant, the difference between your means must be at least 1.684 standard deviations above the mean difference of 0 on the distribution of differences between means.

The *t* Score for the Difference between the Two Actual Means

Here is how you figure the *t* score for Step 4 of hypothesis testing: First, figure the difference between your two samples' means. (That is, subtract one from the other.) Then, figure out where this difference is on the distribution of differences between means. You do this by dividing your difference by the standard deviation of this distribution. In terms of a formula,

$$t = \frac{M_1 - M_2}{S_{\text{Difference}}}$$

(9–6)

For our example, suppose the mean of the first sample is 198 and the mean of the second sample is 190. The difference between these two means is 8 (that is, 198−190 = 8). Earlier we figured the standard deviation of the distribution of differences between means in this example to be 3.04. That would make a *t* score of 2.63 (that is, 8/3.04 = 2.63). In other words, in this example the difference between the two means is 2.63 standard deviations above the mean of the distribution of differences between means. In terms of the formula,

$$t = \frac{M_1 - M_2}{S_{\text{Difference}}} = \frac{198 - 190}{3.04} = \frac{8}{3.04} = 2.63$$

Steps of Hypothesis Testing with a *t* Test for Independent Means

Considering our five steps of hypothesis testing, there are three new wrinkles for a *t* test for independent means: (a) The comparison distribution is now a distribution of differences between means (this affects Step 2); (b) the degrees of freedom for finding the cutoff on the _t_ table is based on two samples (this affects Step 3); and (c) your sample's score on the comparison distribution is based on the difference between your two means (this affects Step 4).

Example of a _t_ Test for Independent Means

Moorehouse and Sanders (1992) studied whether an adolescent boy's sense of how well he is doing in school is related to his mother's work situation. The boys were all in seventh to ninth grades and were all from families in which the mother worked full-time. For purposes of this analysis, the boys were divided into two groups, those in which the mother's work gave her opportunities to solve problems (26 boys) and those in which the mother's work did not give her opportunities to solve problems (17 boys). All 43 boys were given a standard test of perceived academic competence (how successful they see themselves as being at school).

The _t_-test is illustrated in Figure 9–2; the scores and computations are shown in Table 9–1. Let's go through the full five steps of hypothesis testing.

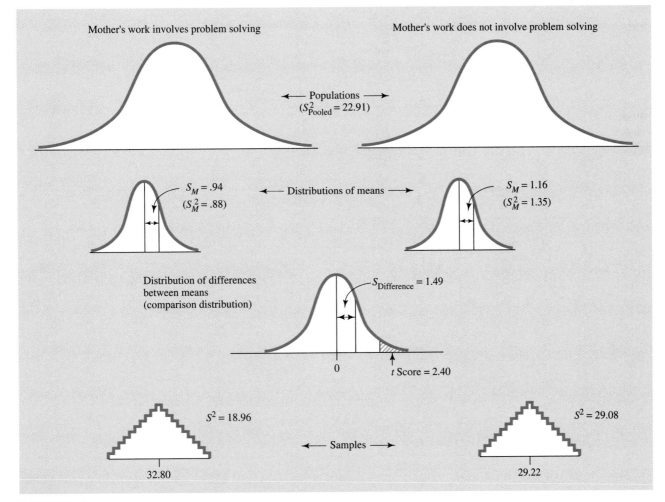

FIGURE 9–2
The distributions involved in the example of a _t_ test for independent means.

TABLE 9–1

***t* Test for Independent Means for a Study of the Relation of the Work Situation of the Mothers of Adolescent Boys to the Boys' Perceived Academic Competence**

Boys Whose Mothers' Work Involves Problem Solving			Boys Whose Mothers' Work Does Not Involve Problem Solving		
Score	*Deviation from mean*	*Squared deviation from mean*	*Score*	*Deviation from mean*	*Squared deviation from mean*
36.9	4.1	16.81	23.5	− 5.7	32.49
34.6	1.8	16.81	22.5	− 6.7	44.89
26.4	− 6.4	40.96	36.4	7.2	51.84
33.3	.5	.25	40.0	10.8	116.64
35.4	2.6	6.76	30.6	1.4	1.96
34.8	2.0	4.00	30.5	1.3	1.69
32.3	− .5	.25	34.5	5.3	28.09
34.5	1.7	2.89	31.3	2.1	4.41
36.0	3.2	10.24	19.4	− 9.8	96.04
24.5	− 8.3	68.89	29.6	.4	.16
31.6	− 1.2	1.44	24.8	− 4.4	19.36
36.1	3.3	10.89	25.0	− 4.2	17.64
36.8	4.0	16.00	28.8	− .4	.16
27.9	− 4.9	24.01	32.5	3.3	10.89
34.4	1.6	2.56	33.3	4.1	16.81
33.8	1.0	1.00	29.6	.4	.16
36.9	4.1	16.81	24.5	4.7	22.09
34.4	1.6	2.56			
31.7	− 1.1	1.21			
29.4	− 3.4	11.56			
34.1	1.3	1.69			
18.2	−14.6	213.16			
34.5	1.7	2.89			
35.3	2.5	6.25			
35.5	2.7	7.29			
33.4	.6	.36			
Σ: 852.7	0.0	473.97	496.8	0.0	465.32

$M_1 = 32.80$; $S_1^2 = 473.97/25 = 18.96$; $M_2 = 29.22$; $S_2^2 = 465.32/16 = 29.08$

$N_1 = 26$; $df_1 = N_1 - 1 = 25$; $N_2 = 17$; $df_2 = N_2 - 1 = 16$

$df_{Total} = df_1 + df_2 = 25 + 16 = 41$

$$S_{Pooled}^2 = \frac{df_1}{df_{Total}}(S_1^2) + \frac{df_2}{df_{Total}}(S_2^2) = \frac{25}{41}(18.96) + \frac{16}{41}(29.08) = .61(18.96) + .39(29.08) = 11.57 + 11.34 = 22.91$$

$S_{M_1}^2 = S_{Pooled}^2/N_1 = 22.91/26 = .88$

$S_{M_2}^2 = S_{Pooled}^2/N_2 = 22.91/17 = 1.35$

$S_{Difference}^2 = S_{M_1}^2 + S_{M_2}^2 = .88 + 1.35 = 2.23$

$S_{Difference} = \sqrt{S_{Difference}^2} = \sqrt{2.23} = 1.49$

Needed *t* with $df = 41$ (using $df = 40$ in table), 5% level, one-tailed = 1.684

$t = (M_1 - M_2)/S_{Difference} = (32.80 - 29.22)/1.49 = 3.58/1.49 = 2.40$

Conclusion: Reject the null hypothesis; the research hypothesis is supported.

Note: Data from Moorehouse & Sanders (1992).

1. Restate the question as a research hypothesis and a null hypothesis about the populations. There are two populations:

Population 1: Boys whose mothers' work involves solving problems
Population 2: Boys whose mothers' work does not involve solving problems

Based on theory and previous research, Moorehouse and Sanders expected that boys whose mothers' work involved solving problems to have higher scores on the test of perceived academic competence. The research hypothesis was that Population 1 boys would score higher than Population 2 boys. (That is, this was a directional hypothesis.) The null hypothesis was that the Population 1 boys would not score higher than the Population 2 boys.

2. Determine the characteristics of the comparison distribution. The comparison distribution is a distribution of differences between means. Its mean is 0 (as it almost always is in a *t* test for independent means, because we are interested in whether there is more than 0 difference between the two populations). The population variance estimated from the two samples comes out to 18.96 and 29.08. The pooled estimate of the population variance is the weighted average of these two: 25/41 times 18.96 and 16/41 times 29.08. This comes out to 22.91. The variance for each distribution of means—this pooled estimate divided by its sample size (22.91/26 and 22.91/17)—comes out to .88 and 1.35. Summing the variance of these two gives the variance of the distribution of differences between means, 2.23. The square root of this variance—the standard deviation of the distribution of differences between means—is 1.49. The shape of this comparison distribution will be a *t* distribution with a total of 41 degrees of freedom.

3. Determine the cutoff sample score on the comparison distribution at which the null hypothesis should be rejected. This requires a one-tailed test because a particular direction of difference between the two populations was predicted. Since the *t* table in Appendix A (Table A–2) does not have exactly 41 degrees of freedom, the next lowest (40) is used. At the .05 level, a *t* of at least 1.684 is needed.

4. Determine your sample's score on the comparison distribution. The *t* score is the difference between the two sample means (32.80–29.22, which is 3.58) is divided by the standard deviation of the distribution of differences between means (which is 1.49). This comes out to 2.40.

5. Decide whether to reject the null hypothesis. The *t* score of 2.40 for the difference between the two actual means is larger than the needed *t* score of 1.684. The null hypothesis can be rejected. The research hypothesis is supported: Boys whose mothers' work involves solving problems see themselves as better at schoolwork than boys whose mothers' work does not involve solving problems.

A Second Example of a *t* Test for Independent Means

Suppose a researcher wants to study the effectiveness of a new job-skills training program for people who have not been able to hold a job. Fourteen people who have not been able to hold a job agree to be in the study. The researcher randomly picks seven of these volunteers to be an experimental group that will go through the special training program. The other seven volunteers are put in a control group that will go through an ordinary job-skills training program. After finishing their training program (of whichever type), all 14 are placed in similar jobs.

A month later, each volunteer's employer is asked to rate how well the new employee is doing using a 9-point scale. The fictional results and the full *t* test analysis are shown in Table 9–2. The analysis is illustrated in Figure 9–3. Let's carry out the analysis, following the hypothesis-testing procedure step by step.

1. Restate the question as a research hypothesis and a null hypothesis about the populations. There are two populations:

Population 1: Individuals who could not hold a job who then participate in the special job-skills program

Population 2: Individuals who could not hold a job who then participate in an ordinary job-skills program

It is possible for the special program to have either a positive or a negative effect compared to the ordinary program, and either result would be of interest.

TABLE 9–2
Computations for a *t* Test for Independent Means for an Experiment Examining the Effectiveness (Using Employers' Ratings) of a New Job-Skills Program for People Who Have Previously Not Been Able to Hold Jobs

	Experimental Group (Receiving Special Program)			Control Group (Receiving Standard Program)		
	Score	Deviation from mean	Squared deviation from mean	Score	Deviation from mean	Squared deviation from mean
	6	0	0	6	3	9
	4	−2	4	1	−2	4
	9	3	9	5	2	4
	7	1	1	3	0	0
	7	1	1	1	−2	4
	3	−3	9	1	−2	4
	6	0	0	4	1	1
Σ:	42	0	24	21	0	26

$M_1 = 6$; $S_1^2 = 24/6 = 4$; $M_2 = 3$; $S_2^2 = 26/6 = 4.33$

$N_1 = 7$; $df_1 = N_1 - 1 = 6$; $N_2 = 7$; $df_2 = N_2 - 1 = 6$

$df_{\text{Total}} = df_1 + df_2 = 6 + 6 = 12$

$$S_{\text{Pooled}}^2 = \frac{df_1}{df_{\text{Total}}}(S_1^2) + \frac{df_2}{df_{\text{Total}}}(S_2^2) = \frac{6}{12}(4) + \frac{6}{12}(4.33) = .5(4) + .5(4.33) = 2.00 + 2.17 = 4.17$$

$S_{M_1}^2 = S_{\text{Pooled}}^2/N_1 = 4.17/7 = .60$

$S_{M_2}^2 = S_{\text{Pooled}}^2/N_2 = 4.17/7 = .60$

$S_{\text{Difference}}^2 = S_{M_1}^2 + S_{M_2}^2 = .60 + .60 = 1.20$

$S_{\text{Difference}} = \sqrt{S_{\text{Difference}}^2} = \sqrt{1.20} = 1.10$

Needed *t* with $df = 12$, 5% level, two-tailed $= \pm2.179$

$t = (M_1 - M_2)/S_{\text{Difference}} = (6.00 - 3.00)/1.10 = 3.00/1.10 = 2.73$

Conclusion: Reject the null hypothesis; the research hypothesis is supported.

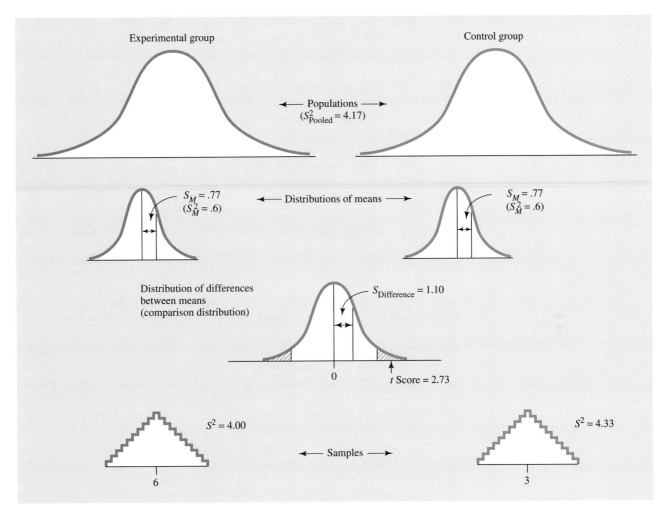

FIGURE 9–3
The distributions involved in the second example of a *t* test for independent means.

Thus, the research hypothesis is that the means of the two populations are different. This is a nondirectional hypothesis. The null hypothesis is that the means of the two populations are the same.

   2. **Determine the characteristics of the comparison distribution.** The distribution of differences between means will have a mean of 0, as usual. We figure its standard deviation by (a) finding the estimated population variance based on each sample; (b) finding the pooled estimate by taking a weighted average of these two estimates (in this example, we have equal numbers in the two samples, so a weighted average comes out the same as an ordinary average); (c) for each population, dividing the pooled estimate by the sample size to get the variance of each distribution of means; (d) adding together the variances of the two distributions of means to get the variance of the distribution of differences between means; and (e) taking the square root of this variance. As shown in Table 9–2, this standard deviation of the distribution of differences between means is 1.10. The shape of the comparison distribution is a *t* distribution with a total of 12 degrees of freedom.

3. **Determine the cutoff sample score on the comparison distribution at which the null hypothesis should be rejected.** The researchers use the ordinary .05 significance level and a two-tailed test (because the hypothesis is nondirectional). Looking this up on the *t* table in the row for 12 degrees of freedom, we need a *t* score of at least ±2.179.

4. **Determine your sample's score on the comparison distribution.** The mean difference divided by the standard deviation of the distribution of differences between means comes out to a *t* score of 2.73.

5. **Decide whether to reject the null hypothesis.** The *t* score of 2.73 is more extreme than the needed 2.179. Thus, the researchers can reject the null hypothesis and conclude that the research hypothesis is supported, that the new job-skills program is effective.

Summary of Steps for Conducting a *t* Test for Independent Means

Table 9–3 summarizes the steps for conducting a *t* test for independent means.[1]

Assumptions of the *t* Test for Independent Means

The first assumption for a *t* test for independent means is the same as that for any *t* test: Each of the population distributions is assumed to follow a normal curve. In practice, this is only a problem if you have reason to think that the two populations are dramatically skewed distributions, and in opposite directions. More generally, the *t* test holds up quite well even when the shape of the population distributions is fairly far from normal.

In a *t* test for independent means, there is also a second important assumption: The two populations are assumed to have the same variance. (We take advantage of this assumption when we average the estimates from each of our two samples.) Once again, however, it turns out that in practice the *t* test gives pretty accurate results even when there are fairly large differences in the population variances, particularly when there are equal numbers of scores in the two samples.

However, the *t* test can give quite misleading results if (a) the scores in the sample suggest that the populations are very far from normal, (b) the variances are very different, or (c) both problems are there. In these situations, there are alternatives to the ordinary *t* test procedure, some of which we will consider in Chapter 11.

---

[1]The steps of figuring the standard deviation of the distribution of differences between means can be combined into a single overall computational formula:

$$S_{\text{Difference}} = \sqrt{\frac{(N_1 - 1)(S_1^2) + (N_2 - 1)(S_2^2)}{N_1 + N_2 - 2} \left(\frac{1}{N_1} + \frac{1}{N_2}\right)} \qquad (9\text{--}7)$$

As usual, we urge you to use the full set of steps and the regular, definitional formulas in your figuring when doing the practice problems in this book. Those steps help you learn the basic principles. However, this computational formula will be useful if a computer with statistics software is not available and you have to compute by hand a *t* test for independent means on actual data from a study with many participants in each group.

TABLE 9–3
Steps for Conducting a *t* Test for Independent Means

1. **Restate the question as a research hypothesis and a null hypothesis about the populations.**

2. **Determine the characteristics of the comparison distribution.**

   a. Its mean will be 0.

   b. Figure its standard deviation.

      i. Figure the estimated population variances based on each sample (that is, figure two estimates).

      ii. Figure the pooled estimate of population variance:

$$S^2_{Pooled} = \frac{df_1}{df_{Total}}(S_1^2) + \frac{df_2}{df_{Total}}(S_2^2)$$

$$(df_1 = N_1 - 1 \text{ and } df_2 = N_2 - 1; df_{Total} = df_1 + df_2)$$

      iii. Figure the variance of each distribution of means: $S^2_{M_1} = S^2_{Pooled}/N_1$ and $S^2_{M_2} = S^2_{Pooled}/N_2$

      iv. Figure the variance of the distribution of differences between means:
      $$S^2_{Difference} = S^2_{M_1} + S^2_{M_2}$$

      v. Figure the standard deviation of the distribution of differences between means:
      $$S_{Difference} = \sqrt{S^2_{Difference}}$$

   c. It will be a *t* distribution with df_{Total} degrees of freedom.

3. **Determine the cutoff sample score on the comparison distribution at which the null hypothesis should be rejected.**

   a. Determine the degrees of freedom (df_{Total}), desired significance level, and tails in the test (one or two).

   b. Look up the appropriate cutoff in a *t* table. If the exact *df* is not given, use the *df* below.

4. **Determine your sample's score on the comparison distribution:**
   $t = (M_1 - M_2)/S_{Difference}$

5. **Decide whether to reject the null hypothesis:** Compare the scores from Steps 3 and 4.

   Many computer programs for figuring the *t* test for independent means actually provide two sets of results. One set of results figures the *t* test assuming the population variances are equal. This method is the standard one, the one you have learned in this chapter. The other method it uses does not make this assumption. It uses an alternative procedure that takes into account that the population variances may be unequal. However, in most situations we can assume that the population variances are equal. Thus, researchers usually use the standard procedure. Using the special approach has the advantage that you don't have to worry about whether you met the equal population variance assumption, but it has the disadvantage that if you have met that assumption, with this special method you have less power. That is, you are less likely to get a significant result using the special method.

Effect Size and Power for the *t* Test for Independent Means

Effect Size

The effect size for the *t* test for independent means is the difference between the population means divided by the standard deviation of the population of individuals. When you have results of a completed study, the effect size is estimated as the difference between the sample means divided by the pooled estimate of the population standard deviation. (The pooled estimate of the population standard deviation is the square root of the pooled estimate of the population variance). Stated as a formula:

$$\text{Estimated Effect Size} = \frac{M_1 - M_2}{S_{\text{Pooled}}}$$

(9–8)

Cohen's (1988) conventions for the *t* test for independent means are the same as in all the situations we have considered so far: .20 for a small effect size, .50 for a medium effect size, and .80 for a large effect size.

Power

Table 9–4 gives the approximate power for the .05 significance level for small, medium, and large effect sizes and one- or two-tailed tests.

For example, suppose you have read a study using a *t* test for independent means that had a nonsignificant result using the .05 significance level, two-tailed. There were 40 participants in each group. Should you conclude that there is in fact no difference at all in the populations? This conclusion

TABLE 9–4

Approximate Power for Studies Using the *t* Test for Independent Means Testing Hypotheses at the .05 Significance Level

Number of Participants in Each Group	Effect Size		
	Small *(.20)*	*Medium* *(.50)*	*Large* *(.80)*
One-tailed test			
10	.11	.29	.53
20	.15	.46	.80
30	.19	.61	.92
40	.22	.72	.97
50	.26	.80	.99
100	.41	.97	*
Two-tailed test			
10	.07	.18	.39
20	.09	.33	.69
30	.12	.47	.86
40	.14	.60	.94
50	.17	.70	.98
100	.29	.94	*

*Nearly 1.
Note: Based on Cohen (1988), pp. 28–39.

BOX 9–1

Two Women Make a Point about Gender and Statistics

One of the most useful advanced statistics books written so far is *Using Multivariate Statistics* by Barbara Tabachnick and Linda Fidell (2001), two experimental psychologists at California State University at Northridge. These two met at a faculty luncheon soon after Tabachnick was hired. Fidell recalls:

> I had this enormous data set to analyze, and out came lots of pretty numbers in nice neat little columns, but I was not sure what all of it meant, or even whether my data had violated any critical assumptions. That was in 1975. I had been trained at the University of Michigan; I knew statistics up through the analysis of variance. But none of us were taught the multivariate analysis of variance at that time. Then along came these statistical packages to do it. But how to comprehend them?

(You will be introduced to the multivariate analysis of variance in Chapter 12.)

Both Fidell and Tabachnick had gone out and learned on their own, taking the necessary courses, reading, asking others who knew the programs better, trying out what would happen if they did this with the data, what would happen if they did that. Now the two women asked each other, why must this be so hard? Were others reinventing this same wheel at the very same time? They decided to put their wheel into a book.

"And so began fifteen years of conflict-free collaboration," reports Fidell. (That is something to compare to the feuds recounted in other boxes in this book.) The authors had no trouble finding a publisher, and the book, now in its second edition, has sold "nicely." In Fidell's opinion, statistics is a field in which women seem particularly to excel and feel comfortable. It is a branch of mathematics that, according to Fidell, women often come to find "perfectly logical, perfectly reasonable—and then, with time, something they can truly enjoy."

In teaching new students, the math-shy ones in particular, she finds that once she can "get them to relax," they often find that they thoroughly enjoy statistics. She tells them, "I intend to win you over. And if you will give me half a chance, I will do it."

Reference: Personal interview with Linda Fidell.

---

seems quite unjustified. Table 9–4 shows a power of only .14 for a small effect size. This suggests that if such a small effect really exists in the populations, this study would probably not show it. Still, we can conclude that if there is a true difference in the populations, it is probably not large. Table 9–4 shows a power of .94 for a large effect size. This suggests that if a large effect exists, it almost surely would have produced a significant result.

Power When Sample Sizes Are Not Equal

For a study with any given total number of participants, power is greatest when the participants are divided into two equal groups. Recall our example where the 42 participants were divided into 11 in the experimental group and 31 in the control group. This study has much less power than it would have if the researchers had been able to divide their 42 participants into two groups of 21.

There is a practical problem in figuring power from tables when sample sizes are not equal. Like most power tables, Table 9–4 assumes equal

harmonic mean

numbers in each of the two groups. What do you do when your two samples have different numbers of people in them? It turns out that in terms of power, the **harmonic mean** of the two unequal sample sizes gives the equivalent sample size for what you would have with two equal samples. The harmonic mean sample size is given by this formula:

$$\text{Harmonic Mean} = \frac{(2)(N_1)(N_2)}{N_1 + N_2}$$

(9–9)

In our example with 11 in one group and 31 in the other, the harmonic mean comes out to about 16.24:

$$\text{Harmonic Mean} = \frac{(2)(N_1)(N_2)}{N_1 + N_2} = \frac{(2)(11)(31)}{11 + 31} = \frac{682}{42} = 16.24$$

Thus, even though you have a total of 42 participants, the study has the power of a study with equal sample sizes of only about 16 in each group. (This means that a study with a total of 32 participants divided equally would have had about the same power.)

Planning Sample Size

Table 9–5 gives the approximate number of participants needed for 80% power for estimated small, medium, and large effect sizes using one- and two-tailed tests, all using the .05 significance level. Suppose you plan a study in which you expect a medium effect size and will use the .05 significance level, one-tailed. Based on Table 9–5, you need 50 people in each group (100 total) to have 80% power. However, if you did a study using the same significance level but expected a large effect size, you would need only 20 people in each group (40 total).

The *t* Test for Independent Means As Described in Research Articles

A *t* test for independent means usually is described in research articles by giving the means (and sometimes also the standard deviations) of the two samples, plus the standard way of giving the *t* numbers—for example, "*t*(18) = 4.72, *p* < .01".

TABLE 9–5

Approximate Number of Participants Needed in Each Group (Assuming Equal Sample Sizes) for 80% Power for the *t* Test for Independent Means, Testing Hypotheses at the .05 Significance Level

	Effect Size		
	Small *(.20)*	*Medium* *(.50)*	*Large* *(.80)*
One-tailed	310	50	20
Two-tailed	393	64	26

TABLE 9–6
t Tests for Means on Passive-Smoking Knowledge, Attitude and Efforts
According to Smoking Status, for Total Group and Men and Women

	Brother Smoker	Brother Nonsmoker	T-Value	Sig.
Total Group	*N =*	*N =*		
Knowledge	2.03 (96)	1.88 (140)	2.61	.01
Attitude	1.95 (94)	1.70 (137)	3.29	.001
Efforts	2.36 (92)	2.23 (133)	1.88	.061
Phys. Resp.*	1.78 (95)	1.61 (142)	2.02	.04
Men				
Knowledge	2.15 (54)	1.92 (69)	2.97	.004
Attitude	2.08 (54)	1.83 (67)	2.12	.036
Efforts	2.50 (52)	2.31 (66)	1.87	.064
Phys. Resp.*	1.81 (54)	1.65 (69)	1.27	.207
Women				
Knowledge	1.87 (42)	1.85 (71)	.30	.767
Attitude	1.77 (40)	1.57 (70)	2.43	.018
Efforts	2.17 (40)	2.15 (67)	.26	.797
Phys. Resp.*	1.76 (41)	1.58 (73)	1.51	.136

*Physician's Responsibility.
Note: From A. S. Frisch, K. Shamsuddin & M. Kurtz, "Family Factors and Knowledge: Attitudes and Efforts Concerning Exposure to Environmental Tobacco Among Malaysian Medical Students, *Journal of Asian and African Studies, 30,* 68–79.

The result of the Moorehouse and Sanders (1992) example might be written up as follows: "The mean perceived academic competence for the boys whose mothers' work involved problem solving was 32.8 (*SD* = 4.27), and the mean for the boys whose mothers' work did not involve problem solving was 29.2 (*SD* = 5.23); *t*(41) = 2.42, *p* < .05, one-tailed."

Table 9–6 is another example, taken from a study conducted by Frisch, Shamsuddin, and Kurtz (1995), in which 293 female medical students in Malaysia were surveyed on their views about smoking and on whether their family members and friends smoked. This table compares those students who have brothers who smoke to those who have brothers who don't smoke. (The article did not explain what the researchers did if a person had two brothers, one who smokes and one who doesn't.) The measures were Knowledge (of the health risks of being around smokers), Attitude (toward being around smokers), Efforts (to avoid being around smokers), and Physician's Responsibility (to inform patients of health risks of being around smokers). All scales were scored so that higher scores were pro-smoking. Lower scores meant more concern about the health risks.

The first line of the table shows that those with a brother who smokes scored higher on the Knowledge scale. This means that such students have less knowledge about the health risks of being around smokers. The second line shows that those with a brother who smokes have a more positive attitude toward being around smokers (that is, they do not see it as being as much of a health risk).

Note that some of these results were not significant. What should we conclude? Consider the students' beliefs about a physician's responsibility. In this comparison, there were 41 with smoker brothers and 73 with nonsmoker brothers. The formula for the harmonic mean indicates that for purposes of computing power, there are 52.5 participants per group. That is,

$$\text{Harmonic Mean} = \frac{(2)(N_1)(N_2)}{N_1 + N_2} = \frac{(2)(41)(73)}{41 + 73} = \frac{5,986}{114} = 52.5$$

Once you know the sample size to use, you can look up power in Table 9-4, using 50 participants (the nearest number of participants in the table to 52.5) and a two-tailed test. From the table, the power of this study to find significance for a small effect size is only .17. On the other hand, the power of the study to find a medium effect size is .70 and a large effect size, .98. Thus, if in fact there is a small effect for having a brother who is a smoker, this would probably not have shown up in this study. On the other hand, suppose there was in fact a medium effect of this kind. In that case, the result of this study probably would have been significant. Almost certainly if there were a large effect, the study would have come out significant. Thus, we can fairly confidently take from this study that having a brother who is a smoker probably does not make a large difference for Malaysian female medical students' beliefs about a physician's responsibility to inform their patients about the risks of being around smokers. However, we cannot conclude that there might not be a small effect of this kind.

Summary

1. A *t* test for independent means is used for hypothesis testing with two samples of scores. The main difference from a *t* test for a single sample is that the comparison distribution is a distribution of differences between means of samples. This distribution can be thought of as being built up in two steps: Each population of individuals produces a distribution of means, and then a new distribution is created of differences between pairs of means selected from these two distributions of means.

2. The distribution of differences between means has a mean of 0 and is a *t* distribution with the total of the degrees of freedom from the two samples. Its standard deviation is figured in several steps: (a) Use each sample to estimate the population variance; (b) assume that both populations have the same variance and make a pooled estimate by taking a weighted average of the two estimates (multiplying each estimate times the proportion of the total degrees of freedom its sample contributes and adding up the products); (c) divide the pooled estimate by each sample's number of scores to give the variances of its population's distribution of means; (d) add these two variances together to get the variance of the distribution of differences between means; and (e) take the square root.

3. The assumptions of the *t* test for independent means are that the two populations are normally distributed and have the same variance. However, the *t* test gives fairly accurate results when the true situation is moderately different from the assumptions.

4. Effect size for a *t* test for independent means is the difference between the means divided by the population standard deviation. Power is greatest when the sample sizes of the two groups are equal. When they are not equal, you use the harmonic mean of the two sample sizes when looking up power on a table.

5. *t* tests for independent means are usually reported in research articles with the means of the two groups plus the degrees of freedom, *t* score, and significance level. Results may also be reported in a table where each significant difference is shown by a star.

Key Terms

distribution of differences between means
harmonic mean
pooled estimate of the population variance (S^2_{Pooled})

standard deviation of the distribution of differences between means $(S_{\text{Difference}})$
t test for independent means

variance of the distribution of differences between means $(S^2_{\text{Difference}})$
weighted average

Practice Problems

These problems involve figuring. Most real-life statistics problems are done on a computer. Even if you have a computer and statistics software, do these by hand (with the help of a calculator) to ingrain the method in your mind.

For practice in using a computer to solve statistics problems, refer to the computer section of each chapter of the Student's Study Guide and Computer Workbook *that accompanies this text.*

All data are fictional (unless an actual citation is given).

Answers to selected problems are given at the back of this book.

1. (a) Explain when you would use a *t* test for dependent means and when you would use a *t* test for independent means.
   (b) Make up an example (not in the book or from your lectures) of a study of each kind.
2. For each of the following experiments, decide if the difference between conditions is statistically significant at the .05 level, two-tailed. Also figure the estimated effect size and find the approximate power (from Table 9–4).

	Experimental Group			**Control Group**		
	N	*M*	S^2	*N*	*M*	S^2
(a)	30	12.0	2.4	30	11.1	2.8
(b)	20	12.0	2.4	40	11.1	2.8
(c)	30	12.0	2.2	30	11.1	3.0

3. A communication researcher randomly assigned 82 volunteers to one of two experimental groups. Sixty-one were instructed to get their news for a month only from television and 21 were instructed to get their news for a month only from the radio. (Why the researcher did not assign equal numbers to the two conditions is a mystery!) After the month was up, all participants were tested on their knowledge of several political issues. The researcher did not have a prediction as to which news source would make people more knowledgeable. That is, the researcher simply predicted that there is some kind of difference. These were the results of the study. TV group: $M = 24$, $S^2 = 4$; radio group: $M = 26$, $S^2 = 6$.

Using the .01 level, what should the researcher conclude? (a) Go through the five steps of hypothesis testing; (b) give the estimated effect size; (c) illustrate your answer with a diagram like Figures 9–2 and 9–3; (d) explain your answers to someone who has never had a course in statistics.

4. A teacher was interested in whether using a student's own name in a story affected children's attention span while reading. Six children were randomly assigned to read a story under normal conditions (using names like Dick and Jane). Five other children read versions of the same story, but with each child's own name substituted for one of the children in the story. The researcher kept a careful measure of how long it took each child to read the story. The results are shown below.

Normal Story		**Own-Name Story**	
Student	*Reading Time*	*Student*	*Reading Time*
A	2	G	4
B	5	H	16
C	7	I	11
D	9	J	9
E	6	K	8
F	6		

Using the .05 level, does including the child's name make any difference? (a) Go through the five steps of hypothesis testing; (b) give the estimated effect size and approximate power based on the results; (c) illustrate your answer with a diagram like Figures 9–2 and 9–3; (d) explain your answers to a person who understands the *t* test for dependent means but does not know anything about the *t* test for independent means.

5. What are the approximate numbers of participants needed for each of the following planned studies to have 80% power, assuming equal numbers in the two groups and all using the .05 significance level. (Be sure to give the total number of participants needed, not just the number needed for each group.)

	Expected Means		**Expected**	
Study	M_1	M_2	*Population SD*	*Tails*
a	107	149	84	1
b	22.5	16.2	31.5	2
c	14	12	2.5	1
d	480	520	50	2

6. Van Aken and Asendorpf (1997) studied 139 German 12-year-olds. All of the children completed a general self-worth questionnaire and were interviewed about the supportiveness they experienced from their mothers, fathers, and classmates. The researchers then compared the self-worth of those with high and low levels of support of each type. The researchers reported that "lower general self-worth was found for children with a low-supportive mother ($t(137) = 4.52$, $p < .001$, $d = 0.78$) and with a low-

supportive father ($t(137) = 4.03$, $p < .001$, $d = 0.69$). . . . A lower general self-worth was also found for children with only low supportive classmates ($t(137) = 2.04$, $p < .05$, $d = 0.35$)." ("*d*" in the above is a symbol for effect size.) Explain what these results mean to a person who has never had a course in statistics. (Be sure to include a discussion of effect size and power. When figuring power, you can assume that the two groups in each comparison had about equal sample sizes.)

7. Do men or women have longer first names? Take out a phone book and use the random numbers given here to select a page. (If your phone book has closer to 100 pages, use just the first two digits.) On the first page, look for the first clearly female name, and write down how many letters it has. Do the same thing (find the page for the numbers, and so on) 16 times. Then continue, getting lengths for 16 male names. (You will have to exclude names for which you cannot tell the gender.) Compute a *t* test for independent means using these two samples. (Be sure to note the city of the telephone book you used.)

121, 798, 107, 971, 534, 740, 156, 55, 741, 128, 571, 939, 946, 731, 682, 516, 609, 569, 72, 932, 435, 912, 573, 581, 381, 120, 514, 338, 571, 743, 982, 471, 385, 663, 201, 323, 609, 430, 788, 296, 398, 174, 314, 120, 612, 100, 801, 352, 312, 993, 226

Introduction to the Analysis of Variance

CHAPTER OUTLINE

Cindy Hazan and Philip Shaver (1987) arranged to have the *Rocky Mountain News,* a large Denver area newspaper, print a mail-in survey. The survey included the question shown in Table 10–1 to measure what is called attachment style. Those who selected the first choice are "secure"; those who selected the second, "avoidant"; and those who selected the third, "anxious-ambivalent." These attachment styles are thought to be different ways of behaving and thinking in close relationships that develop from a person's experience with early caretakers (e.g., Mickelson et al., 1997). Readers also answered questions about various aspects of love, including amount of jealousy. Hazan and Shaver then compared the amount of jealousy reported by people with the three different attachment styles.

With a *t* test, Hazan and Shaver could have compared the mean jealousy scores of any two of the attachment styles. Instead, they were interested in differences among all three attachment styles. The statistical procedure for testing variation among the means of several groups is called the **analysis of variance,** sometimes abbreviated as **ANOVA.** (You could use the analysis of variance for a study with only two groups, but the *t* test, which gives the same result in the two group situation, is simpler.)

analysis of variance (ANOVA)

In this chapter, we introduce the analysis of variance, focusing on the fundamental logic, how to carry out an analysis of variance in the most basic situation, and how to make sense of more complicated forms of the analysis of variance when reading about them in research articles. This chapter assumes you understand hypothesis testing and the *t* test, particularly the material on the distribution of means.

Basic Logic of the Analysis of Variance

The null hypothesis in an analysis of variance is that the several populations being compared all have the same mean. For example, in the attachment style example, the null hypothesis is that the populations of secure, anxious-ambivalent, and avoidant people all have the same average degree of jealousy. The research hypothesis would be that the degree of jealousy differs among these three populations.

Hypothesis testing in analysis of variance is about whether the means of the samples differ more than you would expect if the null hypothesis were true. This question about *means* is answered, surprisingly, by analyzing *variances* (hence the name *analysis of variance*). (Among other reasons, we need to focus on variances because when you want to know how several means differ, you are asking about the variation among those means.)

Thus, to understand the logic of analysis of variance, we turn to considering variances. In particular, we begin by considering two different ways of estimating population variances. As you will see, the analysis of variance is about a comparison of the results of these two different ways of estimating population variances.

Estimating Population Variance from Variation within Each Sample

With the analysis of variance, as with the *t* test, we do not know the true population variances. However, as with the *t* test, you can estimate the variance of each of the populations from the scores in the samples. Also, as with the

TABLE 10–1
Question Used in Hazan and Shaver (1987) Newspaper Survey

Which of the following best describes your feelings? [check one]

[ ] I find it relatively easy to get close to others and am comfortable depending on them and having them depend on me. I don't often worry about being abandoned or about someone getting too close to me.

[ ] I am somewhat uncomfortable being close to others; I find it difficult to trust them completely, difficult to allow myself to depend on them. I am nervous when anyone gets too close, and often, love partners want me to be more intimate than I feel comfortable being.

[ ] I find that others are reluctant to get as close as I would like. I often worry that my partner doesn't really love me or won't want to stay with me. I want to merge completely with another person, and this desire sometimes scares people away.

Note. From C. Hazan & P. Shaver "Romantic Love Conceptualized as an Attachment Process," *Journal of Personality and Social Psychology* 52, 515, 1987.

t test, you assume in the analysis of variance that all populations have the *same* variance. Thus, you can average the estimates from each sample into a single pooled estimate, called the **within-group estimate of the population variance.** It is an average of estimates figured entirely from the scores *within* each of the samples.

within-group estimate of the population variance

One of the most important things to remember about this within-group estimate is that it is not affected by whether or not the null hypothesis is true. This estimate comes out the same whether the means of the populations are all the same (the null hypothesis is true) or whether the means of the populations are very different (the null hypothesis is false). This estimate comes out the same because it focuses only on the variation inside of each population. Thus, it doesn't matter how far apart the means of the different populations are.

Estimating the Population Variance from Variation between the Means of the Samples

There is also a second way to estimate the population variance. Each sample's mean is a number in its own right. If there are several samples, there are several such numbers, and these numbers will have some variation among them. The variation among these means gives another way to estimate the variance in the populations that the samples come from. Just how this works is a bit tricky, so follow the next two sections closely.

When the Null Hypothesis Is True.   First, consider the situation in which the null hypothesis is true. In this situation, all samples come from populations that have the same mean. Remember, we are always assuming that all populations have the same variance (and also that they are all normal curves). Thus, if the null hypothesis is true, all populations are identical. (They have the same mean, variance, and shape.)

However, even when the populations are identical, the samples will each be a little different, and their means will each be a little different. How different can the means be? That depends on how much variation there is within each population. If a population has very little variation in the scores within it, then the means of samples from that population (or any identical population) will tend to be very similar to each other.

What if several identical populations have a lot of variation in the scores within each? In that situation, if you take one sample from each population, the means of those samples could easily be very different from each other. Being very different, those means will have a great deal of variance among them.

The point is that the more variance within each of several identical populations, the more variance there will be between the means of samples when you take a random sample from each population.

Suppose you were studying samples of six children from each of three large classrooms (the populations in this example). If each classroom had children who were all either 9 or 10 years old, the means of your three samples would all be between 9 and 10. Thus, there would not be much variance among those means. However, if each classroom had children ranging from 5 to 15 years old, the means of the three samples would probably vary quite a bit. What this illustrates is that the variation among the means of samples is related directly to the amount of variation within each of the populations from which the samples are taken. The more variation in each population, the more variation among the means of samples taken from those populations.

Look also at our example of the populations of secure, anxious-ambivalent, and avoidant attachment types studied by Hazan and Shaver. There will, of course, be some variance in the degree of jealousy of different people within each of these populations. Let us suppose for the moment that these three populations all have the same mean degree of jealousy (as would be the case if the null hypothesis is true). Even in this situation of all having the same mean, no two samples are likely to have the exact same mean, whether they are taken from the same population or from identical, different populations. Further, the more each population varies within itself, the more the means of samples taken from these populations will vary. Again, they will vary even if, in fact, the populations' means are identical.

This principle we have been considering is illustrated in Figure 10–1. The three identical populations on the left have small variances and the three identical populations on the right have large variances. In each set of three identical populations, even though the means of the three populations are exactly the same, the means of the samples from those populations are not exactly the same. Most important to notice, the means from the populations with less variance are closer together (have less variance among them). The means from the populations with more variance are more spread out (have more variance among them).

We have now seen that the variation among the means of samples taken from identical populations is related directly to the variation of the scores within each of those populations. This has a very important implication: It should be possible to estimate the variance within each population from the variation among the means of our samples. That is, we should be able to use the variation in the means of our samples to figure out how much variation there is in the populations from which these samples come.

between-group estimate of the population variance

Such an estimate is called a **between-group estimate of the population variance.** (It has this name because it is based on the variation between the means of the samples, the "groups." Grammatically, it ought to be *among* groups; but *between* groups is traditional.) We take up how you actually figure this estimate later in the chapter.

So far, all of this logic we have considered has assumed that the null hypothesis is true, so that there is no variation among the means of the *populations*. Let's now consider what happens when the null hypothesis is not true and instead the research hypothesis is true.

When the Null Hypothesis Is Not True.   If the null hypothesis is not true and the research hypothesis is true, the populations themselves have different means. In this situation, the variation among means of samples taken from these populations is still caused by the variation within the populations. However, in this situation in which the research hypothesis is true, the variation among the means of the samples also is caused by the variation between the population means. That is, in this situation the means of the samples are spread out for two different reasons: (a) because of variation within each of the populations and (b) because of variation between the populations. The left side of Figure 10–2 shows populations with the same means and the means of samples taken from them. (This is the same kind of situation as in Figure 10–1a and 10–1b). The right side of Figure 10–2 shows three popula-

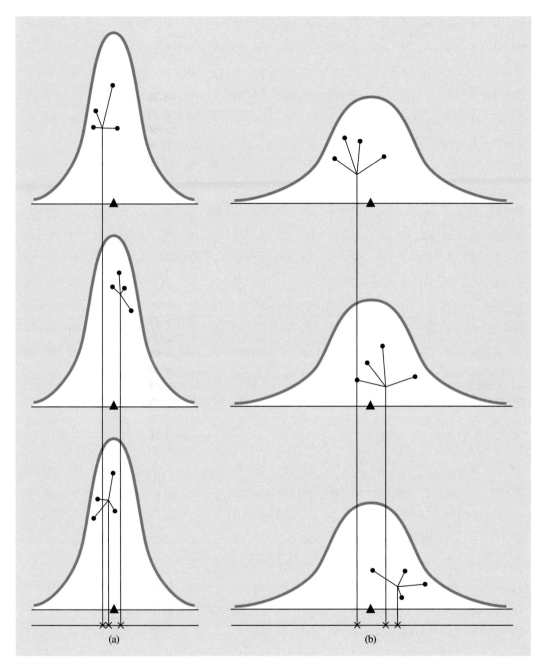

FIGURE 10–1
Means of samples from identical populations will not be identical. (a) Sample means from populations with less variation will vary less. (b) Sample means from populations with more variation will vary more. Population means are indicated by a triangle, sample means by an *X*.

tions with different means and the means of samples taken from them. (This is the situation we have just now been discussing.) Notice that the means of the samples are more spread out in the situation on the right side of Figure 10–2. This is true even though the variations within the populations are the same for the situation on both sides of Figure 10–2. The additional spread

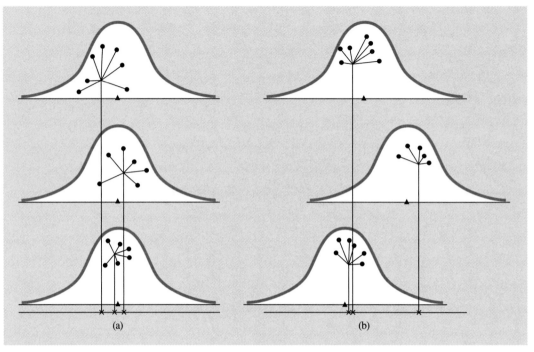

FIGURE 10–2
Means of samples from populations whose means differ (b) will vary more than sample means taken from populations whose means are the same (a). Population means are indicated by a triangle, sample means by an X.

(variance) amount for the means on the right side of the figure is due to the populations having different means.

In summary, the between-group estimate of the population variance is figured based on the variation among the means of the samples. If the null hypothesis is true, this estimate gives an accurate indication of the variation within the populations. But if the null hypothesis is false, this method of estimating the population variance is influenced both by the variation within the populations and the variation between them. It will not give an accurate estimate of the variation within the populations because it also will be affected by the variation between the populations. This difference has important implications. It is what makes the analysis of variance a method of testing hypotheses about whether there is a difference among means of groups.

Comparing the Within-Group and Between-Group Estimates of Population Variance

Table 10–2 summarizes what we have seen so far about the within-group and between-group estimates of population variance, both when the null hypothesis is true and when the research hypothesis is true. When the null hypothesis is true, the within-group and between-group estimates are based on the same thing. Literally, they are estimates of the same population variance.

TABLE 10–2
Sources of Variation in Within- and Between-Group Variance Estimates

	Variation Within Populations	Variation Between Populations
Null hypothesis is true		
Within-group estimate reflects	X	
Between-group estimate reflects	X	
Research hypothesis is true		
Within-group estimate reflects	X	
Between-group estimate reflects	X	X

When the null hypothesis is true, both estimates should be about the same (only *about* the same—these are estimates). Here is another way of describing this similarity of the between-group estimate and the within-group estimate when the null hypothesis is true. In this situation, the ratio of the between-group estimate to the within-group estimate should be approximately 1 to 1. For example, if the within-group estimate is 107.5, the between-group estimate should be around 107.5, so that the ratio would be about 1. (A ratio is found by dividing one number by the other.)

The situation is quite different when the null hypothesis is not true. As shown in Table 10–2, when the research hypothesis is true, the between-group estimate is influenced by two sources of variation: (a) the variation of the scores within each population and (b) the variation of the means of the populations from each other. Yet even when the research hypothesis is true, the within-group estimate still is influenced only by the variation within the populations. Therefore, when the research hypothesis is true, the between-group estimate should be larger than the within-group estimate. In this situation, the ratio of the between-group estimate to the within-group estimate should be greater than 1. For example, the between-group estimate might be 638.9 and the within-group estimate 107.5, making a ratio of 638.9 to 107.5 or 5.94. That is, when we divide the larger, the between-group estimate, by the smaller, the within-group estimate, we get not 1 but more than 1. In this example the between group estimate is nearly six times bigger than the within group estimate.

This is the central principle of the analysis of variance: *When the null hypothesis is true, the ratio of the between-group population variance estimate to the within-group population variance estimate should be about 1. When the research hypothesis is true, this ratio should be greater than 1*. If we figure this ratio and it comes out much bigger than 1, we can reject the null hypothesis. That is, it is unlikely that the null hypothesis could be true and the between-group estimate be a lot bigger than the within-group estimate.

The F Ratio

This crucial ratio of the between-group to the within-group population variance estimate is called an **F ratio.** (The *F* is for Sir Ronald Fisher, an eminent statistician who developed the analysis of variance; see Box 10–1.)

BOX 10–1

Sir Ronald Fisher, Caustic Genius at Statistics

Ronald A. Fisher, a contemporary of William Gosset (see Box 8–1) and Karl Pearson (see Box 11–1), was probably the brightest and certainly the most productive of this close-knit group of British statisticians. In the process of writing 300 papers and 7 books, he developed many of the modern field's key concepts: variance, analysis of variance, statistics (in the sense of describing a sample, as opposed to parameters of a population), significance levels, the null hypothesis, and almost all of our basic ideas of research design, including the fundamental importance of randomization.

It is one of those family legends that little Ronald, born in 1890 in East Finchley, a northern suburb of London, was so fascinated by math that one day, at age 3, when put into his highchair for breakfast, he asked his nurse, "What is a half of a half?" Told it was a quarter, he asked, "What's half of a quarter?" To that answer he wanted to know what was half of an eighth. At the next answer he purportedly thought a moment and said, "Then I suppose that a half of a sixteenth must be a thirty-toof." Ah, baby stories.

As a grown man, however, Fisher seems to have been anything but darling. Some observers ascribe this to a cold and unemotional mother, but whatever the reason, throughout his life the man was embroiled in bitter feuds, even with scholars who had previously been his closest allies and who certainly ought to have been comrades in research. When he was teased, apparently he responded with deadly seriousness; when others were anxious, he joked. William G. Cochran (a well-known statistician in his own right) reported a tale of their crossing a street together at a moment that was obviously unsafe. When Cochran hesitated, Fisher supposedly chided him: "Oh come on, a spot of natural selection won't hurt us." Cochran sheepishly risked his neck.

Fisher's thin ration of compassion extended to his readers as well—not only was his writing hopelessly obscure, but it often simply failed to supply important assumptions and proofs. Gosset said that when Fisher began a sentence with "Evidently," it meant two hours of hard work before one could hope to see why the point was evident. Another statistician sought to excuse him,

---

The *F* Distribution and the *F* Table

F distribution

F table

We have said that if the crucial ratio of between-group estimate to within-group estimate (the *F* ratio) is a lot larger than 1, you can reject the null hypothesis. The next question is, just how much bigger than 1 does it need to be before we can reject the null hypothesis with confidence?

Statisticians have developed the mathematics of an **F distribution** and have prepared tables of *F* ratios. For any given situation, you merely look up in an **F table** how extreme an *F* ratio is needed to reject the null hypothesis at, say, the .05 level. (You learn to use the *F* table later in the chapter.)

For an example of an *F* ratio, return to the attachment style study. The results of that study, for jealousy, were as follows: The between-group population variance estimate was 23.19 and the within-group population variance estimate was .53. (You will learn shortly how to figure these estimates on your own.) The ratio of the between-group to the within-group variance estimates (23.19/.53) came out to 43.91; that is, $F = 43.91$. This *F* ratio is considerably larger than 1. The *F* ratio needed to reject the null hypothesis at the

however, saying that, "Fisher was talking on a plane barely understood by the rest of humanity." It is true that he was invariably admired and respected for his work, if not for his manners.

Indeed, his lack of empathy extended to all of humankind. Like Galton, Fisher was fond of eugenics, favoring anything that might increase the birthrate of the upper and professional classes and skilled artisans. Not only did he see contraception as a poor idea—fearing that the least desirable persons would use it least—but he defended infanticide as serving an evolutionary function. It may be just as well that his opportunities to experiment with breeding never extended beyond the raising of his own children and some crops of potatoes and wheat.

The greatest influence on Fisher was probably his 14 years working at an agricultural experimental station called Rothamsted, in Hertfordshire, 25 miles north of London. At Rothamsted, Fisher, like Gosset at his brewery in Dublin, faced all sorts of practical problems, such as whether yearly applications of manure improved the yield of a field in the long run or was the cause of mysterious declines in production after many decades. Perhaps it was even this isolation from the personality disputes among London academics and this closeness to real issues that helped Fisher concentrate on developing statistics as a powerful research tool.

Although Fisher eventually became the Galton Professor of Eugenics at University College, his most influential appointment probably came when he was invited to Iowa State College in Ames for the summers of 1931 and 1936 (where he was said to be so put out with the terrible heat that he stored his sheets in the refrigerator all day). At Ames, Fisher greatly impressed George Snedecor, an American professor of mathematics also working on agricultural problems. Consequently, Snedecor wrote a textbook of statistics for agriculture that borrowed heavily from Fisher's work at Rothamsted. The book so popularized Fisher's ideas about statistics and research design that its second edition sold 100,000 copies.

While Fisher was at Ames, he also won over E. F. Lindquist, professor of education at the University of Iowa in Iowa City. Lindquist filled his next textbook with Fisher's ideas, introducing them to the fields of education and psychology, where they have played a major role to this day.

.05 level is only 3.01. Thus, the researches confidently rejected the null hypothesis and concluded that amount of jealousy is different among the three attachment styles. (Mean jealousy ratings were 2.17 for secures, 2.57 for avoidants, and 2.88 for anxious-ambivalents.)

An Analogy

Some students find an analogy helpful in understanding the analysis of variance. The analogy is to what engineers call the signal-to-noise ratio. For example, your ability to make out the words in a staticky cell-phone conversation depends on the strength of the signal versus the amount of random noise. With the F ratio in the analysis of variance, the difference among the means of the samples is like the signal; it is the information of interest. The variation within the samples is like the noise. When the variation among the samples is sufficiently great in comparison to the variation within the samples, you conclude that there is a significant effect.

Carrying Out an Analysis of Variance

Having considered the basic logic of the analysis of variance, we will go through an example to illustrate the details. (We use a fictional study to keep the numbers simple.)

Suppose a researcher is interested in the influence of knowledge of previous criminal record on juries' perceptions of the guilt or innocence of defendants. The researcher recruits 15 volunteers who have been selected for jury duty (but have not yet served at a trial). The researcher shows them a videotape of a 4-hour trial in which a woman is accused of passing bad checks. Before viewing the tape, however, all of the research participants are given a "background sheet" with age, marital status, education, and other such information about the accused woman. The sheet is the same for all 15 participants, with one difference. For five of the participants, the last section of the sheet says that the woman has been convicted several times before for passing bad checks—we will call these participants the *Criminal Record Group*. For five other participants, the last section of the sheet says the woman has a completely clean criminal record—the *Clean Record Group*. For the remaining five participants, the sheet does not mention anything about criminal record one way or the other—the *No Information Group*.

The participants are randomly assigned to groups. After viewing the tape of the trial, all 15 participants make a rating on a 10-point scale, which runs from completely sure she is innocent (1) to completely sure she is guilty (10). The results of this fictional study are shown in Table 10–3. As you can see, the means of the three groups are different (8, 4, and 5). Yet there is also quite a bit of variation within each of the three groups. (Population variance estimates from the score in these three groups are 4.5, 5.0, and 6.5.)

We need to do three calculations to test the hypothesis that the three populations are different: (a) a population variance estimate based on the variation of the scores within each of the samples, (b) a population variance estimate based on the differences among the group means, and (c) the ratio of the two, the F ratio. (In addition, we need the significance cutoff from an F table.)

TABLE 10–3
Results of the Criminal Record Study (Fictional Data)

Criminal Record Group			Clean Record Group			No Information Group		
Rating	Deviation from Mean	Squared Deviation from Mean	Rating	Deviation from Mean	Squared Deviation from Mean	Rating	Deviation from Mean	Squared Deviation from Mean
10	2	4	5	1	1	4	−1	1
7	−1	1	1	−3	9	6	1	1
5	−3	9	3	−1	1	9	4	16
10	2	4	7	3	9	3	−2	4
8	0	0	4	0	0	3	−2	4
Σ: 40	0	18	20	0	20	25	0	26

$M = 40/5 = 8$
$S^2 = 18/4 = 4.5$

$M = 20/5 = 4$
$S^2 = 20/4 = 5.0$

$M = 25/5 = 5$
$S^2 = 26/4 = 6.5$

Estimating Population Variance on the Basis of Variation of Scores within Each Group

You can estimate the population variance from any one group (that is, from any one sample) using the usual method of estimating a population variance from a sample. First, you figure the sum of the squared deviation scores. That is, you take the deviation of each score from its group's mean, square that deviation score, and sum all the squared deviation scores. Second, you divide that sum of squared deviation scores by that group's degrees of freedom. (The degrees of freedom for a group are the number of scores in the group minus 1.) For the example, as shown in Table 10–3, this gives an estimated population variance of 4.5 based on the Criminal Record Group's scores, an estimate of 5.0 based on the Clean Record Group's scores, and an estimate of 6.5 based on the No Information Group's scores.

Recall that in analysis of variance, as with the t test, we assume that the populations have the same variance. The estimates based on each sample's scores are all estimating the same true population variance. The sample sizes are equal in this example so that the estimate for each group is based on an equal amount of information. Thus, you can pool these variance estimates by straight averaging. This gives an overall estimate of the population variance based on the variation within groups of 5.35 (that is, the sum of 4.5, 5.0, and 6.5, which is 16, divided by 3, the number of groups).

The estimated population variance based on the variation of the scores within each of the groups is the within-group variance estimate (S^2_{Within}). In terms of a formula,

$$S^2_{\text{Within}} = \frac{S^2_1 + S^2_2 + \cdots + S^2_{\text{Last}}}{N_{\text{Groups}}}$$

(10–1)

In this formula, S^2_1 is the estimated population variance based on the scores in the first group (the group from Population 1), S^2_2 is the estimated population variance based on the scores in the second group, S^2_{Last} is the estimated population variance based on the scores in the last group. (The dots, or ellipses, in the formula show that you are to fill in the population variance estimate for as many other groups as there are in the analysis). N_{Groups} is the number of groups. Using this formula for our computations, we get

$$S^2_{\text{Within}} = \frac{S^2_1 + S^2_2 + \cdots + S^2_{\text{Last}}}{N_{\text{Groups}}} = \frac{4.5 + 5.0 + 6.5}{3} = \frac{16.3}{3} = 5.33$$

Estimating Population Variance from Differences between Group Means

Figuring the between-group estimate of the population variance involves two steps. First, you estimate, from the means of your samples the variance of a distribution means. Second, based on the variance of this distribution of means, you figure the variance of the population of individuals.

Step 1: Estimating the Variance of the Distribution of Means. You can think of the means of your samples as taken from a distribution of means.

You follow the standard procedure of using the scores in a sample to estimate the variance of the population from which these scores are taken. In this situation, think of the means of your samples as the scores and the distribution of means as the population from which these scores come. What this boils down to are the following procedures: You begin by figuring the sum of squared deviations. (You find the mean of your samples' means, figure the deviation of each sample mean from this mean of means, square each of these deviations, and then sum these squared deviations.) Then, divide this sum of squared deviations by the degrees of freedom, which is the number of means minus 1. In terms of a formula (when sample sizes are all equal),

$$S_M^2 = \frac{\Sigma(M - GM)^2}{df_{\text{Between}}}$$

(10-2)

In this formula, S_M^2 is the estimated variance of the distribution of means (estimated based on the means of the samples in your study). M is the mean of each of your samples. GM is the **grand mean,** the overall mean of all your scores, which is also the mean of your means. df_{Between} is the degrees of freedom in the between-group estimate, the number of groups minus 1 (that is, $df_{\text{Between}} = N_{\text{Groups}} - 1$).

grand mean

In the criminal-record example, the three means are 8, 4, and 5. The figuring of S_M^2 is shown in Table 10–4.

Step 2: From the Estimated Variance of the Distribution of Means to an Estimated Variance of the Population of Individual Scores. What we have just figured from a sample of a few means is the estimated variance of a distribution of means. From this we want to make an estimation of the variance of the population (the distribution of individuals) on which the distribution of means is based. We saw in Chapter 6 that the variance of a distribution of means is smaller than the variance of the population (the distribution of individuals) on which it is based. This is because means are less likely to be extreme than are individual scores (because several scores that are extreme in the same direction are unlikely to be included in any one sample). Specifically, you learned in Chapter 6 that the variance of a distribution of means is the variance of the distribution of individual scores divided by the number of scores in each sample.

Now, however, we are going to reverse what we did in Chapter 6. In Chapter 6 you figured the variance of the distribution of means by *dividing*

TABLE 10–4
Estimated Variance of the Distribution of Means Based on Means of the Three Experimental Groups in the Criminal Record Study (Fictional Data)

	Sample Means	Deviation from Grand Mean	Squared Deviation from Grand Mean
	(M)	*(M − GM)*	*(M − GM)²*
	4	−1.67	2.79
	8	2.33	5.43
	5	− .67	.45
Σ:	17		8.67

$GM = \Sigma M / N_{\text{Groups}} = 17/3 = 5.67$; $S_M^2 = \Sigma(M - GM)^2 / df_{\text{Between}} = 8.67/2 = 4.34$.

the variance of the distribution of individuals by the sample size. Now you are going to figure the variance of the distribution of individuals by *multiplying* the variance of the distribution of means times the sample size. That is, to come up with the variance of the population of individuals, we multiply our estimate of the variance of the distribution of means times the sample size. The result of all this is the between-group population variance estimate. Stated as a formula (for when sample sizes are equal),

$$S^2_{\text{Between}} = (S^2_M)(n) \qquad (10\text{--}3)$$

In this formula, S^2_{Between} is the estimate of the population variance based on the variation between the means (the between-group population variance estimate). n is the number of scores in each sample.

Let's return to our example in which there were 5 in each sample and an estimated variance of the distribution of means of 4.34. In this example, multiplying 4.34 times 5 gives a between-group population variance estimate of 21.7. In terms of the formula,

$$S^2_{\text{Between}} = (S^2_M)(n) = (4.34)(5) = 21.7$$

To summarize, the procedure of estimating the population variance based on the differences between group means is (a) figure the estimated variance of the distribution of means and then (b) multiply that estimated variance times the number of scores in each group.

Figuring the F Ratio

The F ratio is the ratio of the between-group estimate of the population variance to the within-group estimate of the population variance. Stated as a formula,

$$F = \frac{S^2_{\text{Between}}}{S^2_{\text{Within}}} \qquad (10\text{--}4)$$

In the example, the ratio of between and within is 21.7 to 5.33. Carrying out the division gives an F ratio of 4.07. In terms of the formula,

$$F = \frac{S^2_{\text{Between}}}{S^2_{\text{Within}}} = \frac{21.7}{5.33} = 4.07$$

The F Distribution

You are not quite done. You still need to find the cutoff for the F that is large enough to reject the null hypothesis. This requires a distribution of F ratios that you can use to figure out what is an extreme F ratio.

In practice, you simply look up the needed cutoff on a table. To understand from where that number on the table comes, you need to understand the *F* distribution. The easiest way to understand this distribution is to think about how you would go about making one.

Start with three identical populations. Next, randomly select five scores from each. Then, on the basis of these three samples (of five scores each), figure the *F* ratio. (That is, you use these scores to make a between-group estimate and a within-group estimate and divide the first by the second.) Let's say that you do this and the *F* ratio you come up with is 1.36. Now you select three new random samples of five scores each and figure the *F* ratio using these three samples. Perhaps you get an *F* of .93. If you do this whole process many, many times, you will eventually get a lot of *F* ratios. The distribution of all possible *F* ratios figured in this way (from random samples from identical populations) is called the *F* distribution. Figure 10–3 shows an example of an *F* distribution. (There are many different *F* distributions and each has a slightly different shape. The exact shape depends on how many samples you take each time and how many scores are in each sample. The general shape is like that shown in the figure.)

No one actually goes about making his or her own *F* distributions in this way. It is a mathematical distribution whose exact characteristics can be found from a formula. Statisticians can also prove that if you had the patience to follow this procedure of taking random samples and figuring the *F* ratio of each for a very long time, you would get the same result.

As you can see in Figure 10–3, the *F* distribution has a long tail on the right. The reason for the positive skew is that an *F* distribution is a distribution of ratios of variances. Variances are always positive numbers. (A variance is an average of squared deviations, and anything squared is a positive number.) A ratio of a positive number to positive number can never be less than 0. Yet there is nothing to stop a ratio from being a very high number. Thus, the *F* ratios' distribution cannot be lower than 0 and can rise quite high.

FIGURE 10–3
An *F* distribution.

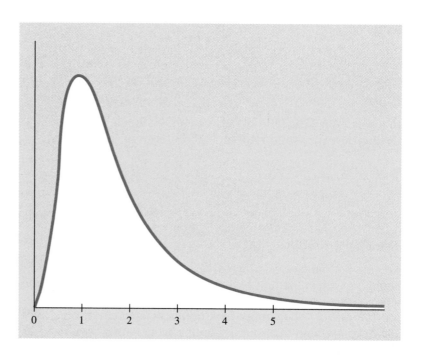

(Most F ratios pile up near 1, but they spread out more on the positive side, where they have more room to spread out.)

The F Table

The F table is a little more complicated than the t table. This is because there is a different F distribution according to both the degrees of freedom used in the between-group variance estimate and the degrees of freedom used in the within-group variance estimate. That is, you have to take into account two different degrees of freedom to look up the needed cutoff. One is the **numerator degrees of freedom.** This is the degrees of freedom you use in the between-group variance estimate, the numerator of the F ratio. The other is the **denominator degrees of freedom.** This is the total degrees of freedom that you use when figuring out the within-group variance estimate, the denominator of the F ratio.

numerator degrees of freedom

denominator degrees of freedom

The numerator degrees of freedom is the number of groups minus 1 (because that is the degrees of freedom used in figuring the between-groups variance estimate). Stated as a formula,

$$df_{\text{Between}} = N_{\text{Groups}} - 1 \qquad (10\text{--}5)$$

The denominator degrees of freedom is the sum of the degrees of freedom for all of the groups (because all of their estimates are included in the pooling). Stated as a formula,

$$df_{\text{Within}} = df_1 + df_2 + \cdots + df_{\text{Last}} \qquad (10\text{--}6)$$

In the criminal record experiment example, the numerator degrees of freedom is 2. (There are 3 means, minus 1.) In terms of the formula,

$$df_{\text{Between}} = N_{\text{Groups}} - 1 = 3 - 1 = 2$$

The denominator degrees of freedom is 12. This is because each of the groups has 4 degrees of freedom on which the estimate is based (5 scores minus 1) and there are 3 groups overall, making a total of 12 degrees of freedom. In terms of the formula,

$$df_{\text{Within}} = df_1 + df_2 + \cdots + df_{\text{Last}} = (5-1) + (5-1) + (5-1) = 4 + 4 + 4 = 12$$

You would look up the cutoff for an F distribution "with 2 and 12" degrees of freedom. As shown in Table 10–5, for the .05 level, you need an F ratio of 3.89 to reject the null hypothesis. (At the .01 level, you would need an F of 6.93.) The full F table appears as Table A–3 in Appendix A.

Hypothesis Testing with the Analysis of Variance

Let's look at how these steps work in the criminal record experiment.

1. **Restate the question as a research hypothesis and a null hypothesis about the populations.** There are three populations:

TABLE 10–5
Cutoffs for the *F* Distribution (Portion)

Denominator Degrees of Freedom	Significance Level	Numerator Degrees of Freedom					
		1	*2*	*3*	*4*	*5*	*6*
10	.01	10.05	7.56	6.55	6.00	5.64	5.39
	.05	4.97	4.10	3.71	3.48	3.33	3.22
	.10	3.29	2.93	2.73	2.61	2.52	2.46
11	.01	9.65	7.21	6.22	5.67	5.32	5.07
	.05	4.85	3.98	3.59	3.36	3.20	3.10
	.10	3.23	2.86	2.66	2.54	2.45	2.39
12	.01	9.33	6.93	5.95	5.41	5.07	4.82
	.05	4.75	**3.89**	3.49	3.26	3.11	3.00
	.10	3.18	2.81	2.61	2.48	2.40	2.33
13	.01	9.07	6.70	5.74	5.21	4.86	4.62
	.05	4.67	3.81	3.41	3.18	3.03	2.92
	.10	3.14	2.76	2.56	2.43	2.35	2.28

Population 1: Jurors told that the defendant has a criminal record
Population 2: Jurors told that the defendant has a clean record
Population 3: Jurors given no information of the defendant's record

The null hypothesis is that these three populations have the same mean. The research hypothesis is that the populations' means differ.

2.   Determine the characteristics of the comparison distribution. The comparison distribution is an *F* distribution with 2 and 12 degrees of freedom.

3.   Determine the cutoff sample score on the comparison distribution at which the null hypothesis should be rejected. Using the *F* table for the .05 significance level, the needed *F* ratio is 3.89.

4.   Determine your sample's score on the comparison distribution. In the analysis of variance, the comparison distribution is an *F* distribution, and the sample's score on that distribution is its *F* ratio. In the example, the *F* ratio was 4.07.

5.   Decide whether to reject the null hypothesis. In the example, our *F* ratio of 4.07 is more extreme than the .05 significance level cutoff of 3.89. Thus, the researcher would reject the null hypothesis that the three groups come from populations with the same mean. This suggests that they come from populations with different means: that people exposed to different kinds of information (or no information) about the criminal record of a defendant in a situation of this kind will differ in their ratings of the defendant's guilt.

You may be interested to know that several real studies have looked at whether knowing a defendant's prior criminal record affects the likelihood of conviction. The overall conclusion seems to be reasonably consistent with that of the fictional study described here. For a review of such studies, see Dane and Wrightsman (1982).

Summary of Steps for Hypothesis Testing Using the Analysis of Variance

Table 10–6 summarizes the steps of an analysis of variance of the kind we have been considering in this chapter.[1]

TABLE 10–6
Steps in an Analysis of Variance (When Sample Sizes Are Equal)

1. **Restate the question as a research hypothesis and a null hypothesis about the populations.**
2. **Determine the characteristics of the comparison distribution.**
   (a) The comparison distribution is an F distribution.
   (b) The numerator degrees of freedom is the number of groups minus 1: $df_{Between} = N_{Groups} - 1$.
   (c) The denominator degrees of freedom is the sum of the degrees of freedom in each group (the number in the group minus 1): $df_{Within} = df_1 + df_2 + ... + df_{Last}$.
3. **Determine the cutoff sample score on the comparison distribution at which the null hypothesis should be rejected.**
   (a) Decide the significance level.
   (b) Look up the appropriate cutoff in an F table, using the degrees of freedom from Step 2.
4. **Determine your sample's score on the comparison distribution.**
   This will be an F ratio.
   (a) Figure the between-group population variance estimate ($S^2_{Between}$).
       (i) Figure the mean of each group.
       (ii) Figure a variance estimate based on the means of the groups: $S^2_M = \Sigma(M - GM)^2/df_{Between}$.
       (iii) Convert this estimate of the variance of a distribution of means to an estimate of the variance of a population of individual scores by multiplying it times the number of scores in each group: $S^2_{Between} = (S^2_M)(n)$.
   (b) Figure the within-group population variance estimate S^2_{Within}.
       (i) Figure population variance estimates based on each group's scores: For each group, $S^2 = \Sigma(X - M)^2/(n - 1)$.
       (ii) Average these variance estimates: $S^2_{Within} = (S^2_1 + S^2_2 + ... + S^2_{Last})/N_{Groups}$.
   (c) Figure the F ratio: $F = S^2_{Between}/S^2_{Within}$.
5. **Decide whether to reject the null hypothesis:** Compare the scores from Steps 3 and 4.

[1]There are some computational formulas that are helpful if you have to do an analysis of variance for a real study without a computer. Also, the procedure you have learned to do in the chapter works (without modification) only if you have equal numbers of scores in each group. These computational formulas also work when there are unequal numbers of scores in each group. These formulas require that you first figure an intermediary for the two variance estimates, called "sum of squares" or SS for short. For the between-group estimate, $S^2_{Between} = SS_{Between} / df_{Between}$. The formula for $SS_{Between}$ is as follows:

$$SS_{Between} = \frac{(\Sigma X_1)^2}{n_1} + \frac{(\Sigma X_2)^2}{n_2} + ... + \frac{(\Sigma X_{Last})^2}{n_{Last}} - \frac{(\Sigma X)^2}{N}$$

(10–7)

For the within-group estimate, $S^2_{Within} = SS_{Within} / df_{Within}$. The formula for SS_{Within} is as follows:

$$SS_{Within} = \Sigma X^2 - \frac{(\Sigma X)^2}{N} - SS_{Between}$$

(10–8)

However, as usual, we urge you to use the definitional formulas we have presented in the chapter to work out the practice problems. The definitional formulas are closely related to the meaning of the procedures. Using the definitional formulas to work out the problems helps you learn the meaning of the analysis of variance.

Assumptions in the Analysis of Variance

The assumptions for the analysis of variance are basically the same as for the *t* test for independent means. That is, you get strictly accurate results only when the populations follow a normal curve and have equal variances. As with the *t* test, in practice you get quite acceptable results even when your populations are moderately far from normal and have moderately different variances. As a rule, if the variance estimate of the group with the largest estimate is no more than 4 or 5 times that of the smallest and the sample sizes are equal, the conclusions using the *F* distribution should be adequately accurate. In Chapter 11, we consider what to do when you have reason to think that your populations are a long way from meeting these assumptions.

Comparing Each Group to Each Other Group

The result of an analysis of variance shows whether the means of three or more populations are, overall, different from each other. This is not quite the same thing as the populations all having different means. It could be that two of the populations have about the same mean but both of these are different from the mean of a third population. Even when the overall analysis of variance is significant, we still do not know which population means are different from which other population means.

For this reason, researchers often do not stop after getting a significant result with an analysis of variance. Instead, they may go on to compare each population to each other population. For example, with three groups, you would compare group 1 to group 2, group 1 to group 3, and group 2 to group 3. You could do each of these comparisons using ordinary *t* tests for independent means. However, there is a problem with using ordinary *t* tests like this. The problem is that you are making three comparisons, each at the .05 level. The overall chance of at least one of them being significant just by chance is more like .15.

Some statisticians argue that it is all right to do three *t* tests in this situation because we have first checked that the overall analysis of variance is significant. These are called **protected *t* tests.** We are protected from making too big an error by the overall analysis of variance being significant. Other statisticians believe that the protected *t* test is not enough protection. Advanced statistics texts give procedures that provide even more protection. (Also, most standard statistics software have options as part of the analysis of variance that provide various ways to compare means that provide strong protection of this kind. One widely used method is called *Tukey's HSD* test.)

protected *t* tests

Effect Size and Power for the Analysis of Variance

Effect Size

Effect size for the analysis of variance is a little more complex than for a *t* test. With the *t* test, you take the difference between the two means and divide by the pooled population standard deviation. In the analysis of variance, you still can divide by the population standard deviation—you can use the square root of the within-group population variance estimate. However, in analysis of variance, we have more than two means, so it is not obvious just what is the equivalent to the difference between the means—the numerator in figuring effect size. Cohen (1988) suggests that in the analysis of variance, we should think of the equivalent of the difference between means as the variation among the means. Specifically, Cohen recommends using the standard deviation of the distribution of means. (This is the square root of the variance you figure as the first step of finding the between-groups population variance estimate.) Thus, Cohen defines the **effect size for the analysis of variance** as the standard deviation of the distribution of means divided by the standard deviation of the individuals. Stated as a formula in terms of estimated variances,

effect size for the analysis of variance

$$\text{Estimated Effect Size} = \frac{S_M}{S_{\text{Within}}}$$

(10–9)

Cohen's conventions for effect size for analysis of variance are .10 for a small effect, .25 for a medium effect, and .40 for a large effect size.

Consider our criminal-record experiment. We figured S_M^2, the estimated variance of the distribution of means based on the means of our three samples, to be 4.34. S_M, the square root of S_M^2, is 2.08. We figured S_{Within}^2, the estimate of the variance of each population of individuals, based on the variance estimates using each group's scores, to be 5.33. S_{Within}, the square root of S_{Within}^2, is 2.31. Applying the formula,

$$\text{Estimated Effect Size} = \frac{S_M}{S_{\text{Within}}} = \frac{2.08}{2.31} = .90$$

This is a very large effect size (thanks to our fictional data).

With a bit of algebraic manipulation, it turns out that the effect size using estimated variances can be figured directly from knowing the F and the number of scores in each group. The formula is

$$\text{Estimated Effect Size} = \frac{\sqrt{F}}{\sqrt{n}}$$

(10–10)

For example, in the criminal record study we had calculated F to be 4.07 and there were five people in each group. Using the formula,

$$\text{Estimated Effect Size} = \frac{\sqrt{F}}{\sqrt{n}} = \frac{\sqrt{4.07}}{\sqrt{5}} = \frac{2.02}{2.24} = .90$$

This formula is very helpful when figuring the effect size of a completed study reported in a published research article.

Power

Table 10–7 shows the approximate power for the .05 significance level for small, medium, and large effect sizes; sample size of 10, 20, 30, 40, 50, and 100 per group; and three, four, and five groups.[2]

Consider a planned study with five groups of 10 participants each. This study has an expected large effect size (.40) and using the .05 significance level, based on Table 10–7, would have power of .56. Thus, even if the research hypothesis is in fact true and has a large effect size, there is only a little greater than even chance (56%) that the study will come out significant.

Planning Sample Size

Table 10–8 gives the approximate number of participants you need in each group for 80% power at the .05 significance level for estimated small, medium, and large effect sizes for studies with three, four, and five groups.[3]

For example, suppose you are planning a study involving four groups and you expect a small effect size (and will use the .05 significance level).

TABLE 10–7
Approximate Power for Studies Using the Analysis of Variance Testing Hypotheses at the .05 Significance Level

		Effect Size	
Participants per Group (n)	**Small (.10)**	**Medium (.25)**	**Large (.40)**
Three groups ($df_{Between} = 2$)			
10	.07	.20	.45
20	.09	.38	.78
30	.12	.55	.93
40	.15	.68	.98
50	.18	.79	.99
100	.32	.98	*
Four groups ($df_{Between} = 3$)			
10	.07	.21	.51
20	.10	.43	.85
30	.13	.61	.96
40	.16	.76	.99
50	.19	.85	*
100	.36	.99	*
Five groups ($df_{Between} = 4$)			
10	.07	.23	.56
20	.10	.47	.90
30	.13	.67	.98
40	.17	.81	*
50	.21	.90	*
100	.40	*	*

*Nearly 1.

[2]More detailed tables are provided in Cohen (1988, pp. 289–354). When using these tables, note that the value of u at the top of each table refers to $df_{Between}$, which for a one-way analysis of variance is the number of groups minus 1, not the number of groups directly as used in our Table 10–7.
[3]More detailed tables are provided in Cohen (1988, pp. 381–389). If you use these, see footnote 2 in this chapter.

TABLE 10–8
Approximate Number of Participants Needed in Each Group (Assuming Equal Sample Sizes) for 80% Power for the One-Way Analysis of Variance Testing Hypotheses at the .05 Significance Level

	Effect Size		
	Small (.10)	Medium (.25)	Large (.40)
Three groups ($df_{\text{Between}} = 2$)	322	52	21
Four groups ($df_{\text{Between}} = 3$)	274	45	18
Five groups ($df_{\text{Between}} = 4$)	240	39	16

For 80% power, you would need 274 participants in each group, a total of 1,096 in all. However, suppose you could adjust the research plan so that it was now reasonable to predict a large effect size (perhaps by using more accurate measures and a more powerful experimental procedure). Now you would need only 18 in each of the four groups, for a total of 72.

Factorial Analysis of Variance

Factorial analysis of variance, an extension of what you just learned, is a wonderfully flexible and efficient approach that handles many types of experimental studies. The actual figuring of a factorial analysis of variance is beyond what we can cover in an introductory book. Our goal in this section is to help you understand the basic approach and the terminology so that you can make sense of research articles that use it.

We will introduce factorial analysis of variance with an example. Lambert and his colleagues (1997) were interested in how stereotypes affect the evaluations we make of others. For example, people often use age or gender stereotypes to evaluate whether someone will be successful in a particular job. Lambert et al. were especially interested in how the influence of stereotypes is affected by (a) awareness that a stereotype is inappropriate for a particular circumstance and (b) our mood. They believed that people are less affected by a stereotype when it is inappropriate and are particularly unaffected by stereotypes when in a sad mood.

Thus, Lambert et al. did the following experiment. Participants were asked to put themselves in the position of a job interviewer. Their task was to "form a preliminary evaluation of the suitability of an individual for a particular job" (p. 1010)—which for all participants was that of a flight attendant. The participants were then given a resume of an applicant that included a photo of a very attractive woman. Based on this information, the participants were asked how likely it was they would hire her, using a scale from 0 (not at all) to 10 (extremely). This experiment used the attractiveness stereotype, a stereotype that includes the tendency to think that good-looking people are especially competent.

The researchers put half the participants in a sad mood prior to reading the resume, supposedly as part of a separate experiment. These participants were asked to think about "an episode in your life that made you feel very sad and continues to make you sad whenever you think about it, even today"

TABLE 10–9
Factorial Design Employed by Lambert et al. (1997)

Stereotype	Mood	
	Sad	Neutral
Appropriate	a	c
Inappropriate	b	d

factorial research design

(p. 1004). This was the *Sad Mood* condition. The other half of the participants were not given any particular instructions. This was the *Neutral Mood* condition.

The other influence of interest to the researchers was appropriateness of the stereotype. Participants were given a description of a good flight attendant that differed according to how important attractiveness was for the job. For half the participants in each of the mood groups, the description emphasized the ability "to solve and analyze problems in a rational and analytic fashion" (p. 1010); this was the *Stereotype Inappropriate Condition*. For the other participants, the description emphasized passenger satisfaction and how appearance contributed to it; this was the *Stereotype Appropriate Condition*.

In sum, there were two experimental manipulations: Sad Mood versus Neutral Mood and the job description being Stereotype Appropriate versus Stereotype Inappropriate.

Lambert and his colleagues could have conducted two studies, one comparing participants put in a sad versus a neutral mood and one comparing participants given the stereotype appropriate versus inappropriate job descriptions. Instead, they studied the effects of both mood and stereotype appropriateness in a single study. They considered four groups of participants (see Table 10–9): (a) those in the Sad Mood and Stereotype Appropriate conditions, (b) those in the Sad Mood and Stereotype Inappropriate conditions, (c) those in the Neutral Mood and Stereotype Appropriate conditions, and (d) those in the Neutral Mood and Stereotype Inappropriate conditions.

Factorial Research Design Defined

The Lambert et al. (1997) study is an example of a **factorial research design** study, in which the effect of two or more variables are examined at once by making groupings of every combination of the variables. In this example, there are two levels of mood (sad and neutral) and two levels of stereotype appropriateness (appropriate and inappropriate). This allows four possible combinations, and Lambert et al. used all of them in their study.

A factorial research design has a major advantage over doing separate studies of each variable—efficiency. With a factorial design you can study both variables at once, without needing twice as many participants. In the example, Lambert et al. were able to use a single group of participants to study the effects of mood and stereotype appropriateness.

Interaction Effects

There is an even more important advantage of a factorial research design. A factorial design lets you study the effects of combining two or more variables. In this example, mood and stereotype appropriateness might affect hiring in a simple additive way. By additive, we mean that their combined influence is the sum of their separate influences—if you are more of one and also more of the other, then the overall effect is the total of the two individual effects. For example, suppose being sad makes you more willing to hire someone; similarly, the stereotype being appropriate makes you more willing to hire a person. If these two effects are additive, then participants in the sad, stereotype appropriate group will be most willing to hire the person; participants in the neutral, stereotype inappropriate group will be least likely to hire the person; and those in the other two conditions would have an intermediate likelihood of hiring the person.

It could also be that one variable but not the other has an effect. Or perhaps neither variable has any effect. In the additive situation, or the one in which only one variable or neither has an effect, looking at the two variables in combination does not give any interesting additional information.

However, it is also possible that the combination of the two changes the result. In fact, Lambert et al. predicted that the effect of stereotype inappropriateness would be especially strong in the sad-mood condition. This prediction was based on the notion that when in a sad mood we are more willing to revise our initial, unthinking, stereotype-based reactions.

A situation where the *combination* of variables has a special effect is called an **interaction effect.** An interaction effect is an effect in which the impact of one variable depends on the level of the other variable. In the Lambert et al. study, there was an interaction effect. Look at Table 10–10. The result was that the participants in the Appropriate-Sad group were most likely to hire the applicant, the Inappropriate-Neutral group was the next most likely, and the two other groups were least likely (to about an equal extent). Consider the bottom row of the results, the Inappropriate Stereotype group. This part of the result supported the researchers' theory that when in a sad mood people are able to counteract their stereotypes. (What about the appropriate-sad being the most likely to hire? The researchers acknowledged that this result was "unexpected and difficult to explain" [p. 1011].)

Suppose the researchers had studied stereotype appropriateness and mood in two separate studies. They would have concluded that each factor had only a slight effect. The average likelihood of hiring for the appropriate is 6.77 (that is, the average of 5.8 and 7.73 comes out to 6.77) and for inappropriate is 6.29. The average likelihood of hiring for those in the sad-mood condition was 6.78 versus 6.28 for those in the neutral-mood condition. Thus, following the approach of two separate studies, they would have completely missed the important results. The most important results had to do with the combination of the two factors.

interaction effect

TABLE 10–10
Mean Likelihood of Hiring in the Lambert et al. (1997) Study

Stereotype	Mood	
	Sad	Neutral
Appropriate	7.73	5.80
Inappropriate	5.83	6.75

Some Terminology

The Lambert et al. study would be analyzed with what is called a **two-way analysis of variance** (it uses a **two-way factorial research design**). By contrast, the situations we considered earlier (such as the attachment style study or the criminal record experiment) were examples of studies analyzed using a **one-way analysis of variance.** Such studies are called one-way because they consider the effect of only one variable (such as a person's attachment style or information about a defendant's criminal record).

In a two-way analysis, each variable or "way" (each dimension in the diagram) is a possible **main effect.** If the result for a variable, averaging across the other variable or variables, is significant, it is a main effect. This is entirely different from an interaction effect, which is based on the combination of variables. In the two-way Lambert et al. study, there was a possibility of two main effects and one interaction effect. The two possible main effects

two-way analysis of variance
two-way factorial design

one-way analysis of variance

main effect

include one for stereotype appropriateness and one for mood. The possible interaction effect is for the combination of stereotype appropriateness and mood. In a two-way analysis of variance, you are always testing two possible main effects and one possible interaction.

cell
cell mean

Each grouping combination in a factorial design is called a **cell.** The mean of the scores in each grouping is called a **cell mean.** For example, in the Lambert et al. study, there are four cells. Thus, there are four cell means, one for each combination of the levels of stereotype appropriateness and mood. That is, one cell is Stereotype Appropriate and Sad Mood (as shown in Table 10-10, its mean is 7.33); one cell is Stereotype Inappropriate and Sad Mood (5.83); one cell is Stereotype Appropriate and Neutral Mood (5.80); and one cell is Stereotype Inappropriate and Neutral Mood (6.75).

marginal means

The means of one variable alone are called **marginal means.** For example, in the Lambert et al. study there are four marginal means, one mean for all the stereotype-appropriate participants (as we saw earlier, 6.77), one for all the stereotype-inappropriate participants (6.29), one for all the sad-mood participants (6.78), and one for all the neutral-mood participants (6.28). (Because we were mainly interested in the interaction, these means were not shown in the tables.)

To look at a main effect, you focus on the marginal means. To look at the interaction effect, you focus on the pattern of individual cell means.

Recognizing and Interpreting Interaction Effects

It is very important to understand interaction effects. In many experiments the interaction effect is the main point of the research.

As we have seen, an interaction effect is an effect in which the impact of one variable depends on the level of another variable. The Lambert et al. study results (Table 10–10) show an interaction effect. This is because the impact of stereotype appropriateness is different with a sad mood than with a neutral mood.

An interaction effect can be made clear in words, in numbers, or in a graph. You can think out an interaction effect in words by saying that an interaction effect occurs when the impact of one variable depends on the level of another variable. In our Lambert et al. example, you can say that the effect of stereotype appropriateness depends on the level of mood. (You can also say that the effect of mood depends on the level of stereotype appropriateness. Interaction effects are completely symmetrical, in that you can describe them from the point of view of either variable.)

You can see an interaction effect numerically by looking at the pattern of cell means. If there is an interaction effect, the differences in cell means across one row will not be the same as the differences in cell means across another row. Consider the Lambert et al. example. In the Stereotype Appropriate row, there is a positive difference in the cell means—the Sad Mood participants rated how likely they were to hire (7.33) much higher than the Neutral Mood participants (5.80). This was a positive difference of 1.93 (that is, $7.73 - 5.80 = 1.93$). However, look at the Stereotype Inappropriate row. Those in a sad mood rated their likelihood of hiring (5.83) lower than those in the neutral mood (6.75). The difference for sad-versus-neutral mood for stereotype inappropriate participants was $-.92$.

Table 10–11 gives cell and marginal means for six possible results of a fictional two-way factorial study on the relation of age and education to income. Age has two levels (younger, such as 25 to 29, versus older, such as 30 to 34) and education has two levels (high school versus college). These fictional results are exaggerated, to make clear when there are interactions and main effects.

In Result A there is an interaction. In the "Younger" row, education makes no difference, but in the "Older" row, the college cell mean is much higher than the high school cell mean. One way to express this in words would be as follows: Education is not related to income for the younger group, but for the older group, people with a college education earn much more than those with less education.

Result B is also an interaction. This is because in the "Younger" row the high-school mean income is higher than the college mean income, but in the "Older" row the high-school mean income is lower. Put in words, this pattern shows that among younger people, those with only a high-school education make more money (perhaps because they entered the workplace earlier or the kinds of jobs they have start out at a higher level); but among older people, those with a college education make more money.

Result C is not an interaction effect. In the "Younger" row, the high-school mean is 40 lower than the college mean, and the same is true in the "Older" row. In words, whether young or old, people with college educations earn $40,000 more.

In Result D, there is also no interaction—in neither row is there any difference. Regardless of education, older people earn $100,000 more.

Result E is an interaction. This is because in the "Younger" row, the college mean is 20 higher, but in the "Older" row, the college mean is 40 higher. So among young people, college-educated people earn a little more, but among older people, those with a college education earn much more.

TABLE 10–11
Possible Means for Results of a Study of the Relation of Age and Education to Income

Result A

	High School	College	Overall
Younger	40	40	40
Older	40	60	50
Overall	40	50	

Result B

	High School	College	Overall
Younger	60	40	50
Older	40	60	50
Overall	50	50	

Result C

	High School	College	Overall
Younger	20	60	40
Older	40	80	60
Overall	30	70	

Result D

	High School	College	Overall
Younger	20	20	20
Older	120	120	120
Overall	70	70	

Result E

	High School	College	Overall
Younger	40	60	50
Older	40	80	60
Overall	40	70	

Result F

	High School	College	Overall
Younger	40	60	50
Older	60	100	80
Overall	50	80	

Finally, Result F is also an interaction effect. This is because there is a smaller difference in the "Younger" row than in the "Older" row. As with Result E, this pattern indicates that for people with a college education, income increases more with age than it does for those with only a high-school education.[4]

Identifying Interaction Effects Graphically

Another common way of making sense of interaction effects is by graphing the pattern of cell means. This is usually done with a bar graph.[5] Figure 10–4 is reproduced from Lambert et al.'s article. The graphs in Figure 10–5 show the graphs for the fictional age and education results we just considered (the ones shown in Table 10–11).

One thing to notice about such graphs is this: Whenever there is an interaction, the patterns of bars on one section of the graph will be different from the pattern on the other section of the graph. Thus, in Figure 10-4, the pattern for inappropriate is a step down, but the pattern for appropriate is a step up. The bars having a different pattern is just a graphic way of saying that the pattern of differences between the cell means from row to row is not the same.

Consider Figure 10–5. First, look at Results C and D. In Result C the younger and older sets of bars have the same pattern—both step up by 40. In Result D, both are flat. Within both Results C and D, the younger bars and the older bars have the same pattern. These were the examples that did not

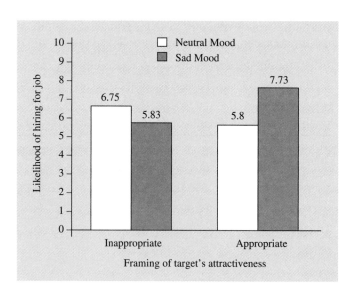

FIGURE 10–4

Judgments of the physically attractive job candidate as a function of framing attractiveness (inappropriate vs. appropriate) and manipulated mood (sad vs. neutral), Experiment 3. Higher numbers indicate a greater likelihood of hiring the target for the job. (Fig. 1 from "Mood and the Correlation of Positive Versus Negative Stereotypes" by A. J. Lambert, S. R. Khan et al. *Journal of Personality and Social Psychology,* 72, 1002–1016. Copyright © 1997 by The American Psychological Association. Reprinted with permission.)

[4]Based on 1990 statistics from the U.S. Department of Education, the actual situation in the United States is closest to Result F, though not as extreme. People with a college education earn more than those with only a high-school education in both age groups, but the difference is somewhat greater for the older group.

[5]The use of bar graphs to show analysis of variance cell means where there is an interaction effect has become the standard in the last few years. Prior to this, it was more common to use line graphs.

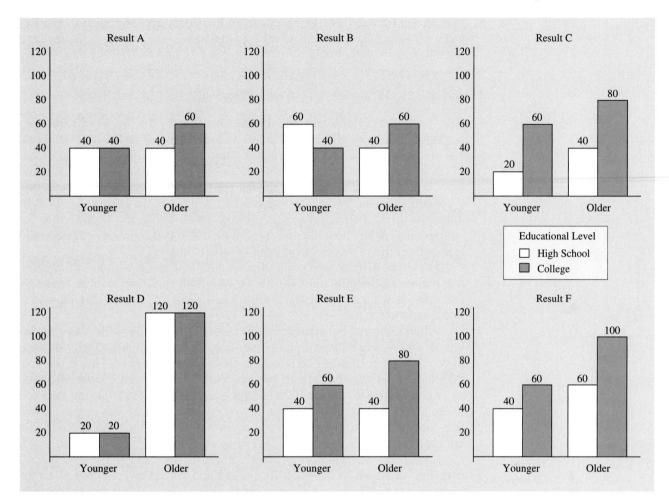

FIGURE 10–5
Graphs for the results of the fictional data shown in Table 10–11.

have interactions. All the other results, which did have interactions, have patterns of bars that are not parallel. For example, in Result A, the two younger bars are flat but the older bars show a step up. In Result B, the younger bars show a step down from high school to college but the older bars show a step up from high school to college. In Results E and F, both younger and older bars show a step up, but the younger bars show a smaller step up than do the older bars.

You can also see main effects from these graphs. In Figure 10–5, a main effect for age would be shown by the bars for younger being overall higher or lower than the bars for older. For example, in Result C, the bars for older are clearly higher than the bars for younger. What about the main effect for the bars that are not grouped together, college versus high school in this example? With these bars, you have to see whether the overall step pattern goes up or down. For example, in Result C, there is also a main effect for education because the general pattern of the bars for high school to college goes up, and it does this for both the younger and older bars. Result D shows a main effect for age (the older bars are higher than the younger bars). But Result D does not show a main effect for education—the pattern is flat for both the older and younger bars.

Relation of Interaction and Main Effects

Any combination of main and interaction effects can be significant. For example, they may all be significant, as in the pattern in Result F of Table 10–11. In this result, older students earn more (a main effect for age), college students earn more (a main effect for level of education), and how much more college students earn depends on age (the interaction effect).

There can also be an interaction effect with no main effects. Result B of Table 10–11 is an example. The average level of income is the same for younger and older (no main effect for age), and it is the same for college and high school (no main effect for level of education).

There can also be one main effect significant along with an interaction, one main effect significant by itself, or no significant main or interaction effects. See how many of these possibilities you can find in the fictional results in Table 10–11.

When there is no interaction, a main effect has a straightforward meaning. However, when there is an interaction along with a main effect, you have to be cautious in drawing conclusions about the main effect. This is because the main effect may be created by just one of the levels of the variable. For example, in Result A the main effect for education (40 vs. 50) is entirely due to the difference for older people. It would be misleading to say that education makes a difference without noting that it really only matters when you are older.

Sometimes the main effect clearly holds up over and above any interaction. For example, in Result F in the age and education example, it seems clear that the main effect for age holds up over and above the interaction. That is, it is true for both people with and without a college education that older people earn more. (There is still an interaction, of course, because how much more older people earn depends on education.)

Extensions and Special Cases of the Factorial Analysis of Variance

Analysis of variance is very versatile. Factorial designs can be extended into three-way and higher designs. There are also procedures to handle situations in which the same participants are tested more than once. This is like the *t* test for dependent means but works with more than two testings. It is called a *repeated measures analysis of variance.*

Analyses of Variance As Described in Research Articles

A one-way analysis of variance is usually described in a research article by giving the F, the degrees of freedom, and the significance level. For example, "$F(3, 67) = 5.21, p < .01$." The means for the groups usually are given in a table. However, if there are only a few groups and only one or a few measures, the means may be given in the regular text of the article. Returning to the criminal-record experiment example, we could describe the analysis of variance results this way: "The means for the Criminal Record, Clean Record, and No Information conditions were 7.0, 4.0, and 5.0, respectively, $F(2, 12) = 4.07, p < .05$."

In a factorial analysis of variance, researchers usually give a description in the text plus a table. The text gives the F ratio and the information that goes with it for each main and interaction effect. The table gives the cell means and sometimes also the marginal means. If there is an interaction effect, there may also be a graph. For example, Lambert et al. described the result we used for our example as follows:

> Analysis of participants' intention to hire the target revealed only one significant effect, the predicted Mood X Job Type interaction, $F(1, 57) = 11.46, p < .001$. Data relevant to this interaction are displayed in Figure [10–4]. (p. 101).

Summary

1. The analysis of variance (ANOVA) is used to test hypotheses about differences among means of several samples. The procedure compares two estimates of population variance. One, called the "within-group estimate," is figured by averaging the variance estimates from each of the samples. The other, called the "between-group estimate," is based on the variation among the means of the samples.

2. The F ratio is the between-group estimate divided by the within-group estimate. The null hypothesis is that all the samples come from populations with the same mean. If the null hypothesis is true, the F ratio should be about 1. This is because the two population variance estimates are based on the same thing, the variation within each of the populations. If the research hypothesis is true, and the samples come from populations with different means, the F ratio should be larger than 1. This is because the between-group estimate is now influenced by the variation both within the populations and between them. But the within-group estimate is still affected only by the variation within each of the populations.

3. When the samples are of equal size, the within-group population variance estimate is the average of the estimates of the population variance computed from each sample. The between-group population variance estimate is done in two steps. First, you estimate the variance of the distribution of means based on the means of your actual samples. (This is figured with the usual formula for estimating population variance from sample scores.) Second, you multiply this estimate times the sample size. This step takes you from the variance of the distribution of means to the variance of the distribution of individual scores.

4. The distribution of F ratios when the null hypothesis is true is a mathematically defined distribution that is skewed to the right. Significance cutoffs are given on an F table according to the degrees of freedom for each population variance estimate, the between-group

(numerator) estimate being based on the number of groups minus 1 and the within-group (denominator) estimate being based on the sum of the degrees of freedom within all samples.

5. The assumptions for the analysis of variance are the same as for the *t* test: The populations must be normally distributed, with equal variances. Like the *t* test, the analysis of variance is considered robust to moderate violations of these assumptions.

6. Effect size in the analysis of variance can be figured for a completed study as the square root of *F* divided by the square root of the number of participants in each group. Power depends on effect size, number of people in the study, significance level, and number of groups.

7. In a factorial research design, participants are put into groupings according to the combinations of the variables whose effects are being studied. Such designs mean that you can study the effects of two variables without needing twice as many participants and also that you can study the effects of combinations of the two variables. An interaction effect is an effect in which the impact one variable depends on the level of the other variable. A main effect is the effect of one variable, ignoring the effect of the other variable.

Key Terms

analysis of variance (ANOVA)
between-group estimate of the population variance ($S^2_{Between}$)
cell
cell mean
denominator degrees of freedom (df_{within})
effect size for the analysis of variance
factorial analysis of variance
factorial research design
F distribution
F ratio
F table
grand mean (GM)
interaction effect
main effect
marginal mean
numerator degrees of freedom ($df_{between}$)
one-way analysis of variance
protected *t* tests
two-way analysis of variance
within-group estimate of the population variance (S^2_{Within})

Practice Problems

These problems involve figuring. Most real-life statistics problems are done on a computer. Even if you have a computer and statistics software, do these problems by hand (with the help of a calculator) to ingrain the method in your mind.

For practice in using a computer to solve statistics problems, refer to the computer section of each chapter of the Student's Study Guide and Computer Workbook *that accompanies this text.*

All data are fictional (unless an actual citation is given).

Answers to selected problems are given at the back of this book.

1. For each of the following studies, decide whether you can reject the null hypothesis that the groups come from identical populations. Use the 05 level. In addition, figure the estimated effect size and approximate power for each. (Be sure to show your calculations throughout. Also, note that studies (b) and (c) provide *S* and not S^2.)

(a)	Group 1	Group 2	Group 3	
n	10	10	10	
M	7.4	6.8	6.8	
S^2	.82	.90	.80	

(b)	Group 1	Group 2	Group 3	Group 4
n	25	25	25	25
M	94	101	124	105
S	24	28	31	25

(c)	Group 1	Group 2	Group 3	Group 4	Group 5
n	25	25	25	25	25
M	94	101	124	105	106
S	24	28	31	25	27

2. For each of the following studies, decide whether you can reject the null hypothesis that the groups come from identical populations. Use the .01 level. In addition, compute the estimated effect size and approximate power for each. (Be sure to show your calculations throughout.)

(a)	Group 1	Group 2	Group 3
	8	6	4
	8	6	4
	7	5	3
	9	7	5

(b)	Group 1	Group 2	Group 3
	12	10	8
	4	2	0
	12	10	8
	4	2	0

3. Do students at various colleges differ in how sociable they are? Twenty-five students were randomly selected from each of three colleges in a particular region and were asked to report on the amount of time they spent socializing each day with other students. The results for College X was a mean of 5 and an estimated population variance of 2; for College Y, $M = 4$, $S^2 = 1.5$; and for College Z, $M = 6$, $S^2 = 2.5$. What should you conclude? Use the .05 level. (a) Carry out the five steps of hypothesis testing. (b) Figure estimated effect size. (c) Explain your answer to someone who understands everything involved in conducting a t test for independent means but who has never heard of the analysis of variance.

4. A social worker at a small mental hospital was asked to determine whether there was any clear difference in the length of stay of patients with different categories of diagnosis. Looking at the last four clients in each of the three major categories, the results (in terms of weeks of stay) were as follows:

Diagnosis Category		
Affective Disorders	Cognitive Disorders	Drug-related Conditions
7	12	8
6	8	10
5	9	12
6	11	10

Using the .05 level, is there a significant difference in length of stay among diagnosis categories? (a) Carry out the five steps of hypothesis testing. (b) Figure estimated effect size. (c) Explain your answer to someone who understands everything involved in conducting a t test for independent means but who is unfamiliar with the analysis of variance.

5. An organizational researcher was interested in whether individuals working in different sectors of the company differed in their attitudes toward the company. The results for the three people surveyed in engineering were 10, 12, and 11; for the three in the marketing department, 6, 6, and 8; for the three in accounting, 7, 4, and 4; and for the three in production, 14, 16, and 13 (higher numbers mean more positive attitudes). Was there a significant difference in attitude toward the company among employees working in different sectors of the company at the .05 level? (a) Carry out the five steps of hypothesis testing. (b) Figure the estimated effect size. (c) Explain your answer to someone who understands everything involved in conducting a t test for independent means but who has never heard of the analysis of variance.

6. A researcher wants to know if the need for health care among prisoners varies according to the different types of prison facilities. The researcher randomly selects 40 prisoners from each of the three main types of prisons in a particular U.S. state and gives exams to determine their need for health care. In the article describing the results, the researcher reported the means for each group and then added: "The need for health care among prisoners in the three types of prison systems appeared to be clearly different, $F(2, 117) = 5.62$, p < .01." Explain what this means to a person who has never had a course in statistics. As part of your discussion, figure the effect size (using Formula 10-10) and discuss its meaning.

7. Each of the following is a table of means showing results of a study using a factorial design. Assuming that any differences are statistically significant, for each table, (a) make a bar graph showing the results; (b) indicate which effects (main and interaction), if any, are found; and (c) describe the meaning of the pattern of means (that is, any main or interaction effects or the lack thereof) in words.

(i) Measured variable: Income (thousands of dollars)

Social Class	Age	
	Young	Old
Lower	20	35
Upper	25	100

(ii) Measured variable: Grade point average

College Type	Major	
	Science	Arts
Community	2.1	2.8
Liberal Arts	2.8	2.1

(iii) Measured variable: Days sick per month

	Gender	
Group	**Female**	**Males**
Exercisers	2.0	2.5
Controls	3.1	3.6

(iv) Measured variable: Rated restaurant quality (10 = high)

	City		
Price	**New York**	**Chicago**	**Vancouver**
Expensive	9	5	7
Moderate	6	4	6
Inexpensive	4	3	5

8. Sinclair and Kunda (2000) conducted a study testing the idea that if you want to think well of someone (for example, because they have said positive things about you), you are less influenced by the normal stereotypes when evaluating them. In this study, participants filled out a questionnaire on their social skills and then received feedback from either a male or female "manager in training." The study was rigged so that the managers gave half the participants positive feedback and half negative feedback. The participants then rated the managers for their skill at evaluating them. The question was whether the usual tendency to stereotype women as less skillful managers would be undermined when people got positive ratings. Sinclair and Kunda described their results as follows:

> Participants' ratings of the manager's skill at evaluating them were analyzed with a 2 (feedback) x 2 (manager gender) ANOVA. Managers who had provided positive feedback ($M = 9.08$) were rated more highly than were mangers who had provided negative feedback ($M = 7.46$), $F(1,46) = 19.44$, $p < .0001$. However, as may be seen in Figure 1 [our Figure 10–6], the effect was qualified by a significant interaction, $F(1, 46) = 4.71$, $p < .05$ . . . (p. 1335–1336).

Briefly describe the meaning of these results to a person who has never had a course in statistics. (Do not go into the computational details, just the basic logic of the pattern of means, the significant results, effect sizes, and issues of interpreting nonsignificant results.)

9. Cut up 100 little pieces of paper of about the same size and write "1" on 16, "2" on 34, "3" on 34, and "4" on 16 of them. (You are creating an approximately normal distribution.) Put the slips into a bowl or hat, mix them up, draw out two, write the numbers on them down, and put them back. Then draw out another two, write down their numbers, and put them back, and finally another two, write down their numbers, and put them back. (Strictly speaking, you should sample "with replacement." That means putting each one, not two, back after writing its number down. But we want to save you a little time, and it should not make much difference in this case.) Compute an analysis of variance for these three randomly selected groups of two each. Write down the F ratio, and repeat the entire drawing process and analysis of variance again. Do this entire process at least 20 times, and make a frequency polygon of your results. You are creating an F distribution for 2 (3 groups – 1) and 3 (2 – 1 in each of three groups) degrees of freedom. At what point do the top 5% of your F scores begin? Compare that to the 5% cutoff given on the F table in Appendix B for 2 and 3 degrees of freedom.

FIGURE 10–6
Participants' ratings of the manager's skill at evaluating them as a function of feedback favorability and the manager's gender (Study 2). (From "Motivated Stereotyping of Women. She's Fine if She Praised Me but Incompetent If She Criticized Me" by Lisa Sinclair and Ziva Kunda. *Personality and Social Psychology Bulletin,* Vol. 26, No. 11, November 2000, p. 1336, copyright © 2000 by Society for Personality and Social Psychology, Inc. Reprinted by permission of Sage Publications Inc.)

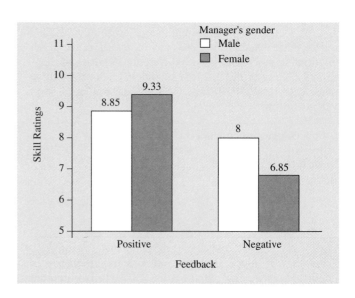

Chi-Square Tests and Strategies When Population Distributions Are Not Normal

11

CHAPTER OUTLINE

T HE hypothesis testing procedures you have learned in the last few chapters (the *t* test and the analysis of variance) are very versatile, but there are many research situations in which these methods cannot be used. One such situation is when the variable measured uses categories (such as a person's region of the country or religion). The *t* test and the analysis of variance all require that the measured variable have scores that are quantitative, such as rating on a 7-point scale or number of years served as mayor. Another research situation in which the ordinary *t* test and analysis of variance do not apply is when the populations do not clearly follow a normal curve.

This chapter examines hypothesis testing in these two situations in which the ordinary hypothesis-testing procedures cannot be used properly. The first half of the chapter focuses on chi-square tests.[1] **Chi-square tests** are used when the scores are on a nominal variable. The second half of the chapter focuses on strategies for hypothesis testing when you cannot assume that the population distributions are even roughly normal.

This chapter assumes you have a solid command of hypothesis testing and are familiar with the *t* test and analysis of variance, and in particular the assumptions required for their use. In addition, you may want to review the Chapter 1 material on kinds of variables and on shapes of distributions.

Chi-square tests

Chi-Square Tests

Consider an example. Harter et al. (1997) were interested in three styles of relating to romantic partners: a self-focused autonomy style, an other-focused connection style, and a mutuality style. Harter et al. conducted a newspaper survey that included items assessing the respondents' styles and also the respondents' perceptions of their partners' styles. One of the researchers' predictions was that men who described themselves as having the self-focused autonomy style would be most likely to describe their partners as having the other-focused style.

Here is what Harter and her colleagues found. Of the 101 self-focused men in their study, 49.5% of the men "reported the predicted pairing, compared to 25.5% who reported self-focused autonomous partners and 24.5% who reported partners displaying mutuality . . ." (p. 156). In terms of raw numbers, of the 101 self-focused men, 50 had other-focused partners, 26 had self-focused partners, and 25 had mutuality-style partners.

Suppose the partners of these men had been equally likely to be of each of the three relationship styles. If that were the situation, then about 33.66 (1/3 of the 101) of the partners of these men should have been of each style. This information is laid out in the "Observed Frequency" and "Expected Frequency" columns of Table 11–1. The Observed Frequency column shows the breakdown of relationship styles of partners actually observed and the Expected Frequency column shows the breakdown you would expect if the different partner styles had been exactly equally likely.

Clearly, there is a discrepancy between what was actually observed and the breakdown you would expect if the partner styles were equally likely.

---

[1]Chi is the Greek letter *X;* it is pronounced *ki,* rhyming with high and pie.

TABLE 11–1
Observed and Expected Frequencies for Relationship Styles of Partners of Self-Focused Autonomous Men

Partner Style	Observed Frequency[a] (O)	Expected Frequency (E)	Difference (O–E)	Difference Squared (O–E)^2	Difference Squared Weighted by Expected Frequency (O–E)^2/E
Other-Focused Connection	50	33.67	16.33	266.67	7.92
Self-Focused Autonomous	26	33.67	–7.67	58.83	1.75
Mutuality	25	33.67	–8.67	75.17	2.23

[a]Data from Harter et al. (1997).

The question is this: Should we assume that this discrepancy is no more than what we would expect just by chance for a sample of this size? Suppose that self-focused men in general (the population) are equally likely to have partners of the three styles. Still, in any particular sample from that population, we would not expect a perfectly equal breakdown of partners' styles. But if the breakdown in the sample is a long way from equal, we would doubt that the partner styles in the population really are equal. In other words, we are in a hypothesis-testing situation, much like the ones we have been considering all along. But with a big difference too.

In the situations in previous chapters, the scores have all been numerical values on some dimension, such as a score on a standard achievement test, length of time in a relationship, an employer's rating of an employee's job effectiveness on a 9-point scale, and so forth. By contrast, relationship style of a man's partner is an example of what in Chapter 1 we called a **nominal variable** (or a **categorical variable**). A nominal variable is one in which the information is the number of people in each category. These are called nominal variables because the different categories or levels of the variable have names instead of numbers. (We have actually used nominal variables before in a sense—which groups a person is in for a *t*-test for independent means or an ANOVA is a nominal variable—but in those situations, the scores themselves in the groups are numeric variables.)

nominal variable (categorical variable)

Hypothesis testing with nominal variables uses what are called chi-square tests. The chi-square test was originally developed by Karl Pearson (see Box 11–1) and is sometimes referred to as the Pearson chi-square.

The Chi-Square Statistic and the Chi-Square Test for Goodness of Fit

The basic idea of any chi-square test is that you compare how well an observed breakdown of people over various categories fits some expected breakdown (such as an equal breakdown). In terms of the relationship style example, you are comparing the observed breakdown of 50, 26, and 25 to the expected breakdown of about 34 (33.67) for each style. A breakdown of numbers of people expected in each category is actually a frequency distribution, as you learned in Chapter 1. Thus, a chi-square test is more formally described as comparing an **observed frequency** distribution to an **expected frequency** distribution. Overall, what the hypothesis testing involves is

observed frequency
expected frequency

BOX 11–1

Karl Pearson: Inventor of Chi-Square and Center of Controversy

Karl Pearson, sometimes hailed as the founder of the science of statistics, was born in 1857, the son of a Yorkshire barrister. Most of both his virtues and his vices are revealed in what he reported to his colleague Julia Bell as his earliest memory: He was sitting in his highchair, sucking his thumb, when he was told to stop or his thumb would wither away. Pearson looked at his two thumbs and silently concluded, "I can't see that the thumb I suck is any smaller than the other. I wonder if she could be lying to me." Here we see Pearson's faith in himself and in observational evidence and his rejection of authority. We also see his tendency to doubt the character of people with whom he disagreed.

Pearson studied mathematics on a scholarship at Cambridge. Soon after he arrived, he requested to be excused from compulsory divinity lectures and chapel. As soon as his request was granted, however, he appeared in chapel. The dean summoned him for an explanation, and Pearson declared that he had asked to be excused not from chapel "but from compulsory chapel."

After graduation, Pearson traveled and studied in Germany, becoming a socialist and a self-described "free-thinker." Returning to England, he wrote an attack on Christianity under a pen name and in 1885 founded a "Men and Women's Club" to promote discussion of the relations between the sexes. The club died out, but through it he met his wife, Maria Sharp.

Pearson eventually turned to statistics out of his interest in proving the theory of evolution, being especially influenced by Sir Francis Galton's work (see Box 3–1). Most of Pearson's research from 1893 to 1901 focused on the laws of heredity and evolution, but he needed better statistical methods for his work, leading to his most famous contribution, the chi-square test. Pearson also invented the method of computing correlation used today and coined the terms histogram, skew, and spurious correlation. When he felt that biology journals failed to appreciate his work properly, he founded the famous journal of statistics called *Biometrika*. In short, he led statistics from its early position as a matter largely ignored to one central to the scientific method, especially in the natural sciences.

Unfortunately, Pearson was a great fan of eugenics, the "improvement" of the human race through selective breeding, and his work was later used by the Nazis as justification for their treatment of Jews and other ethnic minorities. As Pearson aged, his opinions met strong resistance and much discrediting evidence from other, younger statisticians, which only turned Pearson against more and more of his colleagues.

Indeed, throughout his life, Pearson was a man who evoked either devoted friendship or deep dislike. William S. Gosset (see Box 8–1), inventor of the *t* test, was one of his friends. Sir Ronald Fisher, inventor of the analysis of variance and a man associated with even more extreme attitudes (he is described in Box 10–1), was one of Pearson's worst enemies. The kindly, peaceable Gosset, friends of both, was always trying to smooth matters between them. In 1933, Pearson finally retired, and Fisher, of all persons, took over his chair, the Galton Professorship of Eugenics at University College in London. In 1936, the two entered into their bitterest argument yet; Pearson died the same year.

References: Peters (1987); Stigler (1986); Tankard (1984).

(a) figuring a number for the amount of mismatch between the observed frequency and the expected frequency and then (b) seeing whether that number is for a greater mismatch than you would expect by chance.

Let's start with how you would come up with that mismatch number for the observed versus expected frequencies. The mismatch between observed and expected for any one category is just the observed frequency minus the expected frequency. For example, consider again the Harter et al. study. For men with an other-focused partner, the observed frequency of 50 is 16.33 more than the expected frequency of 33.67 (recall the expected frequency is 1/3 of the 101 total). For the second category, the difference is –7.67. For the third, –8.67. These differences are shown in the "Difference" column of Table 11–1.

We do not use these differences directly. One reason is that some differences are positive and some are negative. Thus, they would cancel each other out. To get around this, we square each difference. (This is the same strategy we used in Chapter 2 to deal with difference scores in figuring the variance.) In the relationship-style example, the squared difference for those with other-focused partners is 16.33 squared, or 266.67. For those with self-focused partners, it is 58.83. For those with mutuality-style partners, 75.17. These squared differences are shown in the "Difference Squared" column of Table 11–1.

In the Harter et al. example, the expected frequencies are the same in each category. But in other research situations, expected frequencies for the different categories may not be the same. A particular amount of difference between observed and expected has a different importance according to the size of the expected frequency. For example, a difference of 8 people between observed and expected is a much bigger mismatch if the expected frequency is 10 than if the expected frequency is 1,000. If the expected frequency is 10, a difference of 8 would mean that the observed frequency was 18 or 2, frequencies that are dramatically different from 10. But if the expected frequency is 1,000, a difference of 8 is only a slight mismatch. This would mean that the observed frequency was 1,008 or 992, frequencies that are only slightly different from 1,000.

How do we adjust the mismatch (the squared difference) between observed and expected for a particular category? What we need to do is adjust or weight the mismatch so as to take into account the expected frequency for that category. You can do this by dividing your squared difference for a category by the expected frequency for that category. Thus, if the expected frequency for a particular category is 10, you divide the squared difference by 10. If the expected frequency for the category is 1,000, you divide the squared difference by 1,000. In this way, you weight each squared difference by the expected frequency. This weighting puts the squared difference onto a more appropriate scale of comparison.

Let's return to our example. For men with an other-focused partner, you would weight the mismatch by dividing the squared difference of 266.67 by 33.67, giving 7.92. For those with a self-focused partner, 58.83 divided by 33.67 gives 1.75. For those with a mutuality style partner, 75.17 divided by 33.67 gives 2.23. These adjusted mismatches (squared differences divided by expected frequencies) are shown in the rightmost column of Table 11–1.

What remains is to get an overall figure for the mismatch between observed and expected frequencies. This final step is done by adding up the results for all the categories. That is, you take the result of the squared difference divided by the expected frequency for the first category, add the result of the squared difference divided by the expected frequency for the second category, and so on. In the Harter et al. example, this would be 7.92 plus 1.75 plus 2.23, for a total of 11.90.

chi-square statistic

This final number (the sum of the weighted squared differences) is an overall indication of the amount of mismatch between the expected and observed frequencies. It is called the **chi-square statistic.** In terms of a formula,

$$\chi^2 = \Sigma \frac{(O-E)^2}{E}$$

(11–1)

In this formula, χ^2 is the chi-square statistic. Σ is the summation sign, telling you to sum over all the different categories. O is the observed frequency for a category (the number of people actually found in that category in the study). E is the expected frequency for a category. (In this example, it is based on what we would expect if there were equal numbers in each category.) Applying the formula to the Harter et al. example,

$$\chi^2 = \Sigma \frac{(O-E)^2}{E} = \frac{(50-33.67)^2}{33.67} + \frac{(26-33.67)^2}{33.67} + \frac{(25-33.67)^2}{33.67} = 11.90$$

Summary of Steps for Figuring the Chi-Square Statistic

1. **Determine the actual, observed frequencies in each category.**
2. **Determine the expected frequencies in each category.**
3. **In each category, take observed minus expected frequencies.**
4. **Square each of these differences.**
5. **Divide each squared difference by the expected frequency for its category.**
6. **Add up the results of Step 5 for all the categories.**

The Chi-Square Distribution

The next question is whether the chi-square statistic you have figured is a bigger mismatch than you would expect by chance. To answer that, you need to know how likely it is to get chi-square statistics of various sizes by chance. That is, you need the distribution of chi-square statistics that would arise by chance. As long as you have a reasonable number of people in the study, the distribution of the chi-square statistic follows quite closely a known mathematical distribution—the **chi-square distribution.**

chi-square distribution

The exact shape of the chi-square distribution depends on the degrees of freedom. For a chi-square test, the degrees of freedom are the number of categories that are free to vary, given the totals. In our partners' relationship–style example, there are three categories. If you know the total number of people and you know the number in any two categories, you can figure out the number in the third category. In a study like this example, if there are three categories, there are two degrees of freedom.

The chi-square distributions for several different degrees of freedom are shown in Figure 11–1. Notice that the distributions are all skewed to the right. This is because the chi-square statistic cannot be less than 0 but can have very high values. (Chi-square must be positive because it is figured by adding a group of fractions in each of which the numerator and denominator both have to be positive. The numerator has to be positive because it is

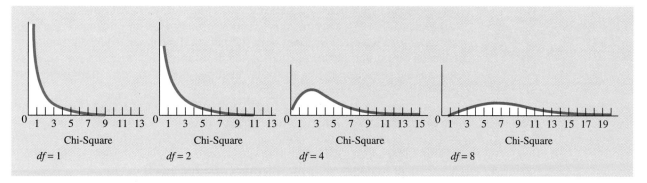

FIGURE 11–1
Examples of chi-square distributions for different degrees of freedom.

squared. The denominator has to be positive because the number of people expected in a given category can't be a negative number—you can't expect less than no one!)

The Chi-Square Table

What matters most about the chi-square distribution for hypothesis testing is the cutoff for a chi-square to be extreme enough to reject the null hypothesis. For example, suppose you are using the .05 significance level. In that situation, you want to know the point on the chi-square distribution where 5% of the chi-square statistics are above that point. A **chi-square table** gives the cutoff chi-square for different significance levels and various degrees of freedom. Table 11–2 shows a portion of a chi-square table like the one in the Appendix (Table A–4). Consider the partners' relationship-style example, where there were two degrees of freedom. The table shows that the cutoff chi-square for the .05 level using a chi-square distribution with 2 degrees of freedom is 5.992.

chi-square table

The Chi-Square Test for Goodness of Fit

You now have all the information you need for hypothesis testing in the Harter et al. example. Recall that the chi-square statistic for this example was 11.90, which is clearly larger than the chi-square cutoff for this example

TABLE 11–2
Portion of a Chi-Square Table

	Significance Level		
df	*.10*	*.05*	*.01*
1	2.706	3.841	6.635
2	4.605	**5.992**	9.211
3	6.252	7.815	11.345
4	7.780	9.488	13.277
5	9.237	11.071	15.087

Note: Full table is in Appendix A.

(using the .05 significance level) of 5.992. Thus, Harter et al. rejected the null hypothesis. That is, they rejected as too unlikely that the mismatch they observed could have come about if in the population of self-focused men there were an equal number of partners of each relationship style. It seemed more reasonable to conclude that the relationship styles of such partners were truly different.

We have just carried out a full hypothesis-testing procedure for the Harter et al. example. This example involved differing numbers of people at three levels of a particular nominal variable (the relationship style of partners of self-focused men). This kind of chi-square test involving levels of a single nominal variable is called a **chi-square test for goodness of fit.**

chi-square test for goodness of fit

Steps of Hypothesis Testing: An Example

Let us review the process of conducting a chi-square test for goodness of fit. We will use the same example, but this time systematically follow our standard five steps. In the process we also consider some fine points.

1. **Restate the question as a research hypothesis and a null hypothesis about the populations.** There are two populations:

    Population 1: Self-focused men like those in the study
    Population 2: Self-focused men whose partners are equally of the three relationship styles

The research hypothesis is that the distribution of people over categories in the two populations is different; the null hypothesis is that they are the same.

2. **Determine the characteristics of the comparison distribution.** The comparison distribution here is a chi-square distribution with 2 degrees of freedom. (Once you know the total, there are only two category numbers still free to vary.)

It is important not to be confused by the terminology here. The comparison distribution is the distribution to which we compare the number that summarizes the whole pattern of the result. With a t test, this number is the t score and we use a t distribution. With an analysis of variance, it is the F ratio and we use an F distribution. Accordingly, with a chi-square test, our comparison distribution is a distribution of the chi-square statistic.

This can be confusing because when preparing to use the chi-square distribution, we compare a distribution of observed frequencies to a distribution of expected frequencies. Yet the distribution of expected frequencies is not a comparison distribution in the sense that we use this term in Step 2 of hypothesis testing.

3. **Determine the cutoff on the comparison distribution at which the null hypothesis should be rejected.** You do this by looking up the cutoff on the chi-square table for your significance level and the study's degrees of freedom. In the present example, we used the .05 significance level, and we determined in Step 2 that there were 2 degrees of freedom. Based on the table, this gives a cutoff chi-square of 5.992.

4. **Determine your sample's score on the comparison distribution.** Your sample's score is the chi-square figured from the sample. In other words, this is the step where you do all the figuring. For each category, you need to figure the expected frequencies, then the squared difference between the observed and expected frequencies, and then divide that result by the ex-

pected frequency. Summing the results of all this for all the categories gives the chi-square statistic for your study. In this example, it came to 11.90.

5. **Decide whether to reject the null hypothesis.** The chi-square cutoff to reject the null hypothesis is 5.992 and the chi-square of our sample is 11.90. Thus, we can reject the null hypothesis. The research hypothesis that the two populations are different is supported. That is, Harter et al. could conclude that the partners of self-focused men are not equally likely to be of the three relationship styles.

The Chi-Square Test for Independence

So far, we have looked at the distribution of one nominal variable with several categories, such as the relationship style of men's partners. In fact, this kind of situation is fairly rare in research. We began with an example of this kind because it provides a good stepping stone to get to the more common actual research situation, to which we now turn.

The most common use of chi-square is one in which there are two nominal variables, each with several categories. For example, Harter et al. might have been interested in whether the breakdown of partners of self-focused men was the same as the breakdown of partners of other-focused men. If that were their purpose, we would have had two nominal variables. Relationship style of partners would be the first nominal variable. Men's own relationship style would be the second nominal variable. Hypothesis testing in this kind of situation is called a **chi-square test for independence.** You will learn shortly why it has this name.

chi-square test for independence

Consider the following fictional study. Researchers at a large university survey 200 staff members who commute to work. The staff members are asked about the kind of transportation they use as well as whether they prefer to go to bed early and awaken early (these are "morning people") or go to bed late and awaken late ("night people"). Table 11–3 shows the results. Notice the two nominal variables: type of transportation (with three levels) and sleep tendency (with two levels).

Contingency Tables

Table 11–3 is an example of a **contingency table**—a table in which the distributions of two nominal variables are set up so that you have the frequencies of their combinations as well as the totals. A contingency table is similar

contingency table

TABLE 11–3
Contingency Table of Observed Frequencies of Morning and Night People Using Different Types of Transportation (Fictional Data)

		Transportation			Total
		Bus	Carpool	Own Car	
Sleep Tendency	Morning	60	30	30	120 (60%)
	Night	20	20	40	80 (40%)
	Total	80	50	70	200 (100%)

to tables used in factorial experiments with analysis of variance (see Chapter 10). However, in a contingency table, the numbers are frequencies, not means. The number in each category or combination of categories is a number of individuals, not an average of scores of some kind. Thus, in Table 11–3, the 60 in the bus-morning combination is how many morning people ride the bus. It is not an average of anything.

Table 11–3 is called a 3×2 contingency table because it has three levels of one variable crossed with two levels of the other. (Which dimension is named first does not matter.) It is also possible to have larger contingency tables, such as a 4×7 or a 6×18 table. Smaller tables, 2×2 contingency tables, are especially common.

Independence

independence

The question in this example is whether there is any relation between the type of transportation people use and whether they are morning or night people. If there is no relation, the proportion of morning and night people is the same among bus riders, carpoolers, and those who drive their own cars. Or to put it the other way, if there is no relation, the proportion of bus riders, carpoolers, and own car drivers is the same for morning and night people. However you describe it, the situation of no relation between the variables in a contingency table is called **independence.**

Sample and Population

In the observed survey results in our example, the proportions of night and morning people in the sample vary with different types of transportation. For example, the bus riders are split 60–20, so three-fourths of the bus riders are morning people. Among people who drive their own cars, the split is 30–40. Thus, a slight majority are night people. Still, the sample is only of 200. It is possible that in the larger population, the type of transportation a person uses is independent of the person's being a morning or a night person. The big question is whether the lack of independence in the sample is large enough to reject the null hypothesis of independence in the population.

Using Chi-Square in a Test of Independence

To test whether the lack of independence in a sample is large enough to reject the null hypothesis of independence in the population, we need two things. First, we need a number for the amount of mismatch between the sample's pattern and what we would expect if the sample pattern perfectly reflected a population in which there was independence. This is a chi-square statistic. Second, we need to know the distribution of that statistic if the null hypothesis were true. That is the chi-square distribution.

Just as we did in the relationship-style example, we have to figure a chi-square statistic and compare it to a chi-square cutoff from a table. What is new are the details of how we figure the chi-square statistic and how we figure the degrees of freedom to look up the cutoff on the chi-square table.

Expected Frequencies

Just as we did before, to figure the chi-square statistic, we compare observed to expected frequencies. One thing that is new is that you now have to figure differences between observed and expected for each combination of categories—that is, for each **cell** of the contingency table. (When there was only one nominal variable, you figured these differences just for each category of that single nominal variable.) The more important new part of the procedure has to do with figuring out what the expected frequencies should be.

cell

Table 11–4 is the contingency table for our example survey. This time we have put in the expected frequency (in parentheses) next to each observed frequency. Follow the logic of the next two paragraphs while looking at these numbers.

To figure expected frequencies we assume that the two variables are independent—that is, in this example we assume transportation and sleep tendency are independent. (We make this assumption when figuring the expected frequencies because it is independence to which we want to compare our observed frequencies.) If they are independent, then the proportions up and down the cells of each of the transportation columns should be the same.

Overall, there are 60% morning people and 40% night people. Thus, if transportation method is independent of being a morning or night person, this 60%–40% split should hold for each column (each transportation type). First, the 60%–40% overall split should hold for the bus group. This would make an expected frequency in the bus cell for morning people of 60% of 80, which comes out to 48 people. The expected frequency for the bus riders who are night people is 32 (that is, 40% of 80 is 32).

Similarly, consider the expected frequencies in the carpool column. If transportation type and sleep tendency are independent, this column should also break down 60%–40%. Thus, its total of 50 people should have a 60%–40% split, giving an expected frequency of 30 morning people who carpool (that is, 60% of 50 is 30) and 20 night people who carpool (that is, 40% of 50 is 20). You figure the own-car column's expected frequencies in the same way, which comes out to 42 and 28, as shown in Table 11–4. Stated as a formula,

$$E = \left(\frac{R}{N}\right)(C)$$

(11–2)

TABLE 11-4
Contingency Table of Observed (and Expected) Frequencies of Morning and Night People Using Different Types of Transportation (Fictional Data)

		Transportation			Total
		Bus	Carpool	Own Car	
Sleep Tendency	Morning	60 (48)[a]	30 (30)	30 (42)	120 (60%)
	Night	20 (32)	20 (20)	40 (28)	80 (40%)
	Total	80	50	70	200 (100%)

[a]Expected frequencies are in parentheses.

In this formula, E is the expected frequency for a particular cell, R is the number of people observed in this cell's row, N is the number of people total, and C is the number of people observed in this cell's column. (If you mix up cells and columns, the expected frequency still comes out the same.) Applying the formula to the top left cell (morning persons who ride the bus),

$$E = \left(\frac{R}{N}\right)(C) = \left(\frac{120}{200}\right)(80) = (.60)(80) = 48$$

Looking at the entire Table 11–4, notice that the expected frequencies add up to the same totals as the observed frequencies. For example, in the first column (bus), the expected frequencies of 32 and 48 add up to 80, just as the observed frequencies in that column of 60 and 20 do. Similarly, in the top row (morning), the expected frequencies of 48, 30, and 42 add up to 120, the same total as for the observed frequencies of 60, 30, and 30. As a check on your arithmetic, it is always a good idea to make sure that the expected and observed frequencies add up to the same row and column totals.

Figuring Chi-Square

Once you know the observed and expected frequencies, you figure chi-square the same as in the chi-square test for goodness of fit, except that you now figure the weighted squared difference for each *cell* and add these up. (Before, you did this for each category and there were no cells for combinations of categories because there was only one nominal variable.) Here is how it works for our survey example:

$$X^2 = \Sigma \frac{(O-E)^2}{E} = \frac{(60-48)^2}{48} + \frac{(30-30)^2}{30} + \frac{(30-42)^2}{42} + \frac{(20-32)^2}{32}$$
$$+ \frac{(20-20)^2}{20} + \frac{(40-28)^2}{28}$$
$$= 3 + 0 + 3.43 + 4.5 + 0 + 5.14 = 16.07$$

Degrees of Freedom

The degrees of freedom in a chi-square contingency table is the number of columns minus 1 times the number of rows minus 1. Put as a formula,

$$df = (N_{Columns} - 1)(N_{Rows} - 1) \tag{11–3}$$

$N_{Columns}$ is the number of columns and N_{Rows} is the number of rows. Using this formula for our survey example,

$$df = (N_{Columns} - 1)(N_{Rows} - 1) = (3-1)(2-1) = (2)(1) = 2$$

A contingency table with many cells may have relatively few degrees of freedom. In our example, there are six cells and 2 degrees of freedom. This is because in a chi-square test the degrees of freedom are the number of categories free to vary once the totals are known. With a chi-square test of independence, the number of categories becomes the number of cells; the totals now include the row and column totals. If you know the row and column totals, you have a lot of information.

Consider our sleep tendency and transportation example. Suppose you know the first two cell frequencies across the top, for example, and all the row and column totals. You could then figure all the other cell frequencies just by subtraction. Table 11–5 shows the contingency table for this example with just the row and column totals and these two cell frequencies. Let's start with the Morning, Own Car cell. There is a total of 120 morning people and the other two morning-person cells have 90 in them (60 + 30). Thus, only 30 remain for the Morning, Own-Car cell. Now consider the three night-person cells. You know the frequencies for all the morning-people cells and the column totals for each type of transportation. Thus, each cell frequency for the night people is its column's total minus the morning people in that column. For example, there are 80 bus riders and 60 are morning people. Thus, the remaining 20 must be night people.

What you can see in all this is that with knowledge of only two of the cells you could figure out the frequencies in each of the other cells. Thus, although there are six cells, there are only 2 degrees of freedom—only two cells whose frequencies are really free to vary once we have all the row and column totals.

Hypothesis Testing

With 2 degrees of freedom, Table 11–2 (or Table A–4) shows that the chi-square you need for significance at the .01 level is 9.211. The chi-square of 16.07 for our example is larger than this cutoff. Thus, you can reject the null hypothesis that the two variables are independent in the population.

Steps of Hypothesis Testing and the Chi-Square Test for Independence: An Example

We have just done a full hypothesis test using the chi-square test for independence. However, once again it will be useful to review the process, but this time systematically follow the five steps of hypothesis testing.

1. Restate the question as a research hypothesis and a null hypothesis about the populations. There are two populations:

TABLE 11–5
Contingency Table Showing Marginal and Two Cells' Observed Frequencies to Illustrate Computation of Degrees of Freedom

		Transportation			Total
		Bus	Carpool	Own Car	
Sleep Tendency	Morning	60	30	——	120 (60%)
	Night	——	——	——	80 (40%)
	Total	80	50	70	200 (100%)

> **Population 1:** People like those surveyed
> **Population 2:** People for whom being a night or a morning person is independent of the kind of transportation they use to commute to work

The null hypothesis is that the two populations are the same, that in general the proportions using different types of transportation are the same for morning and night people. The research hypothesis is that the two populations are different, that among people in general the proportions using different types of transportation are different for morning and night people.

Put another way, the null hypothesis is that the two variables are independent (they are unrelated to each other). The research hypothesis is that they are not independent (that they are related to each other).

2. Determine the characteristics of the comparison distribution. The comparison distribution is a chi-square distribution with 2 degrees of freedom. As we have seen, in a 3×2 contingency table, if you know the numbers in two cells and the row and column totals, all the others can be determined. Or, using the rule for contingency tables, the number of cells free to vary is the number of columns minus 1 times number of rows minus 1.

3. Determine the cutoff sample score on the comparison distribution at which the null hypothesis should be rejected. You use the same table as for any chi-square test. In the example, setting a .01 significance level with 2 degrees of freedom, you need a chi-square of 9.211.

4. Determine your sample's score on the comparison distribution. In the example, we came up with a chi-square statistic of 16.07.

5. Decide whether to reject the null hypothesis. The chi-square needed to reject the null hypothesis is 9.211 and the chi-square for our sample is 16.07 (see Figure 11–2). Thus, you can reject the null hypothesis. The research hypothesis that the two variables are not independent in the population is supported. That is, the proportions of type of transportation used to commute to work are different for morning and night people.

A Second Example

Richard Riehl (1994) studied the college experience of first-year students who were the first generation in their family to attend college. These students were compared to other students who were not the first generation in their family to go to college. (All students in the study were from Indiana

FIGURE 11–2
For the sleep tendency and transportation example, chi-square distribution ($df = 2$) showing the cutoff for rejecting the null hypothesis at the .01 level.

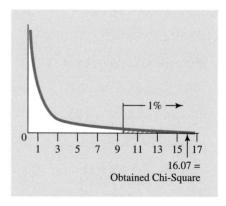

University.) One of the variables Riehl measured was whether or not students dropped out during their first semester.

Table 11–6 shows the results along with the expected frequencies (shown in parentheses) based on these percentages. Below the contingency table are the computations for the chi-square test of independence.

1. **Restate the question as a null hypothesis and a research hypothesis about the populations.** There are two populations:

Population 1: Students like those surveyed
Population 2: Students whose dropping out or staying in college their first semester is independent of whether or not they are the first generation in their family to go to college.

The null hypothesis is that the two populations are the same—that, in general, whether or not students drop out of college is independent of whether or not they are the first generation in their family to go to college. The research hypothesis is that the populations are not the same. In other words, the research hypothesis is that students like those surveyed are unlike the hypothetical population in which dropping out is unrelated to whether or not you are first generation.

TABLE 11–6
Results and Computation of the Chi-Square Test for Independence Comparing whether First Generation College Students Differ from Others in First Semester Dropouts

| | Generation to Go to College | | | |
	First	Other	Total	
Dropped Out	73 (57.7)	89 (103.9)	162	(7.9%)
Did Not Drop Out	657 (672.3)	1226 (1,211.1)	1883	(92.1%)
	730	1315	2045	

Chi-square needed, $df = 1$, .01 level: 6.635

$$\chi^2 = \Sigma \frac{(O-E)^2}{E} = \frac{(73-57.7)^2}{57.7} + \frac{(89-103.9)^2}{103.9} + \frac{(657-672.3)^2}{672.3} + \frac{(1,226-1,211.1)^2}{1,211.1}$$

$$= \frac{15.3^2}{57.7} + \frac{-14.9^2}{103.9} + \frac{-15.3^2}{672.3} + \frac{14.9^2}{1,211.1}$$

$$= \frac{234.1}{57.7} + \frac{222}{103.9} + \frac{234.1}{672.3} + \frac{222}{1,211.1}$$

$$= 4.06 + 2.14 + .35 + .18$$

$$= 6.73$$

Conclusion: Reject the null hypothesis.

Notes:
1. With a 2×2 analysis, differences and squared differences (numerators) for each cell are identical. In this example, the differences are due to rounding error.
2. Data from Riehl (1994). The exact chi-square (6.73) is slightly different from that reported in the article (7.2), due to rounding error.

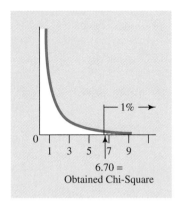

FIGURE 11–3
For the example from Riehl (1994), chi-square distribution (*df* = 1) showing the cutoff for rejecting the null hypothesis at the .01 level.

2. Determine the characteristics of the comparison distribution. This is a chi-square distribution with 1 degree of freedom.

3. Determine the cutoff sample score on the comparison distribution at which the null hypothesis should be rejected. Using the .01 level and 1 degree of freedom, Table 11–2 shows that you need a chi-square for significance of 6.635. This is illustrated in Figure 11–3.

4. Determine your sample's score on the comparison distribution. To figure the chi-square, you need the expected frequencies for each cell. You do this by multiplying the expected percentage in each row times the number in the column. Consider the top row, the first-generation dropouts. Overall, dropouts account for 7.9% of the students. If the null hypothesis were true, they should be 7.9% of the 730 students in this cell's column (the first-generation students). Thus, the expected frequency for the first generation dropouts is 57.7 (that is, 7.9% × 730 = 57.7). Once you have figured the expected frequencies for each cell, the rest of the chi-square analysis follows the usual procedure of finding the difference for each cell, squaring it, dividing it by the expected frequencies, and adding up these results for all the cells. As shown in Table 11–6, this gives a chi-square of 6.73.

5. Decide whether to reject the null hypothesis. Your chi square of 6.73 is larger than the cutoff of 6.635 (see Figure 11–3). Thus, you can reject the null hypothesis. That is, judging from a sample of 2,045 Indiana University students, first-generation students are somewhat more likely to drop out during their first semester than are other students. (Remember, of course, that there could be many reasons for this result.)

Assumptions for the Chi-Square Test of Independence

The chi-square tests for goodness of fit and for independence do not require the usual assumptions of normal population variances and such. There is, however, one key assumption: Each score must not have any special relation to any other scores. Basically, this means that you can't use these chi-square tests if the scores are based on the same people being tested more than once. Consider a study in which 20 people are tested to see if the distribution of their preferred brand of breakfast cereal changed from before to after a recent nutritional campaign. The results of this study could not be tested with the usual chi-square because the distributions of cereal choice before and after are from the same people.

Effect Size for Chi-Square Tests for Independence

In chi-square tests of independence, you can use the chi-square statistic you calculate to figure a number that indicates the degree of association of your two nominal variables. With a 2 × 2 contingency table, the measure of association is called the **phi coefficient (ϕ).** It is the square root of what you get when you divide your chi-square by the number of people in the entire sample. In terms of a formula,

phi coefficient (ϕ)

$$\Phi = \sqrt{\frac{\chi^2}{N}}$$

(11–4)

The phi coefficient has a minimum of 0 and a maximum of 1 and can be considered similar to a correlation coefficient (see Chapter 3).[2]

Cohen's (1988) conventions for the phi coefficient are that .10 is a small effect size, .30 is a medium effect size, and .50 is a large effect size. (These are exactly the same conventions as for a correlation coefficient.)

For example, in the Riehl (1994) study of first generation college students, the chi-square we calculated was 6.73 and there were 2,045 people in the study. Applying the formula for the phi coefficient,

$$\Phi = \sqrt{\frac{\chi^2}{N}} = \sqrt{\frac{6.73}{2,045}} = \sqrt{.00329} = .06$$

This is a very small effect size. The significance results tell us that the greater likelihood of first-generation students dropping out that we saw in our sample is probably not due to the particular people that were randomly recruited to be in this sample. We can thus have some confidence that there is a pattern of this kind in the population. But the phi coefficient tells us that this true population tendency may not be a very important factor in practice. (See Chapter 7 for a discussion of this kind of situation when a result is statistically significant but has a very small effect size.)

You only use the phi when you have a 2×2 situation. **Cramer's phi statistic** is an extension of the ordinary phi coefficient that you can use for contingency tables larger than 2×2. (Cramer's phi is also known as *Cramer's V* and is sometimes written ϕ_C or V_C.) You figure Cramer's ϕ the same way as the ordinary phi coefficient, except that instead of dividing by N, you divide by N times the degrees of freedom of the smaller side of the table ($df_{Smaller}$). Stated as a formula:

Cramer's phi statistic

$$Cramer's \ \Phi = \sqrt{\frac{\chi^2}{(N)(df_{Smaller})}}$$

(11–5)

In the sleep-tendency-and-transportation-preference example, the chi-square statistic was 16.07 and the total number of people surveyed was 200. The degrees of freedom for the smaller side of the table (the rows in this example) was 1. Cramer's phi is the square root of what you get when you divide 16.07 by 200 times 1. This comes out to .28. In terms of the formula,

$$Cramer's \ \Phi = \sqrt{\frac{\chi^2}{(N)(df_{Smaller})}} = \sqrt{\frac{16.07}{(200)(1)}} = \sqrt{.08} = .28$$

Cohen's conventions for effect size for Cramer's phi depend on the degrees of freedom for the smaller side of the table. Table 11–7 shows Cohen's (1988) effect size conventions for Cramer's phi for tables in which the smallest side of the table is 2, 3, and 4. Notice that when the smallest side of

[2]In fact, Φ is identical to a correlation coefficient. Suppose you were to take the two variables in a 2×2 contingency table and arbitrarily make one of the values of each equal to 1 and the other equal to 2 (or any other two numbers). If you then figured a correlation coefficient between the two variables, the result would be exactly the same as the phi coefficient. (Whether it was a positive or negative correlation, however, would depend on which categories in each variable got the 1 and which the 2.)

TABLE 11–7
Cohen's Conventions for Cramer's Phi

Smallest Dimension of Contingency Table	Effect Size		
	Small	Medium	Large
2 ($df_{Smaller} = 1$)	.10	.30	.50
3 ($df_{Smaller} = 2$)	.07	.21	.35
4 ($df_{Smaller} = 3$)	.06	.17	.29

the table is 2, the degrees of freedom is 1. Thus, the effect sizes in the table for this situation are the same as for the ordinary phi coefficient. (The computation also gives the same result, since multiplying by 1 does not change anything. That was the situation in the example we just considered.)

Based on the table, in our example there is an approximately medium effect size (.28), a medium amount of relationship between type of transportation one uses and whether one is a morning or a night person.

Power and Needed Sample Size for Chi-Square Test for Independence

Table 11–8 shows the approximate power at the .05 significance level for small, medium, and large effect sizes and total sample sizes of 25, 50, 100, and 200. Power is given for tables with 1, 2, 3, and 4 degrees of freedom.[3]

TABLE 11–8
Approximate Power for the Chi-Square Test for Independence for Testing Hypotheses at the .05 Significance Level

Total df	Total N	Effect Size		
		Small ($\phi = .10$)	Medium ($\phi = .30$)	Large ($\phi = .50$)
1	25	.08	.32	.70
	50	.11	.56	.94
	100	.17	.85	*
	200	.29	.99	*
2	25	.07	.25	.60
	50	.09	.46	.90
	100	.13	.77	*
	200	.23	.97	*
3	25	.07	.21	.54
	50	.08	.40	.86
	100	.12	.71	.99
	200	.19	.96	*
4	25	.06	.19	.50
	50	.08	.36	.82
	100	.11	.66	.99
	200	.17	.94	*

*Nearly 1.

[3]Cohen (1988, pp. 228–248) gives more detailed tables. However, Cohen's tables are based on an effect size called w, which is equivalent to phi but not to Cramer's phi. He provides a helpful conversion table of Cramer's phi to w on page 222.

TABLE 11–9
**Approximate Total Number of Participants Needed for 80% Power
for the Chi-Square Test for Independence for Testing Hypotheses
at the .05 Significance Level**

Total df	Effect Size		
	Small ($\phi = .10$)	Medium ($\phi = .30$)	Large ($\phi = .50$)
1	785	87	26
2	964	107	39
3	1,090	121	44
4	1,194	133	48

Consider the power of a planned 2×4 study ($df = 3$) of 50 people with an expected medium effect size (Cramer's $\Phi = .30$). The researchers will use the .05 level. From Table 11–8 you can find that this study would have a power of .40. That is, if the research hypothesis is true, and there is a true medium effect size, there is about a 40% chance that the study will come out significant.

Table 11–9 gives the approximate total number of participants needed for 80% power with small, medium, and large effect sizes at the .05 significance level for chi-square tests of independence of 2, 3, 4, and 5 degrees of freedom.[4] Suppose you are planning a study with a 3×3 ($df = 4$) contingency table. You expect a large effect size and will use the .05 significance level. According to the table, you would only need 48 participants.

Strategies for Hypothesis Testing When Population Distributions Are Not Normal

This second main part of the chapter examines some strategies researchers use when the variables are quantitative, but the assumption of a normal population distribution is clearly violated. (This assumption underlies most ordinary hypothesis-testing procedures, such as the t test and the analysis of variance.) First, we briefly review the role of assumptions in the standard hypothesis-testing procedures. Then we examine two approaches researchers use when the assumptions have not been met: data transformations and rank-order tests.

Assumptions in the Standard Hypothesis-Testing Procedures

As we saw in Chapters 8 through 10, you have to make certain assumptions to carry out a t test or an analysis of variance. In these hypothesis-testing procedures, you treat the scores from a study as if they came from some larger, though unknown, populations. One assumption you have to make is that the populations involved follow a normal curve. The other main assumption you have to make is that the populations have equal variances.

[4]More detailed tables are provided in Cohen (1988, pp. 253–267).

You also learned in previous chapters that you get fairly accurate results when a study suggests that the populations even very roughly meet the assumptions of following a normal curve and having equal variances. Our concern here, however, is with the situation where it is clear that the populations are nowhere near normal, or nowhere near having equal variances. In such situations, if you use the ordinary t test or analysis of variance, you can get quite incorrect results. For example, you could do all the figuring correctly and decide to reject the null hypothesis based on your results. And yet, if your populations do not meet the standard assumptions, this result could be wrong—wrong in the sense that instead of there actually being only a 5% chance of getting your results if the null hypothesis is true, in fact there might be a 15% or 20% chance!

Remember:—Assumptions are about populations and not about samples. It is quite possible for a sample not to follow a normal curve even though it comes from a population that does. Figure 11–4 shows histograms for several samples, each taken randomly from a population that follows a normal curve. (Notice that the smaller the sample, the harder it is to see that it came

FIGURE 11–4

Histograms for several random samples, each taken from a normal population with a mean of 0 and a standard deviation of 1.

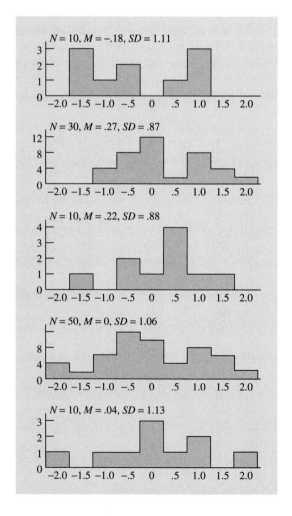

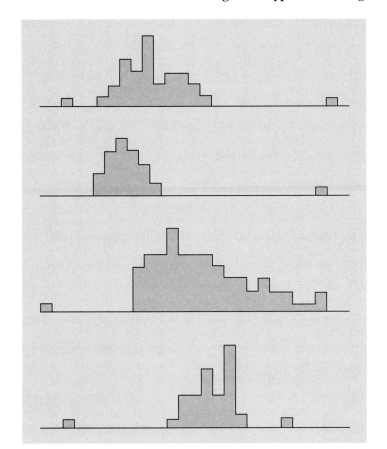

FIGURE 11–5
Distributions with outliers at one or both ends.

from a normal population.) Of course, it is quite possible for non-normal populations to produce any of these samples as well. Unfortunately, the sample is usually all you have when doing a study. One thing researchers do is make a histogram for the sample; if it is not drastically different from normal, the researchers assume that the population it came from is normal. When considering normality, most social and behavioral science researchers consider a distribution innocent until proven guilty.

One common situation where you might doubt the assumption that the population follows a normal distribution is when there is a ceiling or floor effect (see Chapter 1). Another common situation that raises such doubts is when the sample has outliers, extreme scores at one or both ends of the sample distribution. Figure 11–5 shows some examples of distributions with outliers. Outliers are a big problem in the statistical methods we ordinarily use because these methods rely, ultimately, on squared deviations from the mean. Because it is so far from the mean, an outlier has a huge influence when you square its deviation from the mean. The result is that a single outlier, if it is extreme enough, can cause a statistical test to give a significant result even when all the other scores would not. An outlier can also make a result not significant that would be significant without the outlier.

Data Transformations

A widely used procedure when the scores in the sample do not appear to come from a normal population is to change the scores! Not by fudging—although at first it may sound that way, until we explain. The method is that the researcher applies some mathematical procedure to each score, such as taking its square root, to make a non-normal distribution closer to normal. (Sometimes this can also make the variances of two or more groups more similar.) This is called a **data transformation.** Once you have made a data transformation, if the other assumptions are met, you can then go ahead with a usual *t* test or analysis of variance and you will get accurate results.

data transformation

Data transformation has an important advantage over other procedures of coping with non-normal populations that you will learn about. Once you have made a data transformation, you can use familiar and sophisticated hypothesis-testing procedures.

Consider an example. Measures of reaction time (such as how long it takes a research participant to press a particular key when a light flashes) are usually highly skewed to the right. There are many short (quick) responses and a few, but sometimes quite long (slow), ones. It is unlikely that the reaction times shown in Figure 11–6 come from a population that follows a normal curve. The population of reaction-time scores itself is probably skewed.

However, suppose you take the square root of each reaction time. Most reaction times are affected only a little. A reaction time of 1 second stays 1; a reaction time of 1.5 seconds reduces to 1.22. However, very long reaction times, the ones that create the long tail to the right, are much reduced. For example, a reaction time of 9 seconds is reduced to 3, and a reaction time of

FIGURE 11–6
Skewed distribution of reaction times (fictional data).

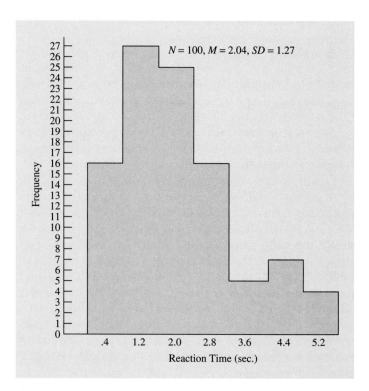

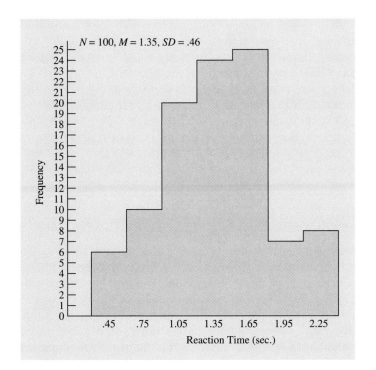

FIGURE 11–7
Data from Figure 11–6 after square-root transformed on.

16 seconds (the person was really distracted and forgot about the task) reduces to 4. Figure 11–7 shows the result of taking the square root of each score in the skewed distribution shown in Figure 11–6. After a **square-root transformation,** this distribution of scores seems much more likely to have come from a population with a normal distribution (of transformed scores).

square root transformation

Legitimacy of Data Transformations

Do you feel that this is somehow cheating? It would be if it were done only to some scores or done in any other way to make the result more favorable to the researcher's predictions. However, in actual research practice, the first step after the data are collected and recorded (and checked for accuracy) is to see if the data suggest that the populations meet assumptions. If the data suggest that the populations do not meet assumptions, the researcher carries out data transformations. Hypothesis testing is done only after this checking and any transformations.

It is important to remember that any transformation of scores has to be done for all the scores on that variable, not just those in a particular subgroup. Most important, no matter what transformation procedure we use, the order of the scores always stays the same. A raw score that is the second highest in a group of scores will still be second highest in the group of transformed scores.

The procedure may seem somehow to distort reality to fit the statistics. In some cases, this is a legitimate concern. Suppose you are looking at the difference in income between two groups. You probably do not care about how much the two groups differ in the square root of their income. What you care about is the difference in actual dollars.

On the other hand, consider a survey question in which the person indicates their agreement with the statement "I am satisfied with local law enforcement" on a 7-point rating from 1, strongly disagree, to 7, strongly agree. Higher scores on this scale certainly mean more agreement; lower scores, less agreement. However, each unit of increase on the scale is not necessarily related to an equal amount of increase in agreement. It is quite possible that the square root of each unit's increase is directly related to the person's agreement. In many research situations, there may be no strong reason to think that the transformed version is any less accurate a reflection of the reality than the original version. Also, the transformed version may meet the normality assumption.

Kinds of Data Transformations

There are several types of data transformations. We already have illustrated a square-root transformation: Instead of using each score, you use the square root of each score. We gave an example in Figures 11–6 and 11–7. The general effect is shown in Figure 11–8. As you can see, a distribution skewed to the right becomes less skewed to the right after square-root transformation. To put it numerically, moderate numbers become only slightly lower and high numbers become much lower. The result is that the right side is pulled in toward the middle. (If the distribution is skewed the other way, you may want to *reflect* all the scores, that is, subtract them all from some high number so that they are now all reversed. Then, using the square root will have the correct effect. However, you then have to remember when looking at the final results that you have reversed the direction of scoring.)

There are many other kinds of transformations you will see in social and behavioral science research articles. One common type is called a *log transformation*. (In a log transformation, instead of the square root, the researcher takes the logarithm of each score.) Some other transformations you might see are *inverse transformations* and *arcsine transformations*. We will not go into examples of all these kinds of transformations here. Just learning the square root transformation will help you get the principle. The main thing to remember about other kinds of transformations is that they all use this same approach of taking each score and applying some arithmetic to it, usually to make the set of scores come out more like a normal curve. Once again, whatever transformation you use, a score that is between two other scores always stays between those two other scores.

FIGURE 11–8
Distribution skewed to the right before (a) and after (b) taking the square root of each score.

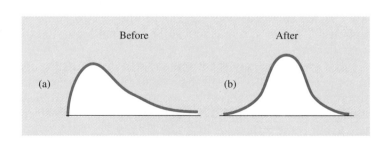

TABLE 11–10
Results of a Study Comparing Highly Sensitive and Not Highly Sensitive Children on the Number of Books Read in the Past Year (Fictional Data)

	Highly Sensitive	
	No	*Yes*
	0	17
	3	36
	10	45
	22	75
Σ:	35	173
$M =$	8.75	43.25
$S^2 =$	95.58	584.00

An Example of a Data Transformation

Consider a fictional study in which four children who score high on a test of being "highly sensitive" are compared on the number of books read in the preceding year to four children who score low on the test. (The general idea of being a highly sensitive person is described in Aron, 1996, and Aron & Aron, 1997.) Based on theory, the researcher predicts that highly sensitive children will read more books. Table 11–10 shows the results.

Ordinarily in a study like this, involving a comparison of two independent groups, you would use a t test for independent means. Yet the t test for independent means is like all of the procedures you have learned for hypothesis testing (except chi-square): It requires that the parent populations of scores for each group be normally distributed. In this study, however, the distribution of the sample is strongly skewed to the right—the scores tend to bunch up at the left, leaving a long tail to the right. It thus seems likely that the population of scores of number of books read (for both sensitives and nonsensitives) is also skewed to the right. This shape for the population distribution also seems reasonable in light of what is being measured. A child cannot read fewer than zero books; but once a child starts reading, it is easy to read a lot of books in a year.

Also note that the estimated population variances based on the two samples are dramatically different, 95.58 versus 584. This is another reason you would not want to go ahead with an ordinary t test.

However, suppose we carry out a square-root transformation on the scores (Table 11–11). The result is that both samples are much more like a

TABLE 11–11
Square-Root Transformation of the Data in Table 11–10

	Highly Sensitive		
	No		*Yes*	
X	$\sqrt{X}$	X	$\sqrt{X}$
0	0.00	17	4.12
3	1.73	36	6.00
10	3.16	45	6.71
22	4.69	75	8.66

TABLE 11–12
Computations for a *t* Test for Independent Means Using Square-Root-Transformed Scores for the Study of Books Read by Highly Sensitive Versus Not Highly Sensitive Children (Fictional Data)

t needed for .05 significance level, $df = (4 - 1) + (4 - 1) = 6$, one tailed = 1.943.

Highly Sensitive

	No	*Yes*
	0.00	4.12
	1.73	6.00
	3.16	6.71
	4.69	8.66
Σ:	9.58	25.49
$M =$	9.58/4 = 2.40	25.49/4 = 6.37
$S^2 =$	12.03/3 = 4.01	10.56/3 = 3.52

$$S^2_{Pooled} = 3.77$$

$S^2_M =$	3.77/4 = .94	3.77/4 = .94

$S^2_{Difference} = .94 + .94 = 1.88$
$S_{Difference} = \sqrt{1.88} = 1.37$
$t = (6.37 - 2.40)/1.37 = 2.90$

Conclusion: Reject the null hypothesis.

normal curve, and the transformation also seems reasonable in terms of the meaning of the numbers. Number of books read is meant as a measure of interest in things literary. Thus, the difference between 0 and 1 book is a much greater difference than the difference between 20 and 21 books. Table 11–12 shows the *t* test analysis using the transformed scores.

Rank-Order Tests

rank-order transformation

Another way of coping with non-normal distributions is to use a special kind of transformation in which you change the scores to ranks. Suppose you have a sample with scores 4, 8, 12, and 64. This would be a rather surprising sample if the population was really normal. A **rank-order transformation** would change the scores to 1, 2, 3, and 4, the 1 referring to the lowest number in the group, the 2 to the second lowest, and so forth. (A complication with a rank-order transformation occurs when you have two or more scores that are tied. The usual solution to ties is to give them each the average rank. For example, the scores 12, 81, 81, 107, and 154 would be ranked 1, 2.5, 2.5, 4, and 5.)

Converting the scores to ranks is a kind of data transformation. But unlike the square-root transformation we just considered, a rank-order transformation is not used to produce a normal distribution. The distribution you get from a rank-order transformation is rectangular, with equal numbers of scores (one) at each value. Ranks have the effect of spreading the scores out evenly.

There are special hypothesis-testing procedures that make use of rank-ordered data, called **rank-order tests.** They also have two other common names. You can transform scores from a population with any shaped distribution into ranks. Thus, these tests are sometimes called *distribution-free tests.* Also, the distribution of rank-order scores is known exactly rather than estimated. Thus, rank-order tests do not require estimating any parameters (population values). For example, there is no need to estimate a population variance because you can determine exactly what it will be if you know that ranks are involved. Hence, hypothesis-testing procedures based on ranks are also called *nonparametric tests.*

The ordinary hypothesis-testing procedures you have learned (*t* test and analysis of variance) are examples of *parametric tests.* Chi-square, like the rank-order tests, is considered a nonparametric test, but it is distribution-free only in the sense that no assumptions are made about the shape of the population distributions. However, the terms *distribution-free* and *nonparametric* are typically used interchangeably; the subtleties of differences between them are a matter of ongoing debate among statisticians.

Rank-order tests also have the advantage that they can be used where the actual scores in the study are themselves ranks.

Overview of Rank-Order Tests

Table 11–13 shows the name of the rank-order test that you would substitute for each of the parametric hypothesis-testing procedures you have learned. (Full procedures for using such tests are given in intermediate statistics texts.) Where more than one possible test is listed, the procedures are approximately equivalent.

Next, we will describe how such tests are done in a general way, including an example. However, we do not actually provide all the needed information for you to carry them out in practice. We introduce you to these techniques because you may see them used in articles you read and because their logic is the foundation of an alternative procedure that we do teach you to use (shortly). This alternative procedure does roughly the same thing as these rank-order tests and is closer to what you have already learned.

Basic Logic of Rank-Order Tests

Consider a study involving an experimental group and a control group. (This is the kind of situation for which researchers would use a *t* test for independent means if all the assumptions were met.) If you wanted to use a rank-

TABLE 11–13
Major Rank-Order Tests Corresponding to Major Parametric Tests

Parametric Test	Corresponding Rank-Order Test
t test for dependent means	Wilcoxon signed-rank test
t test for independent means	Wilcoxon rank-sum test or Mann-Whitney *U* test
Analysis of variance	Kruskal-Wallis *H* test
t test for correlation	Spearman rho or Kendall's tau

order test, you would first transform all the scores into ranks, ranking all the scores from lowest to highest, regardless of whether a score was in the experimental or the control group. If the two groups were scores randomly taken from a single population, there should be about equal amounts of high ranks and low ranks in each group. (That is, if the null hypothesis is true, the ranks in the two groups should not differ.) Because the distribution of ranks can be worked out exactly, statisticians can figure the exact probability of getting any particular division of ranks into two groups if in fact the two groups were randomly taken from identical distributions.

The way this actually works is that the researcher converts all the scores to ranks, adds up the total of the ranks in the group with the lower scores, and then compares this total to a cutoff from a special table of significance cutoffs for totals of ranks in this kind of situation.

An Example of a Rank-Order Test

Table 11–14 shows the transformation to ranks and the computation of the Wilcoxon rank-sum test for the kind of situation we have just described, using the same results as for our data-transformation example of the number of books read by highly-sensitive versus not-highly-sensitive children. The logic is a little different, so be patient until we explain it.

Notice that we first set the significance cutoff, as you would do in any hypothesis-testing procedure. (This cutoff is based on a table you don't have but is available in most intermediate statistics texts.) The next step was to rank all the scores from lowest to highest, then add up the group you expect to have the smaller total. You then compare the smaller total to the cutoff. In the example, the total of the ranks for the lower was not higher than the cutoff, so the null hypothesis was rejected.

TABLE 11–14
Computations for a Wilcoxon Rank-Sum Test for the Study of Books Read by Highly Sensitive Versus Not Highly Sensitive Children (Fictional Data)

Cutoff for significance: Maximum sum of ranks in the not highly sensitive group for significance at the .05 level, one-tailed (from a standard table) = 11.

Highly Sensitive

No		Yes	
X	Rank	X	Rank
0	1	17	4
3	2	36	6
10	3	45	7
22	5	75	8
Σ:	11		

Comparison to cutoff: Sum of ranks of group predicted to have lower scores, 11, equals but does not exceed cutoff for significance.

Conclusion: Reject the null hypothesis.

Using Parametric Tests with Rank-Transformed Data

Two statisticians (Conover & Iman, 1981) have shown that instead of using the special procedures for rank-order tests, you get approximately the same results for the t test and one-way analysis of variance if you transform the data into ranks and then apply all the usual t-test or one-way analysis-of-variance procedures.

The result of using a parametric test with data transformed into ranks will not be quite as accurate as either the ordinary parametric test or the rank-order test. It will not be as accurate as the ordinary parametric test because the assumption of normal distributions is clearly violated. The distribution is, in fact, rectangular when ranks are involved. It will not be as accurate as the rank-order test because the parametric test uses the t or F distribution instead of the special tables that rank-order tests use, which are based on exact probabilities of getting certain divisions of ranks. However, the approximation seems to be quite close.[5]

Table 11–15 shows the computations of an ordinary t test for independent means for the fictional sensitive-children data, using each child's rank

TABLE 11–15

Computations for a t test for Independent Means Using Ranks Instead of Raw Scores for the Study of Books Read by Highly Sensitive Versus Not Highly Sensitive Children (Fictional Data)

t needed for .05 significance level, $df = (4 - 1) + (4 - 1) = 6$, one-tailed = -1.943

Highly Sensitive

	No	Yes
	1	4
	2	6
	3	7
	5	8
Σ	11	25
$M =$	$11/4 = 2.75$	$25/4 = 6.25$
$S^2 =$	$8.75/3 = 2.92$	$8.75/3 = 2.92$

$$S^2_{Pooled} = 2.92$$

| $S^2_M =$ | $2.92/4 = .73$ | $2.92/4 = .73$ |

$S^2_{Difference} = .73 + .73 = 1.46$

$S_{Difference} = \sqrt{1.46} = 1.21$

$t = (2.75 - 6.25)/1.21 = -2.89$

Conclusion: Reject the null hypothesis.

[5]If you want to be very accurate, for a t test or one-way analysis of variance, you can convert your result to what is called an L statistic and look it up on a chi square table (Puri & Sen, 1985). The L statistic for a t test is $([N-1]t^2)/(t^2 + [N-2])$ and you use a chi-square distribution with $df = 1$. The L statistic for a one way analysis of variance is $([N-1][df_{Between}]F)/([df_{Between}]F + df_{Within})$ and you use a chi-square distribution with $df = df_{Between}$. The L for the significance of a correlation (see Chapter 3 appendix) is just $(N-1)r^2$ and you use the chi square table for $df = 1$. It is especially important to use the L statistic when using rank-transformed scores for more advanced parametric procedures, such as factorial analysis of variance (Chapter 10), multiple regression (Chapter 11), and those procedures discussed in Chapter 12. Thomas, Nelson, and Thomas (1999) give fully worked out examples.

instead of actual number of books read. Again we get a significant result. (In practice, carrying out an ordinary procedure like a *t* test with scores that have been transformed to ranks is least accurate with a very small sample like this. However, we used the small sample to keep the example simple.)

Chi-Square Tests, Data Transformations, and Rank-Order Tests as Reported in Research Articles

Chi-Square Tests

The reporting of chi-square tests usually includes the frequencies in each category or cell as well as the degrees of freedom, number of participants, computed chi-square, and significance level. For example, Harter et al. reported their finding for the relationship style of the self-focused men as "$\chi^2(2, n = 101) = 11.89, p < .005$" (p. 156).

Here is another example of a chi-square test for goodness of fit. Sandra Moriarty and Shu-Ling Everett (1994) did a study of television viewing in which graduate students actually went to 55 different homes and observed people watching television for 45-minute sessions. In one part of their results, they compared the number of people they observed who fell into one of four distinct categories:

> Flipping [very rapid channel changing], the category dominated by the most active type of behavior, occurred most frequently, in 33% of the sessions ($n = 18$). The grazing category [periods of browsing through channels] dominated 24% of the sessions ($n = 13$), and 22% were found to be in each of the continuous and stretch viewing categories ($n = 12$). These differences were not statistically significant ($\chi^2 = 1.79, df = 3, p > .05$).

Published reports of chi-square tests of independence provide the same basic chi-square information. For example, John Lydon and his associates (1997) compared long-distance to local dating relationships. Lydon et al. first gave questionnaires to a group of students one month prior to their leaving home to begin their first semester at McGill University (Time 1). Some of these students had dating partners who lived in the McGill area; others had dating partners who lived a long way from McGill. Lydon et al. contacted the participants again late in the fall semester, asking them about the current status of their original dating relationships (Time 2). Here is how they reported their results:

> Of the 69 participants . . . 55 were involved in long-distance relationships, and 14 were in local relationships (dating partner living within 200 km of them). Consistent with our predictions, 12 of the 14 local relationships were still intact at Time 2 (86%), whereas only 28 of the 55 long-distance relationships were still intact (51%), $\chi^2(1, N = 69) = 5.55, p < .02$. (p. 108).

Although Lydon et al. do not give the effect size for their significant result, we can compute it from the information provided:

$$\phi = \sqrt{\frac{\xi^2}{N}} = \sqrt{\frac{5.55}{69}} = \sqrt{.08} = .28$$

This suggests that there is a moderate effect size.

Data Transformations

Data transformations usually are mentioned in the Results section, just prior to the description of the analysis using the data that were transformed. For example, Martinez (2000) studied the link between homicide rates and immigrant status among Latinos in the United States. However, prior to presenting the results, Martinez noted, ". . . . the dependent variables indicated skewed distributions. Thus, all Latino homicide types . . . were logarithmically transformed into natural logs."

Rank-Order Tests

Here is an example of a rank-order test reported in a study by Ford et al. (1997), focusing on the relation of certain personality factors to treatment for post-traumatic stress disorder (a psychological condition resulting from a traumatic event such as might be experienced during war or as a result of a violent attack). The personality factor of interest to the researchers was based on a modern version of Freudian psychoanalytic theory called "object relations." This refers to the psychological impact of our earliest relationships, mainly with our parents (the "objects" of these early relationships). The researchers based their measure of object relations on a clinical interview focusing on such things as ability to invest in a close relationship and the ability to see others in a complex way (e.g., not seeing a person as all good or all bad). In reporting their results, they abbreviated the object-relations-clinical-interview-measure as "OR-C." The distribution of scores on the OR-C was not normal (it was bimodal).

One of their analyses focused on the relation of object relations to whether a person stays in treatment to completion or terminates prematurely. They reported their results as follows:

> Six of the 74 participants prematurely terminated. . . . The six premature terminators did not differ from the rest of the sample on any demographic or pretest variable. . . . They did differ statistically significantly from completers on OR-C ratings, scoring lower as tested by the nonparametric Mann-Whitney U Test ($Z = -3.43$, $p < .001$) (p. 554).

Summary

1. Chi-square tests are used for hypothesis tests involving nominal variables. The chi-square statistic shows the amount of mismatch between expected and observed frequencies over several levels or categories. It is figured by finding, for each category, or combination of categories, the difference between observed frequency and expected frequency, squaring this difference (eliminating positive and

negative signs), and dividing by the expected frequency (making the squared differences more proportionate to the numbers involved). The results are then added up for all the categories or combinations of categories. The distribution of the chi-square statistic is known and the cutoffs can be looked up in standard tables.

2. The chi-square test of independence is used to test hypotheses about the relation between two nominal variables—that is, about whether the breakdown over the categories of one variable has the same proportional pattern within each of the categories of the other variable. The frequencies are set up in a contingency table, in which the two variables are crossed and the numbers in each combination are placed in each of the resulting cells. The frequency expected for a cell if the two variables are independent is the percentage of all the scores in that cell's row times the total number of scores in that cell's column. The degrees of freedom for the test of independence are the number of columns minus 1 times the number of rows minus 1.

3. The estimated effect size for a chi-square test of independence (that is, the degree of association) for a 2 × 2 contingency table is the phi coefficient; for larger tables, Cramer's phi. Phi is the square root of the result of dividing the computed chi-square by the number of persons. Cramer's phi is the square root of the result of dividing the computed chi-square by the product of the number of persons times the degrees of freedom in the smaller side of the contingency table. These coefficients range from 0 to 1.

4. Ordinary hypothesis testing procedures assume that populations follow a normal curve. When samples suggest that the populations are very far from normal (for example, due to outliers), using the ordinary procedures gives incorrect results.

5. One approach when the populations appear to be non-normal is to transform the scores, such as taking the square root of each score so that the distribution of the transformed scores appears to represent a normally distributed population. The ordinary hypothesis-testing procedures can then be applied.

6. Another approach is to rank all of the scores in a study. Special rank-order tests (sometimes called nonparametric or distribution-free tests) use basic principles of probability to determine the chance of the ranks being unevenly distributed across groups. However, in many cases, using the rank-transformed data in an ordinary hypothesis test may give a good approximation.

Key Terms

cell	chi-square test for independence	independence
chi-square distribution		nominal variable
chi-square statistic (χ^2)	contingency table	observed frequency
chi-square table	Cramer's phi statistic	phi coefficient (Φ)
chi-square test	data transformation	rank-order tests
chi-square test for goodness of fit	expected frequency	rank-order transformation

Practice Problems

These problems involve figuring. Most real-life statistics problems are done on a computer. Even if you have a computer and statistics software, do these problems by hand (with the help of a calculator) to ingrain the method in your mind.

For practice in using a computer to solve statistics problems, refer to the computer section of each chapter of the Student's Study Guide and Computer Workbook *that accompanies this text.*

All data are fictional unless an actual citation is given.

Answers to selected problems are given at the back of this book.

1. Compute a chi-square test for goodness of fit for each of the following, using the .05 level for each. In each problem, the expected distribution is equal frequencies in each category.

   (a) 5 10 5
   (b) 10 15 10
   (c) 10 20 10
   (d) 5 15 5

2. A director of a social service agency is planning to hire temporary staff to assist with intake. In making plans, the director needs to know whether there is any difference in the use of the agency at different seasons of the year. Last year there were 28 new clients in the winter, 33 in the spring, 16 in the summer, and 51 in the fall. On the basis of last year's data, should the director conclude that season makes a difference? (Use the .05 level.) Explain your answer to a person who has never taken a course in statistics. (This problem is like the Harter et al. example in which you are doing a chi-square for a single nominal variable. It is not a chi-square test for independence and does not involve any contingency tables.)

3. Carry out a chi-square test for independence for each of the following contingency tables. (Use the .01 level, and compute phi or Cramer's phi for each.)

(a)   10 16   (b)   100 106   (c)   100 160
       16 10   106 100   160 100

(d) 10 16 10   (e) 10 16 16   (f) 10 16 10
    16 10 10   16 10 16   16 10 16

4. A political analyst is interested in whether the community in which a person lives is related to that person's opinion on an upcoming water conservation ballot initiative. The analyst surveys 90 people by phone. The results are shown at the top of the next column. Is opinion related to community at the .05 level? (a) Carry out the five steps of hypothesis testing. (b) Compute Cramer's phi and power. (c) Explain your answer to a person who has never taken a course in statistics.

	Community A	Community B	Community C
For	12	6	3
Against	18	3	15
No opinion	12	9	12

5. The following chart shows the results of a survey of a sample of people attending a ballet, distributed according to the type of seat they purchased and how regularly they attend. Is there a significant relation? (Use the .05 level.) (a) Carry out the five steps of hypothesis testing. (b) Compute Cramer's phi. (c) Explain your answer to a person who has never taken a course in statistics.

		Attendance	
		Regular	*Occasional*
Seating Category	*Orchestra*	20	80
	Dress circle	20	20
	Balcony	40	

6. Johnston (2000) surveyed 45 managers. She hypothesized that "the attachment patterns of managers would be significantly related to the way in which individuals chose to structure their organizations." ("Attachment patterns" refers to attachment style, people's typical way of relating to others in close relationships—we presented an extensive example that used this variable in Chapter 10.) The results are shown in Table 11–16. (a) What does the pattern of results tell us specifically about how managers of particular attachment styles are likely to structure their organization. (b) Explain the statistical analysis (the significance test) to a person who has never had a course in statistics.

TABLE 11–16
Contingency Table of Organizational Structure by Manager's Attachment Type

	Avoidant	Preoccupied	Secure	Total
Centralized	13	5	4	22
Decentralized	0	0	11	11
Disorganized	2	10	0	12
Total	15	15	15	

Chi-square	Value	df	Significance
Pearson	42.64	4	$p < .0001$

From "Delegation and Organizational Structure in Small Businesses" by Michelle A. Johnston, *Group & Organization Management,* Vol. 25, No. 1, March 2000, p. 4, copyright © 2000. Reprinted by permission of Sage Publications Inc.

7. A researcher compares the typical family size in 10 cultures, 5 from Language Group A and 5 from Language Group B. The figures for the Group A cultures are 1.2, 2.5, 4.3, 3.8, and 7.2. The figures for the Group B cultures are 2.1, 9.2, 5.7, 6.7, and 4.8. Based on these 10 cultures, does typical family size differ in cultures with different language groups? Use the .05 level. (a) Carry out a square-root transformation (to keep things simple, round off the transformed scores to one decimal place). (b) Carry out a t test for independent means using the transformed scores. (show your work). (c). Explain what you have done and why to someone who is familiar with the t test but not with data transformation.

8. A researcher randomly assigns participants to watch one of three kinds of films: one that tends to make people sad, one that tends to make people exuberant, and one that tends to make people angry. The participants are then asked to rate a series of photos of individuals on how honest they appear. The honesty ratings for the sad-film group were 201, 523, and 614; the honesty ratings for the angry-film group were 136, 340, and 301; and the honesty ratings for the exuberant-film group were 838, 911, and 1,007. (a) Make a rank transform of the scores. (b) Carry out a one-way analysis of variance using the rank-transformed scores. (Use the .05 significance level.) (c) Explain what you have done and why to a person who understands the analysis of variance but not rank transformations or non-parametric tests.

9. June et, al. (1990) surveyed black students at a Midwestern university about problems in their use of college services. Surveys were conducted of about 250 students each time, at the end of the spring quarter in 1976, 1978, 1980, 1982, and 1987. The researchers ranked the nine main problem areas for each of the years. One of their analyses then proceeded as follows: "A major question of interest was whether the ranking of most serious problems and use of services varied by years. Thus, a Kruskal-Wallis one-way analysis of variance (ANOVA) was performed on the rankings but was not significant. . . ." (p. 180). Explain why the researchers used the Kruskal-Wallis test instead of an ordinary analysis of variance and what conclusions can be drawn from this result.

Making Sense of Advanced Statistical Procedures in Research Articles

12

$\mathbf{M}$OST studies you will read in your social and behavioral science classes use one or more of the statistical procedures you have learned in this book. However, often you will also run into procedures that you will not learn to do yourself until you take more advanced statistics courses. Fortunately, most of these advanced procedures are direct extensions of what you have learned in this book. At the least, after reading this chapter, you should be able to make sense of the general idea of just about any statistical analysis in a research article.

The first part of this chapter considers some widely used advanced statistical techniques that focus on associations among variables. These are basically elaborations of what you learned in Chapter 3 on correlation and regression. After a brief review of multiple regression as a foundation, we introduce hierarchical and stepwise multiple regression, partial correlation, reliability, factor analysis, and causal modeling. The second part of this chapter considers advanced statistical techniques that focus on differences between groups. These are basically elaborations of what you learned in Chapter 10 on the analysis of variance. These procedures include the analysis of covariance, multivariate analysis of variance, and multivariate analysis of covariance. We conclude with a discussion of what to do when you read a research article that uses a statistical technique you have never heard of.

To understand the first part of this chapter, you need a strong grasp of the material in Chapter 3, especially on multiple regression, as well as on the general logic of hypothesis testing from Chapters 4–7. For the second part of this chapter, you need a strong grasp of the material in Chapter 10, including factorial analysis of variance.

Brief Review of Multiple Regression

As you learned in Chapter 3, regression is the prediction aspect of correlation. Multiple regression is about predicting scores on a criterion variable from two or more predictor variables. For example, in the sleep-and-mood study example in that chapter, we discussed predicting a person's mood the next day (the criterion variable) from three predictor variables: number of hours slept the night before, how well the person slept, and number of dreams during the night.

A multiple regression prediction rule has a regression coefficient for each predictor variable. If you know a person's scores on the predictor variables, you multiply each predictor variable's score times that variable's regression coefficient. The sum of these multiplications is the person's predicted score on the criterion variable. With Z scores, the regression coefficients are standardized and are called standardized regression coefficients or beta weights (βs). For example, with three independent variables, the form of the prediction rule is as follows:

$$\text{Predicted } Z_Y = (\beta_1)(Z_{X_1}) + (\beta_2)(Z_{X_2}) + (\beta_3)(Z_{X_3}) \tag{12–1}$$

The overall accuracy of a prediction rule, the amount of variation it accounts for in the criterion variable, is called the proportion of variance accounted for and is abbreviated as R^2. Multiple regression also gives you the statistical significance of both the overall proportion of variance accounted for, R^2, as well as for each beta individually.

Hierarchical and Stepwise Multiple Regression

Hierarchical Multiple Regression

Sometimes researchers focus on the influence of several predictor variables in a sequential way. That is, they want to know what the correlation will be of the first predictor variable with the criterion variable. Then how much is added to the overall variance accounted for (the R^2) by including a second predictor variable on the prediction rule. Then perhaps how much more is added by including a third predictor variable. And so on. Thus, when reporting results, a researcher usually describes the amount that each successive predictor variable adds to the overall prediction in terms of increasing in R^2. The procedure is known as **hierarchical multiple regression.**

    Consider an example. MacDonald and her colleagues (1997) studied the relation of various factors to war veterans' symptoms of posttraumatic stress disorder (PTSD). These researchers studied 756 Vietnam War veterans in New Zealand, including 161 Maori individuals (the Maori are the indigenous Polynesian people of New Zealand). Table 12–1 shows the results of their hierarchical regression analysis. The first variable they considered, Step 1, was combat exposure. This variable by itself had an R^2 of .070; the two stars show that this was significant. The second step was to add a set of variables involving Vietnam military experience. The entire set of variables increased

hierarchical multiple regression

TABLE 12–1
Regression Coefficients, R^2 And R^2 Change Values For Combat Exposure, Vietnam Experience Variables, and Race Predicting to PTSD

	Standardized beta		
Predictor Variable	*Step 1*	*Step 2*	*Step 3*
Combat exposure	.266**	.300**	.297**
Vietnam military experience			
Length Vietnam service		−.035	−.036
Rank		−.316**	−.314**
Combat role		.153*	.154*
Military specialization 1[a]		.015	.017
Military specialization 2[a]		.044	.044
Race[b]			−.024
R^2	.070**	.171**	.171**
R^2 change		.100*	.001*

$*p < .01; **p < .001.$
[a]Dummy variables: military specialization 1 (infantry/non-infantry); military specialization 2 (artillery/nonartillery).
[b]Dichotomous variable (Maori/non-Maori).
Table 2 from "Race, Combat, and PTSD in a Community Sample of New Zealand War Veterans" by C. MacDonald, K. Chamberlain, & N. Long. *Journal of Traumatic Stress,* 10, 123, 1997. Reprinted by permission of Kenny Chamberlain.

the R^2 from .070 to .171, an increase (R^2 change) of .101. (The researchers show the increase as .100 in their table. The discrepancy between .100 and .101 is probably their rounding off the numbers in the table at each stage.) Finally, at Step 3, they added race (Maori or not). Adding race increased the R^2 only slightly, and this slight increased was not significant.

These results are especially interesting because the direct ordinary correlation of race with PTSD symptoms was significant. Thus, the hierarchical regression shows that race does not predict PTSD if you have already taken into account combat experience and military situation. In other words, the apparent effect of race was probably due to Maoris having more exposure to combat and different military experience (such as being more likely to be in the infantry).

Stepwise Multiple Regression

stepwise multiple regression

Sometimes, especially in an exploratory study, a researcher measures many variables that are possible predictors of some criterion variable and wants to pick out which predictor variables make a useful contribution to the overall prediction. This is usually done with a controversial procedure called **stepwise multiple regression.** The most common form of stepwise multiple regression works as follows: A computer program goes through a step-by-step procedure in which it first picks out the variable that has the highest correlation with the criterion variable. If this correlation is not significant, the process stops, since even the best predictor is of no use. However, if this correlation is significant, the process goes on to the next step. The next step is to pick out the predictor variable that, in combination with this first one, has the highest R^2. The computer then checks to see whether this combination is a significant improvement over the best single predictor variable alone. If it is not, the process stops. If it is a significant improvement, the computer goes on. The next step is to pick out which of the remaining predictor variables, when combined with these first two, creates the highest R^2. Then this combination is checked to see if it is a significant improvement in prediction over and above just the first two predictors. The process continues until either all the predictor variables are included or adding any of the remaining ones does not give a significant improvement. We have diagramed this procedure in Table 12–2. It is called "stepwise" because it proceeds one step at a time.

Here is an example. Mooney, Sherman, and Lo Presto (1991) were interested in what predicts women's adjustment to college. They studied 82 women who were in the fourth week of their first semester at college. The women in the study were all living away from home. The predictor variables were distance from home (in miles), perceived distance from home (a scale from *just right* to *too far*), a self-esteem scale, and an "academic locus of control" scale that measures how much a person feels in control over being successful at school. One purpose of the study was to find out whether all of these variables made their own unique contributions to predicting college adjustment. And if not all of them, which ones? The authors describe the procedure they used as follows:

> For this analysis, a stepwise procedure was employed. . . . Three predictors were retained: academic locus of control, perceived distance from home, and self-esteem. . . . With these variables in the equation, 59% of the variance in the

TABLE 12–2
The Process of a Stepwise Multiple Regression

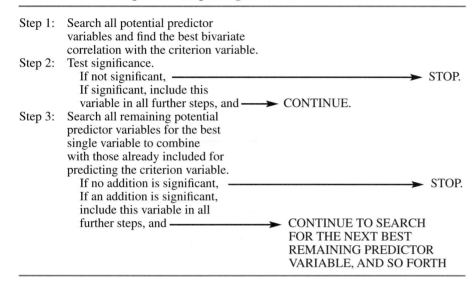

Step 1:   Search all potential predictor variables and find the best bivariate correlation with the criterion variable.

Step 2:   Test significance.
      If not significant, —————————————————————→ STOP.
      If significant, include this variable in all further steps, and ———→ CONTINUE.

Step 3:   Search all remaining potential predictor variables for the best single variable to combine with those already included for predicting the criterion variable.
      If no addition is significant, —————————————————→ STOP.
      If an addition is significant, include this variable in all further steps, and ———————→ CONTINUE TO SEARCH FOR THE NEXT BEST REMAINING PREDICTOR VARIABLE, AND SO FORTH

dependent [criterion] variable was accounted for ($R = .77$, $R^2 = .59 \ldots$). The standardized beta coefficients [of the regression equation including these three predictor variables] indicated that academic locus of control was weighted the most, followed by self-esteem and perceived distance. . . .(p. 447)

What the authors are telling us is that of the four potential predictors, the proportion of variance accounted for by three of these variables was not improved upon by also including the fourth (actual distance from home). Actual distance from home was left out of the final regression equation because it did not add anything to include it.

One caution about stepwise regression. We said earlier that stepwise regression is a controversial procedure. The reason it is controversial is that the prediction formula that results from this procedure is the best group of variables for predicting the criterion variable, *based on the sample studied*. However, it often happens that when the same variables are studied with a new sample, a somewhat different combination of variables turns out to be best. The reason this is likely is that the variable selected at each step is one that adds the most to the overall prediction. It is not required that the variable added be significantly better than the other variables—only that it add the most and that the addition is significant. The next best variable might also make a significant addition, but just not quite as strong an addition. Yet in a new sample from the same population, this slight difference in one adding more than the other could well be reversed.

Hierarchical and Stepwise Regression Compared

Hierarchical and stepwise regression are similar in an important way. In both methods you add variables a stage at a time and check whether the addition significantly improves the prediction. However, there is also a very important difference. In hierarchical regression, the order of adding the predictor variables is based on some theory or plan, decided in advance by the researcher. In stepwise regression, there is no initial plan. The computer simply figures out the best variables to add until adding more makes no additional contribution.

Thus, hierarchical regression is used in research that is based on theory or some substantial previous knowledge. Stepwise regression is useful in exploratory research where you don't know what to expect. It is also useful in applied research where we are looking for the best prediction formula without caring about its theoretical meaning.

Partial Correlation

Partial correlation

Partial correlation is widely used in the social and behavioral sciences. Partial correlation is the amount of association between two variables, over and above the influence of one or more other variables. Suppose a sociologist wants to know whether how much the stress people experience in married life is related to how long they have been married. However, the researcher realizes that part of what might make marital stress and marriage length go together is whether the couples have children. Having children or not could make stress and length go together because those married longer are more likely to have children and having children may create marital stress. Thus, simply figuring the correlation between marital stress and marriage length would be misleading. The researcher wants to know the relation between stress and marriage length that would be found if everyone had the same number of children. Or to put this another way, the researcher wants somehow to subtract out the information provided by number of children from the information provided by marital stress and length. Partial correlation accomplishes this.

**holding constant
partialing out
controlling for
adjusting for**

In this example, the researcher would compute a partial correlation between marital stress and length of marriage, **holding constant** number of children. Holding a variable constant is also called **partialing out, controlling for,** or **adjusting for** the variable held constant (such as number of children). These terms (holding constant, partialing out, etc.) all mean the same thing and are used interchangeably. The actual statistic for partial correlation is called the

partial correlation coefficient

partial correlation coefficient. Like an ordinary correlation coefficient between two variables, it goes from -1 to $+1$. Just remember that unlike an ordinary correlation coefficient, some third variable is being controlled for.

Here is another way to think about partial correlations. In this example, you could figure the ordinary correlation between stress and marriage length using only people who have no children, then figure an ordinary correlation between stress and marriage length using only those with one child, and so on. Each of these correlations, by itself, is not affected by differences in number of children. (This is because the people included within any one of these correlations all have the same number of children.) You could then figure a kind of average of these various correlations, each of which is not affected by number of children. This average of these correlations is the partial correlation. It is literally a correlation that *holds constant* the number of children.

In fact, the calculations for a partial correlation are fairly straightforward and do not require figuring all these individual correlations and averaging them. However, the result of the process amounts to doing this.

Partial correlation often is used to help sort out alternative theoretical explanations for the relations among variables. Suppose the sociologist found an ordinary correlation between marital stress and marriage length. The sociologist might want to use this result to support a theory that the effect of time (marriage length) is to make people feel more stress in their marriage because their partners take them for granted. The sociologist would also be aware that another possible explanation for what is going on is that when people are married longer, they are likely to have more children, and having more children might create stress in the marriage. If the correlation between stress and length holds up, even after controlling for number of children, this alternate explanation about children is made unlikely.

Reliability

In the social and behavioral sciences, most variables are measured with questionnaires or systematic observations of what people do. Measures of these kinds are rarely perfectly consistent or stable over time. The degree of stability or consistency is called its **reliability.** Roughly speaking, the reliability of a measure is the extent to which you would get the same result if you were to give the same measure again to the same person under the same circumstances. You will often see reliability statistics in research articles.

reliability

One way to gauge a measure's reliability is to use the measure with the same group of people twice. The correlation between the two testings is called **test-retest reliability.** However, this approach often is not practical or appropriate. For example, you can't use this approach if taking a test once would influence the second taking (such as with an intelligence test).

test-retest reliability

For many measures, such as most questionnaires, you also can gauge its reliability by correlating the average of the answers to half the questions with the average of the answers to the other half. For example, you could correlate the average score on all the odd-numbered questions with the average score on all the even-numbered questions. If the person is answering consistently, this should be a high correlation. This is called **split-half reliability.**

split-half reliability

A problem with the split-half method is deciding which way to split the halves. Using odd-versus-even items makes sense in most situations, but by chance it could give too low or too high a correlation. Fortunately, there is a more general solution. You can divide the test into halves in all possible ways and figure the correlation using each division. A statistic called **Cronbach's alpha (α)** gives you what amounts to this average. Cronbach's alpha is the most widely used measure of reliability. Cronbach's alpha also can be thought of as telling you the overall consistency of the test, how much high responses go with highs and lows with lows over all the test questions. In general, in the social and behavioral sciences, a measure should have a Cronbach's alpha of at least .6 or .7 and preferably closer to .9 to be considered useful.

Cronbach's alpha (α)

One context in which reliabilities are nearly always discussed is when a research article is mainly about the creation of a new measure. For example, Sellers and his colleagues (1997) developed a questionnaire to assess Black identity among African Americans. In developing the scale they identified a number of aspects of black identity, creating a Multidimensional Inventory of Black Identity (MIBI) that includes several subscales. One of the various methods they used to evaluate its soundness as a measure was to assess the reliability of each subscale, and to do so for African American students at both an all-black university and a predominantly white university. Table 12–3 shows results of this aspect of their study. (The line for Public Regard is blank in the table because this was a subscale they had originally included but later dropped in the process of developing the measure.) Sellers et al. summarize the findings in the table as follows: "The revised MIBI scales and subscales demonstrated adequate internal consistency. . . . The Cronbach's alphas for the subscales ranged from a low of .60 (Private Regard) to .79 (Nationalism). Alphas were similar for each school" (p. 810).

Factor Analysis

factor analysis

factor
factor loading

Suppose you have measured people on a large number of variables (for example, you might have done a survey with questions about 85 different attitudes). You use **factor analysis** to tell you which variables tend to clump together—which ones tend to be correlated with each other and not with other variables. Each such clump (group of variables) is called a **factor.** The correlation of an individual variable with a factor is called that variable's **factor loading** on that factor. Variables have loadings on each factor but usually will have high loadings on only one. Factor loading range from −1, a perfect negative association with the factor, through 0, no relation to the factor, to +1, a perfect positive correlation with the factor. Normally, a variable is considered to contribute meaningfully to a factor only if it has a loading of at least about .3 (or below −.3).

The factor analysis itself involves a relatively complex set of formulas that begin with the correlations among all the variables and end up with a set of factor loadings. There is, however, one subjective part of the process—the name you give to a factor. (When reading a research article reporting a factor analysis, think closely about the name the researcher gives to each factor. Do the names really do a good job of describing the variables that make up each factor?)

TABLE 12–3
Descriptive Statistics for the Multidimensional Inventory of Black Identity (MIBI) by School and for the Full Sample

Scale	Full Sample			Predominantly White University			African American University		
	Cronbach's α	M	SD	Cronbach's α	M	SD	Cronbach's α	M	SD
Centrality	.77	5.23	1.08	.78	5.20	1.14	.75	5.28	.98
Regard-Priv	.60	6.25[a]	.70	.55	6.38	.59	.61	6.05	.81
Regard-Pub	—	—	—	—	—	—	—	—	—
Assimilation	.73	4.92[a]	.91	.66	5.16	.80	.74	4.55	.94
Humanist	.70	5.15[a]	.84	.68	5.33	.80	.69	4.87	.81
Minority	.76	4.78[a]	.82	.75	4.82	.80	.77	4.70	.86
Nationalist	.79	4.27[a]	.99	.78	4.02	.96	.74	4.67	.90

Note. Priv = Private; Pub = Public.

[a]Denotes means that are significantly different between the two samples at $\alpha = .01$.

Consider an example of factor analysis. Clyde and Susan Hendrick (1989) gave 19 different love scales to 391 students. The Hendricks then did a factor analysis of the scores to "determine commonalities among the scales" (p. 791). Table 12–4 shows the results. (On the Love Attitudes Scale, Eros refers to passionate, romantic love; Ludus, to game-playing love; Storge to friendship-based love; Pragma to practical love; Mania to possessive, dependent love; and Agape to altruistic love.)

This particular table leaves blank factor loadings below .35 to make it easy to see which variables go with what factor. Also notice that the last line of this table tells you the percentage of variance that the factor as a whole accounts for (that is, what the R^2 would be of this factor with all the variables). The Hendricks described each factor in some detail. For example, with regard to the first factor:

> The first factor that emerged included the love styles of Eros, Mania, and Agape; Sternberg's Intimacy, Passion, and Commitment; the Passionate Love Scale; and Davis's Viability, Intimacy, Passion, Care, and Satisfaction. The highest loadings on the factor were those of Commitment and the three measures of Passion, although the other variables also had substantial loadings. Passionate love

TABLE 12–4
Factor Analysis of All Love Scales Combined

Individual Measures	Factor Structure and Loadings				
	1	*2*	*3*	*4*	*5*
Attachment Styles					
Avoidant	—	—	—	−.81	—
Anxious-Ambivalent	—	—	.80	—	—
Secure	—	—	—	.83	—
Love Attitudes Scale					
Eros	.76	—	—	—	—
Ludus	—	−.65	—	—	—
Storge	—	—	—	—	.80
Pragma	—	−.39	—	—	.73
Mania	.39	—	.68	—	—
Agape	.54	—	—	—	—
Triangular Theory of Love Scale					
Intimacy	.72	.44	—	—	—
Passion	.85	—	—	—	—
Commitment	.82	—	—	—	—
Passionate Love Scale					
Passionate Love	.80	—	—	—	—
Relationship Rating Form					
Viability	.51	.67	—	—	—
Intimacy	.58	.52	—	—	—
Passion	.82	—	—	—	—
Care	.72	.43	—	—	—
Satisfaction	.78	.38	—	—	—
Conflict	—	−.70	—	—	—
% variance	32	14	8	8	7

Note: Only factor loadings of .35 or larger are shown. $N = 391$.

From Hendrick, C., & Hendrick, S. S. (1989), tab. 4. Research on love: Does it measure up? *Journal of Personality and Social Psychology*, 56, 784–794. Copyright © 1989, by the American Psychological Association. Reprinted by permission of the author.

was certainly a major component of the factor, but intimacy, commitment, satisfaction, and aspects of caring love also appeared to be important. (p. 791)

After describing each factor in this way, they concluded:

In summary, the various love scales primarily tap passionate love (Factor 1); however, two types of bipolar closeness-distance dimensions (Factors 2 and 4) are also important, as well as ambivalence-mania (Factor 3) and practicality-friendship (Factor 5). (p. 791)

Causal Modeling

As with factor analysis, you use causal modeling when you have measured people on many variables. Unlike factor analysis, the goal of causal modeling is to test whether the pattern of correlations among the variables fits with some specific theory of which variables are causing which.

Causal modeling techniques are widely used in the social and behavioral sciences. We first introduce the older (but still common) method of path analysis. It is also often called "ordinary path analysis," to distinguish it from the newer, more elaborate method of structural equation modeling (that is also in a sense a kind of path analysis) that we describe in the next section.

Path Analysis

In **path analysis,** you make a diagram with arrows connecting the variables. The arrows, or **paths,** show what some particular theory predicts as the cause-and-effect connections between variables Then, based on the correlations and the path diagram, you figure path coefficients for each path. The **path coefficient** is like a beta in multiple regression. Specifically, if the path diagram is a correct description of the causal relationship among the variables, the path coefficient tells you how much effect on the variable at the end of the arrow is produced by a one-unit change in the predictor variable at the start of the arrow. (A path coefficient is figured so that it partials out the influence of any other variables that have arrows to the variable at the end of the arrow.)

Here is an example. MacKinnon-Lewis and her colleagues (1997) were interested in predictors of social acceptance by peers of 8 to 10-year-old boys. The main predictors they used were the child's rating of parental acceptance and rejection, peers' ratings of acceptance and aggression, and conflict with siblings as observed in a laboratory interaction. They tried several different possible causal models, and concluded that the best was what they called "Model 1."

The standardized path coefficients of Model 1 are presented in Figure [12–1], which shows that siblings whose mothers were perceived and observed to be more rejecting were observed and reported to be more aggressive with one another than were siblings whose mothers were less rejecting. Moreover, boys who experienced more aggressive sibling interactions were more likely to be nominated by their peers as being aggressive and were less accepted by their peers. Although fathering failed to evince a direct influence on sibling aggression, an indirect effect was evidence as a result of the fact that less accepting fathering was related to more rejecting mothering. (p. 1027)

*path analysis
paths*

path coefficient

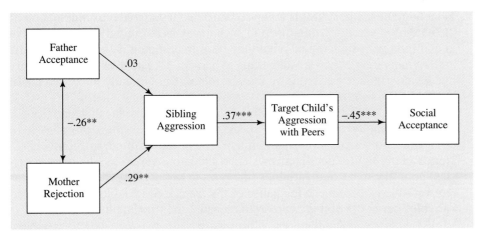

FIGURE 12–1
Path model of associations among parenting variables, sibling aggression, peer aggression, and social acceptance. Standardized path coefficients are given. **$p < .01$. *** $p < .001$.
(From MacKinnon-Lewis, C., Starnes, R., Volling, B., & Johnson, S. (1997), fig. 1. Perceptions of parenting as predictors of boys' sibling and peer relations. *Developmental Psychology, 33,* 1024–1031. Copyright © 1997, by the American Psychological Association. Reprinted with permission.)

In this path diagram, the most important paths had significant coefficients in the predicted directions. Thus, MacKinnon-Lewis et al. considered the results as encouraging support for their theory.

Structural Equation Modeling

Structural equation modeling is a special elaboration of ordinary path analysis. It also involves a path diagram with arrows between variables and path coefficients for each arrow. However, structural equation modeling has several important advantages over the older path analysis method. One major advantage is that structural equation modeling gives you an overall measure of the fit between the theory (as described in the path model) and the correlations among the scores in your sample. This measure of overall fit is called a **fit index** or an index of *goodness of fit*. There are several different fit indexes used, but in general, a fit of .9 or higher is considered a good fit. (The maximum is usually 1.)

In structural equation modeling, you can also do a kind of significance test of this fit. We say a "kind of significance test" because the null hypothesis in this situation is that the theory fits. That is, a significant result tells you that the theory does not fit. In other words, a researcher trying to demonstrate a theory hopes for a nonsignificant result in this significance test!

A second major advantage of structural equation modeling over ordinary path analysis is that it uses what are called **latent variables.** A latent variable is not actually measured but stands for a true variable that you would like to measure but can only approximate with real-life measures. For example, a latent variable might be social class, which the researcher tries to approximate with several measured variables, such as level of income, years of education, prestige of occupation, and home square footage. No one of these measured variables by itself is a very good stand-in for social class. In structural equation

structural equation modeling

fit index

latent variables

modeling, the mathematics is set up so that a latent variable is a combination of the measured variables, combined in such a way as to use only what they have in common with each other. What they have in common is the true score, the underlying variable they are all getting at parts of. (A latent variable is actually like a factor in factor analysis, in that the factor is not directly measured itself, but it stands for a combination of several variables that make it up.)

In a structural equation modeling diagram, the variables that actually are measured usually are shown in boxes; the latent variables are shown in circles or ellipses (ovals). This is illustrated in the example in Figure 12–2. Notice in the figure that the arrows from the latent variables (the ones in circles) go to the measured variables (the ones in boxes). The idea is that the latent variable is the underlying cause of the measured variables, the measured variables being the best we can do to measure the true latent variable.

Also notice that all of the other arrows are between latent variables. Structural equation modeling usually works in this way: The measured variables are used to make up latent variables, and the main focus of the analysis is on the causal relations (the paths) between the latent variables.

An Example of Structural Equation Modeling

This example is from a study by Kwan and her colleagues (1997) of predictors of life satisfaction, focusing on the role of self-esteem and social harmony. In particular they predicted that the relation of self-esteem and social harmony to life satisfaction would be different in different cultures. In more communal cultures, such as many Asian cultures, social harmony would matter more. However, in more individualistic cultures, such as most North American and European cultures, self-esteem would matter more. The researchers also measured independent self-construal (how much a person emphasizes personal development and achievement) and interdependent self-construal (how much a person emphasizes getting along and fitting in with others). The participants were 389 college students from the United States and Hong Kong.

FIGURE 12–2
A structural equation model path diagram.

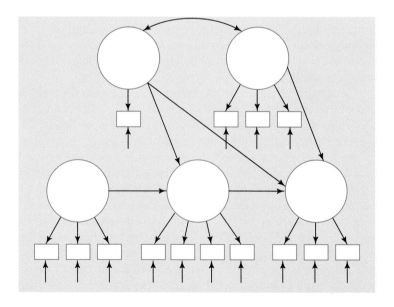

Figure 12–3 shows their basic results, focusing on the paths between the latent variables. In this particular study, the researchers give two sets of standardized path coefficients for each path. The path coefficients not in parentheses are for the Hong Kong sample; those in parentheses, for the U.S. sample. Notice that the impact of self-construals is about the same for the two cultures. For example, participants from the two cultures show about the same degree of association of how much a person emphasizes independence with self-esteem. What is most interesting, however, is that the path from self-esteem to life satisfaction is bigger for the U.S. sample, while the path from relationship harmony to life satisfaction is bigger for the Hong Kong sample.

A Key Limitation Of Causal Modeling

It is important to realize how little magic there is behind these wonderful methods. They still rely entirely on a researcher's deep thinking. All the predicted paths in a path analysis diagram can be significant and a structural

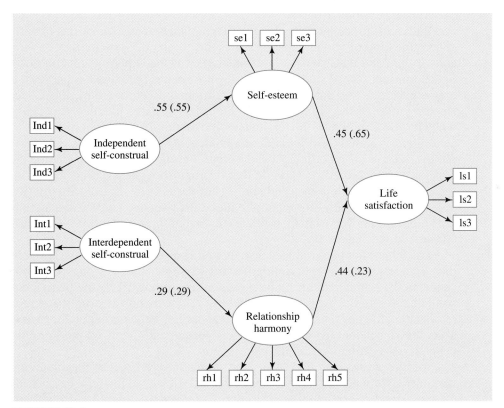

FIGURE 12–3
The final Self-Construal Scale model. $N = 194$ for the Hong Kong sample; $N = 184$ for the U.S. sample. Ellipses represent latent constructs, boxes represent indicators, arrows pointing from latent constructs to indicators depict factor loadings, and arrows relating latent constructs represent path coefficients. Standardized path coefficients are shown; factor loadings and measurement errors are omitted for clarity. Numbers inside parentheses are coefficients for the U.S. sample; numbers outside parentheses are coefficients for the Hong Kong sample. All these coefficients were significant at $p < .05$ or less. (From Kwan, V. S., Bond, M. H., & Singelis, T. M. (1997), fig. 1. Pancultural explanations for life satisfaction: Adding relationship harmony to self-esteem. *Journal of Personality and Social Psychology, 73,* 1038–1051. Copyright © 1997, by the American Psychological Association. Reprinted with permission.)

equation model can have an excellent fit, and yet it is still quite possible that other patterns of causality could work equally well or better.

Alternatives could have arrows that go in the opposite direction or make different connections, or the pattern could include additional variables not in the original diagram. Any kind of causal modeling shows at best that the data are consistent with the theory. The same data could also be consistent with quite different theories. Ideally, a researcher tries out plausible alternative theories and finds that the data do not fit them well. Nevertheless, there can always be alternative theories the researcher did not think of at all.

Procedures that Compare Groups

So far in this chapter, we have looked at statistical procedures that focus on associations among variables and are basically fancy elaborations of correlation and regression. Now we turn to procedures that focus on differences between group means, procedures that are basically elaborations of the analysis of variance (Chapter 10).

With such procedures we need to distinguish between two kinds of variables. One kind of variable distinguishes the groups from each other. A variable of this kind that we used in Chapter 10 was the experimental condition in the criminal-record study (whether the information provided as part of the experiment put the participant in the Criminal Record group, the Clean Record group, or the No Information group). A variable like this, especially when it is determined by the researcher who randomly assigns participants to **independent variable**   conditions, is called an **independent variable.** (Even when there are just two groups, such as an experimental and a control group in an experiment, the independent variable is the variable that distinguishes the experimental from the control group.) In a factorial analysis of variance, there are actually two independent variables—for example, mood (sad versus neutral) and stereotype (appropriate versus inappropriate) in the Lambert et al. (1997) study we considered in Chapter 10.

The other kind of variable in a study that compares groups is the variable that is measured—in the criminal-record example it was ratings of innocence; in the Lambert et al. study, it was ratings of how likely the participant would be to hire the person. A variable like this, which is measured and rep-**dependent variable**   resents the effect of the experimental procedure, is called a **dependent variable.** It is dependent in the sense that any participant's score on this variable depends on what happens in the experiment.

We did not need to introduce these terms before because the situations we considered were relatively straightforward. However, it would be difficult to understand the remaining procedures covered in this chapter without knowing about the difference between independent and dependent variables.

Analysis of Covariance (ANCOVA)

analysis of covariance, or   One of the most widely used of the elaborations on the analysis of variance is
ANCOVA   called the **analysis of covariance,** or **ANCOVA,** for short. In this procedure, you do an ordinary analysis of variance, but one which adjusts the dependent variable for the effect of some unwanted additional variable. The analysis of

covariance does for the analysis of variance what partial correlation does for ordinary correlation. The variable adjusted for (or partialed out) is called the **covariate.** The rest of the results are interpreted like any other analysis of variance.

covariate

Here is an example. Capaldi and Patterson (1991) compared the adjustment of elementary school boys who had experienced different levels of parental transitions since birth. The different levels of parental transition were no transition, loss of father, new stepfather, and two or more new stepfathers. The authors reported, "An ANOVA showed that there were significant differences among the transition groups, $F(3, 170) = 7.53$, $p < .001$." (The pattern of means for the four levels was in the predicted direction of the more parental transitions, the poorer the adjustment of the boy.)

However, Capaldi and Patterson also wanted to take into account the fact that the boys in the four transition levels came from families of different socioeconomic status (SES) and different income levels. Could these differences, and not the differences in transition level, be the underlying cause of the difference in adjustment?

> Next, we tested the hypothesis that the differences among transition groups were primarily a function of the differences in SES and income. To test this assumption, an ANOVA was run with SES and per capita income as covariates. The difference among the transition groups remained significant, $F(5, 167) = 4.0$, $p < .01$. (pp. 492–493)

The pattern of means was also the same in this analysis as in the original. (Although they did not use the term, an ANOVA with covariates is an analysis of covariance.)

Multivariate Analysis of Variance (MANOVA) and Multivariate Analysis of Covariance (MANCOVA)

In all of the procedures we have discussed so far in this book, including in this chapter, there is only one dependent variable. There may be two or more independent variables, as in the factorial analysis of variance. However, in all the situations we have considered, there has been only one dependent variable.

In this section we consider **multivariate statistics,** which are procedures used when you have two or more dependent variables. Specifically, we focus on the two most widely used multivariate procedures. These are multivariate elaborations of the analysis of variance and the analysis of covariance. That is, these are versions of the analysis of variance and covariance that are able to handle more than one dependent variable.

multivariate statistics

Multivariate analysis of variance (MANOVA) is an analysis of variance in which there can be several dependent variables. Usually, these dependent variables are different measures of approximately the same thing, such as three different political involvement scales or three different reading ability tests. You can interpret the results of a MANOVA basically the same as an ordinary analysis of variance. Suppose you study three groups and measure each participant on four dependent variables. The MANOVA would give an overall F and significance level for the difference among the three groups, in terms of how much they differ on the combination of the four variables.

multivariate analysis of variance (MANOVA)

When you do find an overall significant difference among groups with MANOVA, this says that the groups differ on the combination of dependent variables. You will then usually also want to know whether the groups differ on any or all of the dependent variables considered individually. Thus, it is common to follow up a MANOVA with a series of ordinary analyses of variance, one for each of the dependent variables. These individual analyses of variance are called *univariate analyses of variance* (as opposed to the multivariate analyses), because each has only one dependent variable.

Consider an example. DeGarmo and Forgatch (1997) studied a group of divorced mothers, focusing on the support they received from their closest confidant. That confidant was sometimes a close friend, sometimes a family member, and sometimes a cohabiting partner. In the study, both the mothers and the confidants were interviewed on various measures; they were also videotaped interacting in a special laboratory task, and the interaction was systematically coded by the researchers. These various approaches created quite a few measures of the relationship between the mother and her closest confidant, including three measures of confidant support, four measures of confidant negativity, and four measures of the intimacy of their relationship.

One aspect of the study focused on how the relationship with the confidant differed for confidants who were friends, family members, or cohabiting partners. DeGarmo and Forgatch described the analysis as follows:

> Multivariate and univariate analyses of variance were conducted on the indicators of support, negativity, and intimacy for close friends, family members, and cohabiting partners. The mean values, tests of differences, and significant contrasts are displayed in Table [12–5].
>
> Significant differences were found among relationship types in the multivariate analysis of variance (MANOVA) on the indicators, $F(20, 254) = 4.10$, $p < .001$. (p. 340)

TABLE 12–5
Means and Standard Deviations for Construct Indicators by Confidant Relationship Types

Construct Indicator	Friend (1)		Family (2)		Partner (3)		$F(2, 135)$	Significant contrasts
	M	SD	M	SD	M	SD		
Observed confidant support								
Interpersonal	3.34	.67	3.35	.63	2.92	.65	5.93**	1, 2 > 3
Likeability	3.39	.86	3.24	.94	2.68	1.21	6.58**	1, 2 > 3
Emotional	1.04	.36	.96	.37	.69	.35	12.17***	1, 2 > 3
Confidant negativity								
Self-report, irritability	1.91	.84	1.70	.70	2.25	.65	5.27**	0, 3 > 2
Intimacy-report irritability	1.36	.50	1.33	.35	1.48	.40	1.65	
Depressed mood	1.06	.32	.93	.36	.95	.34	2.02**	
Relationship intimacy								
Mother-report intimacy	3.18	.73	3.19	.75	3.65	.58	5.94**	3 > 1, 2
Confidant-report intimacy	3.05	.78	3.29	.69	3.48	.64	4.62**	0, 3 > 1
Mother-report complexity	1.91	.84	2.29	.74	2.87	.33	22.52***	3 > 1, 2
Confidant-report complexity	2.01	.74	2.19	.75	2.73	.55	13.36***	3 > 1, 2

Note. ns = 65, 33, and 40 for the friend, family, and partner relationship types, respectively.
**$p < .01$. ***$p < .001$.

Degarmo and Forgatch then discussed the results of the univariate analyses of variance and follow-up contrasts. For example, they noted that the "analysis of variance showed a pattern in which partners were observed to provide less support" (p. 340).

An analysis of covariance in which there is more than one dependent variable is called a **multivariate analysis of covariance (MANCOVA).** The difference between it and an ordinary analysis of covariance parallels the difference between a MANOVA and an ordinary analysis of variance. That is, a MANCOVA is a MANOVA in which there are one or more covariates (variables adjusted for).

multivariate analaysis of covariance (MANCOVA)

Overview of Statistical Techniques

Table 12–6 shows in a systematic way the various techniques we have considered in this chapter, along with the other parametric procedures covered throughout the book. Just to prove to yourself how much you have learned, you might cover the right-hand column and play "Name That Statistic."

TABLE 12–6
Major Statistical Techniques

Association or Difference	Number of Independent Variables	Number of Dependent Variables	Any Variables Controlled?	Name of Technique
Association	1	1	No	Bivariate correlation/regression
Association	Any number	1	No	Multiple regression (including hierarchical and stepwise regression)
Association	1	1	Yes	Partial correlation
Association	Many, not differentiated		No	Reliability coefficients, Factor analysis
Association	Many, with specified causal patterns			Path analysis, Structural equation modeling
Difference	1	1	No	One-way ANOVA, t test
Difference	Any number	1	No	factorial ANOVA
Difference	Any number	1	Yes	ANCOVA
Difference	Any number	Any number	No	MANOVA
Difference	Any number	Any number	Yes	MANCOVA

BOX 12–1

The Golden Age of Statistics: Four Guys around London

In the last chapter of his little book *The Statistical Pioneers,* James Tankard (1984) discusses the interesting fact that the four most common statistical techniques were created by four Englishmen born within 68 years of each other, three of whom worked in the vicinity of London (and the fourth, Gosset, stuck at his brewery in Dublin, nevertheless visited London to study and kept in good touch with all that was happening in that city). What were the reasons?

First, Tankard feels that their closeness and communication were important for creating the "critical mass" of minds sometimes associated with a golden age of discovery or creativity. Second, as is often the case with important discoveries, each man faced difficult practical problems or "anomalies" that pushed him to the solution he arrived at. (None simply set out to invent a statistical method in itself.)

Tankard also discusses three important social factors specific to this "golden age of statistics." First, there was the role of biometrics, which was attempting to test the theory of evolution mathematically. Biometrics had its influence through Galton's reading of Darwin and his subsequent influence on Pearson. Second, this period saw the beginning of mass hiring by industry and agriculture of university graduates with "high-powered" mathematical training. Third, since the time of Isaac Newton, Cambridge University had been a particular, centralized source for England of brilliant mathematicians. They could spread out through British industry and still, through their common alma mater, remain in contact with students and each other and conversant with the most recent breakthroughs—an interesting time.

Today is also an interesting time for statistics. After little change for thirty years, the computer has made possible all kinds of new statistical methods. The fundamentals developed in the Golden Age are mainly what you have learned in this book. They probably will remain the fundamentals for a long time to come. Yet, what can be done beyond the fundamentals is changing rapidly. If you go on to take an advanced statistics course, much of what you learn will be procedures developed in the last decade or two. These ideas could well revolutionize the research possibilities open to social scientists in the years to come. If we could look back from the future, we would probably say we live now in another Golden Age of Statistics.

How to Read Results Involving Unfamiliar Statistical Techniques

Based on this chapter and what you have learned throughout this book, you should be well prepared to read and understand, at least in a general way, the results in most research articles in the social and behavioral sciences. However, you will still now and then come up against new techniques (and sometimes unfamiliar names for old techniques). This happens even to well-seasoned researchers. So what do you do when you run into something you have never heard of before?

First, don't panic. Usually, you can figure out the basic idea. Almost always there will be a p level and it should be clear just what pattern of results is being considered significant or not. In addition, there will usually be some indication of the degree of association or the size of the difference. If the statistic is about the association among some variables, it is probably stronger as the result gets closer to 1 and weaker as the result gets closer to 0. Do not expect to understand every word in a situation like this, but do try to grasp as much as you can about the meaning of the result.

Suppose you really can't figure out anything about a statistical technique used in a research article. In that situation, you can try to look up the procedure in a statistics book. Intermediate and advanced statistics textbooks are sometimes a good bet, but we have to warn you that trying to make sense of an intermediate or advanced text on your own can be difficult. Many such texts are heavily mathematically oriented. Even quite accessible textbooks will each use their own set of symbols. Thus, it can be hard to make sense of the description of a particular method without having read the whole book. Perhaps a better solution in this situation is to ask for help from a professor or graduate student. If you know the basics as you have learned them in this book, you should be able to understand the essentials of their explanations.

If you are often coming upon statistics you don't understand, the best solution is to take more statistics courses. Usually, the next course after this one would be an intermediate statistics course in your particular major. In fact, some people find statistics so fascinating that they choose to make a career of it. You might too.

More generally, new statistical methods are being invented constantly. Social and behavioral scientists all encounter unfamiliar numbers and symbols in the research articles they read. They puzzle them out, and so will you. We say that with confidence because you have arrived, safe and knowledgeable, at the back pages of this book. You have mastered a thorough introduction to a complex topic. That should give you complete confidence that with a little time and attention you can understand anything further in statistics. Congratulations on your accomplishment.

Summary

1. In hierarchical multiple regression, predictor variables are included in the prediction rule in a planned sequential fashion. This allows you to determine the contribution of each successive variable over and above those already included. Stepwise multiple regression is an exploratory procedure in which potential predictor variables are searched in order to find the best predictor; then the remaining variables are searched for the predictor that, in combination with the first, produces the best prediction. This process continues until adding the best remaining variable does not provide a significant improvement.
2. Partial correlation is the correlation between two variables while holding one or more other variables constant.
3. Reliability coefficients measure how much scores on a test are internally consistent (usually with Cronbach's alpha) or consistent over time (test-retest reliability).
4. Factor analysis identifies groupings of variables that correlate maximally with each other and minimally with other variables.
5. Causal analysis examines whether the correlations among several variables are consistent with a systematic, hypothesized pattern of causal relationships among them. Path analysis describes these rela-

tionships with arrows each pointing from cause to effect and each with a path coefficient indicating the influence of the theorized causal variable on the theorized effect variable. Structural equation modeling is an advanced version of path analysis that includes latent, unmeasured variables (each of which consists of the common elements of several measured variables). It also provides measures of the overall fit of the data to the theorized causal pattern.

6. The analysis of covariance (ANCOVA) is an analysis of variance that controls for one or more variables. The multivariate analysis of variance (MANOVA) is an analysis of variance with two or more dependent variables. The multivariate analysis of covariance (MANCOVA) is an analysis of covariance with two or more dependent variables.

Key Terms

adjusting for
analysis of covariance (ANCOVA)
controlling for
covariate
Cronbach's alpha (α)
dependent variable
factor
factor analysis
factor loading
fit index

hierarchical multiple regression
holding constant
independent variable
latent variable
multivariate analysis of covariance (MANCOVA)
multivariate analysis of variance (MANOVA)
multivariate statistics
partial correlation

partial correlation coefficient
partialing out
paths
path analysis
path coefficient
reliability
split-half reliability
stepwise multiple regression
structural equation modeling
test-retest reliability

Practice Problems

For Problems 1 through 6, you need to explain only the general meaning of the results in the same kind of detail that we used for the various methods in the chapter. You are not expected to explain the logic of the statistical procedures covered here in the way that you have been doing in previous chapters.

Answers to selected problems are given at the back of this book.

1. Part of a study conducted by Lindzey et al. (1997) examined how well mutuality (balance) in father-child interaction predicted social competence in preschool children. In this study, each child and his or her father were observed interacting in a standardized situation. The interactions were rated in ways that gave measures of who initiates play activities and the mutuality of complying with each other's initiation of play activities.

The researchers also had the children's teachers rate each child's social competence. The researchers found a clear correlation between father-child mutuality and the teacher's social-competence rating for the child. However, the researchers were concerned that the measure of mutu-

ality might be mixed up with the amount that children and fathers each initiated individually.

> We therefore conducted a series of hierarchical regression analyses to examine whether father-child mutual compliance . . . made unique contributions to the prediction of children's social competence after taking account of each individual's behavior. . . . Father initiation rate and child initiation rate were entered first and accounted for 3 percent ($p = .57$) of the variance. Father-child mutual compliance was entered second and accounted for an additional, significant 18 percent ($p = .01$) of the variance in teacher-rated social competence. (pp. 532–533)

Explain this method and result to a person who is familiar in a general way with ordinary multiple regression but who has never heard of hierarchical multiple regression.

2. Rusbult et al. (1991) reported a series of studies about the way people deal with a relationship partner doing something destructive to the relationship. The start of their Results section for their first two studies in this article has a section headed "Reliability of Measures." In this section, they explain that they calculated "reliability coefficients"

TABLE 12–7
Varimax Factor Loadings of Tasks

Task	Factor		
	I	*II*	*III*
Tokens	−16	42*	20
Figure recognition	−14	40*	13
Matrices	−14	51*	15
Hand movements	− 8	15	44*
Successive ordering	−28	18	44*
Word recall	− 3	11	43*
Matching numbers	51*	−18	−19
Visual search	54*	−11	− 4
Trails	53*	−21	−12

Note: N = 430. Decimal points are omitted. Loadings > .30 are noted [with asterisks]. Factor I is defined by the three marker tests of planning, Factor II by the three marker tests of simultaneous coding, and Factor III by the three marker tests of successive coding.

From Kirby, J. R., & Das, J. P. (1990), tab. 1. A cognitive approach to intelligence: Attention, coding, and planning. *Canadian Psychology*, *31*, 320–333. Copyright © 1990 by the Canadian Psychological Association. Reprinted by permission.

for their major measures and that "these analyses revealed sizable alphas for the measures of destructive reactions (. . . .91 for Study 1 and .86 for Study 2) and constructive reactions (. . . .61 and .67)." Explain these results to someone who is familiar with correlation but who has never heard of reliability or the statistics associated with it.

3. Kirby and Das (1988) report a study in which participants performed nine different mental tasks related to intelligence. A table (Table 12–7) in their study gives the results of a factor analysis of the scores on these tasks. Explain these results to a person who is familiar with correlation but who knows nothing about factor analysis.

4. Aron et al. (1998) studied experiences of unreciprocated love—that is, loving someone who does not love you. One of the predictions focused on the intensity of the experience (how much you think about it, how much it disrupts your life). The researchers hypothesized that intensity would be predicted by desirability (to what extent the lover perceived a relationship with the beloved would be wonderful), probability (how much the lover felt the beloved had led them to believe a relationship might develop), and desirability of the state (how much the lover felt it was desirable to be in love, even though it was not reciprocated). Aron et al. carried out a structural equation model analysis. The results are shown in Figure 12–4.

(a) Explain the pattern of results. (b) Using this diagram as an example, explain the general principles of interpreting a path diagram (including the limitations) to a person who understands multiple regression in a general way but who knows nothing about path diagrams or structural equation modeling.

5. Carlin and Saniga (1990) compared a group of special education children (mentally retarded or emotionally disturbed) to a group of regular education students. They compared the two groups on their teachers' and their own ratings of voice problems. For the special education students, the mean teachers' rating was 53.2 and the mean self rating was 53.8. For the regular education students, the corresponding ratings were 56.8 and 53.2. (In these ratings, high scores mean fewer voice problems.) The researchers reported:

A two-way analysis of covariance with . . . age as the covariate yielded an F of 4.17 (*df:* 1, 129, p < 0.04) for the main effect of placement [special versus regular education]. . . . The main effect of the teachers' versus the children's ratings was nonsignificant ($F_{1,130}$ = 0.37). . . . The interaction of placement and rate was significant at the .001 level ($F_{1,130}$ = 11.19). (pp. 301–302).

Explain these results to someone who understands the analysis of variance and correlation but not the analysis of covariance.

6. Gire (1997) examined the preferred methods of resolving conflicts, comparing people in individualistic versus collectivistic cultures. Participants were 90 Nigerians (Nigeria was considered an example of a relatively collectivist society) and 95 Canadians (Canada was considered an example of a relatively individualistic society). All participants answered questions about how much they preferred each of five methods of resolving conflicts. Half the participants in each country answered the questions regarding an interpersonal conflict (a conflict between two neighbors) and half regarding an intergroup conflict (between two groups of neighbors). This created a 2 (culture) × 2 (interpersonal vs. intergroup conflict) factorial design, with five measures of conflict resolution preferences.

These data were analyzed by using the multivariate analysis of variance (MANOVA) procedure. The 2-way

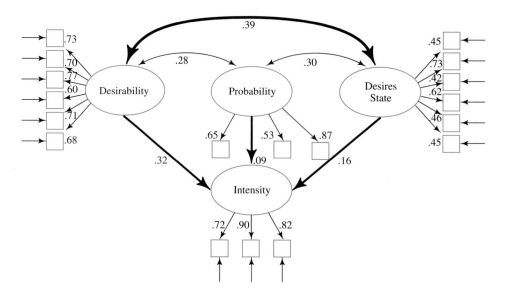

FIGURE 12-4
Latent variable model based on a three-factor framework of motivation in unreciprocated love that was fitted to data for 743 participants who reported experiencing unreciprocated love.
NOTE: Bentler-Bonnett normed fixed index (NFI) = .90; non-normed fit index (NNFI) = .92; average standardized residuals = .04; χ^2 (129) = 430.88; $p < .01$. All parameter estimates shown were significantly different from 0, at least at the .05 level. The key result is that each of the major causal paths to intensity, from desirability, probability, and desirability of the state, were positive and significant, confirming the hypothesis that each of these variables independently predicts intensity. (Figure 1 from "Motivations for Unreciprocated Love" by Aron and Aron, *Personality and Social Psychology Bulletin,* Vol. 24 No. 8, August, 1998, p. 792.)

MANOVA yielded a significant main effect of culture $F(5, 173) = 6.37$, $p < .001$. An examination of the univariate analyses and the means suggests that Nigerians preferred negotiation to a greater extent than Canadians while the reverse was the case on arbitration, as predicted. There was also a significant culture by type of conflict interaction, $F(5, 173) = 3.84$, $p < .002$. The univariate analyses and the means, presented in Table [12–8], reveal that significant differences occurred on three procedures—threats, acceptance of the situation, and arbitration. (p. 41).

Explain these results to someone who understands factorial analysis of variance but not multivariate analysis of variance.

7. For each of the following studies, what would be the most appropriate statistical technique?

(a) A study in which the researcher has a complex theory of the pattern of cause and effect among several variables

(b) A study of the association between two variables

(c) A study of whether a questionnaire scale is consistent internally (that is, that the items correlate with each other) and consistent over time in giving the same result

(d) A 3 × 2 factorial design with three dependent measures

(e) A study in which seven variables have been measured that are thought to predict a particular dependent variable, and the researcher wants to determine which variables contribute significantly to the prediction (but has no theory about which ones might be the most likely)

TABLE 12-8
Method Preferences as a Function of Culture and Type of Conflict

Method	Nigerians		Canadians	
	IP	IG	IP	IG
Threats*	2.09	1.50	1.35	1.61
Accept the situation*	2.72	3.16	3.43	2.71
Negotiation	6.07	6.11	5.56	5.64
Mediation	4.70	4.77	4.87	5.13
Arbitration*	3.05	4.90	5.20	5.42

Note. One asterisk (*) indicates that the means of the culture by type of conflict interaction on a given method was significant at $p < .05$ level. The larger the number, the higher the preference for the method. *ip* = Interpersonal Conflict; *ig* = Intergroup Conflict. Data from Gire, J. T. (1997), tab. 1. The varying effect of individualism-collectivism on preference for methods of conflict resolution. *Canadian Journal of Behavioural Science, 29,* 38–43. Copyright 1997, by the Canadian Psychological Association. Reprinted with permission.

(f) A study in which a researcher measures 16 variables and wants to explore whether there are any simpler groupings of variables underlying these 16

(g) A study in which an experimental group and a control group are being compared on a single dependent variable

(h) A study comparing five groups of individuals on a single dependent variable

(i) A study in which the researcher is studying the effect of several predictor variables on a single dependent variable, has a specific theory about their relative importance, and wants to check whether each successive additional predictor adds anything to what the preceding variables predict.

8. At the library, find an article in a recent issue of a scientific journal in your major that uses one of the statistical procedures described in this chapter. Write a brief summary of the study you found, referring specifically to the statistics. With your answer, include a photocopy of the article, marking clearly the part that reports the statistics you describe.

9. At the library, find an article in a recent issue of a scientific journal in your major that uses a statistical procedure *not* covered anywhere in this book. Write a brief summary of the study you found, referring specifically to the statistics. With your answer, include a photocopy of the article, marking clearly the part that reports the statistics you describe.

APPENDIX

Tables

TABLE A-1
Normal Curve Areas: Percentage of the Normal Curve Between the Mean and the Z Scores Shown

Z	% Mean to Z	Z	% Mean to Z	Z	% Mean to Z
.00	.00	.24	9.48	.48	18.44
.01	.40	.25	9.87	.49	18.79
.02	.80	.26	10.26	.50	19.15
.03	1.20	.27	10.64	.51	19.50
.04	1.60	.28	11.03	.52	19.85
.05	1.99	.29	11.41	.53	20.19
.06	2.39	.30	11.79	.54	20.54
.07	2.79	.31	12.17	.55	20.88
.08	3.19	.32	12.55	.56	21.23
.09	3.59	.33	12.93	.57	21.57
.10	3.98	.34	13.31	.58	21.90
.11	4.38	.35	13.68	.59	22.24
.12	4.78	.36	14.06	.60	22.57
.13	5.17	.37	14.43	.61	22.91
.14	5.57	.38	14.80	.62	23.24
.15	5.96	.39	15.17	.63	23.57
.16	6.36	.40	15.54	.64	23.89
.17	6.75	.41	15.91	.65	24.22
.18	7.14	.42	16.28	.66	24.54
.19	7.53	.43	16.64	.67	24.86
.20	7.93	.44	17.00	.68	25.17
.21	8.32	.45	17.36	.69	25.49
.22	8.71	.46	17.72	.70	25.80
.23	9.10	.47	18.08	.71	26.11

TABLE A-1 (cont.)

Z	% Mean to Z	Z	% Mean to Z	Z	% Mean to Z
.72	26.42	1.29	40.15	1.86	46.86
.73	26.73	1.30	40.32	1.87	46.93
.74	27.04	1.31	40.49	1.88	46.99
.75	27.34	1.32	40.66	1.89	47.06
.76	27.64	1.33	40.82	1.90	47.13
.77	27.94	1.34	40.99	1.91	47.19
.78	28.23	1.35	41.15	1.92	47.26
.79	28.52	1.36	41.31	1.93	47.32
.80	28.81	1.37	41.47	1.94	47.38
.81	29.10	1.38	41.62	1.95	47.44
.82	29.39	1.39	41.77	1.96	47.50
.83	29.67	1.40	41.92	1.97	47.56
.84	29.95	1.41	42.07	1.98	47.61
.85	30.23	1.42	42.22	1.99	47.67
.86	30.51	1.43	42.36	2.00	47.72
.87	30.78	1.44	42.51	2.01	47.78
.88	31.06	1.45	42.65	2.02	47.83
.89	31.33	1.46	42.79	2.03	47.88
.90	31.59	1.47	42.92	2.04	47.93
.91	31.86	1.48	43.06	2.05	47.98
.92	32.12	1.49	43.19	2.06	48.03
.93	32.38	1.50	43.32	2.07	48.08
.94	32.64	1.51	43.45	2.08	48.12
.95	32.89	1.52	43.57	2.09	48.17
.96	33.15	1.53	43.70	2.10	48.21
.97	33.40	1.54	43.82	2.11	48.26
.98	33.65	1.55	43.94	2.12	48.30
.99	33.89	1.56	44.06	2.13	48.34
1.00	34.13	1.57	44.18	2.14	48.38
1.01	34.38	1.58	44.29	2.15	48.42
1.02	34.61	1.59	44.41	2.16	48.46
1.03	34.85	1.60	44.52	2.17	48.50
1.04	35.08	1.61	44.63	2.18	48.54
1.05	35.31	1.62	44.74	2.19	48.57
1.06	35.54	1.63	44.84	2.20	48.61
1.07	35.77	1.64	44.95	2.21	48.64
1.08	35.99	1.65	45.05	2.22	48.68
1.09	36.21	1.66	45.15	2.23	48.71
1.10	36.43	1.67	45.25	2.24	48.75
1.11	36.65	1.68	45.35	2.25	48.78
1.12	36.86	1.69	45.45	2.26	48.81
1.13	37.08	1.70	45.54	2.27	48.84
1.14	37.29	1.71	45.64	2.28	48.87
1.15	37.49	1.72	45.73	2.29	48.90
1.16	37.70	1.73	45.82	2.30	48.93
1.17	37.90	1.74	45.91	2.31	48.96
1.18	38.10	1.75	45.99	2.32	48.98
1.19	38.30	1.76	46.08	2.33	49.01
1.20	38.49	1.77	46.16	2.34	49.04
1.21	38.69	1.78	46.25	2.35	49.06
1.22	38.88	1.79	46.33	2.36	49.09
1.23	39.07	1.80	46.41	2.37	49.11
1.24	39.25	1.81	46.49	2.38	49.13
1.25	39.44	1.82	46.56	2.39	49.16
1.26	39.62	1.83	46.64	2.40	49.18
1.27	39.80	1.84	46.71	2.41	49.20
1.28	39.97	1.85	46.78	2.42	49.22

TABLE A-1 (cont.)

Z	% Mean to Z	Z	% Mean to Z	Z	% Mean to Z
2.43	49.25	2.64	49.59	2.85	49.78
2.44	49.27	2.65	49.60	2.86	49.79
2.45	49.29	2.66	49.61	2.87	49.79
2.46	49.31	2.67	49.62	2.88	49.80
2.47	49.32	2.68	49.63	2.89	49.81
2.48	49.34	2.69	49.64	2.90	49.81
2.49	49.36	2.70	49.65	2.91	49.82
2.50	49.38	2.71	49.66	2.92	49.82
2.51	49.40	2.72	49.67	2.93	49.83
2.52	49.41	2.73	49.68	2.94	49.84
2.53	49.43	2.74	49.69	2.95	49.84
2.54	49.45	2.75	49.70	2.96	49.85
2.55	49.46	2.76	49.71	2.97	49.85
2.56	49.48	2.77	49.72	2.98	49.86
2.57	49.49	2.78	49.73	2.99	49.86
2.58	49.51	2.79	49.74	3.00	49.87
2.59	49.52	2.80	49.74	3.50	49.98
2.60	49.53	2.81	49.75	4.00	50.00
2.61	49.55	2.82	49.76	4.50	50.00
2.62	49.56	2.83	49.77		
2.63	49.57	2.84	49.77		

TABLE A-2
Cutoff Scores for the *t* Distribution

df	One-Tailed Tests .10	.05	.01	Two-Tailed Tests .10	.05	.01
1	3.078	6.314	31.821	6.314	12.706	63.657
2	1.886	2.920	6.965	2.920	4.303	9.925
3	1.638	2.353	4.541	2.353	3.182	5.841
4	1.533	2.132	3.747	2.132	2.776	4.604
5	1.476	2.015	3.365	2.015	2.571	4.032
6	1.440	1.943	3.143	1.943	2.447	3.708
7	1.415	1.895	2.998	1.895	2.365	3.500
8	1.397	1.860	2.897	1.860	2.306	3.356
9	1.383	1.833	2.822	1.833	2.262	3.250
10	1.372	1.813	2.764	1.813	2.228	3.170
11	1.364	1.796	2.718	1.796	2.201	3.106
12	1.356	1.783	2.681	1.783	2.179	3.055
13	1.350	1.771	2.651	1.771	2.161	3.013
14	1.345	1.762	2.625	1.762	2.145	2.977
15	1.341	1.753	2.603	1.753	2.132	2.947
16	1.337	1.746	2.584	1.746	2.120	2.921
17	1.334	1.740	2.567	1.740	2.110	2.898
18	1.331	1.734	2.553	1.734	2.101	2.879
19	1.328	1.729	2.540	1.729	2.093	2.861
20	1.326	1.725	2.528	1.725	2.086	2.846
21	1.323	1.721	2.518	1.721	2.080	2.832
22	1.321	1.717	2.509	1.717	2.074	2.819
23	1.320	1.714	2.500	1.714	2.069	2.808
24	1.318	1.711	2.492	1.711	2.064	2.797
25	1.317	1.708	2.485	1.708	2.060	2.788
26	1.315	1.706	2.479	1.706	2.056	2.779
27	1.314	1.704	2.473	1.704	2.052	2.771
28	1.313	1.701	2.467	1.701	2.049	2.764
29	1.312	1.699	2.462	1.699	2.045	2.757
30	1.311	1.698	2.458	1.698	2.043	2.750
35	1.306	1.690	2.438	1.690	2.030	2.724
40	1.303	1.684	2.424	1.684	2.021	2.705
45	1.301	1.680	2.412	1.680	2.014	2.690
50	1.299	1.676	2.404	1.676	2.009	2.678
55	1.297	1.673	2.396	1.673	2.004	2.668
60	1.296	1.671	2.390	1.671	2.001	2.661
65	1.295	1.669	2.385	1.669	1.997	2.654
70	1.294	1.667	2.381	1.667	1.995	2.648
75	1.293	1.666	2.377	1.666	1.992	2.643
80	1.292	1.664	2.374	1.664	1.990	2.639
85	1.292	1.663	2.371	1.663	1.989	2.635
90	1.291	1.662	2.369	1.662	1.987	2.632
95	1.291	1.661	2.366	1.661	1.986	2.629
100	1.290	1.660	2.364	1.660	1.984	2.626
∞	1.282	1.645	2.327	1.645	1.960	2.576

TABLE A-3
Cutoff Scores for the *F* Distribution

Denom-inator *df*	Signi-ficance Level	Numerator Degrees of Freedom					
		1	*2*	*3*	*4*	*5*	*6*
1	.01	4,052	5,000	5,404	5,625	5,764	5,859
	.05	162	200	216	225	230	234
	.10	39.9	49.5	53.6	55.8	57.2	58.2
2	.01	98.50	99.00	99.17	99.25	99.30	99.33
	.05	18.51	19.00	19.17	19.25	19.30	19.33
	.10	8.53	9.00	9.16	9.24	9.29	9.33
3	.01	34.12	30.82	29.46	28.71	28.24	27.91
	.05	10.13	9.55	9.28	9.12	9.01	8.94
	.10	5.54	5.46	5.39	5.34	5.31	5.28
4	.01	21.20	18.00	16.70	15.98	15.52	15.21
	.05	7.71	6.95	6.59	6.39	6.26	6.16
	.10	4.55	4.33	4.19	4.11	4.05	4.01
5	.01	16.26	13.27	12.06	11.39	10.97	10.67
	.05	6.61	5.79	5.41	5.19	5.05	4.95
	.10	4.06	3.78	3.62	3.52	3.45	3.41
6	.01	13.75	10.93	9.78	9.15	8.75	8.47
	.05	5.99	5.14	4.76	4.53	4.39	4.28
	.10	3.78	3.46	3.29	3.18	3.11	3.06
7	.01	12.25	9.55	8.45	7.85	7.46	7.19
	.05	5.59	4.74	4.35	4.12	3.97	3.87
	.10	3.59	3.26	3.08	2.96	2.88	2.83
8	.01	11.26	8.65	7.59	7.01	6.63	6.37
	.05	5.32	4.46	4.07	3.84	3.69	3.58
	.10	3.46	3.11	2.92	2.81	2.73	2.67
9	.01	10.56	8.02	6.99	6.42	6.06	5.80
	.05	5.12	4.26	3.86	3.63	3.48	3.37
	.10	3.36	3.01	2.81	2.69	2.61	2.55
10	.01	10.05	7.56	6.55	6.00	5.64	5.39
	.05	4.97	4.10	3.71	3.48	3.33	3.22
	.10	3.29	2.93	2.73	2.61	2.52	2.46
11	.01	9.65	7.21	6.22	5.67	5.32	5.07
	.05	4.85	3.98	3.59	3.36	3.20	3.10
	.10	3.23	2.86	2.66	2.54	2.45	2.39
12	.01	9.33	6.93	5.95	5.41	5.07	4.82
	.05	4.75	3.89	3.49	3.26	3.11	3.00
	.10	3.18	2.81	2.61	2.48	2.40	2.33
13	.01	9.07	6.70	5.74	5.21	4.86	4.62
	.05	4.67	3.81	3.41	3.18	3.03	2.92
	.10	3.14	2.76	2.56	2.43	2.35	2.28
14	.01	8.86	6.52	5.56	5.04	4.70	4.46
	.05	4.60	3.74	3.34	3.11	2.96	2.85
	.10	3.10	2.73	2.52	2.40	2.31	2.24

TABLE A-3 (cont.)

Denominator df	Significance Level	Numerator Degrees of Freedom					
		1	2	3	4	5	6
15	.01	8.68	6.36	5.42	4.89	4.56	4.32
	.05	4.54	3.68	3.29	3.06	2.90	2.79
	.10	3.07	2.70	2.49	2.36	2.27	2.21
16	.01	8.53	6.23	5.29	4.77	4.44	4.20
	.05	4.49	3.63	3.24	3.01	2.85	2.74
	.10	3.05	2.67	2.46	2.33	2.24	2.18
17	.01	8.40	6.11	5.19	4.67	4.34	4.10
	.05	4.45	3.59	3.20	2.97	2.81	2.70
	.10	3.03	2.65	2.44	2.31	2.22	2.15
18	.01	8.29	6.01	5.09	4.58	4.25	4.02
	.05	4.41	3.56	3.16	2.93	2.77	2.66
	.10	3.01	2.62	2.42	2.29	2.20	2.13
19	.01	8.19	5.93	5.01	4.50	4.17	3.94
	.05	4.38	3.52	3.13	2.90	2.74	2.63
	.10	2.99	2.61	2.40	2.27	2.18	2.11
20	.01	8.10	5.85	4.94	4.43	4.10	3.87
	.05	4.35	3.49	3.10	2.87	2.71	2.60
	.10	2.98	2.59	2.38	2.25	2.16	2.09
21	.01	8.02	5.78	4.88	4.37	4.04	3.81
	.05	4.33	3.47	3.07	2.84	2.69	2.57
	.10	2.96	2.58	2.37	2.23	2.14	2.08
22	.01	7.95	5.72	4.82	4.31	3.99	3.76
	.05	4.30	3.44	3.05	2.82	2.66	2.55
	.10	2.95	2.56	2.35	2.22	2.13	2.06
23	.01	7.88	5.66	4.77	4.26	3.94	3.71
	.05	4.28	3.42	3.03	2.80	2.64	2.53
	.10	2.94	2.55	2.34	2.21	2.12	2.05
24	.01	7.82	5.61	4.72	4.22	3.90	3.67
	.05	4.26	3.40	3.01	2.78	2.62	2.51
	.10	2.93	2.54	2.33	2.20	2.10	2.04
25	.01	7.77	5.57	4.68	4.18	3.86	3.63
	.05	4.24	3.39	2.99	2.76	2.60	2.49
	.10	2.92	2.53	2.32	2.19	2.09	2.03
26	.01	7.72	5.53	4.64	4.14	3.82	3.59
	.05	4.23	3.37	2.98	2.74	2.59	2.48
	.10	2.91	2.52	2.31	2.18	2.08	2.01
27	.01	7.68	5.49	4.60	4.11	3.79	3.56
	.05	4.21	3.36	2.96	2.73	2.57	2.46
	.10	2.90	2.51	2.30	2.17	2.07	2.01
28	.01	7.64	5.45	4.57	4.08	3.75	3.53
	.05	4.20	3.34	2.95	2.72	2.56	2.45
	.10	2.89	2.50	2.29	2.16	2.07	2.00

TABLE A-3 (cont.)

Denom-inator df	Signi-ficance Level	Numerator Degrees of Freedom					
		1	2	3	4	5	6
29	.01	7.60	5.42	4.54	4.05	3.73	3.50
	.05	4.18	3.33	2.94	2.70	2.55	2.43
	.10	2.89	2.50	2.28	2.15	2.06	1.99
30	.01	7.56	5.39	4.51	4.02	3.70	3.47
	.05	4.17	3.32	2.92	2.69	2.53	2.42
	.10	2.88	2.49	2.28	2.14	2.05	1.98
35	.01	7.42	5.27	4.40	3.91	3.59	3.37
	.05	4.12	3.27	2.88	2.64	2.49	2.37
	.10	2.86	2.46	2.25	2.11	2.02	1.95
40	.01	7.32	5.18	4.31	3.83	3.51	3.29
	.05	4.09	3.23	2.84	2.61	2.45	2.34
	.10	2.84	2.44	2.23	2.09	2.00	1.93
45	.01	7.23	5.11	4.25	3.77	3.46	3.23
	.05	4.06	3.21	2.81	2.58	2.42	2.31
	.10	2.82	2.43	2.21	2.08	1.98	1.91
50	.01	7.17	5.06	4.20	3.72	3.41	3.19
	.05	4.04	3.18	2.79	2.56	2.40	2.29
	.10	2.81	2.41	2.20	2.06	1.97	1.90
55	.01	7.12	5.01	4.16	3.68	3.37	3.15
	.05	4.02	3.17	2.77	2.54	2.38	2.27
	.10	2.80	2.40	2.19	2.05	1.96	1.89
60	.01	7.08	4.98	4.13	3.65	3.34	3.12
	.05	4.00	3.15	2.76	2.53	2.37	2.26
	.10	2.79	2.39	2.18	2.04	1.95	1.88
65	.01	7.04	4.95	4.10	3.62	3.31	3.09
	.05	3.99	3.14	2.75	2.51	2.36	2.24
	.10	2.79	2.39	2.17	2.03	1.94	1.87
70	.01	7.01	4.92	4.08	3.60	3.29	3.07
	.05	3.98	3.13	2.74	2.50	2.35	2.23
	.10	2.78	2.38	2.16	2.03	1.93	1.86
75	.01	6.99	4.90	4.06	3.58	3.27	3.05
	.05	3.97	3.12	2.73	2.49	2.34	2.22
	.10	2.77	2.38	2.16	2.02	1.93	1.86
80	.01	6.96	4.88	4.04	3.56	3.26	3.04
	.05	3.96	3.11	2.72	2.49	2.33	2.22
	.10	2.77	2.37	2.15	2.02	1.92	1.85
85	.01	6.94	4.86	4.02	3.55	3.24	3.02
	.05	3.95	3.10	2.71	2.48	2.32	2.21
	.10	2.77	2.37	2.15	2.01	1.92	1.85
90	.01	6.93	4.85	4.01	3.54	3.23	3.01
	.05	3.95	3.10	2.71	2.47	2.32	2.20
	.10	2.76	2.36	2.15	2.01	1.91	1.84

TABLE A-3 (cont.)

Denom-inator df	Signi-ficance Level	Numerator Degrees of Freedom					
		1	2	3	4	5	6
95	.01	6.91	4.84	4.00	3.52	3.22	3.00
	.05	3.94	3.09	2.70	2.47	2.31	2.20
	.10	2.76	2.36	2.14	2.01	1.91	1.84
100	.01	6.90	4.82	3.98	3.51	3.21	2.99
	.05	3.94	3.09	2.70	2.46	2.31	2.19
	.10	2.76	2.36	2.14	2.00	1.91	1.83
∞	.01	6.64	4.61	3.78	3.32	3.02	2.80
	.05	3.84	3.00	2.61	2.37	2.22	2.10
	.10	2.71	2.30	2.08	1.95	1.85	1.78

TABLE A-4
Cutoff Scores for the Chi-Square Distribution

df	Significance Level		
	.10	.05	.01
1	2.706	3.841	6.635
2	4.605	5.992	9.211
3	6.252	7.815	11.345
4	7.780	9.488	13.277
5	9.237	11.071	15.087
6	10.645	12.592	16.812
7	12.017	14.067	18.475
8	13.362	15.507	20.090
9	14.684	16.919	21.666
10	15.987	18.307	23.209

TABLE A-5
Index to Power Tables and Tables Giving Number of Participants Needed for 80% Power

Hypothesis-Testing Procedure	Chapter	Power Table	Number of Participants Table
Correlation coefficient (r)	3	71	71
t test for dependent means	8	172	173
t test for independent means	9	192	194
One-way analysis of variance	10	218	219
Chi-square test of independence	11	248	249

Answers
to Selected Practice Problems

Answers are provided here for selected practice problems, including at least one example answer to an essay-type question for each chapter.

Chapter 1

1. **(a)** Frequency table.

Number of Hours	Frequency	Percent	Number of Hours	Frequency	Percent
18	1	2	8	5	10
17	0	0	7	11	22
16	0	0	6	4	8
15	1	2	5	2	4
14	0	0	4	3	6
13	2	4	3	4	8
12	1	2	2	2	4
11	3	6	1	1	2
10	5	10	0	1	2
9	4	8			

(b) Frequency polygon based on table in (a).

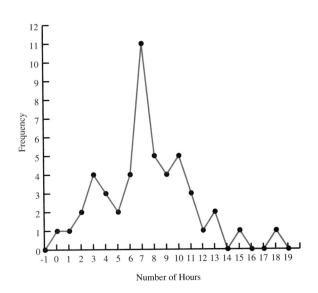

(c) General shape of the distribution: unimodal, somewhat skewed to the right (positively skewed).

4. (a) A distribution is the way a group of numbers is spread out over the different possible values the different numbers can have. One way to describe such a distribution is with a graph, called a histogram. A histogram is a kind of bar graph with one bar for each possible value, in order from lowest to highest; a bar has one unit of height for each time its particular value occurs. In this kind of graph, a symmetrical distribution has a symmetrical shape, meaning that the right and left halves are mirror images. Loosely speaking, this means that there are about as many high numbers as there are low numbers, and the way the number of instances at each value decreases as you move from a middle value to the highest value is the same as the way the number of instances at each value decreases as you move from a middle value to the lowest value. A unimodal distribution is one in which this graph has a single high point, with the other values gradually decreasing around it.

Chapter 2

1. Set A.
  (a) $M = 261/9 = 29$
  (b) Median = 28
  (c) $\Sigma(X - M)^2 = (32 - 29)^2 + (28 - 29)^2 + (24 - 29)^2 + (28 - 29)^2 + (31 - 29)^2 + (35 - 29)^2 + (29 - 29)^2 + (26 - 29)^2$
    $= 3^2 + (-1)^2 + (-5)^2 + (-1)^2 + (-1)^2 + 2^2 + 6^2 + 0^2 + (-3)^2$
    $= 9 + 1 + 25 + 1 + 1 + 4 + 36 + 0 + 9 = 86$
    $SD^2 = \Sigma(X - M)^2/N = 86/9 = 9.56$
  (d) $SD = \sqrt{9.56} = 3.09$

2. The average temperature, in the sense of adding up the 10 readings and dividing by 10, was –7 degrees Celsius. This is called the mean. However, if you were to line the temperatures up from lowest to highest, the middle two numbers would both be –5 degrees. This middle number is called the median. So the median temperature is –5 degrees. Another way of figuring the typical temperature would be to take the specific temperature that came up most often, which is called the mode. In this example, there were two modes, two temperatures that came up most often, –1 and –5. Both of these temperatures came up twice, but the mode is not very useful information in this case

As for the variation, one approach is called the variance. You begin by figuring how much each temperature differs from the average. Then you square each of these "deviation scores." Next, take the average of these squared deviation scores. For example, the first temperature's deviation is 2 (–5 minus –7), which squared is 4. Squaring each deviation and adding up all the results gives 468. Dividing this by 10 gives an average squared deviation of 46.8. This is the variance. The variance is one way of describing how spread out a group of numbers is. The variance is an important part of many statistical calculations. Unfortunately, however, it does not give a very direct sense of how much numbers vary.

You can get a more direct sense of how much a group of numbers vary among themselves if you take the square root of the variance. The square root of 46.8 is 6.84. (The square root of the variance is called the standard deviation.) This means, roughly, that on an average day the temperature differs by 6.84 degrees from the average of –7 degrees.

5. Wife: $Z = (X - M)/SD = (63 - 60)/6 = 3/6 = .5$
   Husband: $Z = (X - M)/SD = (59 - 55)/4 = 4/4 = 1$

The husband has a higher Z score, so he has adjusted better in relation to other divorced men than the wife has adjusted in relation to other divorced women.

Explanation to person who has never had a course in statistics: For wives, a score of 63 is 3 points better than the average of 60 for divorced women in general. (The "mean" in the problem is a statistical term for the ordinary average—the sum of the scores divided by the number of scores.) There is, of course, some variation in scores among divorced women. The approximate average amount that women's scores differ from the average is 6 points: This is the SD referred to in the problem. (Actually, SD, which stands for standard deviation, is only approximately the average amount that scores differ from the average. To be precise, SD is the square root of the average of the square of the difference of each score from the mean.)

The wife's score is only half as far above the mean of wives as wives' scores in general differ from the mean of wives' scores. This gives her what is called a Z score of +.5, which gives her location on a scale that compares her score to that of divorced women in general. Using the same logic to examine the husband's divorce adjustment compared to other divorced men, he is as much above the average as the average amount that men differ from the average; that is, he has a Z score of +1. Therefore, the conclusion is that both have adjusted better than the average for their gender, but the husband has adjusted better in relation to other divorced men than the wife has adjusted in relation to other divorced women.

Chapter 3

1. (a)

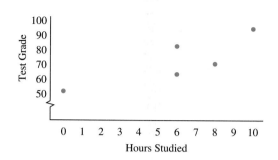

(b) Positive linear correlation—as hours studied goes up, so do test grades.

(c)

Hours Studied		Test Grade		
Raw X	Z_X	**Raw Y**	Z_Y	$Z_X Z_Y$
0	−1.79	52	−1.41	2.52
10	1.19	95	1.48	1.76
6	.00	83	.67	.00
8	.60	71	− .13	− .08
6	.00	64	− .60	.00
				$\Sigma = 4.20$
$M = 6$		$M = 73$		
$SD = 3.35$		$SD = 14.90$		$r = 4.20/5 = .84$

(d) The first step in a correlation problem is to make a graph, putting one variable on each axis, then putting a dot where each score falls on that graph. This is called a scatter diagram, and it gives a picture of the degree of relationship between the two variables. In this case, high scores seem to go with high scores, and lows with lows, making this what is called a positive correlation. (Basically, correlation is the extent to which high scores go with high scores and low scores go with low scores.) Also, because the dots fall roughly near a straight line, this is an example of a positive *linear* correlation.

The next step is to convert all scores to Z scores. This makes it easier to figure how much highs go with highs and lows with lows. Z scores make this easier because they give the best indication of how low or how high a score is in relation to the other scores in its distribution.

The correlation coefficient is a number that tells you the degree of association. You figure it by multiplying the two Z scores for each person times each other, totaling up these products, and then averaging this total over the number of people. This will be a high number if

highs go with highs and lows with lows. This is because with Z scores, highs are always positive (and the higher they are, the more positive), and positive times positive is positive. Also, lows with Z scores are always negative (and the lower the score, the more negative the Z score), and negatives times negatives become positives too.

Statisticians can prove that by following this procedure, the highest number you can get, if the scores for the two variables are perfectly correlated, is +1. If there were no linear relationship between the variables, the result of this procedure would be 0 (that would happen because highs are sometimes multiplied with highs and sometimes with lows, and lows sometimes with highs and sometimes with lows, giving a mixture of positive and negative products that would cancel out).

In the present situation, the total of the products of the Z scores was 4.20, which when divided by the number of people is .84. This is called a Pearson correlation coefficient (r) of .84. It indicates a large, positive linear correlation between hours studied and test grade.

(e) Three logically possible directions of causality: (i) Studying more hours causes improved test grades; (ii) getting a better test grade causes more hours studied (note that although this is theoretically possible, it is not possible in reality to have a future event—the score on the test—cause a previous event—hours studied); or (iii) a third factor, such as interest in the subject matter, could be causing the student to study more and also to do better on the test.

(f) Formulas: Predicted $Z_Y = (\beta)(Z_X)$
Predicted $Y = $ (Predicted $Z_Y)(SD_Y) + (M_Y)$

$Z_X = -2$: Predicted $Z_Y = (.84)(-2) = -1.68$
Predicted $Y = (-1.68)(14.90) + 73 = -25.03$
$+ 73 = 47.97$

$Z_X = -1$: Predicted $Z_Y = (.84)(-1) = -.84$
Predicted $Y = (-.84)(14.90) + 73 = -12.52$
$+ 73 = 60.48$

$Z_X = 0$: Predicted $Z_Y = (.84)(0) = 0$
Predicted $Y = (0)(14.90) + 73 = 0 + 73 = 73$

$Z_X = +1$: Predicted $Z_Y = (.84)(+1) = .84$
Predicted $Y = (.84)(14.90) + 73 = 12.52 + 73$
$= 85.52$

$Z_X = +2$: Predicted $Z_Y = (.84)(+2) = 1.68$
Predicted $Y = (1.68)(14.90) + 73 = 25.03 + 73$
$= 98.03$

(g) $r^2 = .84^2 = .71$

6. This study used a statistical procedure called multiple regression. This procedure produces a formula for predicting a person's score on a criterion variable (in this example, third graders' reading comprehension) from his or her scores on a set of predictor variables (in this example, the three specific measures of reading ability). The formula is of the form that you multiply the person's score on each of the predictor variables by some particular number, called a regression coefficient or beta, and then add up the products. The procedure produces the most accurate prediction rule of this kind.

In this example, the prediction rule for the Z score for reading comprehension -.227 times the Z score for Letter-Word Identification, plus .299 times the Z score for Word Attack, plus .671 times the Z score for Oral Reading Fluency. (These are the numbers in the table next to each predictor variable in the Beta column.)

These regression coefficients suggest that reading comprehension is most strongly related to Oral Reading Fluency. Reading comprehension is also somewhat positively related to Word Attack. However, in the context of this prediction equation, reading comprehension is somewhat negatively related to Letter-Word Identification. This means that for any given level of Oral Reading Fluency and Word Attack, the better the child is at Letter-Word Identification, the child will be somewhat *worse* at reading comprehension!

It is important to note, however, that the regression coefficients for each of these predictors reflect what the scores on each predictor contribute to the prediction, over and above what the others contribute. If we were to consider ordinary correlations between each of the predictor variables with the criterion variable, their relative importance could be quite different. (Those correlations, however, were not provided.)

Another important piece of information in this table is R^2. This number tells you the proportion of variance accounted for in the criterion variable by the three predictor variables taken together. That is, 53.4% of the variation in the third graders' reading comprehension is accounted for by these three measures of specific reading abilities. This is equivalent to a correlation between reading comprehension and these three predictor variables of .73 (the square root at 534).

Chapter 4

1. (a) 50%, (b) 16%, (f) 84%, (g) 2%, (i) 50, (j) 45.

Remember: It is much easier to answer problems like this if you draw a picture of a normal curve and shade it as shown here for problems 1a and 1b.

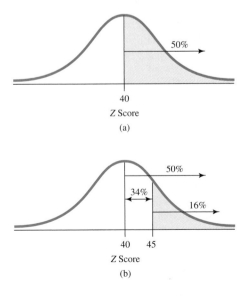

2. (a) From the normal curve table in Appendix A, 3.98% (.398) have Z scores between the mean and .10. By definition a total of 50% have Z scores above the mean. Thus 50% minus 3.98% have Z scores above .10. 50% minus 3.98% is 46.02%.

(b) 3.98% are between the mean and .10. 50% are below the mean. Thus 50% + 3.98% are below .10, for a total of 53.98%.

3. (a) Top 10% means 90% are below; of those, 50% are below the mean. Thus, the top 10% is the point where 40% of scores are between it and the mean. Looking up 40.0 in the normal curve table (the closest actual value is 39.97), you find that this is equivalent to a Z score of +1.28.

4. Needed $Z = 1.64$, which is the same as a raw score of 50 + (10)(1.64) = 66.4.

Explanation: The scores for almost anything you measure, in nature and in the social and behavioral sciences, tend approximately to follow the particular pattern shown here, called a normal curve. In a normal curve, most of the scores are near the middle with fewer but equal numbers of scores at each extreme. Because the normal curve is mathematically defined, the precise proportion of scores in any particular section of it can be calculated, and these have been listed in special tables.

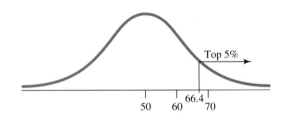

The normal curve tables are based on what are called Z scores. Z scores are in turn based on the mean and the standard deviation. The mean is the ordinary average—the sum of the scores divided by the number of scores. The standard deviation is a measure of how spread out a group of scores are. Roughly speaking, it is the average amount that the scores differ from the average. (To be exact, it is the square root of the average of the squared amounts each score differs from the average.) The Z score is the number of standard deviations a score is from the mean. The normal curve table tells you the percentage of scores in the normal curve between the mean and any particular Z score.

The coordination test scores are known to follow a normal curve. Thus, you can look up in the table the Z score for the point on the normal curve where 45% of the scores are between it and the mean. (The normal curve is completely symmetrical. Thus, 50% of the scores are above the mean, leaving 5% above 45%.) This turns out to be a Z score of 1.64. (Actually, there is not an exact point on the table for 45%, so we could have used either 1.64 or 1.65.)

With a standard deviation of 10, a Z score of 1.64 is 16.4 points above the mean. Adding that to the mean of 50 makes the score needed to be in the top 5% come out to 66.4.

5. (a) 10/50: $p = 10/50 = .2$

Chapter 5

1. (a) A research hypothesis is a statement of the predicted relationship among populations (for example, that they will have different means).
   (d) The comparison distribution is the distribution for the situation if the null hypothesis is true; it is the distribution to which, in hypothesis testing, you compare the score in your sample to decide whether it is so extreme you should reject the null hypothesis..
2. (i)(a) Population 1: Canadian children of librarians; Population 2: All Canadian children.
   (b) Research hypothesis: Population 1 children have a higher average reading ability than Population 2 children.
   (c) Null hypothesis: Population 1's average reading ability is no higher than Population 2's.
   (d) One-tailed, because the question is whether they "do better," so only one direction of difference is predicted.
3. (A) Z score cutoff on the comparison distribution = +1.64
   Z score on the comparison distribution for the sample score = 2
   Conclusion: Reject null hypothesis
4. Reject the null hypothesis: Not having a sense of smell makes for fewer correct identifications.
   Five steps of hypothesis testing:
   1. **Restate the question as a research hypothesis and a null hypothesis about the populations.** The two populations are:

      Population 1: Students who are prevented from using their sense of smell

      Population 2: Students in general

      The research hypothesis is that students prevented from using their sense of smell (Population 1) will do worse on the taste test than students in general (Population 2). The null hypothesis is that students prevented from using their sense of smell (Population 1) will not do worse on the taste test than students in general (Population 2).
   2. **Determine the characteristics of the comparison distribution.** The comparison distribution will be the same as Population 2. As stated in the problem, Population $M = 14$ and Population $SD = 4$. We will assume it follows a normal curve.
   3. **Determine the cutoff sample score on the comparison distribution at which the null hypothesis should be rejected.** At the .05 level, one-tailed, the cutoff is -1.64.
   4. **Determine your sample's score on the comparison distribution.** The sample's score was 5. $Z = (5-14)/4 = -9/4 = -2.25$.
   5. **Decide whether to reject the null hypothesis.** A Z score of -2.25 is more extreme (below) the cutoff of -1.64. Thus, you can reject the null hypothesis. The research hypothesis is supported—not having a sense of smell makes for fewer correct identifications.

      Explanation: In brief, you solve this problem by considering the likelihood that being without a sense of smell makes no difference. Suppose the sense of smell made no difference. In that situation, the probability of the students studied getting any particular number correct is the same as the probability of students in general getting any partic-

ular number correct. We know the distribution of the number correct that students get in general. Thus, we can figure that probability. It turns out that it would be fairly unlikely to get only 5 correct—so the researcher concludes that not having the sense of smell does make a difference.

To go into the details a bit, the key issue is finding these probabilities. We assume that the number correct for the students in general follows a normal curve—a specific mathematical pattern, sometimes called "bell-shaped," in which most of the scores are in the middle and there are fewer as the numbers get higher or lower. There are tables showing exactly what proportion of scores are between the middle and any particular point on the normal curve. These tables use "Z scores," transformed versions of the original scores that are the number of standard deviations above the mean. The mean is the ordinary average (the sum of the scores divided by the number of scores). The standard deviation can be thought of as the average amount that scores differ from the mean. (Strictly speaking, it is the square root of the average of the squares of each score's difference from the mean.)

When considering the result of an experiment, many researchers use a convention of deciding that if a result could have happened by chance less than 5% of the time under a particular scenario, that scenario will be rejected as too unlikely. The normal curve tables show that the top 5% of the normal curve begins with a Z score of 1.64. The normal curve is completely symmetrical. Thus, the bottom 5% includes all Z scores below -1.64. Therefore, even before doing the experiment, the researcher would probably set the following rule: The scenario in which being without the sense of smell makes no difference will be rejected as too unlikely if the number correct (converted to a Z score using the mean and standard deviation for students in general) is less than -1.64.

The actual number correct for the student who could not use the sense of smell was 5. The normal curve for the students in general, we are told, had a mean of 14 and a standard deviation of 4. Getting 5 correct is 9 below the mean of 14; in terms of standard deviation units of 4 each, it is 9/4 below the mean, for a Z score of -2.25.

A Z score of -2.25 is more extreme than -1.64. Thus, the researcher concludes that the scenario in which being without smell has no effect is unlikely. This is illustrated below.

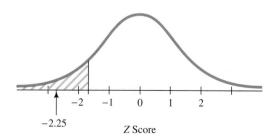

Chapter 6

2. (a) $SD^2 = 10^2 = 100$; $SD^2_M = SD^2/N = 100/2 = 50$; $SD_M = \sqrt{SD^2_M} = \sqrt{50} = 7.07$

3. (a) Characteristics of the distribution of means: $M = 100$; $SD_M = 7.07$; shape = normal
   Z score for top 2.5% = 1.96; Z score for bottom 2.5% = –1.96.
   Upper confidence limit = (1.96)(7.07) + 100 = 13.86 + 100 = 113.86
   Lower confidence limit = (–1.96)(7.07) + 100 = –13.86 + 100 = 86.14

4. The distribution of the population of individual scores is normal, and thus, so will the distribution of means. Based on the normal curve table, a Z score of at least 1.64 is needed to be in the top 5%. For sample (a): $SD_M = \sqrt{(36/10)} = 1.90$. Z (on the distribution of means) = (44 – 40)/1.90 = 4/1.90 = 2.11. Because 2.11 is more extreme than 1.64, this sample is less likely than 5%. The distributions are shown in the following graphs.

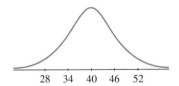

28   34   40   46   52

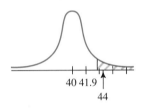

40 41.9
44

5. (a) Five steps of hypothesis testing:
   1. **Restate the question as a research hypothesis and a null hypothesis about the populations.** The two populations are:
      Population 1: Older women receiving the special program
      Population 2: Older women in general (who do not get the special program)
      The research hypothesis is that the population of older women who receive the special program (Population 1) will have shorter reaction time than older women in general (Population 2). The null hypothesis is that Population 1's reaction times will not be shorter than Population 2's.
   2. **Determine the characteristics of the comparison distribution.** The comparison distribution is a distribution of means of samples of 25 taken from the distribution of Population 2. Population $M = 1.8$; $SD_M^2 = SD^2/N = .5^2/25 = .25/25 = .01$; $SD_M = \sqrt{.01} = .1$. Because the population is normal, the distribution of means is normal.
   3. **Determine the cutoff sample score on the comparison distribution at which the null hypothesis should be rejected.** Using a one-tailed test (the researchers predicted a lower reaction time) at the .01 level, the cutoff is –2.33.
   4. **Determine your sample's score on the comparison distribution.** $Z = (1.5–1.8)/.1 = –.3/.1 = –3$.
   5. **Decide whether to reject the null hypothesis.** –3 is lower than –2.33. Thus, you can reject the null hy-

pothesis. The research hypothesis is supported. Older women after taking part in the special program have an average shorter reaction time than the general population of older women.

(b) Confidence interval of 99%: upper limit = $M + (SD_M)(2.57) = 1.5 + (.1)(2.57) = 1.5 + .257 = 1.76$; lower limit = $1.5 + (.1)(–2.57) = 1.24$.

(c) Explanation: This is a standard hypothesis-testing problem, with one exception. You can't compare directly the reaction times for the group of 25 older women tested to the distribution of reaction times for individual older women in general. This is because the distribution of older women in general is a distribution of individual scores, and we have an average of a group of 25 scores. The probability of a group of scores having an extreme mean just by chance is much less than the probability of any one individual having an extreme score just by chance. (This is because when taking scores at random, when you take several scores, any extreme scores are likely to be balanced out by less extreme or oppositely extreme scores). Thus, the proper distribution to use to compare the mean of the group of 25 reaction times is a distribution of what would happen if you were to take many random groups of 25 reaction time scores and find the mean of each group of 25 scores.

Such a distribution of many means of samples has the same mean as the original distribution of individual scores (there is no reason for it to be otherwise). However, it is a narrower curve. This is because the chances of extremes are less. In fact, it is known mathematically that its variance will be exactly the variance of the original distribution of individuals divided by the number of scores in each sample. In this example, this makes a distribution of means with a mean of 1.8 and a standard deviation of .1(that is, $\sqrt{(.5^2/25)}$). This will be a normal distribution because a distribution of many means from a normally distributed population is also normal.

The cutoff for significance, using the .01 level and a one-tailed test, is –2.33. The mean rating of the group of 25 women who received the special program, 1.5, was 3 standard deviations below the mean of the distribution of means, making it clearly more extreme than the cutoff. Thus, we can reject the null hypothesis and conclude that the results support the hypothesis that older women who take part in the special program have lower reaction times.

The confidence interval is an estimate of the range of values that we are reasonably confident includes the true population mean for the group studied (Population 1: in this problem, women who receive the special reaction-time program). A 99% confidence interval is the range of values we are 99% confident includes the true population mean. To figure the upper and lower limit of this interval, we begin by considering that the best single point estimate of the mean of Population 2. This is the mean of our sample of this population (1.5). We then assume that the standard deviation of the distribution of means for this Population 2 is the same as for the known population (which we figured earlier to be .1). Based on this information, if the true population mean were 1.5, 99% of the time, sample means would fall between a Z score of +2.57 (the point on the normal curve that includes 49.5% of the scores above the mean) and –2.57. In our example, these Z scores correspond to raw scores of 1.76 and 1.24.

It turns out that the values figured in this way are the limits of the confidence interval. Why? Suppose the true population mean was 1.76. In this case, there would be a .5% chance of getting a mean as small or smaller than 1.5. (That is, with a mean of 1.76, and a standard deviation of .1, 1.5 is exactly 2.57 standard deviations below the mean. This is the cutoff for the bottom .5%.) Similarly, if the true population mean were 1.24, there would be only a .5% chance of getting a mean larger than 1.5.

Chapter 7

1. (a)

Conclusion from Hypothesis Testing	Real Situation	
	Null Hypothesis True	Research Hypothesis True
Research Hypothesis Supported (Reject null)	*Type I Error* Decide more recess time improves behavior but it really doesn't	*Correct Decision* Decide more recess time improves behavior and it really does
Study Inconclusive (Do not reject null)	*Correct Decision* Decide effect of recess time on behavior is not shown in this study; actually, more recess time doesn't improve behavior	*Type II Error* Decide effect of recess time on behavior is not shown in this study; actually, more recess time improves behavior

3. Effect size = (Population 1 M – Population 2 M) / Population SD
   (a) Effect size = (91 – 90)/4 = 1/4 = .25
4. (a) Not affected. (That is what the significance level tests.)
   (b) Probably of small importance (due to small effect size).
6. (a) Increases power; (b) decreases power

Chapter 8

1. (a) t needed ($df = 63$, $p < .05$, one-tailed) = –1.671
   $S_M = \sqrt{(S^2/N)} = \sqrt{(9/64)} = \sqrt{.141} = .38$
   $t = (M - \text{Population } M)/S_M = (11 - 12.40)/.38$
   $= -1.40/.38 = -3.68$
   Reject null hypothesis.
3. (a) t needed ($df = 19$, $p < .05$, one-tailed) = 1.729
   $S_M = \sqrt{(S^2/N)} = \sqrt{(8.29/20)} = \sqrt{.415} = .64$
   $t = (M - \text{Population } M)/S_M = (1.7 - 0)/.64 = 2.66$
   Reject null hypothesis.
   Effect size = $(M - \text{Population } M)/S = 1.7/\sqrt{8.29} = .59$; medium effect size
4. (a) Steps of hypothesis testing
   1. Restate the question as a research hypothesis and a null hypothesis about the populations.

Population 1: Cities like those who participated in the anti-littering program.
Population 2: Cities who do not change in the amount of litter over a one-year period.
The research hypothesis is that Population 1 has a greater mean decrease in litter than Population 2. The null hypothesis is that Population 1 doesn't have a greater mean decrease in litter than Population 2.
   2. Determine the characteristics of the comparison distribution.
   Population 2: shape = assumed normal; Population $M = 0$; Population SD^2 = unknown; $S^2 = 50/3 = 16.67$; Distribution of means: shape = t (df = 3); $M = 0$; $S_M = \sqrt{S^2/N} = \sqrt{16.67/4} = \sqrt{4.17} = 2.04$
   3. Determine the cutoff sample score on the comparison distribution at which the null hypothesis should be rejected.
   t needed ($df = 3$, $p < .01$, one-tailed) = 4.541.
   4. Determine your sample's score on comparison distribution.
   Change scores = 7, 6, –1, 8;
   $M = 20/4 = 5$; $t = (5 - 0)/2.04 = 2.45$
   5. Decide whether to reject the null hypothesis.
   t from Step 4 (2.45) is not more extreme than cutoff t from Step 3 (4.541).
   Therefore, do not reject the null hypothesis.
   (b) Effect size = $M/S = 5/\sqrt{16.67} = 5/4.08 = 1.23$; very loose effect size
   (c)

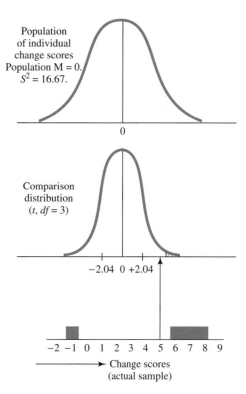

   (d) Explanation: The first thing I did was to simplify by converting the numbers to "change scores"—postprogram (2001) litter minus preprogram (2000) litter for each city. Then I found the mean of these change scores, which was 5. That is, there is an average decrease of five pounds of litter per block per day.

The next step was to see whether this result, found in these five cities, indicates some real difference more generally due to being in this program. The alternative is the possibility that this much change could have happened in four randomly selected cities just by chance even if in general the program has no real effect. That is, we imagine that the average change for cities in general is actually 0, and maybe this study just happened to pick four cities that would have decreased this much anyway.

I then considered just how much a group of four cities would have to change before I could conclude that they have changed too much to chalk it up to chance. This required figuring out the characteristics of this imagined population of cities in which on the average there is no change. Its mean would be 0 change (that is, a mean change of 0 is just how you would describe an average of no change). Since I didn't know the variance in this hypothetical distribution of cities that don't change, I estimated it from the information in the sample of four cities. If the sample were just a chance draw from the hypothetical population, its variance should be representative of the hypothetical population.

However, the variance figured from a sample will in general be slightly smaller than the true population variance. Thus, I had to modify the variance formula to take this into account: Instead of dividing the sum of the squared deviations by the number of scores, I divided it instead by the "degrees of freedom," which is the number of scores minus 1—in this case, 3. (This adjustment exactly accounts for the tendency of the variance in the sample to underestimate the true population variance.) As shown in the calculations in the steps of hypothesis testing, this gave an estimated population variance (S^2) of 16.67.

I was interested not in individual cities but in a group of four. Thus, what I really needed to know was the characteristics of a distribution of means of samples of four taken from this hypothetical population of individual city change scores. Such a distribution of means will have the same mean (since there is no reason to expect the means of such groups of four drawn randomly to be systematically higher or lower than 0). However, such a distribution will have a much smaller variance (because the average of a group of four scores is a lot less likely to be extreme than any individual score). Fortunately, it is known (and can be proved mathematically) that the variance of a distribution of means is the variance of the distribution of individuals divided by the number of individuals in each sample. In our example, this works out to 16.67 divided by 4, which is 4.17. The standard deviation of this distribution is thus the square root of 4.17, or 2.04.

It also turns out that if we can assume that the hypothetical population of individual cities' change scores is normally distributed (and we have no reason to think otherwise), the distribution of means of samples from

that distribution can be thought of as having a precise known shape, called a t distribution (which has slightly thicker tails than a normal curve). Thus, I looked in a table for a t distribution for the situation in which there are 3 degrees of freedom used to estimate the population variance. The table shows that there is a less than a 1% chance of getting a score that is 4.541 standard deviations from the mean of this distribution.

The mean change score for the sample of four cities was 5, which would be 2.45 (that is, 5/2.04) standard deviations above the mean of 0 change on this distribution of means of change scores. This is not as extreme as 4.541. Thus, there is more than a 1% chance that these results could have come from a hypothetical distribution with no change. Therefore, the researcher would not rule out that possibility, and the experiment would be considered inconclusive.

Finally, it is possible to describe the degree of effect in a standardized format, called an effect size. This is just the mean of the change scores divided by the estimated population standard deviation. In this example, it is 5 divided by 4.08, which comes out to 1.23. This means that the change from before to after the program was more than one standard deviation. This is quite a substantial change. However, even with such a substantial amount of change, the result was not significant (no doubt because of the very small sample size of only four cities).

6. **From Table 8–7: (a) .22; (d) .77**
7. **From Table 8–8: (a) 156; (b) 196**

Chapter 9

2. (a) t needed ($df = 58, p < .05$, two-tailed) $= \pm 2.004$;
$$S^2_{Pooled} = S^2_1(df_1/df_{Total}) + S^2_2(df_2/df_{Total})$$
$$= 2.4(29/58) + 2.8(29/58) = 1.2 + 1.4 = 2.6;$$
$$S^2_{M_1} = S^2_{Pooled}/N_1 = 2.6/30 = .087; S^2_{M_2} = .087;$$
$$S^2_{Difference} = S^2_{M_1} + S^2_{M_2} = .087 + .087 = .174;$$
$$S_{Difference} = \sqrt{S^2_{Difference}} = \sqrt{.174} = .417;$$
$$t = (M_1 - M_2)/S_{Difference} = (12 - 11.1)/.417 = .9/.417 = 2.16$$
Conclusion: Reject the null hypothesis.
The difference is significant.
Estimated effect size: $= (M_1 - M_2)/S_{Pooled} = (12 - 11.1)/\sqrt{2.6}$
$= .9/1.6 = .56$

(approximately medium effect size). Power (from table) = .47 (However, a significant result must have power of at least .50. Thus, the approximate figure in the table understimates the true power to some extent.)

3. (a) Steps of hypothesis testing:
   1. **Restate the question as a research hypothesis and a null hypothesis about the populations.**
   Population 1: People who get their news from TV
   Population 2: People who get their news from radio
   The research hypothesis is that the two populations have different means. The null hypothesis is that the two populations have the same mean.

2. **Determine the characteristics of the comparison distribution.**
   Estimated population variance = S^2_{Pooled}
   = (60/80)(4) + (20/80)(6) = 3.0 + 1.5 = 4.5;
   Comparison distribution (distribution of differences between means): Mean = 0; $S_{Difference}$ = .54; Shape = t(80).
   Computation of $S_{Difference}$: $S^2_{M_1}$ = 4.5/61 = .074; $S^2_{M_2}$ = 4.5/21 = .214; $S^2_{Difference}$ = .074 + .214 = .288; $S_{Difference}$ = .54;

3. **Determine the cutoff sample score on the comparison distribution at which the null hypothesis should be rejected.**
   t needed (df = 80, $p < .01$, two-tailed) = ±2.639.

4. **Determine your sample's score on the comparison distribution.**
   t = (24 − 26)/.54 = −2/.54 = −3.70.

5. **Decide whether to reject the null hypothesis.**
   t on 4 (−3.70) is more extreme than cutoff t on 3 (±2.639). Therefore, reject the null hypothesis; conclude that the prediction is supported by the experiment.

(b) Estimated effect size = (24 − 26)/$\sqrt{4.5}$ = −2/2.12 = −.94; large effect size.

(c) See figure below.

(d) Explanation: The mean (M) is the ordinary average (the sum of the scores divided by the number of scores). In this example, the radio group had a higher average score on the test than the TV group. S^2 is the estimate of the variance of scores in the general population based on the variance of scores in the group of people studied (called the sample). The variance (S^2) is a measure of the amount of variation in a group of scores. When estimating the population variance from the variance of the sample, each score's difference from the mean is squared and the sum of these squared differences is divided by the degrees of freedom—the number of participants in the sample minus 1. (The degrees of freedom is the amount of unique information available in the sample to use in estimating the population. Using the sample's variance, which is the sum of squared differences divided by the number of scores, would give too small an estimate of the population variance.) In this situation, I have two estimates, one from each sample.

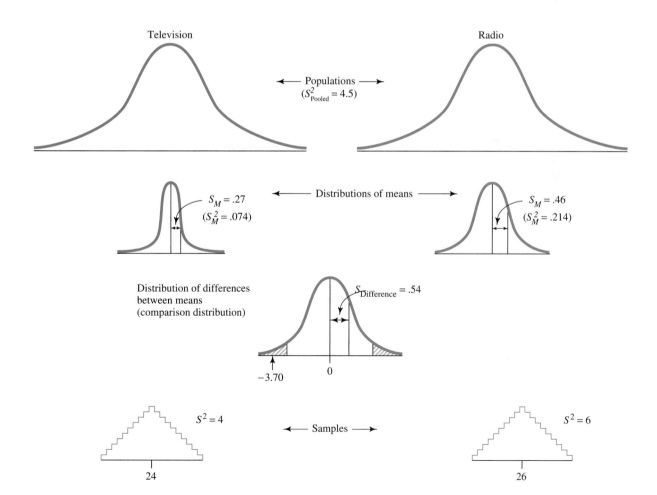

Now that we have considered the results given in the problem, let us turn to the issue of how to draw conclusions. The way to frame the question is to ask: What is the probability of getting this much difference in knowledge scores between the two groups even if radio versus TV made no difference? That is, if the TV and radio groups actually come from two larger populations that were not different, how likely is it that I could have gotten a sample from each population that is this different from the other?

To answer this required figuring out what such non-different populations would look like. The estimates of the population variance that I made apply here. In fact, even if the two groups were from different populations, only the means would be different—I assume the variance to be the same (I have no reason to think it differs). Hence, these are two estimates of the same population variance, and I can average both estimates to get a better estimate still. In averaging, however, I want to give more weight to the estimate based on larger degrees of freedom, so I compute a weighted average, multiplying each estimate by its proportion of the total degrees of freedom and adding up the results. This pooled estimate of the population variance comes out to 4.5. At this point, I had estimated the variance of the populations of individuals' knowledge scores.

Now, because I was interested not in individual scores but in the difference between the mean of a group of 61 and the mean of another group of 21, I needed to figure out what would be the characteristics of a distribution of differences between means of groups of 61 and 21 that are randomly taken from the two identical populations whose variance I just estimated. This required two steps.

First I needed to figure out the characteristics of an intermediate distribution for each sample—the distribution of means of samples of that size taken from its population. For the TV group, this would be a distribution of means of samples of 61 each. Such a distribution will have a variance much smaller than that of the population of individuals from which the samples were taken because any one mean is less likely to be extreme than any single score (because the mean of several scores is likely to include some scores that balance out or reduce the effect of any extremes). In fact, it can be shown mathematically that the variance of a distribution of means will be exactly the variance of the parent population of individuals divided by the number in each sample. For the TV group, this distribution would be 4.5 divided by 61, or .074. The figure for the radio group is .214.

The second step is directly about the distribution of differences between means. It is like a distribution that you would get if you took a mean from the distribution of means for the TV group and took one from the comparable distribution for the radio group and figured their difference; then, after doing this many times, the distribution of the differences you got in this way would create a new distribution—of differences between means.

If radio versus TV made no difference, the two original populations have the same mean. Thus, on average, the difference between a sample taken from the TV group and a sample taken from the radio group should come out to 0. This is because sometimes one will be bigger and sometimes the other, but in the long run these random differences should balance out. The variance of this distribution of differences between means will be affected by the variation in both distributions of means. In fact, it will be the sum of the two. Thus, its variance will be .074 plus .214, or .288. Actually, the variation in such distributions is most often described in terms of what is called the standard deviation (the square root of the variance), which comes out to .54 (that is, $\sqrt{.288} = .54$).

It also turns out that such a distribution of differences between means has a precise known shape. Thus, it is possible to look up in a table the probability of being a certain distance from its mean. The distance is measured in standard deviations. The table shows that for my distribution (with my total of 80 degrees of freedom), there is less than a 1% chance of getting a score (a difference between means) that is 2.639 or more standard deviations from the mean in either direction. (I took into account both directions because I was studying whether there was a difference in either direction between the TV and radio groups. The "1% level" refers to the conventional point at which social scientists, who are very concerned about the risk of concluding in error that an experiment has made a difference, decide that something is too unlikely to have happened by chance.) I have illustrated these various distributions (see the figure on the preceding page).

The difference between my particular two means was –2 (that is, 24 – 26). This would be 3.70 (that is, 2/.54) standard deviations below the mean in the distribution of differences between means. This is clearly more extreme than –2.639. Thus, I could reject as too unlikely the possibility that I could get a difference this large by taking any two groups of participants at random regardless of whether they had been getting their news through TV or radio. Therefore, the researcher can take the results of this study as support for the prediction.

Further, the researcher wanted to know not just that results were not by chance but also how big an effect there was of getting news from radio versus TV. The difference between the two means was 2 points on the knowledge measure. The typical amount of variation in scores on any scale is described by the standard deviation (the square root of the variance, the variance being the average of the squares of each score's difference from the mean). In this case, the standard deviation we would estimate uses the information from both samples, the pooled estimate. The pooled estimate of the variance was 4.5; its square root is 2.12. Thus, a difference of 2 points on the scale is a difference of nearly 1 standard deviation (.94 standard deviations). In social science research in general, an effect size of .80 is considered large, so this is clearly a large effect. Thus, in addition to the conclusion that the result is not likely to have arisen just by chance, the researcher can also conclude that the advantage of radio over TV is quite substantial.

5. (a) Effect size = (107 – 149)/84 = –42/84 = –.5. Medium Effect Size.

Number of participants per group needed for medium effect size, $p < .05$, one-tailed (from Table 9–5) = 50; 100 participants total.

Chapter 10

1. (a) F needed ($df = 2, 27; p < .05$) = 3.36

   $GM = (7.4 + 6.8 + 6.8)/3 = 7$

   $S_M^2 = \Sigma(M - GM)^2/df_{Between}$
   $= [(7.4 - 7)^2 + (6.8 - 7)^2 + (6.8 - 7)^2]/(3 - 1) = .24/2 = .12$

   $S_{Between}^2 = (S_M^2)(n) = (.12)(10) = 1.2$

   $S_{Within}^2 = (S_1^2 + S_2^2 + ... + S_{Last}^2)/N_{Groups}$
   $= (.82 + .90 + .80)/3 = .84$

   $F = 1.2/.84 = 1.43$

   Do not reject the null hypothesis; groups are not significantly different at the .05 level.

   Estimated effect size = $S_M/S_{Within}^2 = \sqrt{.12}/\sqrt{.84} = .35/.92$
   $= .38$

   This is a large effect size. Power (from Table 10–7) = .45

2. (a) F needed ($df = 2, 9; p < .01$) = 8.02

   Group 1: $M = 8, S^2 = .67$; Group 2: $M = 6, S^2 = .67$;
   Group 3: $M = 4, S^2 = .67$

   $S_{Between}^2 = (4)(4) = 16$; $S_{Within}^2 = 67$; $F = 16/.67 = 23.88$

   Reject the null hypothesis, groups are significantly different at the .01 level.

   Estimated effect size = $S_M/S_{Within} = \sqrt{4}/\sqrt{.67} = 2/.82 = 2.44$

   This is a (very) large effect size.

4. (a) Steps of hypothesis testing:

   1. **Restate the question as a research hypothesis and a null hypothesis about populations.**

      Population 1: Patients with affective disorders
      Population 2: Patients with cognitive disorders
      Population 3: Patients with drug-related conditions

      The research hypothesis is that the three population means differ. The null hypothesis is that the three populations have the same mean.

   2. **Determine the characteristics of the comparison distribution.**

      F distribution with 2 and 9 degrees of freedom

   3. **Determine the cutoff sample score on the comparison distribution at which the null hypothesis should be rejected.**

      5% level, $F(2,9)$ needed = 4.26

   4. **Determine your sample's score on the comparison distribution.**

      Within-group population variance estimate (S_{Within}^2) =
      $(.67 + 3.33 + 2.67) / 3 = 2.22$

      Between-group population variance estimate
      ($S_{Between}^2$) = $(5.33)(4) = 21.32$

      F ratio = $21.32/2.22 = 9.60$

   5. **Decide whether to reject the null hypothesis.**

      F from step 4 (9.60) is more extreme than cutoff F from step 3 (4.26).

      Therefore, reject the null hypothesis; the research hypothesis is supported; there is a significant difference.

   (b) Estimated effect size = 1.55

   (c) Explanation: The null hypothesis is that the three groups are from populations of length-of-stay scores with equal means (and, as with a t test, we must be able to assume that they have equal variances). If this null hypothesis is true, then you can estimate the variance of these equal populations in two ways:

(1) You can estimate from the variation within each of the three groups and then average them. (This is just what you would do in a t test for independent means, except now you are averaging three instead of just two. Also in a t test you would weight these variances according to the degrees of freedom they contribute to the overall estimate. However, because all three groups have equal numbers, you can simply average them—in effect weighting them equally.) In this example, the three variance estimates were .67, 3.33, and 2.67, which gave a pooled estimate of 2.22. This is called the within-group estimate of the population variance.

(2) You can estimate the variance using the three means. If we assume the null hypothesis is true, the means of the three groups are based on samples taken from identical populations. Each of these identical populations will have an identical distribution of means of samples taken from that population. The means of our three samples are all from identical populations, which is the same as if they were all from the same population. Thus, the amount of variation among our three means should reflect the variation in the distribution of means that they can be thought of as coming from. As a result, I can use these three means (6, 10, and 10) to estimate the variance in this distribution of means. Using the usual formula for estimating a population variance, I get 5.33.

However, what we want is the variance of a distribution of individuals. So the question is, what would be the distribution of individuals that would produce a distribution of means (of four scores each) with a variance of 5.33? To find the distribution of means from a distribution of individuals, you divide the variance of the distribution of individuals by the size of the samples. In this case, you want to do the reverse. Thus, you multiply the variance of the distribution of means by the size of the samples to get the variance of the distribution of individuals. This comes out to 5.33 times 4, or 21.32. This is called the between-group estimate of the population variance.

If the null hypothesis is true, the two estimates should be about the same because they are estimates of essentially the same population. Thus, the ratio of the between-group estimate divided by the within-group estimate should be about 1.

However, suppose the null hypothesis is false and the three populations from which these groups come have different means. In that situation, the estimate based on the variation among the group means will be bigger than the one based on the variation within the groups. The reason it will be bigger is as follows. If the null hypothesis is true, the only reason that the means of our groups vary is because of the variance inside of each of the three identical distributions of means. But if the null hypothesis is false, each of those distributions of means also has a different mean. Thus, the variation in our means is due to *both* the variation inside of each of these now *not* identical distributions of means, and also to the differences in the means of these distributions of means. Thus, there is an additional source of variation in the means of our groups. If you estimate the variance of the population using these three means, it will be larger than it the null hypothesis were true. On the other hand, the within-group variance is not affected by whether the three groups have different means, because it considers variation only within each of the groups. The within-group variance thus does not get any bigger if the null hypothesis is false. Therefore, when the null hypothesis is false, the ratio of the between-group variance to the within-group variance will be more than 1.

The ratio of the between-group estimate to the within-group estimate is called an *F* ratio. In this example, our *F* ratio is 21.32 to 2.22: 21.32/2.22 = 9.60.

Statisticians have made tables of what happens when you figure *F* ratios based on the situation in which you randomly take a group of four scores from each of three identical populations. This is the situation in which the null hypothesis is true. Looking at these tables, it turns out that there is less than a 5% chance of getting an *F* ratio larger than 4.26. Because our actual *F* ratio is bigger than this, we can reject the null hypothesis.

7. (i) Main effects for class and age; interaction effect. Income is greater in general for upper-class and for older individuals, but the combination of older and upper class has a higher income than would be expected just from the effects of either variable alone.

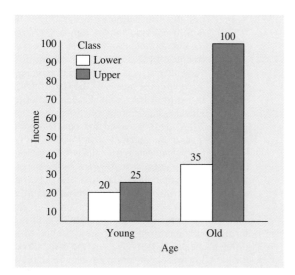

Chapter 11

1. (a) Needed $X^2(df = 3 - 1 = 2, p < .05) = 5.992$.

Category	O	Expected (E)	O − E	(O − E)²	(O − E)²/E
1	5	(1/3)(20) = 6.67	−1.67	2.79	.42
2	10	(1/3)(20) = 6.67	3.33	11.09	1.66
3	5	(1/3)(20) = 6.67	−1.67	1.79	.42

$X^2 = 2.50$

Conclusion: Do not reject the null hypothesis.

3. (a) $df = (N_{Columns} - 1)(N_{Rows} - 1) = (2 - 1)(2 - 1) = 1$
   Needed χ^2 ($df = 1, p < .01$) = 6.635

10 (13)	16 (13)	26 (50%)
16 (13)	10 (13)	26 (50%)
26 26	26 26	52 (100%)

$$X^2 = \frac{(10 - 13)^2}{13} + \frac{(16 - 13)^2}{13} + \frac{(16 - 13)^2}{13} + \frac{(10 - 13)^2}{13}$$

$$= .69 + .69 + .69 + .69 = 2.76$$

Do not reject the null hypothesis.
$\Phi = \sqrt{(X^2/N)} = \sqrt{(2.76/52)} = \sqrt{.053} = .23$

4. (a) Steps of hypothesis testing:
   1. **Restate the question as a research hypothesis and a null hypothesis about populations.**
      Population 1: People like those surveyed
      Population 2: People for whom the community they live in is independent of their opinion on the upcoming ballot initiative

      The research hypothesis is that the two populations are different (the community people live in is not independent of their opinion on the upcoming ballot initiative.) The null hypothesis is that the two populations are the same (the community people live in is independent of their opinion on the upcoming ballot imitative).
   2. **Determine the characteristics of the comparison distribution.**
      Chi-square distribution with four degrees of freedom.
      $df = (N_{Columns} - 1)(N_{Rows} - 1) = (3 - 1)(3 - 1) = 4$
   3. **Determine the cutoff sample score on the comparison.**
      .05 level, $df = 4$: $\chi^2 = 9.488$.
   4. **Determine your sample's score on the comparison distribution.**

	A	B	C	Total
		Community		
For	12 0(9.8)	6 (4.2)	3 0(7)	21 (23.33%)
Against	18 (16.8)	3 (7.2)	15 (12)	36 (40.00%)
No opinion	12 (15.4)	9 (6.6)	12 (11)	33 (36.67%)
Total	42	18	30	90

$$\chi^2 = \frac{(12-9.8)^2}{9.8} + \frac{(6-4.2)^2}{4.2} + \frac{(3-7)^2}{7} + \frac{(18-16.8)^2}{16.8}$$

$$+ \frac{(3-7.2)^2}{7.2} + \frac{(15-12)^2}{12} + \frac{(12-15.4)^2}{15.4} + \frac{(9-6.6)^2}{6.6}$$

$$+ \frac{(12-11)^2}{11}$$

$$= .49 + .77 + 2.29 + .09 + 2.45 + .75 + .75 + .87 + .09 = 8.55$$

5. **Decide whether to reject the null hypothesis.**
   χ^2 in Step 4 (8.55) is less extreme than Step 3 cutoff (9.488) Therefore, do not reject the null hypothesis; the study is inconclusive.
   (b) Cramer's $\Phi = \sqrt{8.55/(90)(2)]} = \sqrt{[8.55/180]} = \sqrt{.05} = .22$.
   (c) Explanation: In this example, 23.33% of all survey respondents were for the ballot initiative. Thus, if community is not related to opinion, 23.33% of the people in each community should be for the initiative. For example, you'd expect 9.8 of the 42 people surveyed in Community C to be for the initiative. Are the survey results so discrepant from these expectations that we should conclude that the community people live in is related to their opinion on the upcoming ballot initiative?

   Chi-square is a measure of the degree of difference between observed and expected results. For each combination of the 3 × 3 arrangement, you figure that discrepancy between observed and expected, square it, and divide by the expected number; then you add up the results. In the For-Community-A combination, 12 minus 9.8 is 2.2, squared is 4.84, divided by 9.8 is .49 (rounded off). Doing the same for the other eight combinations and adding them all up gives 8.55.

   Chi-square uses squared discrepancies so that the result is not affected by the directions of the differences. It is divided by the expected number to adjust for the relatively different numbers expected in the combinations.

   Statisticians have determined mathematically what would happen if you took an infinite number of samples from a population with a fixed proportion of people in each of several groupings and figured the chi-square for each such sample. The distribution of such chi-squares depends only on the number of groupings free to take on different expected values. We always presume you know the row and column totals. Thus, for each community, if you know the numbers For and Against, you can figure out how many have no opinion. Further, you need to know only two of the communities—say A and B for any particular opinion, and you can figure out the third by subtracting these from the total of that row. So only four combinations—say For and Against for Communities A and B—are "free to vary."

   A table of the chi-square distribution when four groupings are free to vary shows that there is only a 5% chance of getting a chi-square of 9.488 or greater. Because our chi-square is smaller than this, the observed numbers in each category differ from the expected numbers less than they would need to before we would be willing to reject the idea that a person's opinion is unrelated to his or her community. The survey is inconclusive.

   We can, however, estimate the actual degree of linkage in this group surveyed between community and opinion. The procedure is called "Cramer's phi," figured by dividing your chi-square by the number of people included in the analysis times the sample side at the table less one, then taking the square root of the results. In this example, this comes out to .22.

   This statistic ranges from 0 (no relationship) to 1 (a perfect relationship—knowing a person's status on one of the dimensions, such as what community they are from, would let you perfectly predict their status on the other dimension, such as their opinion). Thus, .22 is a fairly low figure—although given the amount of other things that affect any relationship, by the standards of social amd behavorial science research, a Cramer's phi of .22 would be considered a medium-sized relation. (To be exact, a Cramer's phi of .21 is the number given for a medium effect size.)

   Looking at this another way, we can ask, if there really is a moderate relationship between opinion and community in the population, what is the chance that this whole process would have led to a positive conclusion? Statisticians have provided tables that give this probability. In this situation, it turns out that there would be about a 66% chance. If there were truly a large effect in the population (which would be a Cramer's phi of about .35), there is a 99% chance we would have come to a positive conclusion. Thus, given the result of this study, if any relationship exists, it is almost surely not a large one.

7. (a) and (b) *t* needed (two-tailed, $p < .05$, $df = 8$) = 2.306

	Square-Root Transformed Scores	
	Group A	*Group B*
	1.10	1.40
	1.60	3.00
	2.10	2.40
	1.90	2.60
	2.70	2.20
$M =$	1.88	2.32
$S^2 =$	.35	.35
$S^2_{Pooled} =$	.35	
$S^2_M =$	.07	.07
$S^2_{Difference} =$	.07 +	.07 = .14
$S_{difference} =$	.37	
$t = (1.88 - 2.32)/.37 = -1.19$		

Do not reject the null hypothesis.
(c) Explanation: It would not have been correct to carry out a *t* test on the numbers as they were (without transform-

ing them). This is because the distributions of the samples were very skewed for both language groups. Thus, it seemed likely that the population distributions were also seriously skewed. That would clearly violate the assumption for a *t* test that the underlying population distributions are normal. Thus, I took the square root of each score. This had the advantage of making sample distributions much closer to normal. This suggests that the population distributions of square roots of family sizes are probably nearly normally distributed. I realize that taking the square root of each family size distorts its straightforward meaning, but the impact for the individuals in the family of each additional child is probably not equal. That is, going from no children to 1 child has a huge impact. Going from 1 to 2 has less, and going from 7 to 8 probably makes much less difference for the family.

In any case, having taken the square root of each score, I then proceeded to conduct an ordinary *t* test for independent means. The result was inconclusive—the null hypothesis could not be rejected. (And because the sample size was so small, the power was also probably low, making it hard to draw any kind of suggestion from the failure to reject the null hypothesis.)

Chapter 12

1. A hierarchical multiple regression is a variation of ordinary multiple regression in which the predictor variables are added to the prediction rule in stages. The additional contribution of the variable is figured. The order the predictor variables are entered is decided by the researcher in advance. In the Lindzey et al. study, the criterion variable was children's social competence. The first two predictor variables considered were father-and child-initiation rates, which accounted for only 3% of the variance in the dependent variable. That is, the R^2 was .03. (This R^2 was not significant—they note that the significance level was far from below .05—it was a huge .57.) So far, this is like an ordinary multiple regression situation with two predictor and one dependent variables.

Then, however, the researchers added an additional predictor variable—father-child mutual compliance. Lindzey et al. report that the overall variance accounted for increased by 18%. This means that the R^2 had to have gone from .03 to .21 (that is, 3% + 18% = 21%). Further, they note that this increase of 18% was significant (with $p = .01$).

What this tells us is that father-and child-initiation rate is not very important in predicting children's competence. Most important, it tells us that even taking those two variables into account, mutual compliance makes an important contribution to predicting social competence.

4. (a) In the context of the proposed model, the key result is that all three hypothesized paths to intensity were significant. However, you can also see that the path from desirability to intensity was strongest and the path from probability to intensity, though significant, was not very strong. This means that how intensely one feels unrequited love is very strongly predicted by how desirable one finds the beloved but that the belief that the other will eventually reciprocate also predicts intensity of the unrequited love, but only weakly.

(b) Structural equation modeling is a statistical technique in which you specify a pattern of causal links among variables, diagrammed with arrows connecting each cause to its effects. You can also specify that some variables measured in the study may actually be indicators of an underlying unmeasured "latent" variable. In this example, the researcher has specified paths from the three motivational factors to intensity. Further, each of the motivational factors and intensity (shown in ovals) are actually latent variables that are seen as the underlying causes of several measured variables (shown here as boxes—if there were not a shortage of space, each of these boxes would have a name for the specific questionnaire items it stands for).

A key statistical aspect of structural equation modeling involves using the correlations among variables to compute a "path coefficient" for each arrow. This tells the degree to which changes on the variable at the tail of the arrow are associated with changes in the variable at the head of the arrow (under conditions in which all other causes for that effect variable are held constant). That is, the path coefficient is a standardized regression coefficient (a "beta") for the causal variable in a prediction model in which the effect variable is the criterion variable and all of the causal variables are predictor variables. For example, the path of .32 from desirability to intensity means that holding constant probability and desires state, for each standard deviation of change in desirability, there would be .32 of a standard deviation of change in intensity.

7. (a) Causal modeling (path analysis or latent variable modeling)
   (c) Reliability statistics, such as Cronbach's alpha and test-retest reliability
   (i) Hierarchical multiple regression

Glossary

Numbers in parentheses refer to chapters in which the term is introduced or substantially discussed.

Adjusting for. In multiple regression, partial correlation, or analysis of covariance, removing the influence of a variable from the association among other variables; same as *partialing out, controlling for,* and *holding constant.* (12)

Alpha (α). Short for *Cronbach's alpha.* Also, probability of a Type I error; same as *significance level* (CS). (12)

Analysis of covariance (ANCOVA). Analysis of variance that controls for the effect of one or more unwanted additional variables. (12)

Analysis of variance (ANOVA). Hypothesis-testing procedure for studies with two or more groups. (10)

Assumption. A condition, such as a population's having a normal distribution, required for carrying out a particular hypothesis-testing procedure; a part of the mathematical foundation for the accuracy of the tables used in determining cutoff values. (8–11)

Beta (β). Standardized regression coefficient. (3, 12)

Between-group degrees of freedom (df_{Between}). Same as *numerator degrees of freedom.* (10)

Between-group estimate of the population variance (S^2_{Between}). In an analysis of variance, the estimate of the variance of the population distribution of individuals based on the variation among the means of the groups studied. (10)

Biased estimate. Estimate of a population parameter that is likely systematically to overestimate or underestimate the true population value. For example, SD^2 would be a biased estimate of the population variance (it would systematically underestimate it). (8)

Bimodal distribution. Frequency distribution with two approximately equal frequencies, each clearly larger than any of the others. (1)

Categorical variable. Same as *nominal variable.* (1, 11)

Causal analysis. Procedure, such as path analysis or structural equation modeling, that analyzes correlations among a group of variables in terms of a predicted pattern of causal relations among them. (12)

Ceiling effect. Situation in which many scores pile up at the high end (creating skewness) because it is not possible to have a higher score. (1, 11)

Cell. In a factorial design, a particular combination of levels of the independent variables; also, in chi-square, the particular combination of categories for two variables in a contingency table. (10, 11)

Cell mean. Mean of a particular combination of levels of the independent variables in a factorial design. (10)

Central limit theorem. Mathematical principle that the distribution of the sums (or means) of scores taken at random from any distribution of individuals will tend to form a normal curve. (4,6)

Central tendency. Typical or most representative value of a group of scores. (2)

Change score. After score minus before score. A kind of *difference score.* (8)

Chi-square distribution. Mathematically defined curve used as the comparison distribution in chi-square tests; the distribution of the chi-square statistic. (11)

Chi-square statistic (χ^2). Statistic that reflects the overall lack of fit between the expected and observed frequencies; the sum, over all the categories or cells, of the squared difference between observed and expected frequencies divided by the expected frequency. (11)

Chi-square table. Table of cutoff scores on the chi-square distribution for various degrees of freedom and significance levels. (11)

Chi-square test. Hypothesis testing procedure that uses the chi-square distribution as the comparison distribution. (11)

Chi-square test for goodness of fit. Hypothesis-testing procedure that examines how well an observed frequency distribution of a nominal variable fits some expected pattern of frequencies. (11)

Chi-square test for independence. Hypothesis-testing procedure that examines whether the distribution of frequencies over the categories of one nominal variable are unrelated to the distribution of frequencies over the categories of another nominal variable. (11)

Comparison distribution. Distribution used in hypothesis testing. It represents the population situation if the null hypothesis is true. It is the distribution to which you compare the score based on your sample results and is made up of the same kinds of numbers as those of the sample's results (such as a sample mean, a difference between sample means, F ratio, or chi square). (5)

Computational formula. Equation mathematically equivalent to the definitional formula that is easier to use for hand computation but does not directly show the meaning of the procedure. (2)

Confidence interval. Roughly speaking, the region of scores (that is, the scores between an upper and lower value) that is likely to include the true population mean; more precisely, the region of possible population means for which it is not highly unlikely that one could have obtained one's sample. (6)

Confidence limit. Upper or lower value of a confidence interval. (6)

Contingency table. Two-dimensional chart showing frequencies in each combination of categories of two nominal variables. (11)

Controlling for. In multiple regression, partial correlation, or analysis of covariance, removing the influence of a variable from the association among other variables; same as *partialing out*, *holding constant*, and *adjusting for*. (12)

Conventional levels of significance ($p < .05, p < .01$). The levels of significance widely used in the social and behavioral sciences. (5, 7)

Correlation. Association between scores on two or more variables. (3)

Correlation coefficient (r). Measure of the degree of linear correlation ranging from -1 (a perfect negative linear correlation) through 0 (no correlation) to $+1$ (a perfect positive linear correlation); average of the cross-products of Z scores of two variables; square root of the proportion of variance accounted for. (3)

Correlation matrix. Common way of reporting the correlation coefficients among several variables in a research article; table in which the variables are named on the top and along the side and the correlations among them are all shown (only half of the resulting square, above or below the diagonal, is usually filled in, the other half being redundant). (3)

Covariate. A variable controlled for in an analysis of covariance. (12)

Cramer's phi. Measure of association between two nominal variables; effect-size measure for a chi-square test of independence with a contingency table that is larger than 2×2; square root of result of dividing chi-square by number of participants times the degrees of freedom of the smaller side of the contingency table; also known as *Cramer's V* and sometimes written as Φ_C or V_c. (11)

Criterion variable (usually Y). In regression, variable that is predicted about. (3)

Cronbach's alpha (α). Widely used measure of a test's reliability that reflects the average of the split-half correlations from all possible splits into halves of the items on the test. (12)

Cross-product of Z scores. The result of multiplying a person's Z score on one variable times the person's Z score on another variable; for a group of individuals, the average of the cross-products of Z scores between two variables is the correlation coefficient for those two variables. (3)

Curvilinear correlation. Relation between two variables that shows up on a scatter diagram as dots following a systematic pattern that is not a straight line; any association between two variables other than a linear correlation. (3)

Cutoff sample score. Point on the comparison distribution in hypothesis testing at which, if reached or exceeded by the sample score, the null hypothesis will be rejected. (5)

Data transformation. Mathematical procedure (such as taking the square root) applied to each score in a sample, usually done to make the sample distribution closer to normal. (11)

Decision error. Incorrect conclusion in hypothesis testing in relation to the real (but unknown) situation, such as deciding the null hypothesis is false when it is really true. (7)

Definitional formula. Equation for a statistical procedure directly showing the meaning of the procedure. (2)

Degrees of freedom (df). Number of scores free to vary when estimating a population parameter; usually part of a formula for making that estimate—for example, in the formula for estimating the population variance from a single sample, the degrees of freedom is the number of scores minus 1. (8–11)

Denominator degrees of freedom (df_{Within}). Degrees of freedom used in the within-group estimate of the population variance in an analysis of variance; denominator of the F ratio; number of scores free to vary (number of scores in each group minus 1, summed over all the groups) in figuring the within-group population variance estimate; *within-group degrees of freedom*. (10)

Dependent variable. Variable considered to be an effect; usually a measured variable. (12)

Descriptive statistics. Procedures for summarizing a group of scores or otherwise making them more comprehensible. (1)

Deviation score. Score minus the mean. (2)

Difference score. Difference between a person's score on one testing and the same person's score on another testing; often an after score minus a before score, in which case it is also called a *change score*. (8)

Dimension. In a factorial design, an independent variables that is crossed with another independent variable; in a contingency table, one of the nominal variables. (10, 11)

Direction of causality. Path of causal effect; if *X* is thought to cause *Y*, then the direction of causality is from *X* to *Y*. (3)

Directional hypothesis. Research hypothesis predicting a particular direction of difference between populations—for example, a prediction that one population has a higher mean than the other). (5)

Distribution-free test. Hypothesis-testing procedure making no assumptions about the shape of the populations; approximately the same as a *nonparametric test*. (11)

Distribution of differences between means. Distribution of differences between means of pairs of samples such that for each pair of means, one is from one population and the other is from a second population; the comparison distribution in a *t* test for independent means. (9)

Distribution of means. Distribution of means of samples of a given size from a particular population (also called a sampling distribution of the mean); comparison distribution when testing hypotheses involving a single sample of more than one individual. (6–10)

Effect size. Standardized measure of difference between groups; separation (lack of overlap) between populations. Effect size increases with greater differences between means and decreases with greater standard deviations in the populations, but it is not affected by sample size. (7)

Effect size conventions. Standard rules about what to consider a small, medium, and large effect size, based on what is typical in social and behavioral science research; also known as *Cohen's conventions*. (7)

Effect size for the analysis of variance. Standard deviation of the means of the groups divided by the standard deviation of the individual scores. (10)

Expected frequency (E). In a chi-square test, number of people in a category or cell expected if the null hypothesis were true. (11)

Expected relative frequency. Number of successful outcomes divided by the number of total outcomes you would expect to get if you repeated an experiment a large number of times. (4)

Factor. In factor analysis, a group of variables that correlate maximally with each other and minimally with variables not in the group. (12)

Factor analysis. Statistical procedure applied in situations where many variables are measured and that identifies groups of variables correlating maximally with each other and minimally with other variables. (12)

Factor loading. In factor analysis, correlation of a variable with a factor. (12)

Factorial analysis of variance. Analysis of variance for a factorial research design; analysis of variance for the differences among the means over the levels of each variable and for the interaction of the variables. (10)

Factorial research design. Way of organizing a study in which the influence of two or more variables is studied at once by setting up the situation so that a group of people are tested for every combination of the levels of the variables; for example, in a 2×2 factorial research design there would be four groups, those high on variable 1 and high on variable 2, those high on variable 1 but low on variable 2, those high on variable 2 but low on variable 1, and those low on variable 1 and low on variable 2. (10)

F distribution. Mathematically defined curve that is the comparison distribution used in an analysis of variance; distribution of *F* ratios when the null hypothesis is true. (10)

F ratio. In analysis of variance, ratio of the between-group estimate of the population variance to the within-group estimate of the population variance; score on the comparison distribution (an *F* distribution) in an analysis of variance; also referred to simply as *F*. (10)

F table. Table of cutoff scores on the *F* distribution for various degrees of freedom and significance levels. (10)

Fit index. In structural equation modeling, measure of how well the pattern of correlations in a sample correspond to the correlations that would be expected based on the hypothesized pattern of causes and effects among those variables; usually ranges from 0 to 1, with 1 being a perfect fit. (12)

Floor effect. Situation in which many scores pile up at the low end of a distribution (creating skewness) because it is not possible to have any lower score. (1)

Frequency distribution. Pattern of frequencies over the various values; what a frequency table, histogram, or frequency polygon describes. (1)

Frequency polygon. Line graph of a distribution in which the values are plotted along the horizontal axis and the height of each point is the frequency of that value; the line begins and ends at the horizontal axis, and the graph resembles a mountainous skyline. (1)

Frequency table. Listing of the number of individuals having each of the different values for a particular variable. (1)

Grand mean (GM). In analysis of variance, overall mean of all the scores, regardless of what group they are in; when groups are of equal size, mean of the group means. (10)

Grouped frequency table. Frequency table in which the number of individuals is given for each interval of values. (1)

Haphazard selection. Procedure of selecting a sample of individuals to study by taking whoever is available or happens to be first on a list; should not be confused with true random selection. (4)

Harmonic mean. Special average influenced more by smaller numbers; in a *t* test for independent means when the number of scores in the two groups differ, the harmonic mean is used as the equivalent of each group's sample size when computing power. (9)

Heavy-tailed distribution. Distribution that differs from a normal curve by being too spread out so that a histogram of the distribution would have too many cases at each of the two extremes ("tails"). (1)

Hierarchical multiple regression. Method of multiple regression in which predictor variables are added, one or a few at a time, in a planned sequential fashion, allowing you to figure the contribution to the prediction of each successive variable over and above those already included. (12)

Histogram. Barlike graph of a frequency distribution in which the values are plotted along the horizontal axis and the height of each bar is the frequency of that value; the bars are usually placed next to each other without spaces, giving the appearance of a city skyline. (1)

Holding constant. In multiple regression, partial correlation, or analysis of covariance, removing the influence of a variable from the association among the other variables; same as *partialing out*, *controlling for*, and *adjusting for*. (12)

Hypothesis testing. Procedure for deciding whether the outcome of a study (results for a sample) support a particular theory or practical innovation (which is thought to apply to a population). (5)

Independence. Situation of no relationship between two variables; term usually used regarding two nominal variables in the chi-square test for independence. (11)

Independent variable (usually X). Variable considered to be a cause, such as what group a person is in in a t test or analysis of variance. (12)

Inferential statistics. Procedures for drawing conclusions based on the scores collected in a research study (sample scores) but going beyond them (to conclusions about a population). (1, 4)

Interaction effect. Situation in the factorial analysis of variance in which the combination of variables has an effect that could not be predicted from the effects of the two variables individually. (10)

Interval. In a grouped frequency table, range of values that are grouped together. (For example, if the interval size was 10, one of the intervals might be from 10.00 to 19.99.) (1)

Interval estimate. Region of scores (that is, the scores between some specified lower and upper value) estimated to include a population parameter such as the population mean; this is in contrast to a *point estimate;* a *confidence interval* is an example of an interval estimate. (6)

Interval size. In a grouped frequency table, difference between the start of one interval and the start of the next. (1)

Inverse transformation. Data transformation using the inverse (1 divided by the number) of each score. (11)

Latent variable. In structural equation modeling, unmeasured variable assumed to be the underlying cause of several variables actually measured in the study. (12)

Level of significance. Probability of getting statistical significance if the null hypothesis is actually true; the probability of a Type I error. (5–7)

Light-tailed distribution. Distribution that differs from a normal curve by being too peaked or pinched so that a histogram of the distribution would have too few cases at each of the two extremes ("tails"). (1)

Linear correlation. Relation between two variables that shows up on a scatter diagram as the dots roughly following a straight line; a correlation of r unequal to 0. (3)

Log transformation. Data transformation using the logarithm of each score. (11)

Long-run relative-frequency interpretation of probability. Understanding of probability as the proportion of a particular outcome that you would get if the experiment were repeated many times. (4)

Main effect. Difference between groups on one variable in a factorial design; result for a variable, averaging across the other variable (sometimes used only for significant differences). (10)

Marginal frequency. In chi-square, frequency (number of people) in a row or column of a contingency table. (11)

Marginal mean. In a factorial design, mean score for all the participants at a particular level of one of the variables; often shortened to *marginal*. (10)

Mean (M). Arithmetic average of a group of scores; sum of the scores divided by the number of scores; also symbolized as $\overline{X}$. (2)

Median. Middle score when all the scores in a distributions are arranged from highest to lowest. (2)

Meta-analysis. Statistical method for combining effect sizes from different studies. (7)

Mode. Value with the greatest frequency in a distribution. (2)

Multimodal distribution. Frequency distribution with two or more high frequencies separated by a lower frequency; a bimodal distribution is the special case of two high frequencies. (1)

Multiple comparisons. Hypothesis-testing procedures for testing the differences among particular means in the context of an overall analysis of variance. (10)

Multiple correlation. Correlation of a criterion variable with two or more predictor variables. (3)

Multiple correlation coefficient (R). Measure of degree of multiple correlation; positive square root of the proportion of variance accounted for in a multiple regression analysis. (3)

Multiple regression. Procedure for predicting scores on a criterion variable from scores on two or more predictor variables. (3, 12)

Multivariate analysis of covariance (MANCOVA). Analysis of covariance with more than one dependent variable. (12)

Multivariate analysis of variance (MANOVA). Analysis of variance with more than one dependent variable. (12)

Multivariate statistics. Statistical procedures allowing more than one dependent variable. (12)

Negative correlation. Relation between two variables in which high scores on one go with low scores on the other, mediums with mediums, and lows with highs; on a scatter diagram, the dots roughly follow a straight line sloping down and to the right; a correlation of r less than 0. (3)

95% confidence interval. Confidence interval in which, roughly speaking, there is a 95% chance that the population mean falls within this interval. (6)

99% confidence interval. Confidence interval in which, roughly speaking, there is a 99% chance that the population mean falls within this interval. (6)

No correlation. No systematic relation between two variables. (3)

Nominal variable. Variable with values that are categories (that is, they are names rather than numbers); same as *categorical variable*. (1, 11)

Nondirectional hypothesis. Research hypothesis that does not predict a particular direction of difference between populations. (5)

Nonparametric test. Hypothesis-testing procedure making no assumptions about population parameters; approximately the same as *distribution-free test*. (11)

Normal curve. Specific, mathematically defined, bell-shaped frequency distribution that is symmetrical and unimodal; distributions observed in nature and in research commonly approximate it. (1, 4)

Normal curve table. Table of percentages of scores in a normally distributed distribution between the mean and various numbers of standard deviations above the mean. (4)

Normal distribution. Frequency distribution following a normal curve. (4)

Null hypothesis. Statement about a relation between populations that is the opposite of the research hypothesis; a statement that in the population there is no difference (or a difference opposite to that predicted) between populations; a contrived statement set up to examine whether it can be rejected as part of hypothesis testing. (5)

Numerator degrees of freedom ($df_{Between}$). Degrees of freedom used in the between-group estimate of the population variance in an analysis of variance (the numerator of the F ratio); number of scores free to vary (number of means minus 1) in figuring the between-group estimate of the population variance; between-group degrees of freedom. (10)

Numeric variable. Variable whose values are numbers (as opposed to a nominal variable). (1)

Observed frequency (O). In a chi-square test, number of individuals actually found in the study to be in a category or cell. (11)

One-tailed test. Hypothesis-testing procedure for a directional hypothesis; situation in which the region of the comparison distribution in which the null hypothesis would be rejected is all on one side (tail) of the distribution. (5)

One-way analysis of variance. Analysis of variance in which there is only one independent variable (as distinguished from a factorial analysis of variance). (10)

Ordinal variable. Same as *rank-order variable*. (1, 11)

Outcome. Term used in discussing probability for the result of an experiment (or almost any event, such as a coin coming up heads or it raining tomorrow). (4)

Outlier. Score with an extreme (very high or very low) value in relation to the other scores in the distribution. (1, 11)

Parametric test. Ordinary hypothesis-testing procedure, such as a t test or an analysis of variance, that requires assumptions about the shape or other parameter (such as the variance) of the populations. (11)

Partial correlation coefficient. Measure of degree of correlation between two variables, over and above the influence of one or more other variables. (12)

Partialing out. In multiple regression, partial correlation, or analysis of covariance, removing the influence of a variable from the association among the other variables; same as *holding constant*, *controlling for*, and *adjusting for*. (12)

Path analysis. Method of analyzing the correlations among a group of variables in terms of a predicted pattern of causal relations; usually the predicted pattern is diagrammed as a pattern of arrows from causes to effects. (12)

Path coefficient. Degree of relation associated with an arrow in a path analysis (including structural equation modeling); same as a regression coefficient from a multiple regression prediction rule in which the variable at the end of the arrow is the criterion variable and the variable at the start of the arrow is the predictor, along with all the other variables that have arrows leading to that criterion variable. (12)

Perfect correlation. Relation between two variables that shows up on a scatter diagram as the dots exactly following a straight line; correlation of $r = 1$ or $r = -1$; situation in which each person's Z score on one variable is exactly the same as that person's Z score on the other variable. (3)

Phi coefficient (Φ). Measure of association between two dichotomous nominal variables; square root of division of chi-square statistic by N; equivalent to correlation of the two variables if they were each given numerical values (for example, of 1 and 0 for the two categories); effect-size measure for a chi-square test of independence with a 2×2 contingency table. (11)

Point estimate. Estimate from a sample of the most likely single value of a population parameter. (6)

Pooled estimate of the population variance (S^2_{Pooled}). In a t test for independent means, weighted average of the estimates of the population variance from two samples (each estimate weighted by the proportion of the degrees of freedom for its sample divided by the total degrees of freedom for both samples). (9)

Population. Entire group of people to which a researcher intends the results of a study to apply; the larger group to which inferences are made on the basis of the particular set of people studied. (4)

Population mean. Mean of the population (usually not known). (4)

Population parameter. Actual value of the mean, standard deviation, and so on, for the population (usually population parameters are not known, though sometimes they are estimated). (4)

Population standard deviation. Standard deviation of the population (usually not known). (4)

Population variance. Variance of the population (usually not known). (4)

Positive correlation. Relation between two variables in which high scores on one go with high scores on the other, mediums with mediums, and lows with lows; on a scatter diagram, the dots roughly follow a straight line sloping up and to the right; a correlation of r greater than 0. (3)

Power. Same as *statistical power*. (7)

Power table. Table for a hypothesis-testing procedure showing the statistical power of a study for various effect sizes and sample sizes. (7–11)

Prediction model. Formula for making predictions; that is, formula for predicting a person's score on a dependent variable based on the person's score on one or more independent variables. (3)

Predictor variable (usually X). In regression, variable that is used to predict scores of individuals on another variable. (3)

Probability (p). Expected relative frequency of a particular outcome; the proportion of successful outcomes to all outcomes. (4)

Proportion of variance accounted for (r^2 or R^2). Measure of association between variables used when comparing associations in different studies or with different variables; correlation squared or multiple correlation coefficient squared; variance of the predicted criterion variable scores (based on a regression formula) divided by the variance of the actual scores. (3, 12)

Protected t tests. In analysis of variance, t-tests among pairs of means after finding that the F for the overall difference among the means is significant. (10).

Quantitative variable. Same as *numeric variable*. (1)

Random selection. Method for selecting a sample that uses truly random procedures (usually meaning that each person in the population has an equal chance of being selected); one procedure is for the researcher to begin with a complete list of all the people in the population and select a group of them to study using a table of random numbers; should not be confused with haphazard selection. (4)

Rank-order test. Hypothesis-testing procedure that makes use of rank-ordered data. (11)

Rank-order transformation. Changing a set of scores to ranks, so that the highest score is rank 1, the next highest rank 2, and so forth. (11)

Rank-order variable. Numeric variable in which the values are ranks, such as class standing or place finished in a race; also called *ordinal variable*. (1, 11)

Raw score. Ordinary measurement (or any other number in a distribution before it has been made into a Z score or otherwise transformed). (2)

Raw-score prediction formula. Prediction model in regression using raw scores. (3)

Raw-score regression coefficient (b). Regression coefficient in a prediction model using raw scores. (3)

Rectangular distribution. Frequency distribution in which all values have approximately the same frequency. (1)

Regression coefficient (b, β). Number multiplied by a person's score on the predictor variable as part of a prediction model. (3)

Regression constant (a). In a prediction model using raw scores, particular fixed number added into the prediction. (3)

Regression line. Line on a graph such as a scatter diagram showing the predicted value of the criterion variable for each value of the predictor variable. (3)

Reliability. Degree of consistency of a measure; the extent to which, if you were to give the same measure again to the same person under the same circumstances, you would obtain the same result. (12)

Repeated-measures analysis of variance. Analysis of variance in which each individual is measured more than once so that the levels of the independent variable(s) are different times or types of testing for the same people. (10)

Repeated-measures design. Research strategy in which each person is tested more than once; same as *within-subject design*. (8, 10)

Research hypothesis. In hypothesis testing, statement about the predicted relation between populations (usually a prediction of difference between population means). (5)

Sample. Scores of the particular group of people studied; usually considered to be representative of the scores in some larger population. (4)

Sample statistic. Descriptive statistic, such as the mean or standard deviation, figured from the scores in a particular group of people studied. (4)

Scatter diagram. Graph showing the relationship between two variables: the values of one variable (often the predictor variable) are along the horizontal axis; the values of the other variable (often the criterion variable) are along the vertical axis, with each score shown as a dot in this two-dimensional space; also called *scatter plot*. (3)

Scatter plot. Same as *scatter diagram*. (3)

Score. Particular person's value on a variable. (1)

Shape of a distribution of means. Contour of a histogram of a distribution of means, such as whether it follows a normal curve or is skewed; in general, a distribution of means will tend to be unimodal and symmetrical and is often normal. (6)

Skewed distribution. Distribution in which the scores pile up on one side of the mean and are spread out on the other side; distribution that is not symmetrical. (1, 11)

Skewness. Extent to which a frequency distribution has more scores on one side of the middle as opposed to being perfectly symmetrical. (1)

Slope. Steepness of the angle of a line on a two-variable graph, such as a regression; number of units the line goes up for every unit it goes across (in raw score regression, slope $= b$). (4)

Split-half reliability. One index of a measure's reliability, based on a correlation of the scores from items from two halves of the test. (12)

Square-root transformation. Data transformation using the square root of each score. (11)

Squared deviation score. Square of the difference between the score and the mean. (2)

Standard deviation (SD). Square root of the average of the squared deviations from the mean; the most common descriptive statistic for variation; approximately the average amount that scores in a distribution vary from the mean. (2)

Standard deviation of a distribution of means (Population SD_M, S_M). Square root of the variance of the distribution of means; same as *standard error (SE)*. (6)

Standard deviation of a distribution of differences between means ($S_{Difference}$). In a *t* test for independent means, square root of the variance of the distribution of differences between means. (9)

Standard error (SE). Same as *standard deviation of the distribution of means;* also called *standard error of the mean*. (6)

Standard score. Z score in a distribution that follows a normal curve; sometimes refers to any Z score. (2)

Standardized regression coefficient (beta, β). Regression coefficient in a prediction model using Z scores; also called a *beta weight*. (3)

Statistical power. Probability that the study will give a significant result if the research hypothesis is true. (7)

Statistically significant. Conclusion that the results of a study would be unlikely if in fact there were no difference in the populations the samples studied represent; an outcome of hypothesis testing in which the null hypothesis is rejected. (3, 5)

Stepwise multiple regression. Exploratory procedure in which all the potential predictor variables that have been measured are tried in order to find the predictor variable that produces the best prediction; then each of the remaining variables is tried to find the predictor variable which in combination with the first produces the best prediction; this process continues until adding the best remaining variable does not provide a significant improvement. (12)

Structural equation modeling. Sophisticated version of path analysis that includes paths with latent, unmeasured, theoretical variables and that also permits a kind of significance test and provides measures of the overall fit of the data to the hypothesized causal pattern. (12)

Sum of squared deviations. Total over all the scores of each score's squared difference from the mean. (2)

Symmetrical distribution. Distribution in which the pattern of frequencies on the left and right side are mirror images of each other. (1)

t distribution. Mathematically defined curve that is the comparison distribution used in a *t* test. (8)

t score. On a *t* distribution, number of standard deviations from the mean (like a Z score, but on a *t* distribution.) (8)

t table. Table of cutoff scores on the *t* distribution for various degrees of freedom, significance levels, and one- and two-tailed tests. (8)

t test. Hypothesis-testing procedure in which the population variance is unknown; it compares *t* scores from a sample to a comparison distribution called a *t* distribution. (8, 9, 11)

t test for a single sample. Hypothesis-testing procedure in which a sample mean is being compared to a known population mean and the population variance is unknown. (8)

t test for dependent means. Hypothesis-testing procedure in which there are two scores for each person and the population variance is not known; it determines the significance of a hypothesis that is being tested using difference or change scores from a single group of people. (8)

t test for independent means. Hypothesis-testing procedure in which there are two separate groups of people tested and in which the population variance is not known. (9)

Test-retest reliability. One index of a measure's reliability, obtained by giving the test to a group of people twice; the correlation between scores from the two testings. (12)

Two-tailed test. Hypothesis-testing procedure for a nondirectional hypothesis; the situation in which the region of the comparison distribution in which the null hypothesis would be rejected is divided between the two sides (tails) of the distribution. (5)

Two-way analysis of variance. Analysis of variance for a two-way factorial research design. (10)

Two-way factorial research design. Factorial design with two independent variables. (10)

Type I error. Rejecting the null hypothesis when in fact it is true; getting a statistically significant result when in fact the research hypothesis is not true. (7)

Type II error. Failing to reject the null hypothesis when in fact it is false; failing to get a statistically significant result when in fact the research hypothesis is true. (7)

Unbiased estimate of the population variance (S^2). Estimate of the population variance, based on sample scores, which has been corrected (by dividing the sum of squared deviations by the sample size minus 1 instead of the usual procedure of dividing by the sample size directly) so that it is equally likely to over-or underestimate the true population variance. (2, 8)

Unimodal distribution. Frequency distribution with one value clearly having a larger frequency than any other. (1)

Value. Number or category that a score can have. (1)

Variable. Characteristic that can have different values. (1)

Variance (SD^2). Measure of how spread out a set of scores are; average of the squared deviations from the mean; standard deviation squared. (2)

Variance of a distribution of differences between means ($S^2_{Difference}$). One of the numbers figured as part of a *t* test for independent means; it equals the sum of the variances of the distributions of means for each of the two samples. (9)

Variance of a distribution of means (Population SD^2_M, S^2_M). Variance of the population divided by the number of scores in each sample. (6)

Weighted average. Average in which the scores being averaged do not have equal influence on the total, as in figuring the pooled variance estimate in a *t* test for independent means. (9)

Within-group degrees of freedom (df_{Within}). Same as *denominator degrees of freedom*. (10)

Within-group estimate of the population variance (S^2_{Within}). In analysis of variance, variance of the distribution of the population of individuals based on the variation among the scores within each of the actual groups studied. (10)

Within-subject design. Same as *repeated-measures design.* (8)

Z score. Number of standard deviations a score is above (or below, if it is negative) the mean in its distribution; ordinary score transformed so that it better describes that score's location in a distribution. (2)

Z test. Hypothesis-testing procedure in which there is a single sample and the population variance is known. (6)

Glossary of Symbols

α Significance level; probability of a Type I error (S, T). Also Cronbach's alpha, a measure of reliability. (12)

β Standardized regression coefficient. (3, 12)

Σ Sum of; add up all the scores following. (2)

Φ Phi coefficient; effect size in a chi-square test for independence with a 2×2 contingency table. (11)

Φ_C Cramer's phi, effect size in chi-square test for independence with a contingency table larger than 2×2. (11)

χ^2 Chi-square statistic. (11)

a Regression constant. (3)

b Raw score regression coefficient. (3)

df Degrees of freedom. (8–11).

df_1, df_2, and so on. Degrees of freedom for the first group, second group, and so on. (9, 10)

df_{Between} Numerator degrees of freedom in analysis of variance. (10)

df_{Smaller} Degrees of freedom for the nominal variable (the row or column in the contingency table) with the smaller number of categories in a chi-square test of independence. (11)

df_{Total} Total degrees of freedom over all groups. (9, 10)

df_{Within} Denominator degrees of freedom in analysis of variance. (10)

F Ratio of the between-group estimate of the population variance to the within-group estimate of the population variance in analysis of variance. (10)

GM Grand mean; in analysis of variance, mean of all scores regardless of what group they are in. (10)

M Mean. (2)

M_1, M_2, and so on. Mean of the first group, second group, and so on. (9, 10)

n In analysis of variance, number of scores within each group. (10)

N Number of scores. (2)

N_1, N_2, and so on. Number of scores in the first group, second group, and so on. (9, 10)

N_{Columns} Number of columns in a contingency table. (11)

N_{Groups} Number of groups in an analysis of variance (11)

N_{Rows} Number of rows in a contingency table. (11)

p Probability. (4)

r Correlation coefficient. (3)

r^2 Proportion of variance accounted for. (3)

R Multiple correlation coefficient. (3, 12)

R^2 Proportion of variance accounted for in multiple regression. (3, 12)

S Unbiased estimate of the population standard deviation. (2, 8)

S^2 Unbiased estimate of the population variance. (2, 8)

S_1^2, S_2^2, and so on. Unbiased estimate of the population variance based on scores in the first sample, second sample, and so on. (9, 10)

S^2_{Between} Between-group estimate of the population variance. (10)

$S_{\text{Difference}}$ Standard deviation of the distribution of differences between means. (9)

$S^2_{\text{Difference}}$ Variance of the distribution of differences between means. (9)

SE Standard error (standard deviation of the distribution of means). (6)

S_M Standard deviation of the distribution of means based on an estimated population variance. (8)

S^2_M Variance of a distribution of means based on an estimated population variance; variance of a distribution of means estimated from the variation among means of groups in analysis of variance. (8, 10)

$S^2_{M_1}$ and $S^2_{M_2}$ Variance of the distribution of means based on a population variance estimated from data in the first sample and in the second sample. (9)

S_{Pooled} Pooled estimate of the population standard deviation. (9)

S^2_{Pooled} Pooled estimate of the population variance. (9)

S^2_{Within} Within-group estimate of the population variance. (10)

SD Standard deviation. (2)

SD^2 Variance. (2)

t score Number of standard deviations from the mean on a t distribution. (8)

X Score on a particular variable; in regression X is usually the predictor variable. (1–3)

X_1, X_2, and so on. First predictor variable, second predictor variable, and so on. (3)

$\bar{X}$ Mean of variable designated X. (2)

Y Score on a particular variable, usually the criterion variable in regression. (3)

$\hat{Y}$ Predicted value of the criterion variable. (3)

Z Number of standard deviations from the mean. (2)

Z_X, Z_Y, and so on. Z score for variable X, for variable Y, and so on. (3)

$\hat{Z}_Y$ Predicted value of the standardized criterion variable.

References

ALTMAN, D. G., LEVINE, D. W., HOWARD, G., & HAMILTON, H. (1997). Tobacco farming and public health: Attitudes of the general public and farmers. *Journal of Social Issues, 53,* 113–128.

ANDERSON, J. E., CAREY, J. W., & TAVERAS, S. (2000). HIV testing among the general US population at increased risk: Information from national surveys, 1987–1996. *American Journal of Public Health, 90,* 1089–1095.

ARON, A., & ARON, E. (1994, 1999). *Statistics for Psychology (1st and 2nd editions).* Upper Saddle River, NJ: Prentice-Hall.

ARON, A., ARON, E. N., & ALLEN, J. (1998). Motivations for unreciprocated love. *Personality and Social Psychology Bulletin, 24,* 787–796.

ARON, A., ARON, E. N., & NORMAN, C. C. (2001). Self-expansion model of motivation and cognition in close relationships and beyond. In M. Clark & G. Gletcher (Eds.), *Blackwell's Handbook of Social Psychology: Vol. 2. Interpersonal Processes.* Oxford: Blackwell Publishers.

ARON, A., ARON, E. N., & SMOLLAN, D. (1992). Inclusion of Other in the Self Scale and the structure of interpersonal closeness. *Journal of Personality and Social Psychology, 63,* 596–612.

ARON, A., NORMAN, C. C., ARON, E. N., MCKENNA, C., HEYMAN, R. E. (2000). Couples' shared participation in novel and arousing activities and experienced relationship quality. *Journal of Personality and Social Psychology, 78,* 273–284.

ARON, A., PARIS, M., & ARON, E. N. (1995). Falling in love: Prospective studies of self-concept change. *Journal of Personality and Social Psychology, 69,* 1102–1112.

ARON, E. N. (1996). *The highly sensitive person.* New York: Carol/Birch-Lane Press.

ARON, E. N., & ARON, A. (1997). Sensory processing sensitivity and its relation to introversion and emotionality. *Journal of Personality and Social Psychology, 73,* 345–368.

BINER, P. M. (1991). Effects of lighting-induced arousal on the magnitude of goal valence. *Personality and Social Psychology Bulletin, 17,* 219–226.

BLOCK, N. (1995). How heritability misleads about race. *Cognition, 56,* 99–128.

CAPALDI, D. M., & PATTERSON, G. R. (1991). Relation of parental transitions to boys' adjustment problems: 1. A linear hypothesis 2. Mothers at risk for transitions and unskilled parenting. *Developmental Psychology, 27,* 489–504.

CARLIN, M. F., & SANIGA, R. D. (1990). Relationship between academic placement and perception of abuse of the voice. *Perceptual and Motor Skills, 71,* 299–304.

COHEN, J. (1988). *Statistical power analysis for the behavioral sciences.* Hillsdale, NJ: Erlbaum.

CONOVER, W., & IMAN, R. L. (1981). Rank transformations as a bridge between parametric and nonparametric statistics. *American Statistician, 35,* 124–129.

COOPER, S. E., & ROBINSON, D. A. G. (1989). The influence of gender and anxiety on mathematics performance. *Journal of College Student Development, 30,* 459–461.

DANE, F. C., & WRIGHTSMAN, L. S. (1982). Effects of defendants' and victims' characteristics on jurors' verdicts. In N. L. Kerr & R. M. Bray (Eds.), *The psychology of the courtroom.* Orlando, FL: Academic Press.

DeGarmo, D. S., & Forgatch, M. S. (1997). Determinants of observed confidant support for divorced mothers. *Journal of Personality and Social Psychology, 72,* 336–345.

Dennenberg, V. H. (1999). A critique of Mody, Studdert-Kennedy, and Brady's "Speech perception deficits in poor readers: Auditory processing or phonological coding?". *Journal of Learning Disabilities, 32,* 379–383.

Drake, C. C. & Michael, W. B. (1995). Criterion-related validity of selected achievement measures in the prediction of a passing or failing criterion on the National Council Licensure Examination (NCLEX) for nursing students in a two-year associate degree program. *Educational and Psychological Measurement, 55,* 675–683.

Dwinell, P. E., & Higbee, J. L. (1991). Affective variables related to mathematics achievement among high-risk college freshmen. *Psychological Reports, 69,* 399–403.

Eppley, K. R., Abrams, A. I., & Shear, J. (1989). Differential effects of relaxation techniques on trait anxiety: A meta-analysis. *Journal of Clinical Psychology, 45,* 957–974.

Evans, R. (1976). *The making of psychology.* New York: Knopf.

Eysenck, H. J. (1981). *A model for personality.* Berlin: Springer-Verlag.

Fiske, S. T. (1998). Stereotyping, prejudice, and discrimination. In D. T. Gilbert, S. T. Fiske, & G. Lindzey, (Eds.) *The handbook of social psychology* (4th ed.). New York: McGraw-Hill.

Ford, J. D., Fisher, P., & Larson, L. (1997). Object relations as a predictor of treatment outcome with chronic posttraumatic stress disorder. *Journal of Consulting and Clinical Psychology, 65,* 547–559.

Frick, R. W. (1995). Accepting the null hypothesis. *Memory and Cognition, 23,* 132–138.

Frisch, A. S., Shamsuddin, K., & Kurtz, M. (1995). Family factors and knowledge: Attitudes and efforts concerning exposure to environmental tobacco among Malaysian medical students. *Journal of Asian and African Studies, 30,* 68–79.

Gable, S., & Lutz, S. (2000). Household, parent, and child contributions to childhood obesity. *Family Relations, 49,* 293–300.

Gallup, D. G. H. (1972). *The Gallup poll: Public opinion, 1935–1971.* New York: Random House.

Gire, J. T. (1997). The varying effect of individualism-collectivism on preference for methods of conflict resolution. *Canadian Journal of Behavioural Science, 29,* 38–43.

Goidel, H. K., & Langley, R. E. (1995). Media coverage of the economy and aggregate economic evaluations: Uncovering evidence of indirect media effects. *Political Research Quarterly, 48,* 313–328.

Greenwald, A. G. (1975). Consequences of prejudice against the null hypothesis. *Psychological Bulletin, 82,* 1–19.

Gunn, B., Biglan, A., Smolkowski, K, & Ary, D. (2000). The efficacy of supplemental instruction in decoding skills for Hispanic and non-Hispanic students in early elementary school. *Journal of Special Education, 34,* 90–103.

Harter, S., Waters, P. L., Pettitt, L. M., Whitesell, N., Kofkin, J., & Jordan, J. (1997). Autonomy and connectedness as dimensions of relationship styles in men and women. *Journal of Social and Personal Relationships, 14,* 147–164.

Hazan, C., & Shaver, P. (1987). Romantic love conceptualized as an attachment process. *Journal of Personality and Social Psychology, 52,* 511–524.

Hendrick, C., & Hendrick, S. S. (1989). Research on love: Does it measure up? *Journal of Personality and Social Psychology, 56,* 784–794.

Hindley, C., Filliozat, A., Klackenberg, G., Nicolet-Meister, D., & Sand, E. (1966). Differences in age of walking in five European longitudinal samples. *Human Biology, 38,* 364–379.

Husserl, E. (1970). *The crisis of European sciences and transcendental phenomenology: An introduction to phenomenological philosophy* (D. C. Carr, Trans.). Evanston, IL: Northwestern University Press.

Jehn, K. A., & Shah, P. P. (1997). Interpersonal relationships and task performance: An examination of mediating processes in friendship and acquaintance groups. *Journal of Personality and Social Psychology, 72,* 775–790.

Johnson, M. A. (2000). Delegation and organizational structure in small business: Influences of manager's attachment patterns. *Group and Organizational Management, 25,* 4–21.

June, L. N., Curry, B. P., & Gear, C. L. (1990). An 11-year analysis of black students' experience of problems and use of services: Implications for counseling professionals. *Journal of Counseling Psychology, 37,* 178–184.

Kagan, J. (1994). *Galen's prophecy.* New York: Basic.

Kirby, R. R., & Das, J. P. (1990). A cognitive approach to intelligence: Attention, coding and planning. *Canadian Psychology, 31,* 320–333.

Kraemer, H. C., & Thiemann, S. (1987). *How many subjects? Statistical power analysis in research.* Newbury Park, CA: Sage.

Kwan, V. S. Y., Bond, M. H., & Singelis, T. M. (1997). Pancultural explanations for life satisfaction: Adding relationship harmony to self-esteem. *Journal of Personality and Social Psychology, 73,* 1038–1051.

Lambert, A. J., Khan, S. R., Lickel, B. A., & Fricke, K. (1997). Mood and the correction of positive versus negative stereotypes. *Journal of Personality and Social Psychology, 72,* 1002–1016.

Lee, K., Byatt, G., & Rhodes, G. (2000). Caricature effects, distinctiveness, and identification: Testing the face-space framework. *Psychological Science, 11,* 379–385.

Lindzey, E. W., Mize, J., & Pettit, G. S. (1997). Mutuality in parent-child play: Consequences for children's peer competence. *Journal of Social and Personal Relationships, 14,* 523–538.

LYDON, J., PIERCE, T., & O'REGAN, S. (1997). Coping with moral commitment to long-distance dating relationships. *Journal of Personality and Social Psychology, 73,* 104–113.

MACDONALD, C., CHAMBERLAIN, K., & LONG, N. (1997). Race, combat, and PTSD in a community sample of New Zealand Vietnam War veterans. *Journal of Traumatic Stress, 10,* 117–124.

MACKINNON-LEWIS, C., STARNES, R., VOLLING, B., & JOHNSON, S. (1997). Perceptions of parenting as predictors of boys' sibling and peer relations. *Developmental Psychology, 33,* 1024–1031.

MARTINEZ, R. (2000). Immigration and urban violence: The link between immigrant Latinos and types of homicide. *Social Science Quarterly, 81,* 363–374.

MCCRACKEN, G. (1988). *The long interview.* London: Sage.

MCLAUGHLIN-VOLPE, T., ARON, A, & REIS, H. T. (2001, February). Closeness during interethnic social interactions and prejudice: A diary study. Paper presented at the Annual Meeting of the Society for Personality and Social Psychology, San Antonio, TX.

MCLEOD, D. M., EVELAND, W. P. & SIGNORELLI, N. (1994). Conflict and public opinion: Rallying effects of the Persian Gulf War. *Journalism Quarterly, 71,* 20–31.

MICKELSON, K. D., KESSLER, R. C., & SHAVER, P. R. (1997). Adult attachment in a nationally representative sample. *Journal of Personality and Social Psychology, 73,* 1092–1106.

MIRVIS, P., & LAWLER, E. (1977). Measuring the financial impact of employee attitudes. *Journal of Applied Psychology, 62,* 1–8.

MOONEY, S. P., SHERMAN, M. F., & LO PRESTO, C. T. (1991). Academic locus of control, self-esteem, and perceived distance from home as predictors of college adjustment. *Journal of Counseling and Development, 69,* 445–448.

MOOREHOUSE, E., & TOBLER, N. S. (2000). Preventing and reducing substance use among institutionalized adolescents. *Adolescence, 35,* 1–28.

MOOREHOUSE, M. J., & SANDERS, P. E. (1992). Children's feelings of school competence and perceptions of parents' work in four sociocultural contexts. *Social Development, 1,* 185–200.

MORIARTY, S. E., & EVERETT, S-L. (1994). Commercial breaks: A viewing behavior study. *Journalism Quarterly, 71,* 346–355.

NORCROSS, J. C., HANYCH, J. M., & TERRANOVA, R. D. (1996). Graduate study in psychology: 1992–1993. *American Psychologist, 51,* 631–643

NOWNES, A. J. (2000). Policy conflict and the structure of interest communities: A comparative state analysis. *American Politics Quarterly, 28,* 309–327.

OLTHOFF, R. (1989). *The effectiveness of premarital communication training.* Doctoral Dissertation, California School of Family Psychology, San Rafael, CA.

PECUKONIS, E. V. (1990). A cognitive/affective empathy training program as a function of ego development in aggressive adolescent females. *Adolescence, 25,* 59–76.

PELLEGRINI, A. D., & BARTINI, M. (2000). An empirical comparison of methods of sampling aggression and victimization in school settings. *Journal of Educational Psychology, 92,* 360–366.

PETERS, W. S. (1987). *Counting for something: Statistical principles and personalities.* New York: Springer-Verlag.

PETTIGREW, T., & MEERTEN, R. W. (1995). *European Journal of Social Psychology, 25,* 57–75.

PURI, M. L., & SENN, P. K. (1985). *Nonparametric methods in general linear models.* New York: Wiley.

REBER, P. J., & KOTOVSKY, K. (1997). Implicit learning in problem solving: The role of working memory capacity. *Journal of Experimental Psychology: General, 126,* 178–203.

RIEHL, R. J. (1994). Academic preparation, aspirations, and first-year performance of first-generation students. *College and University, 70*(1), 14–19.

RUSBULT, C. E., VERETTE, J., WHITNEY, G. A., SLOVIK, L. F., & LIPKUS, I. (1991). Accommodation processes in close relationships: Theory and preliminary empirical evidence. *Journal of Personality and Social Psychology, 60,* 53–78.

SELLERS, R. M., ROWLEY, S. A. J., CHAVOUS, T. M., SHELTON, J. N., & SMITH, M. A. (1997). Multidimensional Inventory of Black Identity: A preliminary investigation of reliability and construct validity. *Journal of Personality and Social Psychology, 73,* 805–815.

SHELINE, Y. I., SANGHAVI, M., MINTUN, M. A., & GADO, M. H. (1999). Depression duration but not age predicts hippocampal volume loss in medically healthy women with recurrent major depression. *Journal of Neuroscience, 19,* 5034–5043.

SINCLAIR, L., & KUNDA, Z. (2000). Motivated stereotyping of women: She's fine if she praised me but incompetent if she criticized me. *Personality and Social Psychology Bulletin, 26,* 1329–1342.

SKINNER, B. F. (1956). A case history in scientific method. *American Psychologist, 11,* 221–233.

SPENCER, S. J., STEELE, C. M., & QUINN, D. M. (1999). Stereotype threat and women's math performance. *Journal of Experimental Social Psychology, 35,* 4–28.

STEELE, C. M. (1997). A threat in the air: How stereotypes shape intellectual identity and performance. *American Psychologist, 52,* 613–629.

STEEN, L. A. (1987). Foreword. In S. Tobias, *Succeed with math: Every student's guide to conquering math anxiety* (pp. xvii-xviii). New York: College Entrance Examination Board.

STIGLER, S. M. (1986). *The history of statistics.* Cambridge, MA: Belknap Press.

TABACHNICK, B. G., & FIDELL, L. S. (2001). *Using Multivariate Statistics* (4th ed.). New York: Harper Collins.

TANKARD, J., JR. (1984). *The statistical pioneers.* Cambridge, MA: Schenkman.

THOMAS, J. R., NELSON, J. K., & THOMAS, K. T. (1999). A generalized rank-order method for nonparametric analysis of data from exercise science: A tutorial. *Research Quarterly for Exercise and Sport, 70,* 11–27.

TOBIAS, S. (1982, January). Sexist equations. *Psychology Today,* pp. 14–17.

TOBIAS, S. (1987). *Succeed with math: Every student's guide to conquering math anxiety.* New York: College Entrance Examination Board.

U.S. DEPARTMENT OF EDUCATION. (1990). *The Condition of Education.* Washington, DC: U.S. Government Printing Office.

VAN AKEN, M. A. G., & ASENDORPF, J. B. (1997). Support by parents, classmates, friends, and siblings in preadolescence: Covariation and compensation across relationships. *Journal of Social and Personal Relationships, 14,* 79–93.

VON FRANZ, M. L. (1979). *The problem of puer aeternus.* New York: Springer-Verlag.

WISEMAN, H. (1997). Interpersonal relatedness and self-definition in the experience of loneliness during the transition to university. *Personal Relationships, 4,* 285–299.

ZEIDNER, M. (1991). Statistics and mathematics anxiety in social science students: Some interesting parallels. *British Journal of Education, 61,* 319–329.

Index